**Neath
Port Talbot
Library &
Information
Services**

Books should be returned or renewed by the last
date stamped above.

NP56

WELSH OUTLAWS AND BANDITS

Palazzo Doria, Rome

Salvator Rosa, Gruppo di Bravi

WELSH OUTLAWS AND BANDITS

Political Rebellion and Lawlessness in Wales, 1400–1603

E. A. Rees

CATERWEN PRESS

Published by
Caterwen Press,
7 Beech Court,
126 Middleton Hall Road,
Kings Norton,
Birmingham B30 1DH

First published 2001

ISBN 0-9540967-0-3

British Library Cataloguing-in-Publication Data

A catalogue record for this book is available from the British Library

Library of Congress Cataloguing-in-Publication Data

Welsh Outlaws and Bandits: Political rebellion and lawlessness in Wales, 1400–1603, author E. A. Rees
p. cm.
Includes bibliographical references
ISBN 0-9540967-0-3
1. Welsh history and politics 1400–1603.   2. Outlaws and bandits

Printed and bound in Great Britain by Antony Rowe Ltd, Chippenham, Wiltshire

Contents

Preface

This study of lawlessness in Wales covers the period from the outbreak of the Glyndŵr rising in 1400 to the death of Elizabeth I in 1603. Its focus is specifically on the problem of government and the way in which the problem of lawlessness was understood and handled in this period. It is not a study of the way in which the judicial process operated or the means by which law was administered, although this is touched upon. It is intended as an exercise in interpretation, examining the nature of the problem of lawlessness in this period and its implications for our wider understanding of Welsh history. In taking this long-term view it is intended to provide the basis for comparison between the fifteenth and sixteenth centuries.

This work examines the nature and extent of lawlessness, the political response of the authorities, and the social-political and cultural context in which this issue arose. It seeks to examine how the problem was structured by other causal factors, how it was perceived and defined. In this, lawlessness is examined in regard to the development of the English state and the fragmentation of authority within Wales itself. Here we are looking also at lawlessness in its social, class and national dimension. As such we are examining not only the effectiveness of the instruments for upholding the law but also the legitimacy of those institutions and of the laws which they administered.

Under the heading of lawlessness a variety of different forms of activities are subsumed, from political insurrection, feuds amongst marcher lords and gentry, organised banditry and border raiding, to ordinary, mundane acts of crime. This approach is deliberately chosen. We shall examine the crisis of lawlessness in Wales in this period in terms of the interrelationship between these different facets of the problem. In this study we draw on the work of Perez Zagorin on revolutions in early modern Europe, Norman Cohn's work on the millenarian dimension of social protest and rebellion, as well as that of E. J. Hobsbawm and F. Braudel on the social and political dimensions of lawlessness and banditry. This work attempts to test some of the hypotheses of these historians in a particular context, and to use their ideas to highlight the specific features of the development of Wales.

Through the study of lawlessness it is possible to explore the changing structures of administration in Wales, the developing power of the English state, the changing relations between the Welsh and the English, the changing structure of Welsh society and the shifting power relations between different groups. This study examines how far lawlessness was a manifestation of political protest or resistance by subordinate social groups, or a form of national rebellion. It explores the interrelationship between the dramatic political upheavals of the period and the problem of social disorder and crime within Welsh society. The crisis of lawlessness in Wales had specific causes, but this period has parallels with other societies. In examining the problem of disorder we are examining also the viability of alternative courses of historical development as contemporaries saw them.

Two main sources are utilised in this study: firstly, the laws passed by the English parliament, which provide the centre's view of the problem, and secondly, the works of the Welsh bards. This work has been undertaken in the belief that the political rebel, the rebellious magnate, the brigand, the outlaw, the border raider – with both their noble and dastardly sides – have been unjustifiably neglected. In concentrating on the problems of instability and lawlessness over such an extended time span, it may be argued that this aspect of life is exaggerated and that the more lawful aspects of daily life are ignored. This study does not seek to sensationalise Welsh history, but to bring out the centrality of these issues for an understanding of the period.

The work does not intend to provide a detailed empirical study of the incidence of criminal activity over time, even if that were possible. Such work, utilising the court rolls of the period, has only begun. Until reliable empirical work is undertaken the precise dimension of the issue will remain uncertain. Even then the significance of lawlessness will remain to be determined. As a preliminary it is necessary to survey the whole terrain, to seek to identify different forms of lawlessness, its incidence over time and its geographic dispersal.

This study draws inspiration particularly from the work of T. Gwynn Jones who highlighted the problem of lawlessness and its relationship to political rebellion as mirrored in the work of the Welsh bards. It seeks to pull together the work of historians and literary critics on banditry and brigandage. The phenomenon under examination often leaves few traces in the historical record. We are often dependent on single accounts, written some time after the event, or on the folk memory of particular localities. These are sources which professional historians naturally regard with some suspicion. In this book an attempt is made to put these various accounts into their historical context, and to draw on parallels with other societies which have experienced similar crisis of order.

Florence   E. A. Rees

Introduction

The fifteenth and sixteenth centuries in Welsh history was characterised by grave disorder and lawlessness. Within the British Isles only the Scottish border and the region of the Irish pale in this period provide comparable instance with the conditions prevailing in Wales and the Marches. The three regions constituted peripheral, frontier regions bordering on an encroaching English state. They were frontiers between culturally distinct peoples in which different traditions and conceptions of law prevailed. The period studied encompasses the Glyndŵr rising, the Wars of the Roses, the Tudor accession, the Reformation, the Acts of Union, and the death of Elizabeth I. All these events had a direct bearing on the crisis of public order in Wales in these two centuries.

Conflicting conceptions of order

The feudal conception of order with mutual obligations between the crown, as the embodiment of the state, and the powerful feudal lords was severely shaken. The legitimacy of royal authority was itself debated. Underlying these discussions lay the question of kingship, its obligations and duties and the need to found authority on consent rather than coercion. These issues were most hotly contested in those peripheral regions on the realm over which the English state sought to extend its control.

Lawful government required some measure of consent; it could not rest entirely on force. Where that legitimacy was questioned political rebellion and resistance in its various forms emerged. One facet of the problem of governance was political resistance and defiance of the law and of the state in its various forms. Saint Augustine discussed the question in the fourth century in the *The City of God Against the Pagans*, a work familiar to learned men in the fifteenth century:

> Remove justice and what are states but gangs of bandits (*latrocinia*) on a large scale? And what are bandit gangs but kingdoms in miniature? The band also is a group of men governed by the orders of a leader, bound by a social compact, and its booty is divided according to a law agreed upon. If by repeated adding desperate men this

1

plague grows to the point where it holds territory and establishes a fixed seat, seizes cities and subdues peoples, then it more conspicuously assumes the name of kingdom, and this name is now openly granted to it, not for any subtraction of cupidity, but by addition of impunity.[1]

Chaucer in the fourteenth century, in a direct paraphrase of Saint Augustine's words, posed the same question in 'The Manciple's Tale':

Right so betwixte a titleless tiraunt
And an outlawe, or a theef erraunt,
The same I seye, ther is no difference.
To Alisaundre was told this sentence,
That, for the tirant is of gretter myght,
By force of meynee [company], for to sleen downright,
And brennen hous and hoom, and make al playn,
Lo, therefore is he cleped a capitayn;
And for the outlawe hath but small meynee,
And may nat doon so greet an harm as he,
Ne brynge a contree to so greet mescheef,
Men clepen hym an outlawe or a theef.[2]

The crown's central responsibility was held to be the defence of the realm and the preservation of law and order. A king who flouted the law, in the view of some, lost all title to rule. The poet John Gower wrote:

What king of lawe taketh no kepe,
Be lawe he mai no regne kepe.
Do lawe awey, what is a king?
Wher is the riht of eny thing,
If that ther be no lawe in londone?[3]

William of Ockham went so far as to proclaim the right of revolution in cases where a ruler had become tyrannical.[4]

At the same time there was recognition of the need to secure the state's integrity, to preserve order and discipline, so as to avoid a collapse into anarchy where no lawful authority could establish itself. This was compounded by the weakness of the medieval state, its restricted administrative and military capabilities, and its reliance on securing the obedience of other powerful magnates. This justified strong state power, as a lesser evil, necessary to prevent revolt and rebellion. The problem of internal disorder was also linked to the danger of foreign invasion.

Political Instability and Lawlessness

The state's struggle against lawlessness was commonly bound up with the attempts by particular social classes or groups to consolidate and legitimise their control over society. Resistance to the imposition of such controls assumed a diversity of forms. Perez Zagorin identifies five categories of revolutions in early modern Europe: i. conspiracy and coup, limited largely to the actions of nobles and aristocratic elites; ii. urban rebellion, either by plebeian and inferior groups against urban elites and governments, or by urban communities against external royal and state authority; iii. agrarian rebellion by peasants and others against landlords and/or against state authorities; iv. provincial, regional and separatist rebellion by provincial societies or dependent realms against their monarchical state centre; v. kingdom-wide civil war against monarchies based on noble and aristocratic leadership and involving the entire society.[5]

Political rebellion was frequently associated with other forms of lawlessness, with the boundary between treason and crime being ill defined. A key concern of the medieval state was with the law breaking by powerful magnates, ecclesiastical as well as lay, the crimes of the gentry and the 'over-mighty subjects' who were often a law unto themselves. A further problem was the activity of more or less organised bands of criminals, whose leaders were often gentry, knights and esquires.[6] Finally there were the acts of individual felons. These forms of lawlessness were often overlapping and interconnected with one another.

Even where criminal activities were not inspired by political motives, however loosely defined, they could themselves pose a threat to established authority, which demanded a political response. Political rebels were outlawed like ordinary criminals. Powerful magnates could pose a challenge to the crown, engaging in bloody feuds and private wars, and themselves acting as patrons and protectors of felons, whilst at the same time being the dispensers of justice in their localities.[7]

Late medieval England was notorious throughout Europe for its high crime rate. L. O. Pike, a pioneer in English criminal history, who examined particularly lawlessness in 1348, the year proceeding the Black Death, described this as a period of widespread depravity.[8] The historical study of lawlessness in medieval England is well developed.[9] For Wales the problem has only been lightly touched on. Here we seek to open up this area for examination, focusing on what was a common problem in both

England and Wales, and at the same time examining what was particular and unique to Wales.

Outlaws and Bandits

At the centre of this study we are concerned both with the perpetrators of crime and those who define what is criminal. Of particular interest are those who are placed outside the bounds of society, namely those who are outlawed. The term outlaw, from the Scandinavian *utlah*, had been incorporated into Anglo-Saxon by the time of King Alfred's laws. The process of outlawing (*utlagare* or *utlegare*) and the rarer process of inlawing pardoned felons (*inlagare* or *inlegare*) were well established.[10]

Alongside the outlaw were those termed as bandits or brigands. Not all outlaws were bandits, and not all bandits had been subject to the process of outlawry. Whilst the term outlaw had a clear legal definition, the term bandit had a specific social connotation, defining a form of organised criminal activity which set itself in opposition to established authority. The term brigand – from the Italian *brigante*, meaning a light-armed foot soldier – had already been incorporated into English by 1387, and the term bandit was in usage by the end of the sixteenth century.

In other countries outlaws and bandits were known by various names. In Spain they were *bandoleros*, in France *bandouliers*, whilst in Italy they were *malandrini, masnadieri* (originally mercenary soldiers), *ladri, fuoruscuti*, and most commonly *banditi* (signifying one who had been banned, banished or outlawed).[11] In the ancient Roman Empire they were called *latrones*. In modern times in the Balkans they went by the name of *haiduks*, in Greece *klephts*, in India *dacoits*, in China *hunghutze* and in Russia *razboiniki*. On the Anglo-Scottish border they were *reivers*, and in Ireland *torai*. In Wales there was a broad category of terms used to cover the phenomenon (see pp. 93–4 below).

Outlaws and bandits provide a focus for studying the wider problem of lawlessness in society. The comparative study of banditry derives from E. J. Hobsbawm's classic studies *Primitive Rebels* and *Bandits*.[12] Hobsbawm's concept of the 'social bandit' as a symbol of resistance by subordinate groups and classes to the oppressive rule of a dominant authority has stimulated research and debate concerning the nature of banditry, its social roots, and its relationship to forms of political rebellion and resistance, and to criminal enterprises generally.

The distinguished French historian Fernand Braudel describes banditry in the Mediterranean basin in the sixteenth and seventeenth century as an episodic but endemic phenomenon. It constituted a form of 'class struggle' which could never quite 'reach boiling point' in a society increasingly polarised between rich and poor, but where class-consciousness was weakly developed. It was, he argues, 'a form of vengeance upon the ruling class and its lopsided justice', 'a latent form of jacquerie, or peasant revolt, the product of poverty and overpopulation' and a 'revenge upon established states'. In this world bandits were often popular folk heroes. At the same time bandit gangs might be headed by noblemen. The gentry offered protection to bandits and might employ them as henchmen, enforcers and bodyguards. The involvement of noblemen in such criminal enterprises Braudel attributes to the 'crisis in noble fortunes' of this period. Inter-class collaboration, national and regional affinities provided another feature of bandit identity and action.[13]

Banditry is often symptomatic of the break down, or embryonic nature, of the state. On account of its organised nature, its capacity to impose control over tracts of territory and to create alternative structures of authority, it poses a direct challenge to established states. In particular instances, such as southern Italy in the nineteenth century, banditry became a mass phenomenon. In societies afflicted by a major breakdown of order specific regions can develop very strong bandit traditions. In Sicily, in Calabria and Abruzzo in southern Italy these traditions were extraordinarily strong and tenacious, and were associated in part with the organisation of the Mafia.[14] This offers some interesting parallels with lawlessness in Wales in the fifteenth and sixteenth centuries, as long as the parallels are not pushed too far.

Banditry shades on the one hand into political rebellion and on the other degenerates into simple acts of organised criminality devoid of political or social significance, except as a problem which has to be contained. Here we are concerned not only with the way bandits are defined by established authority but, a more difficult question, how they conceive themselves and how they are viewed by the wider society of which they are a part.

The extent to which banditry can be viewed as a manifestation of class or national conflict needs to be examined. Hobsbawm's 'social bandit' appears to have been a relatively rare phenomena, although heroic images of the 'social bandit' can be found in folklore and art. More common is the image of the bandit as a scourge who preys indiscriminately on rich and poor alike. Moreover, the association of banditry with powerful local magnates demonstrates that it could just as well be a means of enforcing social control by dominant groups, as a form of retributive justice on the part of subordinate classes, groups and peoples. Banditry is important also on a cultural level, finding expression in folklore, poetry, song and art, reflecting different, sometimes ambiguous, conceptions of political order, justice, duty and obligations. In art the pictorial representations of bandits indicate these very different perceptions – from the heroic view of bandits depicted in some of Salvator Rosa's works, to Goya's representation of bandits as wild, anarchic, diabolic creatures, to Leopold Robert's view of the wan, romantic, picturesque bandits of nineteenth century Italy.[15]

Popular attitudes towards banditry varied enormously, from identification and support on the one hand, to hatred and outright condemnation on the other. The imposition of a class interpretation on the phenomena must thus be approached with care. Other factors must also be addressed. The organisation of late medieval society was based to a large extent on transcendent allegiances – to the crown and to the church, and particularistic allegiances – those between lord and tenant, kinship ties, the bonds of community and locality. The maintenance of social order depended on a combination of coercion and consent, based on conceptions of legitimate authority. These bonds of allegiance defined to some extent what was and was not permissible. Theft was legitimate where individuals felt no obligations to those against whom the crime was perpetrated.[16]

Banditry as a phenomenon appears in many societies over a great time span. Some common circumstances can be identified which facilitate its development. War, civil war, social upheaval and civil commotion provide a fertile soil for such lawlessness. It is associated with remote, agrarian societies, peripheral zones, often mountainous and wild, where the forces of law and order are weak, corrupt or unformed. Distinct cultural or national groups, pitted against neighbouring groups, may find in such activities a means of resistance, defiance and revenge. Traditional patriarchal peasant societies, with strong kinship ties and strict codes of honour, often cultures imbued with a martial ethic, may see brigandage as a legitimate and honourable calling. The fragmentation of state authority, where powerful families or lords exercising jurisdiction in their own territories, allows such lawlessness to gain legitimacy. Dearth, grinding poverty, the disruption of local economies, over-population, and underemployment may provide additional contributory factors.

Wales and England: Historical Background

The crisis of law and order in fifteenth century Wales derived, at least in part, from the peculiar system of administration to which it was subjected. The death of Llywelyn ap Gruffydd, styled Prince of Wales in 1282, and the completion of the Edwardian conquest extinguished the last independent Welsh state. Llywelyn's attempt to create a new feudal state based on Gwynedd to resist further English encroachments was aborted.

By the 'Statute of Wales', Wales was 'annexed and united' to the crown of England.

The royal possessions in Gwynedd were transferred to the English crown. The conquest of Gwynedd saw the construction of the vast castles on the coast – Conwy, Caernarfon, Beaumaris and Harlech – whilst the native Welsh castles were either destroyed or adapted. In the succeeding decades English dominance was challenged by sporadic rebellions by Welsh leaders – Rhys ap Meredydd (1287), Madog ap Llywelyn (1295) and Llywelyn Bren (1316). None of these localised revolts effectively threatened control by the English crown.

Owain Lawgoch, the last descendent of the royal house of Gwynedd, posed one of the most intriguing challenges to the dominance of the English crown in Wales. From 1366 until murdered by an English agent in 1378 he fought in France for the French crown against the English. A famous captain he was accompanied by a retinue of Welsh soldiers, largely drawn from Flintshire. In 1369, 1372 and 1377 Owain Lawgoch, with the support of the French crown, made successive attempts to invade Wales in order to regain his lost patrimony. He was hailed by Welsh bards as the redeemer.[17]

Following the Edwardian conquest Wales was effectively divided between two separate systems of administration, quite distinct from the system of shires in England. The crown itself took over the property of the Welsh princes. The administration of these properties was entrusted to crown officials in Caernarfon for North Wales (Anglesey, Caernarfon, Merioneth) and Carmarthen for South Wales (Cardigan and Carmarthen). Alongside these crown administered shires there coexisted the marcher lordships, established in the wake of the Norman Conquest.[18] The marcher lordships occupied the eastern and southern parts of Wales, acting as a buffer zone between Wales proper (*pura Wallia* as distinct from *Marchia Wallie*) and the neighbouring English counties.

The Marches, derived from the French *marche* (frontier), constituted a mosaic of rival authorities, with each having its own separate jurisdiction, as petty statelets, independent of the crown but owing allegiance to the king.[19] The castles and walled towns of Chester, Oswestry, Shrewsbury, Montgomery, Ludlow, Hereford, Worcester, Gloucester, Monmouth, Newport and Chepstow provided the main line of defence against Welsh incursions. The border was heavily fortified with castles at Hawarden, Holt, Chirk, Whittington, Welshpool, Caus, Clun, Usk, Hay, Wigmore, Grosmont, Skenfrith, Goodrich and Raglan. Fortified bridges protected the main river crossings on the Dee (Chester, Holt), the Severn (Shrewsbury, Bridgnorth, Bewdley, Worcester, Gloucester), the Wye (Hereford), the Usk (Chepstow) and Monnow (Monmouth).

In the century after the conquest the system of rule in Wales underwent a significant change. Having lost their independence the Welsh continued to be ruled locally by the leaders of their own community. Only under the personal rule of Edward III did this system change, with the crown increasingly relying on the English burgesses and English officials, who were often absentee. This process heightened racial animosities.[20] R. R. Davies describes the growing centralisation and uniformity of English administration over its peripheral regions from the thirteenth century onwards as part of a bureaucratisation of government, reflected in a growing intolerance of local and national peculiarities, and an increasingly overbearing attitude towards national cultures and traditions.[21]

The Edwardian conquest established a system of colonial administration in Wales. Edward I's programme of castle building created powerful bastions from which the country could be ruled and protected from foreign invasion. English garrison towns with their settled population of English burgesses sprang up – Caernarfon, Conwy, Beaumaris, Denbigh and Carmarthen. The castles of the marcher lords and the fortified border towns made the Marches one of the most fortified regions in Britain.[22] In times of trouble the garrisons in Wales and on the borders were reinforced from the English counties and ports. This system of rule rested on military force, with the administration in the crown held shires and the marcher lordships often entrusted to English officers, although inevitably at a local level Welsh officials retained an important part in administration.

The division between Wales and England was part of the geographic divide between highland and lowland Britain. The Welsh were mainly pastoralists, cattle herders and sheep breeders, who engaged in limited cultivation of oats and barley. This stood in marked contrast to the agrarian, feudalised towns and villages of their more affluent English neighbours. It was also a cultural divide, reflected in the distinctive language, laws, dress, manners and mores of the Welsh. Pecham, archbishop of Canterbury, portrayed the Welsh as the perfect barbarians, distinguished by their poverty, sloth, moral laxness, brutality and cruelty. They were seen as wild, quarrelsome, treacherous, rebellious and faithless. This cultural stereotype, often based on misconceptions, nevertheless reflected real differences. For the Welsh their own virtues of frugality, love of liberty, hospitality, sharp wittedness and prowess in arms stood in contrast to the alleged vices of the Saxons.[23]

The growth of disorder 1370–1400

Even in the thirteenth century Wales had a reputation as a resort of outlaws, and the Welsh preference for guerrilla warfare was seen as akin to pillage and brigandage.[24] In the century following the Edwardian conquest, coexistence and compromise, R. R. Davies and G. Roberts argue, was the hallmark of relations between the Welsh and the English.[25] This, as A. D. Carr argues, was a precarious coexistence, which could easily break down. The author of *Vita Edwardi Secundi* discussing the revolt of Llywelyn Bren noted 'This habit of the Welsh is a long-standing madness. They keep quiet for ten years and are then suddenly athirst for battle'. The Welsh were reputed for their 'light headedness' and treachery.[26]

In the fourteenth century disputes between the English burgesses and the Welsh erupted periodically into conflict. In 1345 the murders of Henry de Shaldeforde, the king's attorney in North Wales, and of John de Huntingdon, acting sheriff of Merionethshire, killed when holding the county court, prompted great alarm. There were serious disturbances in Caernarfon, Denbigh and Rhuddlan, with attacks on the king's burgesses and tenants.[27] The burgesses of Denbigh petitioned the Prince of Wales:

> The men of Denbigh therefore pray the prince to ordain a speedy remedy, so that the evildoers and their maintainers be chastised in such manner that they may take warning to behave themselves peaceably; for the Prince's English tenants in these parts hardly dare to go out of the towns of the franchise to plough and sow and trade; and his English bailiffs hardly dare to do their work for fear of being slain and plundered, so numerous are the evildoers and rebels who are outlaws in the woods, and are maintained by the greatest men of the land.[28]

The problem of containing disorder was compounded by the threat of foreign invasion. In 1369 the fear of a French invasion, in support of Owen Lawgoch, heightened alarm. The men of Shrewsbury were forbidden to quit their homes on pretence of going on the foreign wars, lest their absence would weaken the town's defences in the event of a Welsh rising. In 1370 the sheriffs of the Welsh counties were ordered to put the castles in Wales in readiness to withstand siege and to arm the English populations of the borough towns to repel a French invasion. In 1377 new orders for the defence of the Welsh coast were issued again inspired by the fears of a French landing.[29]

The lawlessness of the border was compounded by the existence of the marcher lordships as havens for brigands. The county palatine of Chester, whose juridical independence provided a cover for acts of violence and robbery committed by its people in neighbouring counties, posed a particular problem. The Commons in the parliaments of 1379, 1382, 1384 and 1390 condemned these abuses.[30]

The Black Death in 1348–50 severely shook the existing social order. This demographic catastrophe, together with mounting economic problems in England produced the peasants revolt of 1381. The deterioration with regard to the maintenance of law and order was evident during Richard II's reign (1377–1399). Peasant discontent manifested itself in the flight of bondmen, who made up an important part of the community of outlaws. Stringent laws were passed to deal with the problem of disorder and the spreading of seditious ideas, directed either against the crown or the nobility.[31]

Richard II's reign also saw an upsurge of lawlessness on the Anglo-Welsh border. Complaints against these depredations were made in Parliament in 1376.[32] In 1377–8 leading figures from Herefordshire, led by Walter Devereux, John Clifford and Robert de Whyteney, presented a petition to the king, which declared:

> Malefactors from Wales, have come … within these two years … in companies of 40, 60 or 100: and there they have beaten people, and maimed several; more they have killed in the houses of the same and taken their chattels, committing such brutalities and threats in the county as far as the city of Hereford that no man dare indict or take them, for fear of being killed in their house. For which reason they beg there may be ordained sufficient remedy in short time so that the King's lieges may not be entirely destroyed.[33]

The apprehending of English merchants in Wales and the marches was a long-standing source of complaint.[34] In 1378 the burgesses of Bristol, Shrewsbury, Hereford, Gloucester, Worcester and other marcher towns complained to Parliament of the harassment and distress they suffered. The crown ordered the marcher lords to make amends.[35] In the 1380s in one instance the burgesses of Shrewsbury on their way to a fair at Welshpool were arrested by the Earl of Arundel's men, and confined in Oswestry castle.[36] In 1389 the burgesses of the border counties brought similar complaints to Parliament.[37] Frequent complaints were lodged regarding the apprehending of Englishmen who travelled into Wales to recover unpaid debts or other defaults.[38]

The turbulent state of the border in the last decades of the fourteenth century is attested to by an undated law, which prohibited Welshmen from buying or holding land on the English border. These individuals, it was alleged, acted as accomplices of raiders from Wales, so that by the:

procuration, help, counsel and favour of Welshmen buying and possessing land in the English counties on the border, divers malefactors of Wales of their acquaintance in great multitudes, sometimes a hundred or two hundred, and at other times three hundred or more, suddenly entering these counties in war-like array, perpetrate there daily diverse man-slaughters, felonies and other transgressions and enormities, and then retreat in haste to the other side of the border, beyond the jurisdiction of the magistrates of the counties in which the offence was committed.[39]

Retaliatory measures were authorised against Welsh border raiders. Richard II in a charter granted to Hereford in 1394 declared it lawful that in the event of any of the town's citizens being apprehended and unlawfully taken into any Welsh or marcher lordship, they, the town's citizens, were entitled to arrest any inhabitant from the same lordship, and to hold them until their own men were released.[40]

The attacks were by no means one way. In the early 1390s there were raids on Bromfield by Cheshiremen, when 'small groups of former soldiers and landless peasants … crossed the Dee … carrying away livestock, trampling crops, entering barns, assaulting and robbing Welsh peasants and English burgesses at will'.[41] The deterioration in the situation on the border in these decades was part of an unfolding crisis of central authority over the periphery which provided the background against which the Glyndŵr revolt erupted in 1400.

State-building, civility and criminality

For contemporaries viewing the problem of disorder in their society there were various possible ways in which the phenomenon might be addressed. One tendency saw lawlessness as a manifestation of man's sinful nature. Only by strengthening the state and reinforcing social hierarchy could the threat of revolt, rebellion and anarchy be thwarted. This was exemplified by the concept of 'The Great Chain of Being', with each element in the political-social hierarchy assigned its place. This view is outlined in the *Homily of Obedience*: 'Where there is no right order there reigneth all abuse, carnal liberty, enormity, sin and babylonical confusion'.[42]

In the sixteenth century prominent figures such as Sir Thomas More, Raphael Holinshed and senior crown officials sought to identify the social and economic causes of lawlessness and disorder in order to effect a more lasting solution by alleviating the conditions which produced the problem. A central part of the study of lawlessness in Wales involves the examination of the process of English state-building, and the constitutional and administrative incorporation of Wales within the English state. This was one important feature of what G. R. Elton has called the 'Tudor Revolution in Government'.[43] The creation of the modern state involved the transformation of its control over its periphery.[44] Corrigan and Sayer in their study of state formation in the sixteenth century present it as a process of 'revolution from above', but at the same time stress the cultural dimension of state building as part of a process of 'cultural revolution' whereby different groups were incorporated.[45]

Norbert Elias in examining the history of medieval Europe sees the struggle also as a cultural phenomenon in the broadest sense, as nothing less than a struggle for 'civilisation' or 'civility'. It involved not only the establishment of legal and administrative checks to forms of unrestrained behaviour, but the creation of psychological restraints within each individual as to what was permitted or acceptable. The process of state formation and the growth of the concept of 'civility' are thus intimately connected and bound to the growth of 'civil society', in which limits to individual action are accepted, state and legal processes replace personal retribution, and the concept of personal or kin honour is replaced by civil obligations, duties and rights shared by all. This does not exclude a conception of state formation as part of a process of consolidating class, group or national dominance.[46]

The internal political division of a subject people makes it prey to its more powerful neighbours. It makes it, at the same time, incapable of resolving its own internal problems, and thus more likely to seek external support to deal with these difficulties. The twentieth century Neapolitan scholar Schipa writes:

> A society morally and materially, internally and externally, so disintegrated and unfitted to create itself by its own efforts, can have no other state but what is conceded to it or imposed upon it.[47]

These words sumarise the condition of Italy in the centuries prior to its liberation from foreign rule and its unification in the nineteenth century. It is taken from Schipa's account of the ill-fated popular revolution against Spanish rule which was led from Naples by Masaniello in 1647. It was in response to such a dilemma that Machiavelli, a century earlier, had famously sought a solution in his *Prince*, whereby the task of securing national unity would be undertaken by one schooled in warfare and in the brutal arts of politics.[48]

1 The Glyndŵr Rising 1400–1412

In the final decades of the fourteenth century public order in England and Wales deteriorated sharply as a result of the weakening of central authority, the growing conflicts between local magnates and the stirring of peasant discontent. The deposition of Richard II in September 1399 created a crisis of legitimacy. The king on his return from Ireland initially attempted to rally support in Wales before capitulating to the new king Henry IV. These events provided the background to the Glyndŵr rising. This was the most serious challenge to English government of Wales since 1282, and set as its avowed aim the undoing of the settlement imposed on Wales by the Edwardian conquest. This insurrection in its intensity, scope and long duration profoundly influenced life in Wales. As a background to the study of lawlessness in Wales in the fifteenth century a brief outline of this rising is essential.[1]

The rising was fuelled by deep ethnic hatreds, which were stoked by Welsh resentment against English rule. This stemmed in large measure from economic grievances: the pressures of crown and seigniorial exactions; the commutation of dues and services into cash payments ; the requisitioning of provisions and supplies for the English castles; the loss of traditional rights of access to pasture and forests; the dominance of English burgesses over local markets; the heavy charge laid by the mills controlled by the crown and the marcher lords.

Welsh resentments were also shaped by a number of non-economic greivances. The compulsory levying of soldiers for service in the English army imposed a heavy burden on society. In the fourteenth century the Welsh were increasingly excluded from the major offices in civil government and in the church. The displacement of Welsh law by English law was also a source of friction. The privileged position of the English burgesses within the new system of justice, with their claim to be tried only by juries of their own compatriots bred resentment. There are indications also that the severe punishments, including the death penalty, imposed under English law offended Welsh sensibilities.[2]

These asccumulated greivances had the effect of alienating all important sectors of Welsh society, and highlighting the deep ethnic basis on which this system of exploitative, colonial rule operated.

THE OUTBREAK OF THE GLYNDŴR REVOLT, 1400–1402

The rising in Wales stemmed initially from a dispute between Owain ab Gruffydd, Lord of Glyndyfrdwy or Glyndŵr and his neighbour Reginald Grey of Ruthin. Glyndŵr was one of the few Welshmen of large estate at this time. His main seat was at Sycharth. He claimed royal descent from the princes of Deheubarth The high status and authority enjoyed by Glyndŵr, the 'Knight of the Vale' (*marchog y glyn*), was underlined by bards such as Iolo Goch and Rhys Goch Eryri, in poems composed before the insurrection.. He had studied English law at Westminster, and subsequently became squire to the earl of Arundel, who had large estates in north Wales. In 1385 he served in Richard II's Scottish campaign.

Glyndŵr's dispute with Grey arose over a claim to land in the latter's possession. In the Parliament of October 1399 Glyndŵr petitioned for the land to be returned to him. He complained that Grey had failed to deliver a writ summoning him to the Scottish expedition, and had then denouncing him before the king as a traitor for not appearing. In spite of entreaties by John Trevor, bishop of St. Asaph, the Commons cavalierly rejected the petition.

On 16 September 1400 Glyndŵr, supported by leading *uchelwyr* from Glyndyfrdwy, Edernyion and Penllyn, and with at least 250 armed men, descended on Dyffryn Clwyd and burnt Ruthin. On 19 September the king in Nottingham ordered the sheriffs of ten English counties to array 'all fencible men, knights, esquires, archers and others'. They were to join the king at Coventry and proceed to resist the rebels.[3]

The king penetrated as far as Anglesey but was forced to retreat for want of provisions. One of the rebel leaders Goronwy ap Tudur was hung drawn and quartered, and his dismembered limbs displayed in Chester, Ludlow, Hereford and Bristol – 'opening towards Wales'.[4] On 16 October Edward, earl of Rutland was appointed keeper and governor of north Wales with orders to quell the disorder.[5] Orders were issued for the arrest of leading rebels.[6] Glyndŵr's property, on account of his 'high treason against his king's majesty', was forfeited to John Beaufort, earl of Somerset. Others suffered a similar fate.[7]

On 30 November an order of protection was issued in north Wales 'for all Welshmen, lately in insurrection, who may be willing in the presence of the king's son, the prince of Wales, to come to Chester to make submission, and their men and possessions'.[8] Some of the rebels under threat of forfeiture submitted to the crown, and others were pardoned.[9]

In the fortnight following the raid on Ruthin a commission of goal delivery and two inquests were held. Ten individuals were executed. Those involved in the revolt were called to appear before the courts. At the fifth court on 17 May 1401 those who had not appeared, including the leaders of the revolt, were collectively outlawed.[10]

At the outbreak of the rebellion the Welsh castles were weakly garrisoned.[11] The loyalty of Welsh officials and soldiers was also uncertain. John Skydmore complained of the castles and towns in south Wales that 'there be few true men in [t]hem'.[12]

Measures were taken to pacify the country. On 10 March 1401 all the king's lieges in Caernarfonshire, Anglesey, Merionethshire and the lordship of Denbigh were granted pardons, except Owain Glyndŵr, Rhys ap Tudor and Gwilym ap Tudor, and others who had been captured or who were persisting in rebellion.[13] A pardon was granted to Gwilym and Rhys ap Tudur, 'who lately rose in insurrection and took the castle of Conway in north Wales, and burned the town of Conway and despoiled the burgesses'.[14]

On 30 May Henry Percy defeated the rebels at Cader Idris, Merionethshire. Glyndŵr switched his operations to Carmarthen in south Wales. A great assembly of the rebels was held in the district. In May the crown instructed John Chaundos and others to take action against 'evildoers' in the lordship of Abergavenny, where William Beauchamp was besieged in his castle. Numerous homicides had been committed, and the rebels threatened to invade the marches and Herefordshire. The commission empowered Chaundos 'to resist and take all such with the *posse* of the county and the march'.[15]

In spite of these measures a policy of conciliation continued to be attempted. In July 1401 the crown pardoned thirty-five leading Welsh rebels.[16] However, with the seizure of Aberystwyth castle, a more repressive policy was applied. At the end of August the sheriff of Gloucester was instructed to array the *posse comitatus* to support the prince of Wales in putting down the insurrection in south Wales.[17] Henry IV hurried to Worcester, but finding the threat exaggerated, returned to London.

Welshpool, the stronghold of Edward Charlton, was attacked. In June John Charlton in Powys defeated Glyndŵr. In the late summer of 1401 Glyndŵr won an important battle at Hyddgen (Hyddgant) on the northern slopes of Pumlumon against an army from south-west Wales sent to crush the rebellion.[18] By the autumn Gwynedd, Ceredigion and Powys were in rebellion.

In September writs were issued to the sheriffs of 23 English counties and the county palatine of Lancaster, against Owain Glyndŵr who had 'risen in insurrection'. They were required to send all knight, squires and archers to Worcester by 1 October 'to march with the king to Wales for protection and succour of his faithful subjects and repression of the rebels'.[19]

The king, assisted by Prince Henry, invaded Gwynedd, ravaged the country for a month, proceeding to Bangor and Caernarfon, then south into Merioneth and Ceredigion. Strata Florida was despoiled and Ceredigion temporarily submitted. On 2 November, Glyndŵr with a great host was threatening Caernarfon. In September and December commissions of oyer and terminer were appointed for North and South Wales and the marches.[20]

Attempts to conclude a peace between Glyndŵr and the crown, with Northumberland acting as a mediator, failed. At this time Glyndŵr sought support from the Scots, the Irish and the French.[21] He also sought allies amongst the English magnates on the border.

In the winter of 1401/2 Glyndŵr established control over Caernarfonshire and Merionethshire. The lordship of Ruthin was ravaged, although Denbigh (the property of the earl of March was spared). Reginald Grey of Ruthin was seized, with the crown agreeing to license a ransom of 10,000 marks for his release.[22] A key role in the suppression of the rebellion was assigned to the sons of the earl of Northumberland, long experienced in dealing with the Scots; in March 1402 Thomas Percy was appointed king's lieutenant for south Wales, whilst Henry Percy was appointed lieutenant for north Wales.[23] Measures were taken to replenish the supplies and arms in the castles of south Wales.[24]

A second invasion to put down the insurrection was planned. The king instructed the sheriffs of the English counties to array knights, squires and yeoman, and to assemble in Lichfield by 7 July 'to march with him to Wales and resist the wanton malice of Owen Glyndourdy and other rebels of those parts, who have traitorously risen against the king's majesty'.[25] A three-pronged attack on the Welsh rebels was proposed for August from Chester, Shrewsbury and Hereford. They ravaged the land, but after three weeks returned having accomplished little.

Glyndŵr's attention was directed to the southern Marches. In June at the battle of Pilleth Sir Edmund Mortimer, with levies from Herefordshire and Maelienydd, attacked Glyndŵr's forces and suffered heavy losses. Sir Robert Whitney and Sir Kinard de la Bere were slain; Sir Edmund Mortimer and Sir Thomas Clanvow were captured. The king refused to licence Mortimer's ransom. Mortimer decided to throw his lot in with the rebels. In a letter to his tenants he declared that their intention was to oust the usurper Henry IV, and restore Richard II to the throne if he was still alive. If he was dead his own nephew Edward Mortimer (earl of March) should inherit the English crown, and Glyndŵr should have Wales.[26] In November Mortimer cemented the alliance by marrying Glyndŵr's daughter.

Animosities between the Welsh and English were rekindled. Welsh labourers hurriedly returned from England to join Glyndŵr with what weapons they could find.[27] In February 1401 the Commons were warned that Welsh students at Oxford and Cambridge were leaving for home. In July 1402 a commission, headed by the sheriff of Oxfordshire, was established to investigate allegations of seditious night-time assemblies by the Welsh students.[28]

The revolt directly threatened the border English counties.[29] In July Thomas, earl of Arundel, was appointed as the king's lieutenant 'on the frontier of those parts viz from the castles of Holt to Wygemore', with the power to receive the surrender of the rebels, and to punish those supplying them with victuals. The able-bodied men of Herefordshire, Shropshire, Staffordshire were mobilised to defend the border, whilst Hereford, Leominster, Ludlow, and Montgomery were ordered to prepare their defences.[30] In September John Greyndour was given charge of the Herefordshire frontier, whilst Richard Grey was appointed king's lieutenant, with responsibility for the castles of Brecon, Aberystwyth, Cardigan, Carmarthen, Buelt and Hay.[31]

Legislative enactments against the Welsh 1401–2

What initially started as a dispute between two marcher lords quickly assumed the dimensions of a national rising. The conflict acquired parti- cular force on account of the racial enmity between the Welsh and English fostered since the conquest. The revolt was further fuelled by the govern- ment's response. The cautious policy of accommodation and compromise attempted in the early months of the rebellion was jettisoned. In 1401–02 parliament in a panic passed six Acts which imposed punitive penalties against the Welsh collectively.

One Act addressed the problem of cattle-lifting by Welshmen in the border English counties, 'sometimes by day and sometimes by night', and the seizure of Englishmen travelling in Wales. These actions, it noted, were 'to the great impoverishing and utter undoing of the people' of the English counties. The Act empowered the officers of the English counties to demand the restitution of stolen goods from the marcher lordships within seven days. If they were not returned all men and goods from the lordship could be apprehended until the goods had been returned and costs and expenses paid.[32]

Another Act forbade Welshmen, 'wholly born in Wales', from buying or holding land in or about Chester, Shrewsbury, Bridgnorth, Ludlow, Leominster, Hereford, Gloucester, Worcester or other market towns on the English side of the border, or of being elected freemen or holding any franchise in them.[33] No Englishman was to be convicted on the suit of a Welshman. The marcher lords were instructed to fully provision their castles to deal with riots and disturbances.[34]

Another Act ordained that Welshmen who entered the English counties to 'burn, kill, ravish or commit any other felony or trespass' who had not been apprehended were to be outlawed or should abjure the realm in accordance with English law. Where these felons fled back into Wales, the JPs in the English counties were empowered to demand of the marcher lords and their officers where they resided their prosecution and execution.[35]

Additional measures were appended to the ordinances approved by Parliament as a result of discussions held in Prince Henry's Council at Chester on 14 June 1401. These clauses, which appear in the *Record of Caernarvon*, provided that no English man or woman should marry or consort with any Welsh man or women; that no Englishman or woman should send their children to be fostered among the Welsh; that no Welshman bearing arms should enter a town or fortified castle; and that no Welshman or man of mixed blood be granted the rights of burgess.[36]

In 1402 parliament passed nine further Acts to eliminate the remnants of the political and civil rights, which the Welsh had hitherto enjoyed. These ruled that no Englishmen were to be convicted by Welshmen within Wales but only by their fellow countrymen. Welshmen were prohibited from bearing arms in market towns, churches and congregations or on the highways. Welshmen were forbidden to hold castles, walled towns or fortified houses. Welshmen were barred from holding official posts as justice, chamberlain, treasurer, sheriff, steward, constable, receiver, escheator, chief forester, keeper of the records nor lieutenant. Even Englishmen married to Welshwomen, who were considered sympathetic to the rebels, were to be put out of office in Wales and the Marches.

Three of the Acts passed in 1402 dealt with specific aspects of the rebellion. One Act forbade the carrying of victuals into Wales except under license, with the exception of supplies for the castles and English towns. Another Act forbade Welshmen from holding congregations, whilst another specifically referred to the subversive influence of the Welsh bards, 'who by their divinations, lies and exhortations are partly cause of the insurrection and rebellion now in Wales'.[37] This measure was also directed at the *gwestwyr* or purveyancers, employed by Glyndŵr to collect money and provisions to sustain the revolt.

These laws were incorporated into the charters of Denbigh, Hereford, Welshpool, Holt and other English boroughs, at the behest of their burgesses.[38] These laws threw fuel on the flames, creating even wilder rumours of what the English parliament intended towards the rebellious

Welsh. The Welsh chronicler Adam of Usk believed that a decision had been taken to destroy the Welsh tongue, but that this law had then been revoked.[39] The basis for the always precarious trust established between the English and the Welsh since the conquest was destroyed, opening the flood-gates to mutual recriminations and enflamed racial hatred; the basis for compromise was destroyed, whilst violence begat violence transforming a localised revolt into a national rising.

THE MILITARY CAMPAIGN AGAINST GLYNDŴR 1403–1412

In 1403 Welsh incursions turned the border into a war zone. In March the Prince of Wales was appointed 'king's lieutenant in Wales' with power to array the men of Shropshire, Worcestershire, Herefordshire and Gloucestershire to protect the border, investigate treasons and prevent the supply of arms and victuals to the rebels. All those with lands in the Welsh March were to return thither to protect them from invasion. A similar warning was issued to the authorities in Carmarthenshire and Pembroke.[40] From 1406 onwards the prince of Wales was confirmed, renewed quarterly, as lieutenant in north and south Wales and the marches.[41] He was to make war on the rebels, to punish them, and to grant pardons in return for fines.

In the summer Prince Henry launched a campaign against Glyndŵr's strongholds. His two residences were sacked; supporters were captured and executed; Edernyion in Merionethshire and parts of Powys were devastated.[42] The prince clamoured for men and money to relieve the hard-pressed garrisons of Harlech and Aberystwyth.[43] In a counter move, Glyndŵr, with 'a great force of rebels', swept into south Wales and lay siege to Dinefwr castle. Kidwelly castle was besieged by Henry Don (Dwn). Llanymddovery castle was captured. Carmarthen and the lordships of Kidwelly, Iscennen and Carnwyllion, submitted to him. His forces attempted to overawe Pembrokeshire but were repulsed by the Baron of Carew in a battle on 12 July in which 700 of the rebels were killed.[44] Having taken and burnt Carmarthen the rebels marched on Brecon.

John Faireford, receiver of Brecon, urgently appealed to the authorities in Herefordshire for support, declaring that 'all the Welsh nation (*toute la natioun Galoie*) … is adhering to this evil purpose of rebellion'. The rebels, having devastated Cantrefselyf and Bronllys, 'purpose all of them together to burn and destroy all pertaining to the English in these same parts'. Faireford pleaded with the king to ordain 'a final destruction of all the false nation' of the Welsh, warning that the king's liegemen were on the point of being 'utterly ruined'.[45]

John Bodenham, sheriff of Herefordshire, lifted the siege of Brecon, killing over 240 rebels, but warned the king that a renewed attack could be expected. Richard Kingeston reported to the king that the rebels four hundred strong had entered Herefordshire and carried away many men and beasts in violation of a truce which had been concluded. He appealed to the king himself to come to resist the rebels, warning that the gentlemen of the county were fleeing for their safety.[46]

In the summer of 1403 the rising acquired a new dimension. Henry Percy, son of the earl of Northumberland, who had been played a prominent role in suppressing the rebellion, himself turned against the crown, and sought an alliance with Glyndŵr and the Scots.[47] Percy's army was defeated and he himself was killed at the battle of Shrewsbury on 21 July, when Glyndŵr's army failed to rendezvous with him in time.[48] The Prince of Wales was empowered to punish those in Flint, Chester and the lordship of Denbigh who had risen in his support.[49] John Kynaston, steward of Ellesmere, had his lands forfeited for seeking by guile to bring his tenants over to Percy's side.[50] In November Chester was fined 3,000 marks for having supported Percy.[51]

After the battle of Shrewsbury Glyndŵr's forces ravaged parts of Herefordshire and Shropshire. In July the earl of Arundel was empowered 'to govern the marches of England towards Wales and resist the invasion of 'Owin de Gleyndourdy and other rebels there'.[52] In August Hugh Burnell was charged with protecting Shrewsbury from the rebels, 'who prepare to invade it and the adjoining parts'.[53]

The crown planned a third military campaign aimed at recapturing Carmarthen. Instructions were sent out to the sheriffs of the English counties on 6 September to provide men. The king, from Worcester, ordered the owners of 22 castles in south Wales to fortify and re-stock their castles. A loan of £2,000 was raised from the City of London to finance the operation.[54] The king reached Carmarthen by 24 September but quickly withdrew. A French and Breton fleet appeared in Carmarthen Bay, raising panic in Kidwelly.

New orders were issued to Hereford, the marches and other border counties to prepare for a possible invasion by Glyndŵr's forces. The earl of Arundel's commission to defend the border was confirmed.[55] At the end of October the rebels beseiged Cardiff castle, which they finally took and burnt. In November Thomas, earl Marshall, was given charge of Chepstow castle to protect the border against rebel incursions, and to put down the insurrection in south Wales.[56]

Glyndŵr travelled north with his French and Breton allies. In January 1404 the constables of the castles in North Wales were warned that French vessels had been sighted off Lleyn, that Harlech was in jeopardy, that

Caernarfon was under attack.[57] In Anglesey a force of 200 rebels ambushed and captured the sheriff, killed 50–60 men in his company, and besieged Beaumaris castle.[58] Cattle and men were taken out of Anglesey to Caernarfonshire out of the king's reach. If the castles, depleted by losses and plague, were properly manned, Reynald Bayldon claimed, the people of Anglesey, Caernarfonshire and Merionethshire would submit, having suffered much under the rebels and 'misdoers'.[59] In 1404, however, Harlech and Aberystwyth castles fell to the rebels.

In Herefordshire the estates of Edmund Mortimer, earl of March, were devastated. In Shropshire the neighbourhood of Whitchurch and Ellesmere were attacked, and Whittington manor, the seat of the powerful FitzWaryn family, was despoiled.[60] In February orders were again issued to landowners in the Welsh Marches to repair thither to protect their lands from the rebels. Those with lands on the coast were ordered to do likewise in anticipation of a French invasion.[61]

With the revolt at its height Glyndŵr on 10 May 1404 issued from Dolgellau letters patent as 'prince of Wales by the grace of God'. He appointed Griffith Yong as his Chancellor and John Hanmer, his own brother-in-law, as his special ambassador to conclude an alliance with the French. Glyndŵr also summoned a Welsh parliament to Harlech or Machynlleth consisting of 'four of the most sufficient persons of every cwmwd [commote] under his obedience'.[62] John Trevor, bishop of St. Asaph, defected to Glyndŵr in 1404. The Cistercian abbot of Strata Florida and the whole Franciscan order, sided with the rebels. Plans were advanced to establish an independent state, to establish the autonomy of the Welsh church from Canterbury, and for the creation of two universities, one in North and the other in South Wales.

The rebels continued to press their advantage in the border region and South Wales. In August Shropshire made a three-month truce with Glyndŵr. In October John Oldcastle was instructed to take measures to prevent the Welsh rebels trading cattle in return for victuals in the border region, and similar measures had to be instituted twelve months later.[63] In June urgent orders were sent to the sheriffs of the border counties to relieve Abergavenny, 'in the way of perdition through the assault of the Welsh rebels'.[64]

The crown's military efforts in 1404 were hampered by a lack of funds. Grants and loans were sought from various sources.[65] The English boroughs and lordships were held responsible for their own defences. Subsidies were sought for the Welsh war from the archbishop of York, the bishop of Durham, and English abbots and priors with Welsh possessions.[66]

The rising continued into 1405 unchecked. In January the Prince of

Wales warned the king of the massing of a large Welsh force around Builth, under Glyndŵr's leading captain Rhys Gethin, who intended a major assault on Herefordshire. Most of the leading officers and gentry had left the county leaving the border's defences gravely weakened.[67] In February Glyndŵr signed the famous Tripartite Indenture with Mortimer and the earl of Northumberland for dividing up the kingdom in three. It gave Glyndŵr all of Wales and a large part of the border region from the Mersey to the Severn, 'to fulfil the prophecy' of Merlin.[68]

In March Glyndŵr's forces suffered their most serious set back. Having burnt Grosmont castle, they encountered an army led by Lord Talbot, William Newport and John Greyndour at Pwll Melyn near Usk. The force of 8,000 men, led by Glyndŵr's son Gruffydd, was routed with 800–1,000 killed and as many captured. Gruffydd was taken prisoner and sent to the Tower. Glyndŵr's brother Tudur was killed.[69] Later in the year his 'chancellor' Gruffydd Yonge and John Hanmer were also captured and sent to the Tower.

The threat to the border English counties, however, remained. In June John Greyndour was appointed keeper of Chepstow to resist the 'invasions and hostilities of the Welsh rebels'.[70] In July Thomas de Berkeley was commissioned to muster the fencible men of Gloucester, Bristol and Somerset to repulse another anticipated invasion of the marches and English counties by rebel forces.[71]

At Aberystwyth castle on 12 January 1405 Glyndŵr ratified his treaty with the French. On 7 August a French force, under Marshal de Rieux and the Lord de Hugevyle, landed in Milford Haven in support of Glyndŵr.[72] They captured Carmarthen and marched on Worcester. On 24 August the English sheriffs were ordered to bring men to the king at Worcester 'for the defence of the realm'.[73] The Welsh with their French allies were repulsed within miles of Worcester and forced to retreat.[74] By September the king was at Hereford preparing a fourth invasion of Wales. He relieved Coety castle in Glamorganshire, but after losing transport and supplies in floods he returned to Worcester.[75] In west Wales Glyndŵr forced Francis de Court, lord of Pembroke, to purchase a truce.[76]

In January 1406 the king summoned his council to Gloucester, so that he should be near the prince of Wales, who was shortly to march upon Wales' and make war on the rebels.[77] Soldiers and archers were to be mustered in south Wales and the marches in support of the prince's campaign.[78] At this time collusion between the Welsh rebels and the earl of Northumberland was mooted. The English sheriffs were instructed to intercept and arrest these men, who were resting by day and riding by night to join Glyndŵr on the pretence that they were travelling to join forces with the prince of

Wales against the rebels.[79]

In March 1406 Glyndŵr summoned a parliament at Pennal where he recognised the French pope at Avignon, Benedict XIII, with the aim of establishing St. David's as an autonomous episcopate. Lewis Byford was consecrated as bishop of Bangor. The hope of founding an independent Welsh state, however, was quickly overtaken by events. In a battle with the prince's army in April Glyndŵr's forces were routed and one of his sons killed.[80] This marked a turning point in the war. The French force in Wales departed in Lent, indicating a waning of resistance.

In September the sheriffs of the English counties were ordered to muster men at Evesham by 10 October to accompany the king to besiege Aberystwyth castle.[81] This was the fifth military campaign against the rebels. Aberystwyth, under Rhys Ddu, held out on Glyndŵr's insistence but fell in 1408. Harlech was the last Welsh castle to fall in February 1409, with the capture of Glyndŵr's daughter Catrin. The loss of these two strongholds delivered a crushing blow to the rising.[82]

As the situation became more precarious the earl of Northumberland and Bardolf, who had sought protection in Wales the previous year, left for Scotland, taking with them Glyndŵr's two bishops, with the aim to enlist Scottish support for the Welsh rebels. In 1408 Northumberland was defeated and killed in battle, and Lewis Byford was captured.

In 1407 two new Acts of Parliament were passed to deal with the problem of felonies and robberies in Wales. One required the neighbours of felons to turn them in to the authorities on pain of bearing the costs of the crimes committed by them. A second Act forbade felons from disclaiming felonies out of the lordship where the felony was done, but should answer the charges made against then in the lordship concerned.[83]

Repeated attacks by Glyndŵr's men into the border counties, in search of urgently needed food supplies, wrought devastation. It was reported in 1406 that Buildwas abbey, Shropshire, the 'great part burned and destroyed by the Welsh rebels'.[84] In 1408 Shrewsbury and Montgomery were pardoned a grant due to the crown, because of the losses sustained.[85]

In 1409 the crown ordered some of the marcher lords in the northern marches to repudiate their private truces with Glyndŵr.[86] Glyndŵr still held control of Edeirnion, Chirkland on the border, and most of Snowdonia.[87] On 16 May 1409 parliament required the lords of Powys, Ewyas Lacy, Oswestry, Gower, Ruthin, Maelienydd, Glamorgan, Pembroke and Abergavenny to reside in their Welsh domains and castles and devote themselves to suppressing the revolt.[88] In November 1409 Arundel, Roger le Strange, Edward Charlton and Grey were ordered in person to return to their lordships to wage war against the rebels. Officers in the principality and the marcher lordships, Grey complained, could not be trusted, 'been kin unto this meignee (company) that be risen. And till ye put those officers in better governance, this country of North Wales will never have peace'.[89]

In 1410 the rebels suffered further serious reverses. A raid by Glyndŵr's men into Shropshire, again apparently to secure provisions, was routed with the loss of some of his leading captains, including Rhys ap Gruffydd (Rhys Ddu), Philip Scudamore and Rhys ap Tudur. Rhys Ddu was executed at Tyburn, Philip Scudamore at Shrewsbury and Rhys ap Tudur at Chester.[90] In September the prince of Wales was commissioned to identify and punish the king's lieges of north and south Wales and the marches 'who have favoured any Welsh rebels in their rebellion'.[91]

Within Wales the disorder persisted. From 1406 onwards substantial forces were maintained at Bala, Cymer and Strata Florida 'for the safe keeping of North Wales'.[92] In 1411 large English forces were still kept in Wales to supplement the resources of the local lords.[93] On 21 December 1411 the king at the request of parliament issued a pardon to all his subjects, except Glyndŵr and the impostor Thomas of Trumpington.[94]

ASPECTS OF THE RISING

The Glyndŵr rising for a period of ten years was a major concern for the English crown. The duration and intensity of this revolt posed a threat not only to the English border counties, but, allied to the threat of foreign invasion and the threat of the internal fragmentation of England, it posed a thereat to the survival of the English state itself.

The border towns served as bastions against the Welsh rebels as did the English castles and boroughs in Wales itself. Murage was granted to Ruthin, Shrewsbury, Hereford, Ludlow, Worcester and Bristol to enable them to reinforce their defences.[95] The authorities were also concerned with the danger of internal subversion within the border town in support of the rebels.

Large numbers of men were mobilised from the English shires for the succession of military campaigns aimed at crushing the rising, Those serving in Wales found it prudent to appoint attorneys to manage their affairs in their absence.[96] The crown issued *clause volumus* as a form of insurance for those employed in the king's service in Wales. Individuals arrested or outlawed gained pardons as as result of service in Wales. This included five Irish rebels who were pardoned in 1406 on account of their services against the Welsh rebels.[97]

The lands and properties of the leading rebels were forfeited and granted by the crown to its supporters and to Welsh loyalists, such as Dafydd Gam.[98] With the upsurge in the rebellion confiscations in 1403–4 reached a peak. These including the lands of prominent Glyndŵr supporters – Edmund Mortimer, Robert Pillesdon (Pulesdon), and William Lloyd – who had acted as messenger between Glyndŵr and Percy. In 1404 it was ordered that the goods and chattels of 15 Welsh rebels in Somerset and Dorset be seized.[99]

In 1404 it was reported that 7 Welsh rebels were held in the Tower, and 57 in Newgate gaol. The authorities in Bristol in 1404 were ordered to deliver the gaol of Welsh rebels held for treason. In 1409 ten of the leading rebels were held in Windsor castle. In 1410 and 1411 other rebels were held in the Tower or in the Marshalsea prison, including Glyndŵr's son Gruffydd who was held in the Tower. Some of these individuals were pardoned in this period.[100]

Both sides seized and ransomed captives.[101] In June 1412 John Tiptofte, steward of Brecon, was licensed to treat with Glyndŵr and his appointees, for the ransoming of Dafydd Gam, who had been seized by the rebels. Tiptofte was also to attempt to seize leading rebels to trade in ransom for the release of Dafydd Gam.[102]

In 1403 and again in 1404 commissions were issued to the great lords empowering them to grant pardons to the rebels in the lordships in south Wales under their control, if they surrendered, and gave up their weapons.[103] In 1406 Prince Henry was empowered to pardon rebel Welshmen in return for fines and redemptions.[104] The collection of fines was entrusted to Richard Grey.[105] In July 1406 the tenants of the earl of Arundel's lordships were pardoned.[106] In 1406 Gower, Towy and Ceredigion submitted to the king.[107] Eifionydd in Caernarfonshire also submitted in 1406, but was ruthlessly plundered by Thomas Barneby, chamberlain of north Wales.[108] In September the lordship of Denbigh submitted, and Flintshire surrendered soon afterwards, although sporadic resistance continued.[109] In November Anglesey submitted to the Prince's commissioners for a fine. They listed Glyndŵr and 95 others as outlaws.[110]

In June 1407 the duke of York persuaded Glamorgan and Morgannwg to surrender to the king's grace in return for a fine.[111] In September the tenants of 'Avensloand' and its commotes were pardoned. In November Abergavenny lordship were pardoned for a fine of 500 marks. In Powys Edward Charlton's tenants submitted and received charters of pardon. In December the tenants of Brecon and Cantrefselyf lordships received similar pardons.[112] Cardiganshire and Carmarthenshire paid fines for their pardon in 1407 and in 1409.[113]

In January 1408 the tenants of the lordships of South Wales were pardoned. In November the tenants of Whittington, by the supplication of

Elizabeth de Botreaux, were pardoned. In January 1409 the tenants in a number of central Wales lordships were pardoned. These were described as being almost desolate, with tenants having fled for fear of punishment. In February 1410 the tenants of Ogmore lordship were pardoned.[114] In these pardons to communities specific rebels were excluded from its provisions. Some rebels were subsequently granted individual pardons in return for fines.[115]

In 1409 pardons were granted to Howel ap Gwilym, abbot of Conwy, and Lewis Byford, bishop of Bangor.[116] Pardons were also granted to several other leading rebels, including in March 1411 Adam of Usk, whom it was said had been 'against his will' in the company of Glyndŵr, but had escaped as quickly as he could into the king's grace. In February 1412 a pardon was granted to Treherne ap Philip ap Llywelyn 'an adherent of Owyn de Glyndourduy, traitor'.[117]

The war devastated the native economy, leaving large areas depopulated and wasted. Towns, castles, manors, abbeys and churches were destroyed or ruined. Mills were destroyed in large numbers. Economic warfare and trade embargoes were an essential part of the tactics deployed to crush the rebellion. Tenants were killed or fled, leaving rents in 'decay'. The destruction caused was still noted by Leland in the 1530s.[118] Bishop Richard Davies in Elizabeth's reign lamented the destruction of books and libraries, and the loss of culture and learning.[119]

The rebellion seriously effected the church. In 1400 protection was extended to Conwy, Bardsey and Cymer abbey against the depredations of the rebels.[120] The Franciscan friary of Llanfaes near Beaumaris was reportedly desolated, with 'certain Friars of the house have been separated and dispersed as rebels'.[121] After 1404 the crown granted protection to individual priories (Carmarthen, Ewenny, Abergavenny), and convents and to the whole Cistercian order. Tintern abbey and Llanthony Prima, which had been damaged as a result of the rebellion, had also to be pardoned arrears.[122]

Glyndŵr's captains employed tactics of lightning raids and guerrilla warfare, disappearing and emerging out of the woods and mountains; their knowledge of the land a key advantage in their survival. Once pitched battles were engaged in the cause was lost. As well as the widespread destruction wrought by the rebellion, the revolt also witnessed terrible atrocities. Both sides used terror to intimidate and cow the opposition into submission. The mutilation of wounded English soldiers by Welshwomen after the battle of Bryn Glas in 1402 was recalled with a shudder by the Tudor historian Holinshed, and cited in Shakespeare's Henry IV.[123]

Glyndŵr was supposedly inspired by the prophecies of the bards such as

Crach Ffinnant. It was also held that he, as often with the legends of other famous rebels and outlaws, possessed magical powers. It was these powers of necromancy, referred to by Shakespeare, which supposedly accounted for the disastrous weather conditions, which beset the king's campaigns in 1402 and 1405.[124]

For the crown Glyndŵr and his followers were traitors, rebels, outlaws and robbers. Adam of Usk, the Welsh chronicler, who initially sided with the rebels, but later won his way back into royal favour, recounted how

All this summer (1401) Owain Glyndŵr, with many Welsh chiefs who were considered outlaws and traitors to the king, hiding in the mountains and the woods, now looting, now killing their enemies who laid traps and attacked them, greatly harassed the districts of West and North Wales…[125]

Another Welsh chronicler recounted how Glyndŵr in the autumn of 1400 had to flee to the woods with his followers, but the next summer with '120 reckless men and robbers' again arose, winning great fame, and rallying large numbers to his banner.[126]

G. A. Williams emphasised the strong and sustained peasant support for the rising which reflected chronic economic and social discontent.[127] This was underlined by peasant revolts against the earl of Arundel in Chirk and Oswestry, against Edward Charleton in Powys, and against the Fitzwaryn's in Whittington. R. R. Davies, emphasises the diversity of support for the ruising. Central to its initial success was his support amongst the *uchelwyr* (squirearchy). Those who allied with Glyndŵr from 1403 onwards included the leading families of the area-substantial landowners, important office holders and many, like Glyndŵr himself, with military experience with the English crown in France and Scotland. They were bound together also by complex kinship ties and family alliances. These proved extremely strong, with internal family feuds being the exception. The commitment of these men to the rising was vital to his success. After 1405 that support fragmented.

R. R. Davies neatly summarises the intricate coalescence of forces behind the rising: the peasantry provided the overwhelming military support; the Welsh students at Oxford and the exiled wage labourers brought to the movement the greatest idealism; ecclesiastics such as John Trevor and Gruffydd Yonge created the blueprint for an independent Welsh state; the propagandists were the Cistercians, the Franciscans and the bards; but the central role was provided by the squirearchy.[128]

Although this was largely an ethnic based conflict, like all national risings it was also in part a civil war. A number of prominent Welshmen remained firmly loyalist, whilst a small number of Englishmen sided with Glyndŵr. Most supported the rising out of commitment, others out of self-interest, others out of mere expediency. The impact was felt throughout Wales, although in much of the country during the insurrection the system of administration continued to function.[129] The rising in the end failed as a result of military weakness and economic exhaustion. But its fate was intimately bound up with the fate of England. Whilst the English state remained unified the rising was ultimately doomed to defeat. The failure of the Tripartite alliance sealed its fate.

CONCLUSION

The English authorities viewed Glyndŵr as an outlaw, a robber chief and lawless brigand. Most of his Welsh contemporaries revered him as a great leader. For Welsh loyalists he was a vainglorious dreamer who brought ruin on his people.[130] Whatever the judgement on Glyndŵr himself, the rising was one of the major political revolts in late medieval Europea. In Zagorin's classification of revolutions it conforms to the category of 'Provincial, regional and separatist rebellion by provincial societies or dependent realms against their monarchical state centre'. It was infused also with a strong nationalistic feeling, and set as its avowed aim the creation of a separate state.[131] Under Glyndŵr Wales achieved an unprecedented degree of unity, albeit the unity of a people at war, a war which imposed great sacrifices and costs.

George Owen of Henllys, the Elizabethan historian, deplored the discriminatory character of the Lancastrian penal code enacted between 1401 and 1404, which he argued, was more punitive than any laws enacted against 'any other capital enemies of the realm'.[132] Moreover, he asserted that the 'laws made by King Henry IV most unnaturally against Welshmen, not only for their punishment but also to deprive them of all liberty and freedom'. As a result 'there grew about this time ... deadly hatred between them and the English nation insomuch that the name of a Welshman was odious to the Englishmen, and the name of Englishmen woeful to the Welshmen'.[133] David Powel in his *Historie of Cambria*, first published in 1584, described the laws as 'more heathen than Christian'.[134]

These ill-considered laws exacerbated the crisis in 1401–2. In the longer term, many of these laws proved difficult to enforce, and could only be applied selectively. But the rising stemmed also from deep resentment against the system of English colonial rule, which had alienated all major sector of Welsh society. These new laws codified discriminatory legislation against the Welsh, and nurtured lasting resentment. The legal, civil and political rights of the Welsh were curtailed, defining them as a subjugated and conquered people. The defeat of the rising re-instituted a form of military administrative control over a re-conquered territory. The legacy of the rising, in terms of racial hatred, economic dislocation, the break down in government and the administration of justice, persisted for decades.

2 A Turbulent Land 1413–1450

It is impossible to set an exact date on the ending of the Glyndŵr rebellion. By 1410 most of Wales had been granted pardons by the crown. Guerrilla warfare continued as a form of resistance, particularly in the remoter mountain regions. The crown sought to impose order, through military occupation and by gaining the submission of the population. This was in many ways a society exhausted after the prolonged years of warfare and the devastation of the native economy. But it was a society also in which ethnic hatreds remained enflamed. As the military threat subsided Wales ceased to be a dominant concern of the English crown. The legacy of the revolt, however, remained a vital factor which shaped the crisis of public order in the marcher lordships and in the crown controlled shires of north and south Wales.

STABILISATION AND SPORADIC RESISTANCE 1413–1422

Henry V ascended in the throne on 21 March 1413. In April 1413 a royal proclamation granted a general pardon to the king's subjects of England, Wales, Scotland and Ireland who wished to 'drink of his grace', excepting those who had committed murder and rape. This was intended to still the 'whirlwinds of discord in the realm'.[1] The first parliament in May 1413 submitted petitions for urgent measures to restore order throughout the realm. The Leicester parliament of 1414, called on the king to institute 'bone governance', and in particular to pacify the Welsh rebels and establish order in the Welsh Marches.[2]

The first part of the country to which Henry turned his attention was Wales and the Welsh marches, adopting a policy which combined repression with conciliation.[3] Commissions of oyer and terminer were appointed for different parts of Wales to receive rebels, and to investigate offences committed by agents of the crown.[4] Welsh loyalists were entrusted with responsible posts in Wales.[5]

Pardons were granted to a number of rebels who had surrendered.[6] In May and June 1413 pardons were granted to eight prominent Welsh rebels, including Henry Dwn, who had led the siege of Kidwelly castle in 1403. Dwn's lands, which had been confiscated, were returned to him.[7] Over fifty former rebels were tried for treason in the Lancastrian lordship of Kidwelly. All were condemned to death by hanging and beheading, but were reprieved on payment of fines, and had their confiscated lands restored to them.[8] On his release from prison in 1413 Dwn waged a campaign against his neighbours, seizing lands, and demanding fines from 200 Welshmen who had failed to followed him in his revolt.[9]

Exasperated by the continuing resistance in Wales the crown on 6 September 1413 ordered the sheriffs of London that all men born in Wales should leave England before Christmas, on pain of forfeiture. In November and December about 40 Welshmen, including Adam of Usk and David Holbache, purchased licenses exempting them from this law, allowing them to remain in residence in England and to practice their professions. Provisions were also made allowing Welsh students (clerks) to buy licenses to study in England.[10] Another Act prohibited Welshmen from pressing actions in respect of injuries sustained by them during the rebellion, upon pain of paying treble damages and being imprisoned for two years. In 1414 a further Act dealt with the recurrent problem of raids by Welshmen into the neighbouring English counties.[11] In the following years many individual rebels were pardoned, with forfeited lands and possessions returned.[12]

At the end of 1413 a royal ordinance was issued for the return of tenants and bondmen who had fled, particularly from Merionethshire, into the marcher lordships and south Wales. A grant of £200 was allowed for the restocking of Caernarfonshire and Merionethshire with sheep and cattle. Debts incurred before 1411 were cancelled.[13] The economic effect of the rebellion, however, was long felt, reflected in the crisis of crown and seigniorial revenues, with communities unable to meet their dues.[14]

Alongside these concessions went a more repressive policy. From 1411 onwards the Crown imposed heavy fines on the communities involved in the rebellion.[15] In 1413 Cardiganshire and Carmarthenshire paid 400 and 800 marks respectively, on top of the payments which they had made in 1407 and 1409. In 1414 Cardiganshire paid a further fine of 1,000 marks. The Lancastrian lordships paid a total of 2,260 marks.[16] In November 1413 fines were levied on the north Wales counties – Caernarfon 500 marks, Anglesey 800 marks, Merioneth 300 marks, and Flint 500 marks – to be paid over a period of 6 to 8 years.[17]

The process of submission had its own ritual. At Bala, Merionethshire, in March 1414, 600 inhabitants of the county appeared before Arundel and his fellows. Prostrating themselves to the ground, they begged for the king's mercy, acknowledging that according to the strict letter of the law they deserved conviction and death as traitors. The plea roll recorded that on receipt of a communal pardon, they thanked God on their knees for granting them such a magnanimous king. They were required to pay the fine of 300 marks over three years. A similar practice of submission was followed at Caernarfon and Beaumaris.[18] The crown in November 1414 confirmed these general pardons, and in response to petitions from North Wales decreed that everyone be restored to the lands they had held before the revolt broke out.[19]

As a result in two years Henry V raised just over £5,000 in collective fines from his Welsh lands. This did not include the fines paid by individual rebels, in the case of Henry Don 400 marks, in other cases more modest fines up to £5. This compared with a total annual income from Wales before the outbreak of the revolt of £1,000.[20] This provoked opposition from Merionethshire in 1416 and Cardiganshire in 1417.[21] A similar situation existed in the marcher lordships.

Efforts were made to curb official corruption. Thomas Barneby, chamberlain of north Wales since 1406, in May 1412 was pardoned 'treasons, insurrections, rebellions, felonies, trespasses, offences and misprisons' committed by him before 7 December 1411.[22] In 1413–14, however, Barneby, was arraigned before the judicial commission, headed by the earl of Arundel, investigating official corruption. Representatives of the communities of Anglesey, Caernarfon and Merioneth accused him of rallying support for the Percy rebellion in north Wales in 1403, of consorting with the adherent of Glyndŵr, supplying the rebels in return for money, and empanelling juries which included unpardoned rebels to prosecute royal officials. Further, he was accused of appropriating confiscated lands and livestock for his own profit – including the despoiling of Eifionydd in Caernarfonshire in 1406 which led to the flight of tenants, embezzlement, and a host of other offences. In spite of attempts to bribe the jurors, the king's justice dismissed him as chamberlain on 19 March 1414.[23]

Thomas Walton was appointed chamberlain of north Wales in his stead. Barneby was treated leniently, although he was required to repay the crown part of the money he had appropriated. He became treasurer of Harfleur in Normandy, but retained the constableship of Caernarfon until his death in 1427.[24]

The judicial commission into official corruption also took measures against officials in the lordship of Kidwelly.[25] Pardons were granted to crown officials for offences committed during the Glyndŵr rising, and arrears of revenues by stewards in charge of the crown lordships were waived.[26] In February 1415 lands confiscated from the tenants of St. Asaph, on account of their rebellion, were granted, on the petition of bishop Robert of Lancaster, to the bishop for a payment of 10 marks.[27]

The crown after 1413 sought to tighten up the system of financial control, through the appointment of crown auditors to monitor the work of the Exchequers in Caernarfon and Carmarthen.[28] The crown also sought to assist in protecting seigniorial revenues. It instructed Gilbert Taylor and others in February 1416 to secure the payment of arrears of rents and others debts by the ministers and tenants of the lordships of Bromfield and Yale, and Oswestry to the widow of the late earl of Arundel.[29]

After 1413 the crown confirmed charters and letters patent granted to Tenby, Haverford and Newport in south Wales.[30] In May 1415 the crown granted Carmarthen *murage* for five years to rebuild the town-walls, razed by the Welsh rebels, since 'the inhabitants are robbed at night for lack of enclosure'.[31]

An important idication that the situation had not been fully normalised were the restrictions imposed on travel. In 1413 the Beaumaris ferry was instructed that no Welshman should on any account be transported to Anglesey except with the special mandate of the Prince of Wales or his Justices. This injunction was reinvoked in 1438.[32]

The rebellion blurred the distinction between politically motivated offences and simple criminality. The tasks of crown and manorial officers were severely complicated. Sometime between 1407 and 1413 the prince's lieutenant sought to impose a fine of 100 marks on the prince's tenants of Netherwent for failing in the court of Caerleon to impose the correct punishment on 'certain persons outlawed'.[33] Measures had to be instituted to protect officials travelling in Wales.[34] Rebels continued to make depredations at night.[35] The Commons ascribed the lawlessness to the fact that tenants could pass from one lordship to another by becoming advowry tenants.[36] Daring attempts, some successful, were made to release prisoners from the goals.[37] Individuals were outlawed and their protectors prosecuted.[38]

The rebellion had long since passed its peak. Resistance continued to flare up periodically, but, deprived of effective leadership, it increasingly lost its focus. In 1415 Owain Glyndŵr disappeared. According to a Welsh chronicle:

Owen went into hiding on St Mathew's Day in Harvest (September 21st), that he died: the seers (brudwyr – i.e. the bards) maintain he did not and thereafter his hiding place was unknown.[39]

The leader of this incipient proto-nationalist movement became a hunted outlaw, a guerrilla leader on the run. There developed around Glyndŵr an extraordinarily tenacious set of beliefs, strongly propagated by the bards; that he had not died and that 'Owain' would again return as a national redeemer.[40] This belief recurs in other millenarian movements, and, as Hobsbawm notes, is associated also with some famous bandit legends. In 1415, 1416 and 1417 attempts were made to secure the surrender, with the prospect of pardon, of Glyndŵr, his son Meredydd and other rebel leaders.[41] Conscious that they were fighting a hopeless cause, they could not and would not submit. As with all guerilla wars the problem of securing supplies and of living off the land, was solved by the inevitable recourse to brigandage.

During the Agincourt campaign three hundred men were considered sufficient to protect the whole of Wales. The earl of Arundel was dispatched there to hold musters and to report on the situation.[42] The main concentration of English troops was at Cymer and Strata Florida.[43] In February 1416 Humphrey, duke of Gloucester, was granted Llanstephan Castle, forfeited by William Gwyn, who had supported Glyndŵr, and whose son, Henry Gwyn, had fought for the French against the English.[44] In June 1416 Robert Hill, king's justice of south Wales, was commissioned to investigate cases of treason and insurrection in Cardiganshire, and the lordships of Pembroke and Cilgerran, and to fine and ransom the offenders.[45] Further commissions were appointed to the lordships of Pembroke and Cilgerran in 1419 and 1421.[46]

Resistance was strongest and most tenacious in the mountainous regions of north Wales, the stronghold of the rising. In 1416–17 Meredydd ap Owain made a final attempt to rally opposition in north Wales with the support of the Scots.[47] In 1416 John Salghall, constable of Harlech, warned the chamberlain of north Wales of the anticipated landing in Merioneth-shire. In north Wales young men were preparing for war, procuring arms, stealing horses, and assembling in remote and hidden regions.[48] Hywel ap Meilyr, one of those implicated in this plot, was seized, held at Pool castle, tried by the justices in Conwy and hanged.[49]

In 1414 Sir John Oldcastle of Herefordshire was accused of having organised a Lollard plot to overturn the government. Orders were issued for his arrest, and his goods were seized. On his non-appearance in court he was outlawed. Oldcastle may have attempted to broker an alliance with Meredydd ap Owain. He lived the life of a fugitive in Herefordshire and the Marches until 1417 when he was apprehended at Broniarth and imprisoned in Welshpool.[50]

In May 1417 Henry V ordered that the sheriffs in Anglesey, Caernarfon-shire and Merionethshire should be resident, and that castle constables should be of English birth, and be required to carry out their duties conscientiously. Bondmen who had fled north Wales into the marcher lordships were to be returned.[51]

In January 1420 John, duke of Bedford, was empowered to treat with Meredydd ap Owain regarding the possibility of his serving under the king in Normandy. In April 1421 his pardon was confirmed. The pardon repeated the common legal fiction in such documents that Meredydd had not followed his father's malice, but had lived peaceably amongst the king's subject and had submitted himself to the king as soon as he could.[52] Thomas Walton, chamberlain of north Wales, was granted full powers to receive into the king's grace all the Welsh rebels who were prepared to surrender themselves for a fine.[53] Harsh justice continued to be meted out to the most recalcitrant rebels. In Shrewsbury in 1421 a Welsh squire Rees ap Doe was hung, drawn and quartered for treason.[54]

THE REIGN OF HENRY VI 1422–1450

When the child king Henry VI ascended the throne in 1422 the problem of maintaining civil order intensified. The king's council met at Windsor on 28 September and declared its purpose to guarantee peace, particularly on the Welsh border. Parliament six weeks later confirmed this commitment.[55] Fear of rebellion in Wales persisted. In 1424 it was rumoured that Sir John Mortimer, the imprisoned traitor, was planning to raise 40,000 [sic] men in Wales and the marches to overturn the government.[56] In 1426 the government admitted that criminal bands were perpetrating open and notorious robberies and misdeeds throughout the realm. The king's councillors were required to take an oath not to protect criminals, either by influencing judges or jurors, or by taking them into their service. Those who defaulted were to be excommunicated.[57]

Wales was governed through the appointment of a powerful magnates, with proconsular powers. In this period the role was given to Humphrey, duke of Gloucester. In 1414 he had been appointed earl of Pembroke, and became a powerful patron of the gentry of south-west Wales. In 1427 he was appointed justice for north Wales. He was engaged in bitter rivalry with the duke of Suffolk. Offices in Wales often served as sinecures for powerful English magnates.[58] Sir John Radcliffe was made chamberlain of north Wales in February 1434 to allow him to recoup the debt owed him by the crown for his services in France.[59]

In the administration of justice recourse was had to the use of commissions of oyer and terminer. In June 1424 James Audeley, Edward Stradling and William Rede were commissioned to inquire into all treasons and felonies in South Wales.[60]

The laws enacted in 1401 and 1402, which excluded the Welsh from holding office or owning lands in the English boroughs in Wales and in the towns in England, remained in force.[61] In the 1420s the charters of various towns and lordships were renewed – Cardigan (1426), Tallacharn (1428), St Clears (1428), Denbigh (1427) – which reaffirmed the rights of the burgesses, particularly stressing that English burgesses and tenants who inhabited the said towns and lordships could only be tried and convicted by a jury of their compatriots.[62]

In 1429 the Commons, in a petition to the king, noted attempts by the Welsh to inveigle themselves into public office in the boroughs by bribery and by concealment of their backgrounds. Once in office they allowed their fellows to purchase lands and to occupy public office, threatening the English burgesses' hold on the boroughs. The petition demanded that in view of the 'ancient malice and enmity' towards the English in Wales, heightened by the Glyndŵr rising, the provisions of the laws should be strictly enforced. Similar petitions were presented to Parliament in 1433.[63]

A statute of 1430 ruled that Englishmen married to Welshwomen, who were allied to Glyndŵr and his confederates, should be barred from office in Wales and the marches. It confirmed all the previous judgements and processes against Owain Glyndŵr, his relations and heirs, on account of the 'horribility of his many treasons'.[64] In 1433 Sir John Scudamore, Glyndŵr's son in law, was dismissed as sheriff of Herefordshire. Scudamore had incurred the wrath of Somerset, then imprisoned in France, by petitioning that Glyndŵr's former lands in Sycharth and Glyndyfrdwy be entailed to him.[65] The Somerset family retained these lands until 1461.[66]

These measures reflected a growing unease regarding the situation in Wales. In February 1431 a commission was set up into treasons and felonies in Cardiganshire and other parts of south Wales. In March 1432 a similar commission was established for north Wales.[67] In 1433–4 the nobility and the gentry were asked to take an oath that they would not maintain criminals, not support other men's quarrels, overawe juries, officers or judges, nor give criminals livery nor take them into their service. In Wales 'love days' were to be organised for the swearing ceremony.[68]

Uchelwyr sought to sttrengthen their position by drawing outlaws into their service. In 1435 one complainant to the king's council claimed that he dare not 'sue the common law' out of fear of violence because Morgan ap Dafydd Vaughan, recently a royal official in Carmarthenshire, 'draweth unto him outlaws and diverse misruled men the which obey not our law [and] neither our officers'.[69]

Lawlessness amongst the Welsh resident in England also drew the attention of the authorities.[70] The lawlessness of Welsh scholars at Oxford and Cambridge university was notorious, with the Welsh siding with the English southerners against the northerners in periodic riots.[71]

Rebels and brigands

The Glyndŵr rising and the crown's efforts to suppres it left a legacy of disorder which persisted for decades. Antipathy towards English rule remained intense. The form of guerrilla warfare deployed by the Welsh rebels in time degenerated into brigandage. Those who would not submit to the crown sought to create their own redoubts in the more inaccessible mountainous regions of north Wales.

It is very difficult to document this process. We might, however, surmise, that one of the main bastions for these rebel forces, was the region of the Berwyn mountains. This region neighboured Glyndŵr's territory in Glyndyfrdwy and Edernion. It is situated between Merionethshire and the marcher lordships of Powys, including the lordship of Mawddwy. Berwyn and Mawddwy in the fifteenth and sixteenth centuries were notorious as bandit redoubts (pp. 100–1, 209–17 below).

In the lordship of Mawddwy in 1415–6, the local courts imposed entry fines for rebels seeking to return to their farms, with large forfeitures imposed on those rebels who remained loyal to Glyndŵr.[72] Here we appear to have evidence which suggests strong connections between the rebels of the Glyndŵr rising and subsequent generation of brigands who populated this region. Through the fifteenth into the sixteenth century we have extensive documentation of the problem of raiding between the lordships of Powys and Merionethshire. One means of dealing with the problem of raiding between different jurisdictions was the convening of 'love days' or *le day de redresse*.

In February 1430 Henry IV issued orders to Humphrey, duke of Gloucester, justice of north Wales, to the chamberlain of north Wales and the sheriff of Merioneth, concerning serious disturbances (*grandes debates dissensions et riotes*) between the men of Principality and those of Powys. It ordered the convening of a parliamentum between the men of Powys and Merioneth at Bwlch Oerddrws; a site described as *auncienement accustumez pur convenir et traiter amaiablement de les trespasses, oppressions et iniuries qeconques faites de lune et lautre.*[73]

During the financial year 1431–2 three such parliamentum were held at Bwlch Oerddrws. During the next four years there were assemblies at Bwlch Oerddrws and at Carnedd Hywel. These assemblies were attended by representatives of the crown, the officers of the lordships of Powys, and members of the communities directly concerned. As a result of a royal mandate in November 1448 an order was issued requiring the restitution of cattle stolen in Mawddwy and the other lordships of Powys and taken into Merionethshire and Caernarfonshire. The lords of Powys (Sir Henry Grey,

Lord John Tippetofte, Lord John Dudley) and John Burgh, lord of
Mawddwy, were to enforce reciprocal arrangements for the restitution of
cattle stolen in their lordships. The ordinance was to be effective for seven
years. In 1449–50 Henry Norris, deputy chamberlain of north Wales and
other crown officials (*generosi et officiarii regis*) visited the region to
secure peace between the men of the principality and those of Powys.

The deepening crisis 1437–1450

In 1437 the young and infirm Henry VI came of age, and quickly became
the focus of contending factions. Parliament convened on 21 January 1437
with the principal aim of restoring peace and justice amongst the king's
subjects.[74] A plan mooted at this time for the establishment of a Council to
deal with the affairs of Wales and the Marches came to naught.[75]

The crown administration in Wales was entrusted to powerful notables.
By June 1438 William, duke of Suffolk was justiciar of south Wales and
soon afterwards transferred to north Wales. South Wales was effectively
controlled by the king's uncle Humphrey, duke of Gloucester, appointed as
justiciar in February 1440 'to ease the great debates' there.[76] He was later
succeeded by Lord Beauchamp. In south Wales Lord Audley was chamberlain from 1439 until he was killed at the battle of Blore Heath in September
1459. Lord Stanley, with large estates in Cheshire and Lancashire, was
appointed justiciar and chamberlain of north Wales until his death in
February 1459, when Lord Dudley succeeded him.[77]

The governance of Wales was hampered by administrative fragmentation, and the struggle between factions. It was also gravely undermined by
the crown's policy of appointing officials from the royal household to
offices in north and south Wales. Grooms of the cellar and pages of the
kitchen were transformed into armourers, master carpenters and masons,
who held these posts as absentees but received their salaries.[78]

In August 1440 Gloucester, as Justice of south Wales, was commissioned to investigate all offences committed under the late and present king
in Cardiganshire, Carmarthenshire and Pembroke. In February 1441 the
duke of Suffolk was commissioned to make inquisitions into treason and
felonies in the Duchy of Lancaster lordships of south Wales.[79]

The crisis of royal authority in Wales was reflected in the difficulties
encountered in raising revenue. Resistance by the tenantry to the levying
of rents and taxes was very strong. In the crown controlled shires of north
Wales there was continuing difficulties in gathering revenue. In 1446 the
crown pardoned James, Lord Audley, for a debt of £146, on account of the
fact that his officials had failed to collect revenue in south Wales. Some of

the officials and debtors were deceased, some depressed by poverty, whilst others had left the county, been outlawed, or had fled into the mountains.[80] People fled from Carmarthenshire and Cardiganshire in order to avoid paying taxes.[81]

Conflict between the great lords Somerset and Warwick, over the custody of land in Glamorgan in 1443, brought the area to the brink of a private war. There were 'great gatherings, congregations and assemblies unlawful' in Cardiff, and Cowbridge Castle was strongly manned 'as it were in a land of war'. Somerset and Warwick were cited before the king and ordered to surrender the disputed lands to lord Dudley as temporary keeper, until the council could determine who should have their custody.[82]

Gloucester's rivals, the duke of Suffolk and Lord Saye, accused him of raising rebellion in Wales against the king. In February 1447 he was executed at Bury St Edmonds.[83] Forty-two of his followers, mostly Welsh-men, were arrested and imprisoned, including Gruffydd ap Nicholas, Henry Wogan, Owain Dwn and Thomas Herbert. The most prominent were saved from execution by royal pardon. Gloucester's death provoked angry reaction in Wales. It may be connected with the decision to reinforce the garrison in Beaumaris in 1447 against a possible landing by Scots, Bretons and other enemies, at a time when it was said that the Welsh were much agitated.[84]

Gruffydd ap Nicholas of Dinefwr, with his sons Owain and Thomas, assumed a central role in the administration of south west Wales.[85] They were strongly opposed by a rival faction led by John ap Rhys and Meredydd ap Owain. In 1439 there were serious disturbances and outrages committed as a result of rivalry between the two factions. Attempts by two commissions of oyer and terminer, in 1440 and 1441, to call Gruffydd ap Nicholas to account were contemptuously rebuffed. From 1443 onwards he served as deputy chamberlain and lieutenant justiciar of south Wales. Having survived Gloucester's demise, Gruffydd ap Nicholas after 1447 had virtual control of the government of the principality of south Wales.

Legislative enactments against the Welsh

The laws enacted against Welshmen under Henry IV remained in force. Relations between the Welsh and the English in the Marches and in the towns of Wales remained fractious. It produced sporadic outbursts of violence, such as the Black Affray of Beaumaris in the 1440s.[86] In the decades following the rising the English border counties fell constant prey to raiders from Wales (see chapter 7).

Parliament in 1441 ruled that Welsh raiders into the border English shires be judged guilty of treason, and punished accordingly, i.e. executed. Foreign merchandise brought into Wales without paying customs duty was to be forfeited. The Privy Council in October 1442 instructed the marcher lords to proceed home to quell the disturbances and riots in Wales and the Marches. Should they flout these orders, it warned, the king would take matters into his own hands.[87]

In 1442 and 1444 the English burgesses of north Wales petitioned the King's Council for more rigorous application of Henry IV's penal statutes against the Welsh. The Commons concurred, noting that the securing by Welshmen of the rights of denizenship was to the 'utter destruction of all Englishmen in the said towns' in the northern principality, and declared that 'no manner Welshmen of whole blood nor half blood on the fathers side ... be made denizen or English' and that no Welshman was to hold office on pain of a fine of 200 marks.[88]

In March 1446 the crown freed the king's bondmen in Anglesey, Caernarfonshire and Merionethshire of the obligation which had been placed on them for the execution of felons. This in the past had been done under the sheriff's supervision. As a result, it noted, many bondmen had fled from the counties to various parts of England, leaving towns desolate and rents and services unpaid. In Flintshire, by contrast, executions were carried out by the sheriffs before the justices.[89] This was a highly sensitive issue since native Welsh law had no provision for capital punishment, which was viewed as a barbaric feature of English law.

In 1447 the mayors, aldermen, bailiffs and burgesses of the English boroughs of north Wales again petitioned the king to ratify all statutes made against Welshmen and to declare void all grants or franchises for markets and fairs, buying and selling, baking and brewing granted to them in these towns. It demanded also that the king's bondmen in north Wales be bounded to do 'such labours and services of right as they have used to do of old times, not withstanding any grant made of them or any usage used by them of late time to the contrary'.[90] Another petition of 1447 from the 'English people of Wales' to the king deplored the efforts of 'diverse Welshmen' to harass and destroy the English in Wales, on account of the 'great hate which the Welsh still have for the English since the late rebellion in Wales'.[91] The Welsh, it charged, inveigled their way into the English towns by purchasing rights, through marriage and royal dispensations. They oppressed the English burgesses, compelled many of them to depart, threatened to take over the boroughs and undermined the stability of the realm.

Parliament in 1447 confirmed all statutes against Welshmen, and declared all grants and privileges made to them in north Wales void.

Moreover, it ruled that all the king's villeins in north Wales were to be compelled to do such labour and services as they had been accustomed to do, including presumably the execution of felons.[92] A petition presented to Parliament in 1449 maintained that in Wales – in the shires, the royal lordships and in the Duchy of Lancaster properties – that 'misgoverned people' were taking 'diverse persons and cattle, under colour of distress'. This had provoked resistance with 'great assemblies of people, riots, maims and murders' 'whereof the people of the said parts daily abound and increase in evil government'. The taking of goods, cattle and persons without warrant was to be deemed a felony.[93]

The reimposition of the anti-Welsh legislation of Henry IV's reign in the 1440s doubtlessly hardened attitudes. The abbot of Coldingham, Dunfermline in a letter to bishop Kennedy of St. Andrews denounced English tyranny in terms that many Welshmen might have echoed – 'tyranny and cruelty of the English are notorious throughout the world, as manifestly appears in their usurpations against the French, Scots, Welsh, Irish, and neighbouring lands'.[94]

LAWLESSNESS AND THE CHURCH 1413–1450

The Glyndŵr rebellion left the church in a severely weakened state for decades thereafter. Many churches, monasteries and other properties were left wasted and in ruins. Abbots and churchmen who had sided with the rebels were obliged to sue for pardons. In the fifteenth century senior positions in the church, with some exceptions, continued to be asigned to absentee English clerics. After the rebellion church property fell prey to the lawless elements in society, whilst churchmen resorted to armed force to settle disputes, where there was no strong central authority capable of imposing order.[95]

The crown in 1413 extended protection to Robert Clyfton, monk, travelling in 'diverse parts of Wales' to collect dues from Pembroke priory. In 1414 the abbot of Vale Royal was pardoned dues owing to the crown from the abbey's holding of the church of Llanbadarn Fawr, since no revenue had been collected 'on account of the rebellion in the arch-deaconry'. In 1414 the crown provided aid to re-establish the Franciscan friary at Llanfaes, Anglesey, 'lately desolated by the rebellion of the Welsh and the wars there'. The same year the bishop of St. Asaph was pardoned dues, owing to 'the burning and destruction of the cathedral church of St. Asaph by the rebellion of the Welsh'. In 1418 the crown provided aid to restitute 'goods and benefices of poor nuns and hospitallers' in Wales 'destroyed or diminished by hostile incursions'.[96]

A number of incidents point to a significant break down in law and order. In August 1415 the bishop of Llandaff reported to his superiors that he had been unable to assemble the clergy of his diocese for array 'owing to the dangers of the roads and the ambushes of robbers, who are more than usually active'.[97] In 1422 Thomas, abbot of Margam, and John, abbot of Neath, were granted by the crown safe-conduct to enter Carmarthenshire and Cardiganshire to visit their properties. In 1423 Pope Martin V in a Papal Bull ordered the abbot of Margam to excommunicate the 'sons of iniquity' who had despoiled the monastery of Neath, unless restitution was made by a certain date.[98]

The church continued to suffer from the depradations of local magnates. In August 1424 John ap Philip Morgan, a Welshman from Netherwent, who was constable of Berkeley castle in Gloucestershire, attacked the grange of the Benedictine priory of Goldcliff (Gwent). A large herd of cattle was rustled and taken by him to Berkeley. Two weeks later the priory itself was attacked, causing the prior and monks to flee. The prior, having failed to find redress in the court of the marcher lordship of Caerleon, the property of the earl of March, appealed in November 1424 to the king's council.[99]

The rebellion left the Welsh Cistercian order in a parlous state, with open conflict between individuals for control of the abbeys.[100] In 1427–28 John, abbot of Strata Florida, petitioned the king, complaining that John ap Rhys, abbot of Aberconwy, accompanied by other monks of his house and by a large band of armed men and archers, had seized Strata Florida by force. They left after forty days, taking with them all the books, vestments, gold and silver and other movables belonging to the monastery, and driving away horses, cows and sheep to the value of 2,000 marks. The petitioners prayed the king for a remedy against this 'horrible trespass'.[101] The abbots of Margam and Whitland were entrusted with protecting Strata Florida from thieves and robbers.

In 1430 the crown granted protection to the abbot of Talley, which had been ruined by misrule and vexatious suits. In 1431 similar protection was extended to St. Mary's convent in Chester, whose Welsh lands had been devastated by the rebels, and in 1432 protection was granted to the priory of St. John's in Carmarthen.[102] The abbot of Strata Florida in 1435 was bound over for £500 to appear in the court of Chancery and to desist from offering violence to his brother abbot of Vale Royal (Cheshire), or the latter's servants in the parish of Llanbadarn Fawr.[103]

In 1442–3 John ap Rhys, who had led the raid on Strata Florida in 1427–8, as abbot of the impoverished abbey of Cymer in Merionethshire, was again harassing another abbot of Strata Florida, William Morys, and claiming the abbacy for himself.[104] In 1443 protection was granted to the abbot of Cymer, who was daily disturbed and unable to celebrate divine service.[105]

Powerful magnates competed with each other for control over the church. In a dispute concerning the appointment of a new prior to Goldcliff in 1441 Sir William ap Thomas of Raglan provided one claimant, John Twining, a monk of Gloucester, with a band of eighty armed men. They broke into the priory, seized the rival prior and imprisoned him in chains in Usk castle. Thereupon he ordered the prior to resign 'if not, he would make him, with violence, even if he were on the high altar of the priory'.[106] The abbot of Vale Royal, who had possessions in Llanbadarn and elsewhere in Wales, complained of Welshmen who had taken him to court on false accusations because he had not given them 'rewards and fees'. Moreover, he 'could not pass through certain lordships without being assaulted and beaten'.[107] In the early 1440s the abbot of the Cistercian abbey of Basingwerk complain to the king's council of his losses as a result of riots and robberies.[108]

The embers of rebellion continued to flicker. Priests and monks, as seen during the Glyndŵr rising, were not cut off from contemporary political struggles, but were often intimately involved as social leaders and opinion formers. In June 1427 James Audley and others were commissioned to investigate charges of treason against Mathew ap Llywelyn Ddu, canon of the abbey of Talley (Talyllychau) who was accused of stirring up rebellion.[109] The Privy Council in 1443 ordered that an unnamed monk of Whitland, the motherhouse of the Cistercians, who had traversed north and south Wales, holding riotous assemblies and stirring the people to rebellion, should be 'found and taken'.[110]

The other source of subversion was provided by the bards. In July 1442 Edmund Beaufort and Lord Audley headed a commission inquiring into a long list of offences in west Wales, including the activity of the bards who were relating 'Chronicles at Commorthas and other gatherings etc., to the motion of the people'.[111]

CONCLUSION

The system of rule instituted in the decades following the Glyndŵr revolt was based on the granting of proconsular powers to powerful English magnates. It was in part a system of military occupation, and of central control through a plethora of commissions of oyer and terminer. The rebellion left a bitter legacy of animosity. The English parliament renewed its harsh legislation against the native population in the 1420, 1430s and

1440s, and these laws were reinforced by the charters granted to the boroughs in Wales and on the border.

The problem of disorder was compounded by the weakness of central government, administrative fragmentation and reliance on local magnates in dispensing justice[112] Lawlessness was not an aberration but was rooted in the conditions of the time and in the particularities of Welsh society and the system of government to which it was subjected. Lawlessness was also symptomatic of an endemic social ferment, a form of resistance against alien rule, which after the embers of the Glyndŵr rebellion had cooled could never again find its central focus.

Brigandage was a feature of life, which assumed various forms: the depredations of rebels deprived of their lands and rights; the actions of powerful magnates and their retinues engaged in struggles with their neighbours; the actions of outlaw gangs and raiders. These different forms of brigandage were closely interconnected, the crimes of powerful magnates linked to that perpetrated by their retinues and their tenantry, the hiring of outlaws by magnates, the toleration and encouragement of lawbreakers. One feature of this period was the prevalence of acts of violence and robbery directed against the English in the borough towns, the border counties or lone travellers in Wales. But the main victims of this disorder were the Welsh themselves, particularly the weak and defenceless not only at the hands of criminals and outlaw gangs, but also at the hands of the powerful local magnates and their retinues.

3 State, Law and Society

The crisis of disorder, which engulfed large parts of England and Wales for much of the fifteenth century, derived from certain common sources. Here we shall try to disentangle some of the factors that contributed to that crisis. Wales was not unique in the acute disorder which it experienced. But Wales in vital respects was decidedly different. Wales constituted a separate geographic entity, on the English state's periphery, remote, mountainous and difficult to govern. In its language, culture and mores it constituted a distinct society. It was a society which had been conquered in the thirteenth century, and newly re-conquered with the defeat of Glyndŵr. Large parts of the country were seriously disrupted and economically damaged by the war. The prolonged experience of guerrilla warfare created its own problems in restoring order. It was a land in which the evidence of military occupation, by what was perceived as an alien, oppressive and illegitimate force, was readily apparent. Animosity towards the ruling power, whose discriminatory legislation defined the Welsh as a conquered and subject people, remained intense.

The Medieval State

The problem of disorder reflected in part the limited capacity of the medieval state, its decentralised character and its need to take account of rival foci of power, both secular and ecclesiastical, at local level. The problem in Wales was compounded by the lack of uniformity between different jurisdictions. Wales comprised a mosaic of different administrative and judicial authorities. The principality shires were organised into two groups, Anglesey, Caernarfon and Merioneth in north Wales, and Carmarthen and Cardigan in south Wales. They were governed directly by the crown, through its chief justices and chamberlains. The chamberlain was responsible for administration, dispensing justice, collecting taxes and managing the crown's properties. The Exchequers in Caernarfon and Carmarthen, were the chief administrative centres.[1]

These shires were administered in the main like English counties, though the 'Statute of Wales' had preserved some Welsh laws and customs. From 1284 the upholding of law in these counties was the responsibility of the sheriff, who was assisted also by coroners and bailiffs.[2] The Great Sessions were held in these counties, but manorial courts also remained important. Below the sheriffs were the sergeants of the peace (in Welsh *cais* or seekers/searchers)[3] and the officers of the *rhingyll* and *rhaglaw*. Alongside the Principality shires were the Palatines of Glamorgan and Pembroke which were also governed by the laws and customs of England, and Flintshire which was subject to the Exchequer and Chief Justice of Chester.[4]

The Anglo-Norman marcher lordships of the March (in Welsh *Y Mars*) provided a peculiar administrative entity. Glanmor Williams calculates that there were about 45 lordships and A. C. Reeves gives a figure of about 40.[5] The Duchy of Lancaster owned a string of lordships across south Wales: Kidwelly (including Carnwyllion and Iscennen), Ogmore, Ebbw, Brecon, Monmouth, Grosmont, Skenfrith, Whitecastle and Caldicot.[6] The earldom of March controlled a number of lordships from north to south Wales. At the beginning of the fifteenth century the lords Beauchamp of Abergavenny, the Despenser of Glamorgan, and Grey of Ruthin were the dominant families. Other major marcher lords were the earls of Warwick (Beauchamp, from 1449 Nevilles), Buckingham (Staffords), Somerset (Beauforts), Shrewsbury (Talbots), March (Mortimer), lord Abergavenny (Beauchamp), Lord Stanley and Fitzalan. Other Anglo-Norman settlers (*advenae*) like the Wogans and Stradlings intermarried with the Welsh.

The marcher lordships existed as miniature statelets with their own laws (*lex et consuetudo Marchiae*). They were, however, not entirely free from outside interference. The crown gave authorisation to the marcher lords to enter their estates in Wales. In cases of severe disorder the crown could threaten to bring the marcher lords to account. On occasions these lordships fell into the hands of the crown by escheat or forfeiture. During the minority of heirs (*nonage*) lordships came under the wardship of the crown, and were usually given to other powerful lords for their management, which often meant their ruthless exploitation.

Throughout the Anglo-Welsh borderland dozens of small castles and fortresses testified to the power of the marcher lords. They maintained armed retinues (in Welsh *sawdwyr* or *iwmyn*) to deal with recalcitrant peasants or neighbouring lords. Tudur Penllyn speaks of the silk liveried retainers of Watcyn Vaughan of Hergest (*Mae sidan am ei sawdwyr*).[7] Guto'r Glyn notes the damask livery of the yeomen of Sir Walter Herbert (*Mae damasg am dy iwmyn*).[8] Welshmen found employment in the retinues of Welsh magnates and English marcher lords.

Within the lordships the General Receiver or Chamberlain was responsible for finances, the Constable for the administration of the castle, the Chief Seneschal for the administration of justice, and the Chief

Forester for the forests and parks. Beneath the Chief Seneschal were his deputies – the coroner, sheriff and escheator. Below the sheriff were the constable (*rhaglaw*), the beadle (*rhingyll*) and the chief sergeant or keeper of the peace (*pencais*).[9] Lordships had their own courts, whilst borough courts exercised their own jurisdiction.

The system of administration in the shires and lordships, in the civil and ecclesiastical realm, shared certain common characteristics. It was a fragmented and devolved system of administration, which was cliental in nature. In this system powerful patrons were responsible for their clients, and their clients, exercising considerable autonomy in their own realm, owed allegiance to their patrons. At each level individuals faced the challenge of those contending for their position, and the challenge of keeping subordinates in line.

The Social Order

The population of Wales by 1530s is variously estimated at about a quarter of a million.[10] Medieval Welsh society differed significantly from that of English society.[11] The Welsh *uchelwyr* (the high men) approximated very loosely to the English conception of gentry, gentlemen and squires. Whilst no Welsh family could claim noble status, there were substantial Welsh landowners designated as *uchelwyr*. The rise of this stratum, R. A. Griffiths argues, was one of the key aspects of Welsh society in the later Middle Ages. They were the leaders of society at a local level, the patrons of the church and of Welsh culture. They also provided political leadership as officers of the Crown and marcher lords. They constituted an assertive class, closely bound by ties of kinship.[12]

The church and the monasteries were the other important landowners in society. Urban development was very limited and there was no significant merchant class outside of the main seaports, castle and border market towns. In the castle towns the English burgesses predominated. Below the *uchelwyr* were the free tenants and cottars. At the bottom of the social hierarchy lay the villein and bondmen (*taeogion*), who constituted the largest section of the population. In the remoter mountain areas the manorial system had not taken root, and the pastoral economy nurtured a sturdy, independent stratum of free tenants, who clung to their right to bear arms.

This was a society marked by strict codes of social hierarchy. For the gentry social pedigree was highly valued, and the martial virtues highly esteemed, as were the obligations of charity to the weaker elements in society. Following the Edwardian conquest the civil and military administration of the Principality was entrusted into the hands of Englishmen. The marcher lords showed a similar preference for English officials as stewards, bailiffs and receivers. At a local level the employment of native Welsh officials with knowledge of the language, and familiarity with Welsh laws and legal practice was a necessity. The co-option and integration of Welsh families into the system of crown and lordship administration provided opportunities for advancement.

Leading Welsh families rose to prominence in this period. The fortunes of the Herberts of Raglan were founded by Sir William ap Thomas, known to the bards as the blue knight of Gwent (*y marchog glas o Went*). He fought at Agincourt, built up his estate through marriage, and in the 1430s rebuilt Raglan castle on the model of a French chateau. The rival family of Dinefwr, headed by Gruffydd ap Nicholas, dominated west Wales. Other families such as the Games, Dwnns, and the Vaughans of Tretower governed their own territories.

Society was shaped by contradictory impulses of upward and downward mobility. The Welsh custom of partible inheritance (*cyfran* – similar to the English law of gavelkind) resulted in the fragmentation of holdings, with men claiming descent from the *uchelwyr* being forced into penury. The Glyndŵr rebellion caused acute social dislocation and large-scale de-population. Bondmen fled from servitude. Through the fifteenth century there was a move from bond to free labour. The crown, the church and individual landowners increasingly leased land to tenants, who in turn often sublet. The acute labour shortage in the century following the Black Death brought a rise in real living standard for labourers and artisans, which was only reversed in the sixteenth century. The old social order was disrupted by the emergence of a money economy, the development of the Welsh wool and cattle trade, and the growth of a market in land.

The Cultural Universe

Wales in the fifteenth century was strongly Catholic, infused with ritual, with its quasi-magical belief in miracles and visions. It was a world of pilgrimages to local and national shrines – St Davids, St Winifreds, Pen Rhys (Penrice), Llandderfel, and abroad to Santiago De Compostella in Spain, Rome and even the Holy Land. It was a world of richly ornamented churches, of wayside shrines, of holy wells and religious relics. The cults of the Virgin and of local saints flourished. The church and monasteries, impoverished and weakened by the Glyndŵr revolt, stood as unequal counter weights to the power of local magnates and gentry. This Catholic world-view was infused with the values of a strongly patriarchal society in which allegiance to family and kin remained strong. The priests, together with the *uchelwyr* and the bards, were the main moulders of opinion.

For the bards the failure of the Glyndŵr rising dramatised the status of the Welsh as a defeated and subjugated people. Hatred of the English is a recurrent theme running through the poetry of the period. The English garrisons and burgesses in the fortified towns in Wales, the neighbouring English towns and the March were objects of particular hatred. In a poem to Rhys ab Siôn of Glyn Nedd (Glyn Neath), Lewis Glyn Cothi lauds his patron's determination to exclude the English from positions of influence in his domain.

Ni welir Sais didirwy
Na Saeson mewn Sessiwn mwy
Na dyn o Sais yn dwyn swydd.[13]

No longer will you see the arrogant Saxon
Nor Saxons presiding over the Sessions
Nor Saxon holding office amongst us.

Ieuan Deulwyn appeals to one of his patrons to debar Englishmen from holding office (*Roi klo ar Sais rhag cael swydd*).[14] Those of English nationality enjoyed a privileged position in court and could demand that they be tried only by their compatriots. Lewis Glyn Cothi, Guto'r Glyn and Tudur Aled complained that the courts were loaded in favour of the English burgesses, and that English juries showed little sympathy for Welshmen on trial.

Welshmen petitioned for English denizenship to escape these disabilities.[15] The first grant of denizenship was made in 1413.[16] In the fifteenth century dozens of prominent Welshmen, such as Owain Tudor in 1432, and Gruffydd ap Nicholas, were granted denizenship. Guto'r Glyn refers scathingly to the way in which the Welsh *uchelwyr* had been reduced to supplicants, like wandering bards seeking favours from their betters. In another poem he inveighs against Welshmen who purchased English denizenship.

Ac eraill gynt a gerais
A bryn swydd a breiniau Sais.[17]

And others who once I loved
Buy office and the privileges of Saxons.

At the same time the bards supported those Welsh notables who

succeeded in gaining positions of influence under the English crown, and
looked to them to use their power to improve the lot of their people. Tudur
Penllyn praised William Vaughan of Penrhyn, who became in the 1440s
the first Welshman to hold the office of constable of Caernarfon castle and
chamberlain of north Wales, as the 'lock and sword' of Gwynedd, the man
who ensured that the Welsh would not be disadvantaged.

Os un a gawn dros Wynedd
Efo ydyw'n clo a'n cledd:
Os helpu Cymru rhag cam,
......
Cledd i wyr Gwynedd yw'r gŵr.[18]

At a local level individual *uchelwyr* shouldered responsibility for
preserving order. The bard Siôn Cent presents a jaundiced account of the
rapacity of many of these individuals, in marked contrast to their professed
ideals of charity and chivalry. Enjoying the bounteous life, they ruthlessly
pillaged and repressed their weaker brethren:

Goresgyn ar gwrs gweiniaid,
O'u blaen a gostwng y blaid,
Ymofyn am dyddyn da,
Ei ddau ardreth oedd ddirda,
Gostwng gwan yn ei eiste,
Dan ei law a dwyn ei le,
A dwyn tyddyn y dyn dall,
A dwyn erw y dyn arall;
Dwyn yr ŷd oedd dan yr on,
A dwyn gwair y dyn gwirion;
Cynnull arian dan cannyn,
Cyrchu'r da, carcharu dyn.[19]

Oppressing in their course the poor,
The multitude must bow before him,
Requesting a good cottage,
His two rents were profitable
Oppressing the poor in his seat
Beneath his hand and stealing his place
And stealing the blind-man's cottage
And stealing the other man's acre
Stealing the corn from beneath the ash

And stealing the hay of the innocent
Gathering money by false pretext
Pursuing the good, imprisoning men

The bard reminds them of the grave and perdition which awaits them, calling upon them to respect the rights of charity.[20]

It was upon the *uchelwyr* that responsibility for maintaining order devolved. The death or incapacity of a powerful *uchelwyr* could topple the balance of power in a region, and generate new conflicts. The bard Deio ab Ieuan Du in his lament to the dead Rhys of Towyn anticipates fresh eruptions of localised warfare between the men of Uwch and Is Aeron, which his patron had suppressed:

Ar Dowyn mawr fu'r dial,
O flaenau Deau hyd Iâl.
Lliaswyd a llaw Iesu,
Lladdfa fawr lle'dd wyf a fu.
Lladd sir, lluoedd Is Aeron,
Lladdiad, gwae wlad, gwial on.
Yn Uwch Aeron ni chweiriant,
Un dyn, na thelyn na thant.[21]

On Towyn great was the vengeance
From the Bleanau of the South to Yale.
Abandoned by the hand of Jesus
Where I stand was a great slaughter.
A county killed, by Is Aeron's hosts,
A massacre, woe country, the ash spear.
In Uwch Aeron they do not play,
No man, neither harp nor chord

Disorder and localised warfare were encouraged by the absence of mechanisms for the effective enforcement of the law. It was enflamed also by a lack of any shared identity or sense of mutual obligation between social groups and communities. The breakdown in the system of mutual obligations could precipitate the most violent feuds between comunities and even within families, as Sir John Wynn of Gwydir recounts.[22]

Taxation and revenue

The crown also exerted financial control over the shires of north and south

Wales.[23] The Exchequers at Caernarfon and Carmarthen were charged with gathering the revenues from the king's properties, with stewards appointed to manage these properties. Crown appointed auditors in Caernarfon and Carmarthen oversaw this work. In spite of such controls the fifteenth century saw a drastic decline in crown and seigniorial revenues with growing resistance by the tenantry to these exactions.[24]

The king and the prince of Wales required the tenants in the principality to pay *donum* on their entry into their estate. Similarly the marcher lords imposed mises on first entering their lordships. Revenue was raised from farms, rents and tolls, and profits from the courts – fines, the goods and chattels of felons and outlaws, and the goods of intestates. The main tax to the lords was the annual twnc pound, paid to the lord for his sustenance. Distinctive Welsh taxes included *ebediw* a succession duty, paid on entry into a father's property. Other taxes included 'reapsilver' (*arianmedy*) paid in lieu of field service during harvest time; chevage (headpenny) paid for permission to live outside the lord's demesne – important for migrant workers; tolecester – a licence for brewing. Tenants were also required to sustain the cais, the searcher, through the contribution *porthyant cais*.[25]

Amobr or *les lerwytes* was the payment paid to the lord in the event of a daughter's marriage or loss of virginity. Significantly, only Welsh tenants were required to pay this tax. Throughout the fifteenth century the right of amobrage in the principality in north and south Wales, was often granted to English crown officials.[26]

Cymhortha was a traditional practice of mutual assistance by the community. It was closely related to agricultural practices, with neighbours assisting each other during busy seasons. It was employed also to assist neighbours, through the provision of gifts and services, in the face of misfortune and distress and on important family occasions such as the marriage of a daughter, or bereavement. This practice was increasingly abused, reflecting the breakdown of older communal values and traditions. Powerful local magnates summoned assemblies of tenants to extort tribute in the guise of *cymhortha*.[27] It became a form of illegal, private taxation.

The Administration of Justice

In north and south Wales the administration of justice was the responsibility of the Justiciar in Carmarthen and Caernarfon. The administration of justice in the Principality's shires was entrusted to the Great Sessions or Sessions in Eyre, which were held annually. Through the Great Sessions itinerant justices were dispatched through the respective territories. The Great Sessions were empowered to hear complaints against crown or marcher officials, and to try criminal and civil causes. The sessions might last three or four days; all males between sixteen and seventeen were bound to attend, and where they failed might be amerced or outlawed.[28] From the late fourteenth century onwards, similar Sessions in Eyre were held in the marcher lordships ever three to four years, and in some cases every seven years. At a lower level were the county courts, the hundred courts and the manorial courts. Throughout the fifteenth century the frequent recourse to commissions of oyer and terminer, appointed by the crown, to investigate abuses, reflects the weakness of the administration of justice at local level.

Under Henry IV the practice was instituted in Carmarthenshire and Cardiganshire of suspending or redeeming the annual Great Sessions in return for a substantial collective fine (*tallage*) paid by the whole community. The inhabitants were granted 'white books', pardoning offences and remitting debts. In effect this became another form of taxation.[29] From 1422 to 1485 only twelve out of 52 of the sessions in Carmarthenshire, for which records survive, ran their full course, and in Cardiganshire for the same period only seven out of 42 sessions were completed. The practice spread to most marcher lordship in south and central Wales, and to the marcher lordships of Denbigh, Bromfield and Yale in north Wales.[30] This became a bitter source of complaint, as felons were allowed to escape justice, whilst the whole community was forced to bear the fine for all crimes committed.

The problem of lawlessness was compounded by, what Professor R. A. Griffiths calls, 'royal and seigniorial withdrawal' from direct involvement in Welsh affairs. Already in the fourteenth century many marcher lords were absentee. The Mortimers concentrated their attention on their Irish estates. The Bohun inheritance was divided, whilst the Despensers, Mortimer and Stafford families were blighted by minorities.[31]

The bishop of St. David's was acknowledged the rights of a marcher lord. Bishops, abbots and the order of the Knights of St. John had the power to hold their own courts.[32] In 1448 a royal charter renewed the rights of the abbot and convent of Margam to hold court, imprison felons in Ogmore castle, and to seize the goods and chattels of felons and fugitives.[33]

Braudel describes the system of justice of the middle ages as 'lopsided'. There was no conception of equality before the law. In the localities powerful magnates were largely a law unto themselves, and were entrusted with enforcing justice on their social inferiors. Whilst the full rigour of the law might be applied to these subordinate groups, powerful magnates could often flout the law with impunity.

English and Welsh law

With the Edwardian conquest of Wales, native Welsh laws were in part retained, whilst others were abolished or amended. English law alone was to be used in cases of felony. Trial by jury was increasingly introduced. The practice of kindred responsibility was increasingly supplanted by individual responsibility of the offender. Trial by jury replaced *rhaith* (compurgation) by which members of the accused's kindred might swear to his innocence in cases of theft. By producing 300 compurgators who would vouch for the honour of a man charged with crime the person indicted would be released. The practice persisted into the fifteenth century. The English parliament in 1413 prohibited the use of *rhaith*, by which felons and rebels were escaping punishment, and by which loyalist were being persecuted.[34] A petition presented to Parliament in 1427 complained of the use of *rhaith* by Welsh rebels to convict loyalists on trumped up charges.[35]

Welsh tenants petitioned for the restoration of their ancient laws and rights, but English law continued to make great advances.[36] Some Welsh legal customs survived such as the holding of land by Welsh mortgage (*tir-prid*). Particularly significant was *sarhad* – a fine imposed for defaming an individual, reflecting the key importance of personal honour in this society.[37] The right of the illegitimate to succeed to land in return for fee (*cynnwys*) also survived, as did the Welsh custom of partible inheritance (*cyfran*).

Whilst English legal practices made advances, the old Welsh laws traditional practices continued to survive. Trial by combat or trial by ordeal, which had been introduced into Wales by the Normans, was but a memory.[38] Nevertheless, in one instance Gruffydd ap Nicholas, as deputy justiciary of south Wales, brought together two contending parties for an organised joust at Dinefwr castle – Owain ab Ieuan ap Philip had accused Ieuan ap Gruffydd Goch of felony. Owain killed Ieuan in the encounter, and was then himself beheaded on Gruffydd ap Nicholas' order.[39]

In Wales, as in England, law was still partly based on the community and on the network of kinship. The practice of levying collective fines on communities for the crimes committed by individuals was common to both. The English practice of summoning the *posse comitatus*, the tradition of hue and cry established the responsibility of the community to apprehend felons. Outlawry placed individuals outside the law and in a sense outside society. Alongside the judicial machinery for dealing with crime there persisted unofficial devices. Private treaties and arbitration were widely used in Wales as in England to settle legal disputes, avoiding recourse to the courts.[40]

Love days

The enforcement of the law was compounded by the fragmentation of Wales between the crown – controlled shires and the independent marcher lordships. One means of dealing with the problems caused by conflicting jurisdictions was the letter of the March (*littera Marchie*) a kind of passport for tenants travelling outside their lordship, requesting that judicial immunity be accorded the bearer and identifying his lordship of residence.[41]

The means used for settling disputes between different judiciaries was the parliament or day of the March (*parliamentum, dies marchie*), or love days (*dies amoris* or *le day de redresse*). They involved the convening of meetings of the officers of the territories involved, at some designated and accustomed spot on their frontier. In some instances members of the communities themselves attended so as to secure communal assent for any agreement entered into. The *parliamentum* was used to resolve frontier disputes, to extradite criminals, to grant safe conducts, and to arrange the prosecutions of cases in other territories.[42]

Following the Glyndŵr rebellion the regulation of relations between different territories assumed particular importance. Assemblies were held at Bwlch Oerddrws for drafting a compact (*cydfod*) between Gwynedd, Powys and Deheubarth in 1421, another at Pontgamarch between the men of Presteigne, Gwerthrynion, Norton and Deuddwr. There is evidence also for a compact being concluded between Deheubarth and Powys at Eisteddfa Curig, between Powys, Elfail, Buellt, Gwerthrynion and Deuddwr at Aber Diwlas and between Maelienydd and Powys at Rhuddwr.

The practice of outlawry

The practice of outlawing felons had a long history. In the early Middle Ages an outlaw had been regarded as a 'wolf's head'. They could be hunted down and the bounty on their heads claimed. In Wales, with the escape of felons into the marches beyond the control of the crown, outlawing was a common practice.[43] The penalties for outlawry varied according to the offence. The property of outlaws was escheated either to the crown or to the marcher lord. According to Welsh law the property of an outlaw could also revert to the commons. An outlaw could not put the law in motion for his own benefit without first reversing the outlawry. Being outlawed implied the loss of a former status. According to English law, women, having no legal status of their own and not being bound as members of the community, could not be outlawed but only 'waived' or abandoned.[44]

By the fifteenth century the practice of outlawry had lost some of its more draconian connotations. It was widely resorted to, for dealing with felons who failed to present themselves at court to answer charges made against them.[45] Outlaws, however, could present themselves to the court and by payment of a fine have the outlawry lifted.[46] Following the Glyndŵr rebellion it was employed against rebels, who had taken to the woods and mountains to continue the struggle. As a result the stigma of outlawry became instead a badge of honour.

The Great Sessions in the lordship of Newport in 1476 followed the customary practice whereby persons accused were summoned five times, and if they did not appear they were pronounced outlaws. At these sessions over sixty individuals were outlawed.[47] In the lordship of Maelienydd rewards of forty shillings were regularly paid to officers for the capture of notorious outlaws and felons.[48] Officers, however, could not always be trusted to uphold the law. In 1467 the constable of Holt castle, was required to ensure the imprisonment of offenders in the castle goal. If he permitted outlaws and those already tried and convicted of certain crimes to escape he was to be fined £100.[49]

In the marcher lordships at the courts of Great Sessions amnesties were offered to outlaws for a fixed fine, 2s in Newport and 11s in Brecon.[50] The Duke of Buckingham in 1500 confirmed instructions to his council concerning the fines to be levied on outlaws in Newport lordship:

> Also diverse outlaws be coming in and have made general fines, every each at 2s, according to the custom, which was done upon this consideration, that all tenants and resiauntes standing out of the lordship should come in and fine surety of good aberring and appearance and so live under the laws or else to forfeit their penalties.[51]

The outlawing of felons for non-appearance in court remained extensively used.[52]

The right of sanctuary

The administration of justice was complicated by the operation of the privilege of sanctuary. This had two aspects. Firstly was the sanctuary afforded by those jurisdictions outside the control of the crown, or who had received the right of sanctuary by royal grant. As a result the county palatine of Cheshire, the town of Bewdley and the lordship of Wigmore, became notorious as the haunts of criminals and outlaws.[53] *Arddel* was the practice by which strangers, settlers or itinerant workers became tenants in a lordship and were granted legal protection by a lord.[54] This practice was increasingly abused in the Middle Ages and became a device for the harbouring of felons fleeing from one lordship to another. Those who brought protection in this way were known as men of avowal (*gwyr arddelw*) or arthelmen (*advocarii or adventicii*).[55] In some regions, such as Flintshire, the arthelmen had officers (*rhaglaw* or *raglot advocariae*) responsible for them.

The second form of sanctuary was ecclesiastical, provided by consecrated buildings and lands. In Wales there were a number of notable ecclesiastical sanctuaries (*sintor* or *noddfa*) – St. David's, Llanbadarn Fawr, Llanddewi Brefi (Noddfa Brefi), St Cybi's in Holyhead, Aberdaron, Pennant Melangell, Gelli Gaer (Dinas Noddfa) as well as the properties of the Knights of St. John, such as Amroth (with its fifty acres of sanctuary land attached to the church), Penrhys, Loughor and Ysbyty Ifan (Dinas Noddfa).[56] Monasteries, when at their height in the Middle Ages, had their own courts and prisons, and in some instances had the power to execute felons. The Cistercian Order provided sanctuary at its houses such as Tintern, Margam, Neath, Strata Marcella, Cassa Abbatis (St. Dogmael's) and St. Bernachius at Nevern in Cemais. John Leland, writing in the 1530s, noted that at Tintern and Margam the provision of sanctuary had for some time ended, precisely when is unclear.[57] The abuse of ecclesiastical sanctuary, with criminals seeking a safe haven, was a long-standing problem. On account of the violation of sanctuary the master of St. Mary's College, St. David's and the abbot of St. Dogmael's were compelled in this period to seek papal confirmation of those privileges.[58]

The lay authorities could not apprehend those taking sanctuary in a church or churchyard. Anyone who surrendered himself to the clergy could remain there for forty days. He could confess his crime to the coroner and agree to abjure the realm, when he would be sent from constable to constable to the port assigned for him to depart the realm never to return. If, however, he refused, he could after forty days be starved out, or seized and brought to justice. Parishioners were required to keep guard whilst the felon was in sanctuary and could be fined, if by default, he escaped.[59] The fragmentation in the administration of justice was underlined also by the position of the ecclesiastical courts. The problem was compounded by the right of those in holy orders and those who could demonstrate an ability to read the scriptures to plead benefit of clergy and thus to be tried before the more lenient ecclesiastical courts.[60]

The forest laws

A further complicating factor was the special judicial powers exercised in the forests and parklands of Wales. Large forests such as Snowdonia,

Narberth, Glyn Cothi, Mochtre, Devynock (Brecon), Machen, Wyeswode Trelech and Pennallt covered extensive areas. The forests were the resorts of outlaws. The administration of the forests also dealt with breaches of law, but in turn became itself a cause of abuse.

The forests were a vital part of the medieval economy, supplying fuel and timber for the castles, and game for hunting.[61] The administration of the forests was an important royal prerogative, and it was the crown who appointed the master foresters, keepers, foresters, woodwards or coederships.[62] In 1466 Sir William Herbert was appointed chief forester of the forest of Usk and Caerleon and all the king's forests in south Wales.[63] In 1483 the duke of Buckingham was appointed chief forester of the king's forests in Wales.[64] Sir Richard Huddlestone, constable of Beaumaris castle, was made master forester of Snowdonia in 1484.[65]

Foresters went heavily armed and had a reputation for ruthlessness, although the bards depict their forester patrons as models of propriety.[66] The foresters had the power to levy tolls, to fine trespassers, to confiscate any money which they had on them, to amputate offenders' arms where fines could not be paid, and to take possession of stray cattle found in the forests. Some of these draconian laws were softened over time. Under Richard III the tenants of the lordship of Brecknock were released from tolls on entering and leaving the Forest of Devynock.[67]

The blood feud and blood fine (*galanas*)

This was a society in which the notion of retribution and vengeance remained powerful. The concept of *galanas*, already acknowledged in the laws of Hywel Dda of the ninth century, involved monetary compensation in the case of homicide paid by the murderer's kin to the kin of the murdered. This blood fine was assessed by the value of a person's life according to his status. This notion of a distributive blood fine (*galanas wasgarog*) was comparable to the Anglo-Saxon concept of *wergild*.[68] Central to the original notion of *galanas* was the concept of kin honour, responsibility and duty. Moreover, social order was upheld by the threat of retribution.

The growing reluctance of individuals to recognise kin obligation and to contribute to the fine served to undermine the practice. Dafydd ap Llywelyn in the thirteenth century had annulled the law of *galanas* but the practice persisted in a debased form even into the sixteenth century in parts of Wales. *Galanas* came also to mean blood feud or vendetta. The concept of *galanas* is recorded also in Welsh proverbs – 'Long will old feuds remain bitter' (*Hir y bydd chwerw hen alanas*); 'Betrothal from near, vengeance from afar' (*Dyweddi o agos, galanas o bell*).[69]

Lewis Glyn Gothi in the fifteenth century declared that it was better for disputes to be settled by a trial of arms than by feud:

Gwir yw diarheb y gwŷr dewrion
'Gwell yw hen hawl gwayw llinon
No hen alanas hen elynion'.[70]

True is the proverb of the brave men
'Better the ancient rights of the spear
Than ancient blood feuds of old enemies'.

One aspect of English law which the Welsh strongly disapproved of was capital punishment. They considered monetary compensation to the aggrieved party more just: in the case of homicide this involved the payment of a blood fine (*galanas*). This is reflected in Dafydd ap Edmwnd's elegy to the harpist Siôn Eos in the second half of the fifteenth century. Siôn Eos had killed a man in a brawl. He was found guilty by a Chirkland jury and hanged. The poem castigates the jurors for employing the 'law of London' instead of the 'law of Hywel'.[71]

Sir John Wynn in his *History of the Gwydir Family* provides a graphic illustration of the practice of *galanas* in north Wales in the late fifteenth century: 'So bloody and ireful were quarrels in those days and the revenge of the sword at such liberty as almost nothing was punished by law whatsoever happened'. Howell as Rees having murdered one Griffith ap John ap Gronow was 'fain to leave the country to avoid the fury of the revengement of blood'. Men of substance turned their homes into small fortresses, as can still be seen at Gwydir and Tretower, to withstand attacks and sieges. Moreover, 'in that wild world every man stood upon his guard, and went not abroad but in sort and so armed as if he went to the field to encounter with his enemies'.[72]

Rivalries between local families for the 'sovereignty of the country' frequently developed into wars of attrition and blood feuds.

In those days in Chirkland and Oswestryland two sects of kindreds contended for the sovereignty of the country, and were at continual strife one with another, the Kyffins and Trevors, they had their allians, partisans and friends in all countrys round thereabouts, to whom as the manner of that time was they sent such of their followers as committed murder or manslaughter which were kept as very precious jewels and they received the like from their friends. These kind of people were stowed in the day time in chambers in their houses, and in the night they went to the next wine house that belonged to the gent(leman) or to his tenants houses not far off to make merry and to wensh.[73]

Out of this struggle native gentry families were to climb into positions of dominance.

Lawlessness and warfare

Wales was an important recruiting ground for soldiers for the English army, for service on the continent and in the campaigns against the Scots. In the thirteenth century the Ghent chronicler Lodewyk van Velthem, described how the Welsh soldiers went about bare legged, even in winter, dressed in linen tunics. Their weapons were bows, arrows, swords, javelins and billhooks or 'walshe billes or glayves'. Another favourite weapon was the *twca* (English tucke or tuke) which was a kind of rapier.[74] They had a reputation as great drinkers and a name for lawlessness, seizing what they needed from the local population.[75] Welsh soldiers played a prominent role in the English armies during the Hundred Years War, from 1337 onwards. The French historian Chotzen described the Welsh mercenaries as *bon vivants et Don Juans*, with a reputation for hard drinking and wild living. It may be no coincidence that the term *compagnon gallois* came to mean a boon companion, or that a prostitute in medieval Paris was sometimes called a *galloise*.[76]

Welsh society was imbued with a strong martial ethic, but enforced conscription in the English armies was often a source of resentment. Whilst the wars served to siphon off a surplus population of reckless young men the reintegration of these individuals into the society posed its own problems. Military service also attracted rootless, criminal elements. One historian notes that 'from two to twelve per cent of most armies of the period consisted of outlaws'. Military service was a means by which pardons could be earned.[77]

Following Glyndŵr's defeat Welsh soldiers, particularly long-bowmen, were again enlisted into the English armies on the continent. In the Agincourt campaign in 1415 over 500 Welshmen, from south Wales served under John Merbury, chamberlain, earning for themselves a grim reputation for their ferocity. Dafydd Gam, Glyndŵr's adversary was killed at Agincourt. A small number of Welshmen fought on the French side. In the French wars of the 1420 and 1430s leading members of the Welsh gentry played a prominent part. These included Roger Vaughan, Sir Richard Gethin, Sir Gruffydd Vaughan, Sir William ap Thomas, Sir

William Herbert and Owain Tudor. The most famous was the legendary Mathew Gough, who was killed in putting down the rebellion of Jack Cade in London in 1450.[78]

The Glyndŵr rebellion exacerbated animosities between Welsh and English, and between Welsh rebels and loyalists. It reared a generation inured to the brutalities of war. The system of military control through the castles remained a central feature of rule in Wales in the fifteenth century. Rhys Goch Eryri sang the praises of Gwilym ap Griffith's home at Penrhyn, contrasting it with the nearby castle of Caernarfon, the symbol of military subjugation, with its 'sad Greystone Tower of the Eagle, seat of anger', 'whose purpose was', he states

Gyrch dig, i gael gwarchae dyn,
Ac i ostwng ag ystyr
Calonnau a gwarrau gwŷr.[79]

Wrathful attempt, to confine a man,
And to subdue with intent
The hearts and napes of men.

CONCLUSION

Wales of the fifteenth century shared many of the same characteristics as other societies which suffered high level of disorder and banditry. A fragmented, corrupt and oppressive system of colonial rule, which was characterised by the exploitation of the native economy and discrimination against the native population, provided a breeding ground for disorder. It nurtured a culture of resistance, which in some of its forms was a culture of disorder, deceit and duplicity. Here we might draw a parallel with the bandit regions of the Mediterranean world, distinguished by their fragmented political structures, alien rule, Catholicism, powerful magnates and condotierre, strong bonds of kinship, and traditions of retributive justice and blood feud. The parallel is striking in the account of this society given by Sir John Wynn.

The weakness of the state, the experience of failed rebellion and of civil war, created a form of social involution, in which individuals and groups were thrown back on their own resources. Not only the powerful magnates, but also gentlemen and lesser squires took the law into their own hands. Thus kinship and family loyalties were strengthened, and traditional conceptions of justice revived. This reinforced the dependence of individuals on force of arms, strengthening their attachment to ideas of retributive justice, vengeance, *galanas*, or private treaty. Individuals and families sought the protection of more powerful patrons; cemented by marriage alliances, the fostering of sons, and by bonds of mutual dependence. The weakness of state structures was thus mirrored in the very psychology of the society.

4 The Wars of the Roses 1450–1471

In 1450 the Commons complained that the realm was troubled by an unprecedented wave of lawlessness.[1] This collapse of public order affected large parts of the country, with bitter feuds in the West Country and the north.[2] The crisis was compounded by a deep crisis of political authority. The ill health and questionable mental competence of the king Henry VI reopened the question of the legitimacy of Lancastrian rule and the issue of the succession. The defeat of English imperial ambitions in France, weakened royal authority, unleashed feuds amongst the leading magnates and propelled the country towards civil war.[3] The Wars of the Roses, which deeply divided the Welsh gentry, exacerbated the problem of disorder in Wales. The war was fought out mainly in the Marches. Both Lancastrians and Yorkists used Wales as a strategic bridgehead for military campaigns in England and both sides recruited soldiers heavily from Wales and the Marches.

The Yorkist claim to the throne dated back to Henry IV's deposition of Richard II in 1399. Richard, duke of York, was heir to the Earldom of March (in Welsh *Iarllaeth y Mars*), based on Ludlow. His mother Anne Mortimer claimed descent from, amongst others, Llywelyn the Great. York controlled a string of lordships through eastern Wales and the Marches, including Denbigh, Chirbury, Clun, Maelienydd, Caerleon and Usk. His principal allies were the earl of Warwick, and the duke of Norfolk. York's allies included his powerful neighbours William Herbert of Raglan, Sir Walter Devereux of Weobley, Roger Vaughan of Tretower, and the Dwnn family of south-west Wales. These individuals played a central role in marcher politics and had seen military service in France. The alliance between York and Herbert had interesting connotation regarding recent history. Edward Mortimer, earl of March, in 1402 had allied with Glyndŵr, married his daughter, and sought his support for his bid to displace the usurper Henry IV. Sir William ap Thomas, the founder of the fortunes of the Herbert family of Raglan, had married the daughter of Dafydd Gam, Glyndŵr's bitter enemy.

The Tudors of Penmynydd in Anglesey provided the main support for the Lancastrians in Wales. Owain Tudor had married Catherine of Valois, widow of Henry V. Their sons Edmund and Jasper, half brothers to Henry

VI, were created earls of Richmond and Pembroke respectively. Lancastrian support was strongest in south-west Wales, where Gruffydd ap Nicolas of Dinefwr exercised a dominating influence. In the Marches the duke of Buckingham, the earl of Shrewsbury as well as gentry families such as the Scudamores and Pulestons also supported the Lancastrians.

The Yorkist challenge 1450–1460

York's return from Ireland in 1450 was seen as a direct challenge to the king. He had won distinction in the wars in France and Ireland and enjoyed powerful support amongst the nobility. One incident, which illustrates the deepening crisis, was the murder of William Tresham, the Speaker of the Commons, who had fallen foul of powerful Lancastrian magnates, such as the duke of Suffolk. In August 1450, following York's return, Tresham set out from his home in Rushton, Northamptonshire, to rendezvous with him. He was waylaid and murdered.[4]

Tresham's assassination was plotted by Simon Norwich, a squire of Rutland, who procured the assistance of Lord Grey's retainers, namely Evan ap Rice [Rhys], John Dee, Thomas Tudur Maddock the younger (all 'late of Wales, yeomen'), and seven other accomplices. Evan ap Rice assembled 'diverse misdoers and murderers of men to the number of 160 persons or more, arrayed in form of war' and ambushed Tresham at Thorpland, near Moulton in Northamptonshire. He killed Tresham, robbed his victim and rode his horse around Northamptonshire with his companions 'avanting themselves of the said murder' with the sheriff of the county not daring to arrest them. An investigating commission was intimidated into silence. Tresham's widow petitioned Parliament in November for her husband's murderers to be brought to justice.[5]

The mounting disorder was reflected in the Welsh Marches. The duke of Buckingham, one of the most powerful of the English barons, encountered great difficulty in gathering revenue from the lordships of Newport, Caus, Hay, Huntingdon and Brecon. In 1452 the duke's Exchequer had to excuse the tax gatherer his arrears because of the 'great rebellions, stirrings and disobediences of the tenants of the said manors'.[6] Difficulties were also encountered in collecting the fine for redeeming the Great Sessions. The lordship of Brecon was reputed for its disorder and its cattle raiders. At Cantref Selyf, which was contested by the crown and Buckingham, violence was rife, whilst the tenants went in constant fear of armed raiders and other 'misgoverned persons' from the duke of York's retinue.[7]

In 1452 York with a large army marched on London but was prevailed on to disband his forces. In March, having made a solemn affirmation of his loyalty to the king in St.Paul's Cathedral, York was set free. His release may also have been prompted by rumours that an army of 10,000 Welshmen was descending on London. York's liege John Sharp was accused of being the leader of this conspiracy. The duke of Somerset descended on Ludlow, York's stronghold, and presided over trials of his tenants and retainers. Sharp was executed at Tyburn on a charge of murder.[8] Henry VI and Queen Margaret toured the south-west and the Welsh borderlands, visiting Monmouth, to quell disturbances.[9]

In 1453 York was appointed Protector displacing his major rival Somerset. With the recovery of the king in 1454 York's appointment was revoked and Somerset returned to favour.

In 1454 Gruffydd ap Nicholas entered Buckingham's lordship of Brecon and it was alleged 'did receive, maintain and comfort' wrongdoers in York's own lordship of Maelienydd. On 24 May the protectorate council, under York, resolved to remove Gruffydd ap Nicholas and his relatives from all offices in the principality shires and the adjacent lordships. He was found guilty at Shrewsbury and in August apprehended at Hereford, but was rescued from the clutches of the law by his son in law Sir John Scudamore.[10] At the end of August York visited Montgomery and the central Marches. Contemporary chronicles refer to his suppression of 'great trouble' in Wales. At Montgomery York dealt with a disruptive boundary dispute between his own tenants of Chirbury and those of Buckingham's lordship of Caus. He may also have sought to resolve the dispute between the men of Caus and the tenants of the lord of Powys, Richard Grey.[11]

The opening skirmish of the civil war, the first battle of St.Albans of 1455, ended in victory for York, and in the death of his bitter rival Somerset. Parliament was summoned and appointed York again as Protector, but with the king's recovery he was deprived of his title in February 1456. The direction of the Lancastrian government was taken over by the formidable Queen Margaret, York's implacable enemy.

In south Wales the rivalry between Gruffydd ap Nicholas of Dinefwr and William Herbert of Raglan gave the conflict a sharper edge. In the early 1450s Gruffydd ap Nicholas and his sons sought to extend their control over Pembroke. The crown reported that large numbers of armed men from Cardiganshire and Carmarthenshire were invading Pembroke, robbing officials and tenants, capturing others and holding them to ransom 'in contempt of our authority and estate royal'.[12]

The crown's attempts in 1452 to curb the lawlessness of Gruffydd ap Nicholas and his sons failed. With Somerset's death the balance of power shifted to York and his allies. Warwick became steward and constable of

Monmouth, Edward Bouchier steward of Kidwelly, and York himself became constable of Carmarthen and Aberystwyth castles.[13]

York as Protector attempted to curb misrule in Wales and to shore up the central government's authority. Parliament in July 1455 set up a committee, consisting of marcher lords (*Domini Marchearum*) and the crown's legal advisers, to work out measures 'to ordain and purvey for the restful and sad rule in Wales, and set apart such riots and disobedience as have been there before this time used'.[14]

In 1455 a petitioner, Gruffydd ap David ap Thomas, urged York to take possession of Carmarthen and Aberystwyth and to expel Gruffydd ap Nicholas' garrison. Parliament decreed that if he was in either castle without York's licence on 1 March following he be attainted for high treason.[15]

These disorders in Wales were compounded by the threat of foreign invasion. The low calibre of crown officers in the administration of the principality, and the high incidence of absenteeism made matters worse. One contemporary clerk lamented what improvements might be achieved 'if it were that the king had two good sheriffs abiding upon their offices in Caernarvonshire and Angelsey'.[16]

In January 1452 the chamberlain of north Wales Thomas Stanley was pardoned arrears in revenue to the crown.[17] In July a commission was issued to John, bishop of Bangor and other notables, to inquire as to why the king's tenants in these counties had withheld their rents since 1450, and had refused to present themselves at audits. The commissioners were to compel payment, and where tenants were unable to pay to mortgage arrears and to provide pardons.[18] On 12 August 1453 the crown demanded further contributions from north Wales. Merionethshire, which was perpetually in arrears with its dues, was required to offer a subsidy in return for a pardon of its accumulated debt.[19] In September a commission was instituted into the activities of negligent officials in the three shires.[20] In May 1457 the three shires of north Wales were required to offer a gift to Prince Edward of £12,667, payable over six years, as mises on his entry into his Welsh properties. In 1458–9 north Wales managed to pay only £58.[21]

The Lancastrians fended off the Yorkist challenge from 1455 to 1460. The Yorkists lordships in Wales were penalised and used as a source of revenue to strengthen the Lancastrian forces. In 1456 Queen Margaret dispatched Edmund, earl of Richmond, to bring west Wales to order. Edmund Tudor and Gruffydd ap Nicholas were soon thereafter reported to be 'greatly at war'. The latter had seized Carmarthen, Carreg Cennen and Kidwelly castles. By August 1456 Edmund Tudor was in control of Carmarthen castle.

William Herbert, and his father-in-law Sir Walter Devereux, both retainers of York, took matters into their own hands. On 10 August 1456 mobilising a force of 2,000 men from York's lands in Herefordshire and Radnor, they marched on Carmarthen, successfully besieged the castle, and took Edmund Tudor prisoner. They also seized Aberystwyth castle. Herbert and Devereux held judicial sessions, releasing many alleged outlaws and felons.[22] Even Gruffydd ap Nicholas appeared willing to submit to Sir William Herbert.

The queen determined to take resolute action to curb York's Welsh proxies. Devereux and Herbert were summoned to the king's great council at Coventry at the end of September 1456. Devereux was confined in Windsor Castle. The council censured Herbert for his actions in Hereford and south Wales, and advised the king to incarcerate him in the Tower. A full pardon was granted to Gruffydd ap Nicholas and his sons on 26 October 1456, with the aim to isolate York, and win their loyalty.[23]

In 1457 William Herbert, having secured bail, fled to south Wales, and began enlisting men in York's and Warwick's lordships. He was proclaimed a rebel and outlawed for the 'mischief and grievance he had brought upon the King's liege subjects in diverse parts, robbing some of them, beating and maiming some, and causing the death of many'.[24] A reward of 500 marks was offered for his capture. At the end of March the king's court moved to Hereford. Most of Herbert's associates appeared before a commission of oyer and terminer on 28 April 1457 at Hereford. Herbert himself surrendered to the king at Leicester and on 7 June he and his accomplices received a general pardon.[25] The Paston letters reveal that he had 'his life granted and goods, so make amends to them he hath offended'.[26] The crown was loath to outlaw a powerful figure like Herbert, and preferred instead to cultivate him.

In 1457 the Queen travelled through the border counties and granted a pardon to Gruffydd ap Nicholas, who had resisted Edmund Tudor in west Wales. Edmund Tudor had died in November 1456 and his brother Jasper assumed the leadership of the Welsh Lancastrians. In 1457 Jasper Tudor strengthened the castles of Pembroke and Tenby, and took possession of Aberystwyth, reinforced Carreg Cennen and Carmarthen castles, which had been attacked by York's sympathisers.

In 1457 the infant Prince Edward was invested with his patrimony including the principality of Wales. The prince's council, dominated by Queen Margaret's appointees, sought to tighten up administration and the collection of revenues in Wales, albeit with little success.[27]

The Loveday of 24 March 1458 failed to affect reconciliation between the king and York, and the crisis deepened. In the skirmish at Blore Heath,

Staffordshire in 1459, Salisbury defeated the Lancastrian forces. However, at Ludford Bridge in October the Yorkists forces were put to flight, and York himself 'fled fro[m] place to place in Wales, and broke down the bridges after him that the king's maynny [company] should not come after him. And he went unto Ireland'.[28] On 30 October a commission of oyer and terminer was issued for the west midlands and Welsh borderland for the arrest of those implicated in York's treason.[29]

The Coventry parliament of 1459 drew the king's attention to 'the great and lamentable complaints of your true poor subjects universally through-out every part of your realm' regarding robberies, riots, extortions, fines and ransoms.[30]

In 1460 the crown renewed its efforts to crush the Yorkists in Wales. On 5 January Jasper Tudor was appointed constable of Denbigh castle, which was still in Yorkist hands.[31] In February a commission led by Jasper Tudor was established to inquire into the granting of livery and the summoning of unlawful assemblies in the Principality of Wales, Flint and Cheshire, and to recover the castles in Yorkist hands.[32] Canons and munitions were transferred to Wales. Denbigh fell in March 1460 and in May Jasper made his way to south Wales to secure the coast from invasion from Ireland.

In June 1460 the earls of Warwick, March and Salisbury crossed over from France to England in a bid to depose the enfeebled Henry VI. In July Warwick defeated the king's forces at Northampton, taking the king prisoner. Queen Margaret fled to Harlech and then to Pembroke, and finally sailed for Scotland. Warwick used his power to consolidate Yorkist control. Henry VI's name was invoked to transfer power to Yorkist supporters and to disarm the Lancastrians. In August the Privy Council ordered Sir William Herbert, Walter Devereux and Roger Vaughan to take all castles in Wales into the king's hands, to suppress riot, and to apprehend the ringleaders.[33]

York, who had fled to Ireland in 1459, made his way back to London in September 1460 via Shrewsbury, Ludlow and Hereford. Jean de Waurin states that he was encouraged by the gentry of the border region and by 'seigneurs du pays de Galles' (presumably Devereux, Herbert and Vaughan) to take the throne.[34] He was again recognised as Protector, but with the right to succeed Henry VI on his death.[35] However, in December 1460 York's armies were defeated at Wakefield where he was killed and Salisbury was executed. In February 1461 Queen Margaret with an army of Scots, Welshmen and men from the north of England defeated Warwick at the second battle of St.Albans, and re-established Lancastrian control.

York was succeeded by his son Edward, earl of March, who proceeded to mobilise troops in the marcher estates, Herefordshire and south Wales.

The Lancastrian forces arrayed to suppress them were organised by James Butler, earl of Wiltshire, who landed in Milford Haven with a force of French, Breton and Irish soldiers. He was supported by a Welsh contingent recruited from Pembroke and Carmarthenshire and led by Jasper Tudor, Owain Tudor and the sons of Gruffydd ap Nicholas and other local gentry.

The two forces met at Mortimer's Cross on 2 or 3 February 1461. March, supported by Sir Walter Devereux, William Herbert and Sir John Wenlock, and with an army drawn from the south-eastern marches, vanquished the outnumbered Lancastrian forces. Owain Tudor was taken, and executed at Hereford. Jasper Tudor escaped, and in a letter to the north Wales gentry he deplored the treason of March, Herbert and Dwn and swore to avenge the death of his father.[36] The bard Robin Ddu lamenting the execution of Owain Tudor (the swallow) took satisfaction in the thought that the 'earl' Jasper (the great eagle) remained at large (*Er torri pen y wenol/Mae'r iarll, eryr mawr ar ol*). Ieuan ap Rhydderch implored him 'Do not sheathe the sword of Owain Y Glyn'.[37] Lewis Glyn Cothi called on him to free the Welsh from their abject subjugation (*Truan yw'n rhwym, tro ni'n rhydd*).[38]

The reign of Edward IV 1461–1470.

March proceeded in triumph to London, where on 3 March 1461 he was crowned Edward IV. The king's real base of support lay in the Welsh marches, he depended heavily on Welsh magnates such as Sir William Herbert. His family, the Mortimers, had allied with Glyndŵr, and he was considered almost an honorary Welshman.

Edward IV granted William Herbert (Gwilym Ddu) proconsular powers in Wales, over his bitter rival Warwick.[39] In May 1461 he was appointed Chief Justice and Chamberlain of Carmarthen and Cardigan counties, as well as steward and chief forester. He was commissioned to take into the king's hands the possessions of Jasper Tudor, the earl of Shrewsbury and the former earl of Wiltshire. He was made a privy councillor. He was elevated to the peerage as Lord Herbert, and the lordship of Raglan was created for him, the last Marcher lordship to be created in Wales. He was also given custody of Henry, Edmund Tudor's son, captured at Pembroke.[40]

Herbert's supporters were also rewarded. His brother Richard Herbert was made deputy justice in south Wales. Devereux was recognised as Lord Ferrers in 1461, given grants of land, and in 1463 was appointed captain of Aberystwyth castle.[41] Sir William Hastings was created Lord Hastings, and appointed as chamberlain of north Wales. The earl of Worcester was made chief justice of north Wales. John Dwnn became constable of

Aberystwyth and Carmarthen castles and sheriff of Carmarthenshire and Cardiganshire. The Yorkist bards, Guto'r Glyn, Huw Cae Llwyd and Hywel Swrdal, trumpeted their praises of Lord Herbert and his allies, the Vaughans, Harvards and Gamses.

In August 1461 Walter Devereux and William Herbert were commissioned to receive the submission of the rebels who still supported the deposed king in south Wales.[42] Similarly George, duke of Clarence, was commissioned to inquire into all treasons, insurrections and rebellions in south Wales.[43] The earl of Warwick was commissioned to array the men of Shropshire to defend the county against the rebels, who supported the deposed king, and to bring an army to Hereford by the Nativity of the Virgin (8 September).[44] Edward journeyed through the Marches, via Hereford to Ludlow,[45] but resolved to entrust the Welsh campaign to his two lieutenants who 'with diverse many other gentlemen' proceeded before him 'to cleanse the country'.[46]

The Lancastrians in 1461 still retained Pembroke, Tenby, Carreg Cennen, Denbigh and Harlech castles. Tenby quickly fell. Sir William Herbert defeated Jasper Tudor at Tuthill outside Caernarfon forcing him to flee to Ireland. Henry Wyndesore reported to John Paston in October 1461 'and all the castles and holds in south Wales, and in north Wales, are given and yielden up into the King's hands. And the Duke of Exeter (Henry Holland) and the earl of Pembroke (Jasper Tudor) are flown and taken the mountains, and diverse of gentlemen and men of worship are comen in to the King, and have grace, of all Wales'.[47] The Yorkists took Denbigh castle, leaving only Carreg Cennen and Harlech castles in Lancastrian hands.

Gruffydd ap Nicholas held Carreg Cennen from 1455, for the Lancastrians. Following the Lancastrians' defeat at Mortimer's Cross in 1461 Gruffydd's two sons, Owain and Thomas, took refuge in the castle. Edward IV charged Sir William Herbert to bring the country to order. He was empowered to commandeer ships from Bristol for the campaign.[48] In April 1462 Sir William Herbert sent his brother Sir Richard Herbert and Sir Roger Vaughan of Tretower to take the castle. The castle surrendered in May 1462.

The Yorkists garrisoned Carreg Cennen through the summer of 1462 'for the safeguard of the same, forasmuch as the said castle was of such strength that all the misgoverned men of that country there intended to have inhabited the castle and to have lived by robbery and spoiling of the people'. In August Sir William Herbert ordered that the castle be rendered indefensible, on the grounds that it was a '*spelunca latronum*' (a den of thieves), and thus 'to avoid the inconvenience of this kind happening there in time to come'.[49]

The Lancastrian garrison at Harlech held out from 1461 to 1468. The captains who held the castle, such as Dafydd ap Siencyn and Rheinallt ap Gruffudd, were lauded by the Lancastrian bards. The garrison sought to bring the adjoining territory under its control. The 'Tenants and Commons of North Wales' in a petition to Parliament in 1461, complained that many of them had 'been daily taken prisoners and put to fine and ransom as it were in a land at war, and many and diverse of them daily robbed and spoiled of their goods and cattle'. Moreover, the rebels 'reputed in all their doings the said late king [Henry VI] for their sovereign lord and not the king our sovereign lord that now is' and would not recognise any 'such persons as the late king has deputed to be constable'.[50]

In June 1463 Sir William Herbert was appointed chief justice of Merionethshire, general receiver of the king's farms and rents, and constable of Harlech castle.[51] This was a warning to the Lancastrian garrison at Harlech and to the king's tenants in Merionethshire who were withholding rents. The duke of Somerset from Harlech maintained contact with the deposed Henry VI at Bambrough, Nothumberland. Somerset in 1463 travelled north to co-ordinate plans for a revolt. Jasper Tudor was active in orchestrating the campaign. In north Wales Roger Puleston and John Hanmer led the opposition, whilst in south Wales the leaders were Philip Mansel and Hopkyn ap Rhys.[52]

In 1464 the duke of Norfolk was sent to north Wales to put down the planned rising. Paston anticipated a policy of moderation – 'yet they shall have grace'. Prominent rebels who were expected to surrender were John Hanmer, his son William Hanmer, Roger Puleston and Edward Madok.[53] In south Wales John Dwn and Roger Vaughan defeated the Lancastrians at the battle of Dryslwyn on 4 March 1464. The duke of Somerset and the Welsh troops accompanying him, advancing from the north, were defeated at Hedgley Moor in April and Hexham in May, where Somerset was killed. Jasper Tudor was forced into hiding. According to Edward Hall 'he moved from country to country in Wales, not always at his heart's ease, nor in security of life or surety of living'.[54] He finally fled to Brittany.

In 1464 the clergy and people of the diocese of north Wales in a petition to the pope, reported that because 'in those parts the number of murders and ravishers of virgins and other women, thieves and robbers had so much increased that unless their boldness was repressed, good and just men would hardly be safe in future, the said clergy, with the consent of the people, had made and published diverse statutes and ordinances in the matter'.[55]

In October 1464 Herbert was given a commission to treat with the rebels in Harlech and Merionethshire, and to receive them into the king's obedience, saving the most prominent leaders.[56] A proclamation calling for the surrender of Harlech was read out in the north Wales towns on 21 January 1465.[57] In March 1466 the earl of Warwick wass commissioned to inquire into the non-payment of rents and other dues by the king's tenants in Caernarfonshire and Merionethshire, and the failure of tenants in Anglesey and Caernarfonshire to pay the fine of the 'great turn'.[58] The earl of Worcester, chief justice of north Wales, led an expedition into the area but failed to subdue it.[59]

The Lancastrian garrison at Harlech in 1466 embarked on a raid, which took them as far as Wrexham, seventy miles distant. The crown reassured the alarmed Yorkist captains of Beaumaris, Caernarfon, and Conwy that reinforcements would be sent 'for the safeguarding of our strongholds, considering our rebels be daily in the country'.[60] In 1468 Jasper Tudor, with the backing of Louis XI of France, landed at Barmouth, and with an expeditionary force of 2,000 men made an unsuccessful attack on Denbigh.

Lord Herbert replaced Worcester as chief justice of north Wales on 28 January 1467.[61] In July 1468 he was empowered to raise a contingent of 7,000 to 10,000 men, from the Marches and the border counties, and to take Harlech. Herbert, according to Sir John Wynn writing more than a century later, 'wasted with fire and sword all Nanconway and all the country lying between Conway and Dovey', and added that 'the whole borough of Llanrwst and the vale of Conway besides carried yet the colour of fire'.[62] Harlech surrendered in August 1468 after a month's siege. Jasper Tudor evaded capture and fled. His title as earl of Pembroke was conferred upon Lord Herbert as his reward.[63]

The Yorkist bard Guto'r Glyn warned Lord Herbert not to overstretch his authority in retaliation against his countrymen who had supported the Lancastrian cause. He appealed to him as 'King of our People (Language)' (*Brenin ein iaith*) not to tax Anglesey excessively, not to allow unchecked oppression, to expel the English from Gwynedd and Flint, not to confer offices on Englishmen, nor to grant pardons to English burgesses brought before the courts.

Na fwrw dreth yn y fro draw
Ni aller ei chynullaw;
Na friw Wynedd yn frynar,
Nâd i Fôn fyned i fâr.
Nâd y gweiniaid i gwynaw,
Na brad na lledrad rhag llaw;
Nâd trwy Wynedd plant Ronwen

Na phlant Hors yn y Fflint hen
Na, ad f'arglwydd, swydd i Sais,
Na'i bardwn i un bwrdais;
Barn yn iawn, brenin ein iaith,
Bwrw yn tân eu braint unwaith.[64]

The poem concludes with an extraordinary appeal to Lord Herbert to appoint Welshmen as constables to all the castles from Barnstable to Anglesey, and to unite Wales. If England and her Dukes take offence, he pledges, that the whole of Wales will rally to his cause (*rhaid*).

Cymer wŷr Cymru'r awron,
Cwnstabl o Farnstabl i Fôn,
Dwg Forgannwg a Gwynedd,
Gwna'n un o Gonwy i Nedd;
O digia Lloegr a'i dugiaid,
Cymru a dry yn dy raid.

This subversive poem, a manifesto for a crusade to expel the English from Wales, provides confirmation of the suspicions, which many Englishmen had regarding the ambitions, and intentions of those close to Herbert. Guto'r Glyn saw no incompatibility between loyalty to the person of Edward IV as king, and a deep animosity towards the English.

The crown in October 1469 ordered Lord Hastings, Chamberlain of north Wales to make a proclamation amongst the people of the three shires 'that they and each one of them obey our laws and pay their duties of the country there yearly growing as hath been of old time due and accustomed'. Failure to obey this order would incur the crown's 'great indignation'. The chamberlain was to report the names of all defaulters.[65]

Herbert's star was now at its zenith. Even the Lancastrian bard Lewis Glyn Cothi praised him as 'the great ear of Wales in London' (*unclust holl Gymru'n y Gwindy gwyn*) and as Edward IV's master lock in Wales (*unclo'r King Edward yw'r Herbard hwn*). He hailed Edward IV as a royal or privileged Welshman (*Cymro breiniol*) descended from Gwladys Ddu. Dafydd Llwyd, another Lancastrian, urged Herbert to marry his daughter to his young charge Henry Tudor. The concern of these bards appears to have been what they perceived as common national interests above factional allegiances. The bards believed that in Lord Herbert they had found their own 'Prince', as Machiavelli thought he had found his in Cesare Borgia.

The crown's position was further challenged by the revolt in the north

led by Robin of Redesdale, a kinsman of Warwick. The king called up
reinforcements from Wales and the West Country, organised by Lord
Herbert and Henry Stafford, earl of Devon. Herbert mobilised a large army
from south-east Wales and Pembrokeshire. They were feasted at Raglan
castle before embarking on the march north. Guto'r Glyn in a poem
celebrating the event, extolled Herbert as the king's right-hand man, 'the
guardian of Edward's peace' (*A cheidwad heddwch Edwart*) who could
impose order on Wales and the Marches. He is a Charlamagne, Roland,
Hector and Arthur. But, the bard warns, that he is the object of English
jealousy and hatred

Blino y maent o'm blaenawr
Blant Ronwen, genfigen fawr.
Gwenwyn gantun' ugeinwaith
Gael yr iarll ŵr glew o'n iaith[66]

The two armies, from Wales and the West Country, were to rendezvous
in the Cotswolds. Disagreement between Herbert and Stafford prevented
the two forces joining. At Edgecote Lodge near Banbury in July 1469
Herbert's forces clashed with Warwick's army, led by John Clapham.
Herbert's army was routed with losses estimated at between 2,000 and
5,000, amongst them 168 members of the south Wales gentry. Lord
Herbert and his brother Richard were captured and the following day, on
Warwick's orders, were executed as traitors, on the charge that the army
was to be used against the crown.

Lord Herbert had a reputation for ruthlessness and he inspired fear as
English contemporaries, such as William of Worcester, well recognised.[67]
The Croyland Chronicle described him as a 'cruel man' who was 'prepared
for any crime and, it was said, they plotted to subdue the realm of England
and totally plunder it'. The Welsh represented a greater threat than even the
detested Northerners. Herbert and his followers had been inspired by
prophecy, but 'by the providence of God' they had been disappointed.[68]

The Welsh bards both Yorkists and Lancastrians, in part victims of their
own hubris, depicted the battle of Banbury as a national calamity, a product
of English treachery.[69] Despite this calamity Guto'r Glyn continued to
defend the unity of Wales and England under Edward IV's rule (*Mae'r
Nordd a Chymru yn un*). But he called on Sir William Herbert's heir to
wreak vengeance on his killers. He called on him to harry, waste and
punish the men of Gwent, Gloucester and the Forest of Dean (*Ffrystia dir
Fforest y Dên*) who had betrayed him.[70] Lewis Glyn Cothi called on his
patrons to wreak vengeance on the English: he called on Sir Roger

Vaughan of Tretower to hang all of the English tongue (*A gwyr y gregen oll a grogir*), and on his son Sir Thomas Vaughan to string up the tribe of Rowenna (*A chrog lwyth Ronwen wrth gangenau*).[71]

Warwick now wielded enormous power. He quickly assumed his rival's posts of chief justice and chamberlain of south Wales, and constable of Carmarthen and Cardigan.[72] In November 1469 Edward IV moved to check Warwick's power and installed his own brother Richard, duke of Gloucester, as chief justice of north Wales, and chief steward and surveyor of the Principality of Wales and the earldom of March.[73] In February 1470 Gloucester was appointed chief justice and chamberlain of south Wales. The king also built up the power of other figures – Sir Walter Devereux, Sir Roger Vaughan, Sir William Stanley and John Dwnn.[74] Dwnn's elevation provoked Gruffydd ap Nicholas who seized Carmarthen and Cardigan castle, from which he had to be evicted by Gloucester.[75]

Alarmed at the moves to cut back his powers, Warwick, together with the duke of Clarence, in the spring of 1470 fled to France. There Louis XI formed an alliance between them and Margaret of Anjou and Jasper Tudor. They landed at Dartmouth in September intent on reinstating Henry VI on the throne. The civil war between Yorkists and Lancastrians in Wales again flared into life. In September 1470 Edward IV commissioned Lord Ferrers to put down a feared Lancastrian rebellion in south Wales.[76] In January 1471 Henry VI issued a commission of array to the duke of Clarence, Jasper Tudor, Warwick and Salisbury in Wales and the marches to resist the usurper Edward IV.[77]

Warwick was killed at the battle of Barnet. The Welsh bards rejoiced at his death, as revenge for Banbury. The defeat of Margaret of Anjou at the battle of Tewkesbury sealed the fate of the Lancastrian challenge. After the battle the Prince of Wales was executed and Henry VI died mysteriously in the tower, possibly with the connivance of Richard of Gloucester. Jasper Tudor withdrew to Chepstow where he encountered Sir Roger Vaughan of Tretower, reputedly the man who had led Owain Tudor to the block, and put him to death. Thereafter Jasper Tudor, with Henry Tudor his nephew, fled via Tenby to Brittany. Commissions were established to receive and pardon the Lancastrian rebels, save their most prominent leaders. Edward IV's position was firmly secured for the last decade of his life.

CONCLUSION

For G. M. Trevelyan 'The Wars of the Roses were to a large extent a quarrel between Welsh Marcher Lords, who were also great English nobles, closely related to the English throne'.[78] The crown's weakness gave rise to a dynastic civil war, which at local level was reflected in warfare between contending magnates. Civil war unleashed the tensions already simmering within society, and unravelled the bonds which had held lawlessness in check. The crown constituted the capstone, which held together the political structure of late medieval society, which once weakened caused the structure to fall in on itself.

The civil war had a far less disruptive impact on the economic and social life of Wales than the Glyndŵr rebellion. Its impact was more localised, with its worst effects being in the Marches and Gwynedd. From the 1450s onwards, Glanmor Williams argues, there was a substantial recovery in the Welsh economy.[79] The impact of the Wars of the Roses, however, cannot be reduced to the direct impact of the military campaigns of the period. The weakening of central authority and the rise in the power of local magnates fostered lawlessness and brigandage. The recruitment of armies by both sides in the conflict placed a strain on the society, which is difficult to assess. In south west Wales the struggle between Yorkists and Lancastrians led to a major breakdown of law and order. In north-west Wales, with the Lancastrian garrison holding Harlech, the crown lost effective control of the region for seven years in the 1460s.

5 Bards and Rebels

The century 1430 to 1530 was the golden age of Welsh medieval poetry. This rich fund of literary material sheds a great deal of light on the bards' perceptions of lawlessness and on their views of the role of the *uchelwyr* in combating it. In analysing this work, however, care is needed and proper account taken of the particular social function of poetry in this period, and the bards' relations with the *uchelwyr* and the rest of society. It also invites comparison between the treatment of banditry in Welsh literature and the depiction of bandits in other countries. How far individual bandits corresponded to E. J. Hobsbawn's definition of 'social banditry', the representatives of subordinate classes or subject groups in their struggle against oppressive authority, needs also to be considered.[1]

The Bards in Welsh Society

Following the Edwardian conquest the Welsh *uchelwyr* became the chief patrons of the bards. The *uchelwyr* were landowners and often warriors, but they were also expected to possess a certain refinement of culture. They were not only patrons of the bards, but often aspired themselves to become bards in their own right. The bards, by virtue of their profession, belonged to the *uchelwyr* class. Whilst Gutun Owain, Dafydd Llwyd and Tudur Aled were themselves drawn from this strata, and sang at their own table, most had to seek employment as bards to prominent families. Others were of more humble origin. Tudur Penllyn was at various times farmer, wool merchant and drover. Guto'r Glyn served as a soldier in his youth in France under Mathew Goch.[2] The bards enjoyed their privileged lifestyle, and many considered themselves connoisseurs of wine and the good things in life.[3]

The bardic profession was hierarchically organised, with admission and promotion carefully regulated. Through periodic eisteddfodau, virtually conferences of the bardic guild, the rules of the craft were laid down, standards upheld through competition, and admission into the profession controlled. The bards retained a strong sense of identity, as carriers of traditional values. The craft was passed on from father to son. Particular regions, most notably the Dee valley in north-east Wales, produced a large number of bards. The courts of Raglan and Dinefwr in south Wales vied with one another to lure many of these bards to work for them.[4]

The bards constituted an educated coterie within the society, many having been schooled in the monastic houses, and trained as bard apprentices by established bards. The training of a bard was a complex and lengthy process. This was an oral craft. They were versed in the poetry of the past, as well as in the work of their contemporaries. They were particularly interested in the history of the British. They were familiar with the Arthurian legends. They had knowledge of Latin and some knowledge of classical myths and legends. All knew the scriptures, the lives of the saints and the calendar of religious observance. They were well-informed about current affairs. The bards were also experts in genealogy and heraldry.[5]

Bards undertook itineraries between the houses of their patrons (*clera*). They visited their patrons at Christmas, Easter and on special occasions – weddings, funerals, and the patron's saints day (*gwyl mabsant*). The *uchelwyr* on such occasions would be entertained not only by the bards, but also by musicians, minstrels, acrobats, jugglers and conjurors. Romances and tales would be recited by professional storytellers (*cyfarwyddiaid*), whilst bards might employ their own declaimers (*datgeiniaid*).

The poetry of this period was very diverse in form and style. One category of verse was the prophetic or vaticinatory verse (*canu brud*) divining the future through astrology, omens and portents. A millenarian strand prophesied the coming of new leader to liberate the enslaved Welsh. The tradition of vaticinatory or prophetic verse in Wales dates back at least to *Armes Prydein Vawr* in the tenth century, with ancient heroes – Cynan, Cadwaladr or Arthur – presented as the deliverers of their people. The sense of national pride was bolstered by a powerful origin myth of the ancient Britons, drawing on Geoffrey of Monmouth's *Historia Regum Britanniae* and his *Prophetia Merlini*. These held that the Welsh descended from Brutus and his Trojans, who had settled in Britain. The prophecies foretold how the Britons would re-conquer their lost patrimony and expel the Saxons.[6]

In the fifteenth century the bards retained the role of seers and prophets (*brudwyr*), foretelling the coming of a mythic national saviour who would inaugurate a national reawakening in accordance with the ancient prophecies (*daroganau*).[7] Glyndŵr consulted Hopkin ap Thomas ab Einion (*Maister of Brut*),[8] William Herbert in 1469 was allegedly inspired by prophecy, whilst Henry Tudor in 1485 consulted the bard Dafydd Llwyd. A Spanish diplomat at the end of the fifteenth century compared Wales' reputation as the home of prophets, seers and soothsayers with that of Galicia in Spain, another Celtic enclave.[9]

In contrast to these highly politicised poems, much of the verse of the period was otherworldly, religious and high-minded, reflecting the strongly Catholic faith of the society. Poems were dedicated to Christ, the Virgin Mary, local saints and religious shrines. Many bards had close links with the church, with abbots acting as important patrons. Siôn Cent concentrated on religious poetry, preaching a stark, austere message of penitence, renunciation of the world and reconciliation with God.[10]

Another major category of poetry was the praise-poem (*cywydd moliant*) dedicated to local notables and abbots, lauding their virtues, their noble lineage, (*gwaedoliaeth dda or bonedd*) courage, charity and largesse (*perchentyaeth*). Another aspect of the bards' work was to compose elegies (*marwnadau*) to deceased patrons. Asking poems (*cywydd gofyn*) comprise another category, in which bards request gifts for themselves or on behalf of others, in the process describing the gift itself and praising the virtues of their patrons. Bards could also act as intercessors in disputes between feuding families through the composition of verses of reconciliation (*cymodi*).

On a lighter note Llywelyn ab y Moel and Tudur Penllyn followed the style pioneered by Dafydd ap Gwilym, concentrating on love poems, nature poems, and humorous, picaresque verse about love exploits, tavern life, the lot of the minstrels, and the life of the English border towns. The lighter verse included lampoons, satires and jesting verse (*dychan*) often with the bard himself or a rival bard the butt of humour. There were also bawdy and erotic verse, such as those exchanged between Dafydd Llwyd and Gwerful Mechain, one of the few women bards of the age.[11] Verse competitions (*ymryson*) between bards, often involving the exchange of jests and insults, were also common.

Prophetic/vaticinatory verse

Few poems dealing with the Glyndŵr rising survive. The number composed must have been immense, and their disappearance reflects the precariousness of this oral craft.[12] After 1415 most bards and *uchelwyr* prudently dissociated themselves from the revolt. Even bards closely associated with Glyndŵr avoided the subject or referred to it only by allusion, with some adopting pseudonyms apparently to avoid persecution. Much of the poetry of the period is concerned with glorifying the achievements and virtues of the *uchelwyr*. Underlying this conformist stance there runs also a streak of rebellion that often breaks to the surface – criticism of the *uchelwyr*, animosity towards the English, and the search for a saviour to redeem the nation's fortunes.

The rising may be fleetingly referred to in an elegy on the death of Rhys ap Tudur, one of the sons of the Penmynydd family of Anglesey, problematically attributed to Gruffydd Grug. Rhys ap Tudur was one of Glyndŵr's leading captains, who was executed in 1411 or 1412. The bard asserts that Rhys ap Tudur reduced the English to compost (*Gwnaeth Eingl yn fraennar*) and refers to him as the 'Guardian of Snowdonia's stags' (*Ceidwad ... ceirw Eryri*). Some have interpreted this as an allusion to the office of Forester of Snowdonia, but there is no evidence that Rhys ap Tudur ever held this post. The term stags was used to designate local magnates and it was also a code term for outlaws.[13]

Rhys Goch Eryri in his poem to Robert ap Meredydd, who fought with Glyndŵr, makes no mention of the rising. According to Sir John Wynn in his *History of the Gwydir Family* his ancestor is not specifically mentioned in the poem for 'he durst not name him therein, for that it seemeth he was an outlaw at that time when the song was made'.[14]

The bards often vented their wrath against the English, the descendants of Hengist and Horsa, the children of Alice (*plant Alice*), the off-springs of Rowenna (*Rhonwen*), who had deprived them of their patrimony in the rich lowlands of what was now England. A praise poem to Rhys Gethin, one of Glyndŵr's leading captains, protests at how the ancient Britons had been expelled from their own lands to their enduring suffering (*Lle bu'r Brython, Saeson sydd,/A'r boen ar Gymru beunydd*).[15]

In 'The Prophecy of the Sacred Oil' (*Darogan yr Olew Bendigaid*) the author bemoans how the Welsh are in servitude to the English (*yn geith dan Season*), having lost their own princes, and lacking a leader (*heb pennadur*). The author recalls how he threw himself into studying the books of prophecy, which foretold how the Welsh would again be raised to a glorious estate and kingly honour. Another contemporary work laments the loss of Welsh independence on account of treason, for which the Welsh ever since have had to 'suffer pain, want and exile in their native land' (*yn godef poen ac achenocit ac alltuded yn eu ganedic dayar*).[16]

Other bards were much more sceptical regarding the powers of prophecy. Meredydd ap Rhys recounted how he had once sold his property to buy arms for the battles foretold by the prophecies, but had come to regard them with disdain, accusing the *brudwyr* of raising false hopes, duping people with the supposed wisdom of Merlin and misleading the credulous into reckless adventures.[17]

The messianic leader in the fifteenth century was 'Owain' a reference to the myth that Owain Glyndŵr had not died and would one day return. The bards venerated Glyndŵr, the symbol of heroic resistance, who encapsulated an unrealised yearning for freedom. The name Owain was invested with almost magical properties.[18] Lewis Glyn Cothi in his poem to Owain ap Gruffydd ap Nicholas of Dinefwr lists the great 'Owains' of the past including Owain ab Urien, Owain Gwynedd, Owain Cyfeiliog, Owain Lawgoch and Owain Glyndŵr.[19] Tudur Penllyn compared Rheinallt ap Gruffydd ap Bleddyn with Owain ab Urien (*Iarll y Ffynnon*) the hero of the medieval romance The Lady of the Lake (*Iarlles y Ffynnon*).[20]

As Norman Cohn, in *The Pursuit of the Millennium*, has shown, this millenarian belief in a hero who would save his people in their darkest hour was common in many European countries.[21] It forecast a return to a golden age, after a period of suffering, in which the deliverer would be the prophesied one. In most parts of Europe these millenarian beliefs were couched in religious terms. For E. J. Hobsbawm this faith in a messianic deliverer, sometimes in the guise of the noble outlaw, reflects a fragmented society, unable to redress its own grievances.[22]

Vaticinatory verse, as Glanmor Williams argues, is common amongst subjugated people and offers a hope of some millenarian transformation of the world.[23] The work of the Welsh brudwyr exemplifies this combination of hope, frustration and despair. It is full of antipathy towards the English. Bards like Rhys Fardd (who also used the pseudonyms The Little Bard – Y Bardd Bach – or the Sleeping Bard-Bardd Cwsg) composed fiercely anti-English vaticinatory verse in the tradition of earlier bards such as Adda Fras and Y Bergam. In fifteenth century Wales millenarianism seems to have been entirely secular and political. Similarly striking is the absence of any belief that the new millennium would involve social justice or equality.[24]

Bards and monks transcended local allegiances and were the carriers of a collective memory and of a sense of national identity. The Welsh bards, like the English minstrels, were potentially a subversive force. In 1449 measures were decreed to deal with the corruption of the minstrel profession in England, at a time when the authorities were alarmed at mounting social unrest and disorder.[25] The same motive may have lain behind the organisation of the Carmarthen eisteddfod c. 1451, under the auspices of Gruffydd ap Nicholas of Dinefwr.

In the turbulent politics of fifteenth century Wales the bards were required to hold often competing or contradictory views as the occasion required. A bard such as Guto'r Glyn was capable of celebrating the family connections of some of his patrons with Glyndŵr, whilst at the same time celebrating the descent of others, most notably his chief patron Sir William Herbert of Raglan, from Dafydd Gam, Glyndŵr's deadly enemy. The political views of the bards and of the *uchelwyr* also reflected the shifting fortunes of the competing dynastic families in the Wars of the Roses.

The outlaw tradition in literature

The prevalence of outlaws and bandits already in the fourteenth century
was such that they became part of the imagery of the bards. Dafydd ap
Gwilym in one of his love poems to Morfudd depicts himself as an outlaw
untainted by *galanas* (*Herwr glan heb alanas*), an outcast lover. In another
poem the bard has been slayed by his lady, for which she is obliged to
become an outlaw, and as penance to undertake a pilgrimage to St
David's.[26] In 'The Burial of the Poet Who Died of Love' (*Claddu'r bardd
o gariad*) the bard threatens vengeance (*galanas*) on the woman who has
spurned and mortally wounded him.[27]

Guto'r Glyn in his early poems addressed to his patron the abbot of
Ystrad Fflur (Strata Florida) describes himself as a 'talentless outlaw'
(*herwr diddawn*), a 'dumb outlaw' (*Wtla mud es talm ydwyf*), referring to
his travels in south Wales when the muse had temporarily deserted him. In
another poem he calls his hated rival, the bard Dafydd ap Edmwnd, a 'little
outlaw' (*wtla bach*) and 'fugitive' (*gŵr ar ffo*) when the latter had for some
reason been forced to flee. He had sunk so low as to seek shelter amongst
the English in Denbigh (*Aeth i Ddinbech i lechu*) and had hidden out in the
rocks and woods. Guto'r Glyn suggests that he be hunted down like a fox.[28]

Tudur Aled in his early love poetry at the end of the sixteenth century
compares himself to the forlorn lover and the bandit (*gwylliad*). Both were
men of the night, wronged, persecuted, imprisoned and unjustly tried,
awaiting the verdict of a hostile jury of English burgesses like the verdict
of his love.

Gwylliad, ym mraint i golli,
Yng nharchar dan far wyf i,
Yn aros cael, gafael cas,
Dedryd y deuddeg didras.[29]

The same theme of the lover as outlaw is taken up in the love poems of
Bedo Aerddrem and Bedo Brwynllys.[30] Even at the end of the sixteenth
century bards like Thomas Prys still employed the convention of the lover
as outlaw.[31]

Outlaw imagery is also attached to animals. Dafydd ap Gwilym
describes a female hare as an outlaw (*herw wraig*), a possible reference to
the supposed ability of witches to transform themselves into hares. Ieuan
Gethin in his 'Poem to the bees' nest' (*Cywydd y Bydafe*) compares a
swarm of enraged bees, who have had their honey stolen, to a horde of
bandits

Myn dyw nef myned a wnan
Mal wylliaid are mel allan
Dwyn o'r mel di drafael dro).[32]

Frequently outlaws are referred to as stags (*ceirw*), the noble, elusive and hunted creatures of the forests.

The bard as outlaw: Llywelyn ab y Moel

The situation on the Anglo-Welsh border in the early fifteenth century is reflected in the poetry of Llywelyn ab y Moel, who himself led the life of an outlaw.[33] His poetry belongs to either the period of the Glyndŵr rising itself or to the 1420s. It contains bitter anti-English views, with its invective directed at the 'Normans' i.e. the men of the North (*y Nordd*) and the children of Alice (*plant Alis*). Like other bards, he composed verse prophesying the destruction of the English, and the return of 'Owain', who would restore to the Britons their rights and dignities.

Llywelyn ab y Moel, was the son of the bard Moel y Pantri, and father of the bard Owain ap Llywelyn ab y Moel. He came from Llanwnnog, Montgomeryshire. He composed love poems to a maiden named Euron, and a number of controversy (*ymryson*) poems, but his most interesting poems deal with his life as an outlaw. They are distinguished by vibrancy and wit, displaying an aristocratic disdain for the gentry and bards who had abandoned the struggle against alien rule.

In his poem 'To the Greyrock Woods' (*I Goed y Graig Lwyd*) Llywelyn sings the praise of his outlaw lair, situated at Llanymynech, on the border with Shropshire. The wood he describes as 'a fort', 'a warrior's playground', 'a snug lair', 'a fair castle' with 'leafy turrets' and 'tapestries' of woven leaf. It has replaced both the poet's patron and his hall as the true seat of his affections. Freedom and nobility can only be found in the outlaw's life. He compares the lordly opulence of his retreat with the despised hovel of the serf, and lauds the outlaw's life away from the comforts of an enslaved gentry and its bardic sycophants.

Gwell o lawer no chlera
I ddyn a chwenycho dda,
Dwyn Sais, a'i ddiharnesio
Dan dy frign, dien dy fro.[34]

Better than wandering minstrelsy
For one anxious to prosper

To seize and unharness a Saxon
Under your bough, o sweet glade.

The political message is explicitly drawn in the poem's conclusion, which invokes Owain's name in a rallying call for renewed resistance.

Llydan sercl uwch aberclwyd
Llundain gwerin Owain wyd
Llwgr ystad Lloegr ystodiau
Llwyddid Duw'r lluyddiaid tau
Llwyr fendith ymhlith fy mhlaid
Llawn dal, llu Owain deiliaid

Wide circle above our perch
To Owain's men you're London
Whilst, England's fate is marred
God grant our fight goes forward
All good fortune amidst my band
All reward to Owain's hosts

The bard's retinue or band (*plaid*) becomes part of an army of resistance, a rallying point and the promise of future victory.

In his poem 'To the Purse' (*I'r Pwrs*) he converses with his purse in a well-established bardic convention. He notes the purse's sickly looks and sunken cheeks. The purse complains that it cannot live on the meagre earnings from harvesting and that it is dying for want of gold (*Marw o ddig am aur ydd wyf*). It urges the bard to return to the Greyrock Woods, to buckle on the outlaw's sword (*Gwisgio herwgledd, gwisgi hirglaer*) and under cover of night to resume his old calling. The purse recalls earlier successful raids on neighbouring Ruyton Eleven Towns in Shropshire, in the earl of Arundel's lordship. The bard tells the purse to desist, and recalls how they were once nearly captured. The purse chides him for his cowardice and threatens to abandon him. The bard seeks to reason with the purse, promising to seek gold to fill its empty pouches again as a harvester in Maelienydd, and implores it to flee the Greyrock Woods lest it be caught and hanged.[35]

In another humorous poem 'The Battle of Mare's Heath' (*Brwydr Waun Gaseg*) he recounts an episode from his outlaw life. The Waun Gaseg referred to appears to be that situated near Cwm Hir, in the bandit redoubt of Y Drum Ddu. The bard with a raiding party sets off in high humour, recounting tales of 'Owain' and boasting of his past exploits. Suddenly a mounted party of armed men appears before them, led by one with the mouth of an ape who sounds the clarion like a cannon. Without waiting to give battle the bard and his companions scatter in confusion, with Llywelyn himself leading the undignified flight.[36]

Llywelyn ab y Moel was buried at Strata Marcella monastery, north of Welshpool, amidst the lords and abbots. Rhys Goch Eryri in his lament praised his artistry and courage.[37] Guto'r Glyn in a moving elegy paid tribute to his courage in battle, his prowess with the sword and his mastery of love poetry. Owain's songthrush has been stilled (*A thewi bronfraith Owain*).[38] Llywelyn ab y Moel provides the classic illustration of the bard as outlaw and hero.

The bard as outlaw: Lewis Glyn Cothi

The Wars of the Roses deeply divided the Welsh gentry and the bardic fraternity. Lewis Glyn Cothi was one of the leading bards of his day and a Lancastrian supporter. A native of Carmarthenshire, he worked mainly in south Wales. He was a fervent patriot whose poems are full of bile against the English. Several of his poems were aimed at inspiring Welsh chieftains to take up the struggle against alien rule.[39] He was apparently twice forced to take up the life of an outlaw. In one poem he thanks Owain ap Gruffydd of Dinefwr for providing him with shelter when outlawed.

A mi'n nhiredd Gwynedd gynt
Yn herwa yno hirhynt:
Owain i gadw vy einioes
Ei aur a'i win ym a roes.[40]

When formerly I traversed Gwynedd
Outlawed there, long endurance,
Owain to preserve my life
His gold and wine on me bestowed.

In the same poem he inveighs against the overbearing gentry, the decline of Welsh law and custom, and stresses the need to protect the lowly.

Rhoi cyvraith berfaith i'r beilch
Rhoi devawd i'r rhai diveilch[41]

Mete out perfect justice to the proud,
Restore the ancient rights of the lowly

Lewis Glyn Cothi ardently supported Jasper Tudor, earl of Pembroke, and uncle of the future Henry VII. Following Jasper's defeat by the earl of March at the battle of Mortimer Cross in 1461 the bard, like his master, fled into hiding. In his poem to Meredydd ap Meredydd of Trefeglwys he recounts how as a fugitive (*dydechwr celliau*) he hid in the oak groves of Allt y Brain. In a spine-tingling line he adds that there he walked in the footsteps of Owain's men.

Mi'n ddydechwr celliau
A drig a'i wal mewn dâr gau.
Y'nghoedwig brig Allt y Brain,
A'i bro, y bu wŷr Owain;
Minnau yn y man yno
Drwy vedw'r allt a roav dro.[42]

He then hid in the rocks and forests of Pennant Bach, amongst the heather of Cwm Buga, and out on the mountains of Pumlumon.

Rheinallt ap Gruffydd ap Bleddyn

One incident from Lewis Glyn Cothi's eventful life casts further light on the dividing line between banditry and the actions of local chieftains.[43] The bard had married the widow of a citizen of Chester, without obtaining the permission of the magistrates, as Welshmen were obliged to do. His household goods were seized and he was compelled to flee the town. In a poem addressed to Rheinallt ap Gruffydd ap Bleddyn, the young lord of Tower (Y Tŵr) near Mold in Flintshire, he requests his aid in revenging the insult.[44] In another poem he requests a sword from a patron with which to avenge himself on the men of Chester. Yorke in his *Royal Tribes of Wales* says that 'Reinallt being ripe for the enterprise, collected his people, went to Chester, and put the citizens, as many as fell into his hands, to the sword'.

In 1465 according to this tradition a dispute between Rheinallt's men and citizens of Chester at Mold fair led to great slaughter on both sides. Rheinallt took prisoner Robert Bryne, ex-mayor of Chester, whom he hung from a staple in his great hall at Tower. An army of two hundred men from Chester attempted to seize Rheinallt. According to tradition, he lured them into his house and having fastened the doors set the place alight, burning them without mercy, and pursuing the rest into the sea. He was subsequently pardoned during the reign of Edward IV.

Rheinallt's reckless exploits made him the darling of the bards. Gutun

Owain depicts him as a knight of chivalry; he is 'steel in the rock' (*dur yn y graig*); 'Adroit with a lance astride a wild steed' (*Abl a gwayw ar ebol gwyllt*); the 'White dragon of the prophecies' (*Draic wenn y daroganau*); and the shield in Henry Tudor's cause (*Tarian wyd yn rraid Harri*).[45] Tudur Penllyn's vivid description of Rheinallt's encounter with the men of Chester descends into gruesome humour at the expense of those slain.[46] Hywel Cilan describes him as the terror of the March (*braw'r Mars*) and recounts the bloody battle which left the English dead bespattered with the colour of wine (*A lliw'r gwin oll ar eu gwallt*).[47]

Rheinallt was one of the Lancastrian captains who defended Harlech castle in 1468 against Lord Herbert. He died two years later at the age of twenty-eight, with an elegy in his honour being composed by Ieuan ap Tudur Penllyn.[48] For the Lancastrian bards Rheinallt was no brigand but a rebellious chieftain of noble lineage who symbolised resistance to English and Yorkist rule.

The Outlaw as Hero: Dafydd ap Siencyn

The fascination and allure of the outlaw's life is well illustrated by the case of Dafydd ap Siencyn, who operated in the Conwy Valley, which during the Wars of the Roses became a battleground between contending factions. Dafydd ap Siencyn was a Lancastrian partisan and guerrilla fighter. From his eyrie on Carreg y Walch (Hawk Rock) near Llanrwst he kept the Yorkists out of the commote of Nanconwy until 1468 and raided the surrounding countryside. He was of noble stock: his father descended from Marchudd, and his mother was the daughter of Glyndŵr's famous captain – Rhys Gethin, lord of Rhos.

His exploits are related in Sir John Wynn's *History of the Gwydir Family* where he is described as 'a famous outlaw' and a 'a man of great valour'.[49] Together with Rheinallt ap Gruffydd, he was one of the Lancastrian captains who held Harlech castle. In 1468 Dafydd ap Siencyn, Ieuan ap Robert ap Meredith and other Lancastrian captains 'wasted with fire and sword the suburbs of Denbigh and all the lordship of Denbigh'. He was responsible for the murder of the English crown officials Henry Heaton and Richard Pemberton and was supposedly the author of 'many foul deeds'. In retaliation the king sent Lord Herbert with a 'great army' 'to waste the mountain countries of Caernarvonshire and Merionethshire' and to besiege Harlech, which finally yielded in 1468.[50]

Dafydd ap Siencyn also contended with Hywel ap Evan ap Rhys Gethin, who at the beginning of Edward IV's reign lived in Dolwyddelan castle, and is described as 'captain of the country' and an 'outlaw'. Dafydd ap

Siencyn is said to have been supported by the 'English officers'. By a ruse
using a drugged potion he captured Hywel ap Evan in his bed at Pennamen
and took him to Conwy castle. Subsequently he was obliged to 'flee the
country and go to Ireland where he was a year or thereabouts'.[51] He
returned to Wales in the summer 'having himself and all his followers clad
in green, which being come into the country he dispersed here and there
amongst his friends lurking by day, and walking in the night for fear of his
adversaries. Such of the country as happened to have sight of him and his
followers, said they were fairies and so ran away'.[52]

Tudur Penllyn depicts Dafydd ap Siencyn as a heroic symbol of revolt
and independence. Dafydd lives in the sheltered forest, he is the tall Kai of
the greenwoods, his castle is the grove, the oaks are his turrets; he is the
stags' (i.e. the outlaws') friend; he is a skilful warrior, a second Roland; he
is the king of his own land, Gwynedd is at his back and he has followers
in the south; eight score kinsmen form his guard and eight hundred are
faithful to him.

Dy gastell ydyw'r gelli
Derw dôl yw dy dyrau di...
Glanaf a medrit, Dafydd
Gerddwriaeth, herwriaeth hydd;
Caredig i'r ceirw ydwyd
Câr i'r iarll, concweriwr wyd
Tithau, gleddau arglwyddi,
Teyrn wyd yn ein tir ni.
Gwylia'r trefydd celfydd call
A'r tiroeddd o'r tu arall...
Da yw ffin a thref ddinas,
Gorau yw'r glyn a'r graig las...
Cadw o'r dref, cadw'r coed a'r drws
Cadw batent coed y Betws.[53]

Your castle is the grove
The glade's oaks are your turrets...
The finest and accomplished, Dafydd,
In the artistry and lore of outlawry
You are the stags' friend
The Earl's liegeman, and conqueror
The swords of lords
You are king in our land.
Watch the towns discreetly

And the lands from your look out
The border and walled towns are fair
Far better the vale and the blue rock
Avoid the towns, keeper of the woods and door
Protect the woods of Bettws.

This brave forester (*Coedwr dewr*) is no simple brigand, but a man of noble stock. Moreover, the outlaw is possessed of almost magical powers (*herwriaeth hydd*). His outlawry is part of a just struggle on behalf of the Lancastrian cause. He is the blood relative of the earl of Richmond (*Câr i'r iarll*). This poems is related to Tudur Penllyn's vaticinatory poems, which prophesy the coming of Henry Tudor, his poems to Jasper Tudor and other Lancastrian partisans.

The bard Ifan ap Gruffydd Leiaf describes Dafydd ap Siencyn and his followers as 'birds of crime' (*adar o greim*), derisively adopting the garrison men's expression for such outlaws. He is a mighty spear, a golden knight of a warrior race, he and his men outlaws in the land of Grwst.

Mawr ydwyd, wayw mawrydos,
Marchog aur rhyfelog Rhos!
A'th wyr a thithau, herw-wst.
'Adar a greim' ar dir Grwst![54]

Dafydd ap Siencyn is described as of the stock of Rhys Gethin, as the true lord of Rhos; his court is roofed with green twigs and is like Merlin's glass house; his hall is above the bright waters of the glen; groves of holly are its portcullises. With Dafydd were the young warriors of the Trojan race; they had hounds and blades of Gascon steel; they ate seated on the green sward, and lived on vegetables and wine.

The portrait drawn of Dafydd ap Siencyn invites comparison with the paintings of bandits by the seventeenth century Italian artist Salvator Rosa, depicting them as noble, heroic figures, defiant supermen and natural anarchists at war with an unjust order. Salvator Rosa's painting 'Gruppo di Bravi' with the bandit chief standing atop a rock blowing a trumpet to summon his men, could easily be taken for an illustration of Tudur Penllyn's poem to Dafydd ap Siencyn.[55]

Like some other notable outlaws Dafydd ap Siencyn died with honour. Having been pardoned after 1468 he became constable of Conwy castle, having killed the post's previous occupant. Like Llywelyn ab y Moel he was both a man of action and a poet. Tudur Penllyn sang his praises as a poet. Three of his *englynion* survive, one addressed to Tudur Penllyn and

two others composed on his deathbed, from which it appears that his death
was caused by wounds received in a fracas.

The Robin Hood dimension

The Welsh bards were familiar with the traditions of the noble outlaw of
medieval English literature, including Hereward the Wake, Guy of
Warwick, Fulk Fitzwarin, Gamelyn and Robin Hood.[56] Fulk Fitzwarin, lord
of Whittington on the Shropshire border in the thirteenth century, and
famously outlawed, was revered by the Welsh bards who often invoked his
name as a model of knightly valour. Tudur Penllyn's poem to Dafydd ap
Siencyn, like the Robin Hood ballads, extols virtues associated with the
gentry – courage, generosity, charity, care for the poor and oppressed.

In the Welsh chronicles there existed a similar idealisation of the outlaw.
In a manuscript from the Peniarth collection, recounting the life of a cleric,
there is short story similar to that of William Tell or the English tales
associated with William of Cloudisly in the ballad of Adam Bell

> Gwedy saethu yr afal ar ben Madoc Vychan y vab, o arch a
> gorchymyn Mallt Walbri, arglwyddes Brycheiniog, ac wedy taro yr
> afal a diank y mab, y dauth Madoc a'r Rhingyll Du, i gefnder, ac y
> dalyassant hi ai crogyssant hi a'i mab yn y thwr ehun, ac yna y
> daethant ar herw y fforest Lyn Cothi.[57]

> (After shooting the apple on the head of Madoc Vychan the son, by
> the order and direction of Mallt Walbri, the lady of Brycheiniog, and
> after striking the apple, leaving the boy unharmed, Madoc came with
> the Black Judge, his cousin, and they caught her and they hung her
> and her son in this tower, and then they went as outlaws in the forest
> of Glyn Cothi')

It is now generally accepted that the Robin Hood ballads were part of
gentry culture, rather than that of a rebellious peasantry, although they may
have initially been part of peasant folk culture.[58] Wales never developed a
literary genre similar to the Robin Hood ballads in England. One bard,
possibly Ieuan Tew Brydydd Ieuanc, describes an encounter with two
outlaws at a place called Rhyd Goch (Red Ford). The outlaws entertain the
bard, and provide shelter and protection to minstrels and to the poor. They
were haughty, handsome and generous; the green earth their table, spring
water their wine. The bards invokes the example of Robin Hood to justify
theft from the rich.

Dygwch, o'r lle bo digon
Dwyn benthig, ddiddig ddeuddyn,
Dwyn a rhoi, nid anair hyn.
Hudol oedd Robin Hwd lan,
Herwr a fu'n heu arian
O breibiwch, moeswch im' win,
Breibiwch fel y bu Robin.
Ysbario ansyberwyd
A wna byw'n yn y byd;
Kneifiwch, cawn ninnau yfed,
Kybyddion a Saeson sied;
Crist o'ch blaen, er i fraen fron.
Cerddwch, gochelwch, haelion.[59]

Steal from those who have plenty,
Borrow, you amiable pair,
To take and give is no reproach.
Kind Robin Hood was a magician,
An outlaw who scattered money.
Offer bribes, fetch me wine,
Bribe as Robin used to bribe.
By avoiding discourtesy
We may live in this world.
Shear, so we may drink,
Misers and escheated Saxons.
Christ before you, for his pierced breast
Walk on, be wary you generous ones.

This poem offers some insight into the treatment of the subject by lesser bards, reflecting perhaps more closely popular tastes than the work of bards tied to the *uchelwyr*.

Such poems stress the importance of honour, dignity, valour, courage and camaraderie. Life becomes an exhilarating game of chance in which the senses are heightened where life itself may be transient. The outlaws set themselves in defiance to the garrison men (*gwyr y caerau*) and disdained the life of the burgesses (*bwrdais*). The outlaws supplant the gentry as dispensers of patronage to the bards and the lowly.

CONCLUSION

The theme of the noble outlaw in the poetry of the fifteenth century grew out of specific circumstances. The subjugation of Wales under English rule remained a source of rancour. But the bards and the *uchelwyr* were obliged to come to terms with the realities of their time. At the same time the dynastic struggle for power in England allowed the bards the possibility of wresting something from this situation. The tradition of the noble outlaw was associated directly with Glyndŵr and his supporters. It was subsequently associated with the Lancastrian struggle against the alleged Yorkists usurpers, and was to culminate in Henry Tudor's bid for the throne in 1485. These were both presented as struggles for power by those who had a legitimate claim to rule by dynastic right. In both cases they were also projected as part of a struggle to gain either national independence, or to remove the more oppressive features of the existing system of alien rule.

The bards drew a clear distinction between political rebels fighting for what was perceived as a just cause and ordinary bandits and criminals. Although in the circumstances of civil war it was often difficult to distinguish between these categories. The bards were themselves part of the *uchelwyr* strata in society and their poetry served their needs. Whilst the noble outlaws of Welsh poetry reflected to a notable extent nationalistic or dynastic aspirations, there is no evidence in the poetry which survives that the bards identified with the struggle of the peasantry against an oppressive social order. On the contrary the bards of the *uchelwyr* in the main upheld an idealised image of a strongly hierarchical society, in which justice and order was secured by the rule of strong but compassionate leaders, who had a God given right to rule.

6 Bandits and Bandit Redoubts

In the civil wars of the fifteenth century, as in all civil wars, the boundary between political rebellion and criminality became hopelessly obscured. Those lauded as upholders of the law by some were often regarded by others as the perpetrators of lawlessness. These problems have to be borne in mind when we come to address the way in which particular offenders were designated as criminals or bandits. In this we rely to a large extent on the accounts provided in the poetry of the period. The bards treat banditry primarily from the perspective of the *uchelwyr* as bandit fighters, staunch upholders of the law and protectors of the weak. Whilst these accounts cannot be taken at face value they nevertheless provide important evidence concerning the extent of the problem of banditry in the fifteenth century, and the way the bards and their gentry patrons perceived it.

One of the main verse forms was the praise poem, which explicitly served the social and cultural needs of the *uchelwyr*. The poems are highly stylised, with the virtues of strength, valour and generosity lauded. Patrons are compared with eagles, hawks, lions and stags. They are described as guardians (*ceidwad*), doors (*drws*), tor (*tor*), mighty forts (*caer*), ramparts (*allt serth*), shields (*tarian*), great oaks (*caterwen*) which protect their lands and people. Extravagant comparisons are made with figures from history, legend and folklore – Fulk Fitzwarin, Guy of Warwick, King Arthur's knights, Charlemagne, Roland, Hector and Caesar. The bards also stress the social obligations of the *uchelwyr* to protect the weak (*gweiniaid*) by exercising pity and charity.[1] In invoking the values of a lost chivalric age, the bards also drew a veil over the darker side of reality. Siôn Cent, the monk and bard, upbraided his fellow bards for flattering their patrons, arguing that their proper office was to praise God, and condemn the rapacity of the *uchelwyr*. Hywel Dafi rebuked Guto'r Glyn for flattering his patrons for money.[2] The same complaints were voiced a century later.

OUTLAWS AND BANDITS IN WELSH POETRY

Civil disorder is a common theme in the poetry of the period, and was clearly a major preoccupation of the bards and their gentry patrons. The outlaw phenomenon generated its own lexicon. There are frequent references to traitors (*traeturiad* or *bradwyr*), outlaws (*herwyr* or *wtlawyr* – a direct borrowing of *utlah*), robbers (*lladron*), inveterate robbers (*carnlladron*), plunderers (*ysbeilwyr* or *cribddeilwyr*), night-stalkers (*cyrchwyr nos* or *rhodwyr nos*), fugitives (*gwibiad or sglentwyr*), the deceitful (*hocedwyr*), the false (*ffeils*) and brigands and bandits (*gwylliaid*, more rarely *brigawns*).³ The terms foresters or woodmen (*fforestwyr, coedwyr*) also often denote outlaws.

Bandits were not always outlaws, nor were all outlaws bandits. The word for outlaw (*herwr*) is related to the verb to challenge (*herio*) and is also used to refer to fugitives and victims of persecution. It is even used in religious poems concerning Christ's persecution by Herod.⁴ It was used by Siôn Cent to describe the Christians life in this world (*Rhodiwn dir yn hir ar herw*).⁵ It is thus a neutral term, and implied no judgement regarding the cause of the outlawry. In many cases individuals were considered to have been unjustly outlawed or persecuted by those who themselves lacked a legitimate right to rule.

With the term for bandits (*gwylliaid* or *brigawns*) there is no ambiguity. Dafydd Llwyd wrote *Ofn sawdwyr, bradwyr gerbron\Brigawns mwy na berw eigion* (They feared retainers, traitors at hand\And brigands more than hell [the boiling depths]).⁶ Bandits were considered far more serious offenders than common robbers – as Dafydd Llwyd notes *Mwy no lleidr mae'n wylliedydd* (More than a robber, he's a bandit).⁷ The derivation of *gwylliaid* is uncertain, interpreted by some as creatures of the dusk (*gwyll*), but more convincingly as wild men (from *gwyllt*).⁸ *Gwylliaid* were an anonymous, amoral and anarchic force. Whereas bards often entertained sympathy for particular noble outlaws, the word *gwylliaid* is almost invariably used as a term of opprobrium. The noun *gwylliaid* provided the verb *gwyllianta*, to brigandise. Lawlessness was especially acute in border areas between different jurisdictions, between the lordships, the Welsh and English shires. The Welsh word for borderland (*gorwledydd*) became a synonym for disorder.

Attitudes to lawlessness

The Wars of the Roses from 1455 to 1485 deeply divided the Welsh gentry and the bards. Whilst the civil war contributed directly to the problem of lawlessness in Wales, it is interesting to note that the bards were highly critical of the disorder and lawlessness which plagued the country. They extolled the virtues of local notables, particularly those on the Anglo-Welsh border, who they claimed sought to suppress this disorder. They describe also with relish the punishment that was meted out to wrongdoers.

Lewis Glyn Cothi, a bard who was himself outlawed and whose works are full of anti-English invective, leaves no doubt as to his attitude to the endemic lawlessness of the age, which he presents as a scourge, which it is the duty of the *uchelwyr* to root out. After 1468, and the fall of the Lancastrians' last bastion in Harlech, Lewis Glyn Cothi saw the English crown as providing a possible solution to the endemic lawlessness. He came to see Sir William Herbert, the leading Welsh magnate of his day, as a possible champion of Welsh interests. He praised him for his ruthless dealing with wrongdoers, which caused many to flee to the woods (*Rhai i goed a redan rhag ei drydar*).[9] Guto'r Glyn, Huw Cae Llwyd and Iorweth Fynglwyd also praised Sir William Herbert's work in this regard. Amongst the English inhabitants of Herefordshire, however, Sir William Herbert had a very different reputation.

Lewys Glyn Cothi returns repeatedly to this theme in poems addressed to his patrons. He lauds Rhys ap Dafydd Llwyd, Edward IV's steward (evidently during the minority of Lord Grey) of the notoriously lawless lordships of Cedewain, Ceri, Cyfeiliog and Arwystli in Powys for his work in suppressing robbers.

Mae'n dovi gwylliaid llonaid pob llwyn;
Mae'n diva lladron mewn dwy afwyn;
Mae'n rhwymaw'r ddwywlad mewn un gadwyn
Yn mhenau rhai from y mae'n rhoi frwyn.[10]

He tames the bandits which infest each vale
He destroys the robbers in two reins
He unites the two lands in one chain
He bridles the heads of the wild.

The deceased Owain Fychan ab Gruffydd of Llanbrynmair, he says, lay about the transgressors with his sword, tortured the lawless and mercilessly pursued the false and deceitful.

Henry ab Gwilym of Court Henry, sheriff of Carmarthenshire, expended money and effort to apprehend outlaws, bringing them in twos and threes to be tried and executed:

Rhoi aur, a dal herwyr a'u dilyd,
Y mae y sieryv o mesurid,
Bob ddau, bob dri, 'n eu dodi wrth did,
A mynu dadl i'r man y dodid.[11]

The bard calls on Watcyn Vaughan of Talgarth, as constable of Carmarthen castle, to protect the town from the depredations of the foresters, i.e. the outlaws (*Cadw'r dref rhag coedwyr y drin*). Dafydd ap Siôn of Bro Gwyr (Gower) near Swansea is a lamb among the weak and innocent, but is death to the unjust and a mighty conflagration taming the wild and lawless (*Gwalldan yw'n dovi rhai gwylltion diriaid*).[12]

This concern with lawlessness was shared also by the Yorkist bards. Guto'r Glyn or Guto ap Siancyn y Glyn, one of the outstanding bards of the century, frequently refers to the role of his patrons in suppressing lawlessness, and protecting the weak. Thomas Salbri of Lleweni governs the deceitful (*Ceidwad rhag pob hocedwr*). Ieuan ap Einion of Cryniarth is a heavenly lamb in times of peace but a ferocious lion in dealing with bandit hoards (*A llew traws i wylliaid trwch*). Hywel ap Dafydd of Raglan chastised outlaws with his spear and pursued the deceitful (*A phoen herwyr ffyn hirion. Rhai ffeils a rydd her â ffon*).[13]

Guto'r Glyn addressed praise poems to a number of Welsh magnates in the disordered lordships of central Wales. Siôn Dafi of Cemais, who served as a soldier for Edward IV, waged a merciless struggle against criminals, his long arm apprehending outlaws (*Dy law hir yn dal herwyr*). Although loyal to the crown (*Llewpard i Edward ydwyd*), he was also a check on English influence in Wales (*Llaw gref yn erbyn Lloeger oedd*). Sir John Burroughs of Mawddwy, notorious as a haunt of outlaws, protects the upright and innocent, but hunts with spear the deceitful and false (*Helpu cywir a gwirion. Holi ffals a'i hely a ffon*). He praises the work of Hywel ab Owain of Llanbrynmair in Cyfeiliog, Hywel ab Ieuan of Moelyrch in Cynllaith, and Dafydd Llwyd of Newtown in Cydewain and Ceri in combating disorder.[14]

In a poem to Sir Walter Herbert, son of Sir William Herbert of Raglan, Guto'r Glyn stresses the need for order and good government, and declares that it his patron's appointed duty to suppress banditry, to draw out the plague from their midst, to harry the outlaws like a thunderbolt and to protect the weak.

Dewraf undyn drwy fendith,
I dynnu pla wyd o'n plith.
Ymlid herwyr mal taran,
Oll yw'ch gwaith, a llochi gwan.[15]

He is a tor commanding the seething land (*Tor flaen y tir aflonydd*).

Despairing of any solution to this accursed problem Guto'r Glyn appealed impassionedly to Edward IV himself to intervene to impose order in Wales. The king, as a descendant of the Welsh princes, was expected to show particular solicitude towards the Welsh. The bard paints a bleak picture of life in Wales.

Gwae ni o'n geni yn gaeth
Gan ladron, gwna lywodraeth.
Dyred dy hun Edwart hir
I ffrwyno cyrph rhai anwir

Tor bennau a gyddfau gwŷr
Traeturiaid, tro ar herwyr
Dod williaid i dywyllwg
Dilea'r draul, dal rhai drwg[16]

Woe to us born the captives
Of robbers; establish government
Come thyself, valiant Edward
And bridle the deceitful ones

Break the traitors' heads and
Necks, turn on the outlaws
Cast bandits into darkness
Cut our losses, seize the wicked.

Banditry far from being a form of resistance to alien rule was a curse, for which alien rule was the only source of redress. The dominance of the English crown was preferable to lawlessness and anarchy. This was the same Guto'r Glyn who wrote a heartfelt elegy to the famous outlaw bard Llywelyn ab y Moel.

The Lancastrian bard Tudur Penllyn, who wrote praise poems to the rebel chieftain Rheinallt ap Gruffydd ap Bleddyn and to the celebrated outlaw Dafydd ap Siencyn (see chapter five), also condemned common lawlessness. The traditional respect for strong magnates who can impose order is clearly reflected in his work. He advises Gruffydd and Elisau Fychan of Corsygedol, once the pillars of Lancastrian support in Merionethshire, to carefully select officers and to punish outlaws (*Rhoi'r swyddau gorau i'r gwŷr. Rhoi cywiriaid rhag herwyr*). In his poem to Watcyn Vaughan of Hergest he notes that the weak need fear nothing from his silk-liveried retainers, but that outlaws should beware (*ciliwch herwyr*).[17]

The problem of bandits recurs in Tudur Penllyn's other poems. In one poem he requests a horse from a patron to replace one stolen by thieves, and in another requests a sword to defend himself from outlaws.[18] In

another instance he describes how thieves, like a plough, turn over everything in their path (*Dyfod aradr o ladron*).[19] Outlaws provide inspiration
for one of his wittiest poems – a satirical praise poem to one Gruffydd
ap Deicws Chwith, thief. This boastful outlaw (*wtla bostus*), the bard
declares, despoils and pillages all in his wake; storming through
Mawddwy, he robs his neighbours and his own father. Tudur warns that he
will end his days on the gibbet. His corpse will be laid out without the
customary candles, in accordance with the practice for such felons. His
death will be unmourned; with only the cattle, sheep, pigs and dogs which
he stole left to pray over his grave.[20]

The Yorkist bard Huw Cae Llwyd celebrated the achievements of Sir
William Herbert and Sir Richard Herbert in suppressing disorder. He
praised their love of government and enmity towards robbers (*Gwar i'r
llywodraeth, garw i'r lledrad*) and lauded their work in punishing bandits
(*Cosbai gwaith gwallus, casbeth gwylliaid*). In his elegy to the two,
following their execution in 1468, he laments their loss to the struggle to
tame the wildness of Wales (*gwylltined Cymru*). The suppression of
wickedness (*drygioni*) is a recurrent theme in his poetry. In praising Sir
Dafydd of Pen-Rhys, Gower (where a local sanctuary sheltered felons) he
claims that even outlaws will not keep him from his patron's lavish court.
He praises Siôn ap Rhys ap Siancyn of Glyn Nedd (Glyn Neath) for his
courage in taming the wild land (*y tir gwyllt*); his home is a mighty fortress
against disorder (*Caer lydan rhag gorwledydd*) and no outlaws are
entertained at his court.[21]

Owain ap Llywelyn ab y Moel, the son of the famous outlaw bard of the
post-Glyndŵr era (see chapter five), reflects the same concern. Owain,
significantly named, was a minor bard whose work dates from the second
half of the fifteenth century, and comprises praise poems to the heads of
the leading Welsh families in the central March. His work lacks the
political passion of his father's verse and reflects a desire for peace and
order. He describes Dafydd Llwyd of Hafodwen as a valiant judge, defending his neighbourhood against treason and providing a strong fortress to
deter and correct outlaws.

Brawdwy hir i'r brodir hwn.
A bar traws er bwrw treswn.
Ac un castell gwell na gwyr
I'r cywiriaid rhag herwyr.[22]

Banditry in Wales, like raiding on the Anglo-Scottish border, was
seasonal.[23] In a remarkable poem on the months of the year (*Englynion y*

Misoedd) the annual cycle of the seasons is also combined with the cycle of lawlessness. The poem dates from the late fourteenth century, but the latter part was composed in the fifteenth century by Gutun Owain. In October: Plunderers make war, Robbery becomes unrestrained (*Knawd ysbeilwyr yn rryfel, Knawd lledrad yn ddiymgel*). For February the poem contains the elusive line: A dog's head (or dogfish) on a spring morning (*Pen ki ar fore wanwyn*). This is associated with references to murder and conspiracy. It may not be too fanciful to suggest that the dog's head is in fact the wolf's head, i.e. an outlaw. In July: Brigands do not like to associate too long (*Ni char gwylliaid hir gyngrair*). In August and harvest time: Better the work of the sickle than the bow (*Gwell gwaith cryman na bwa*).[24]

At the beginning of the seventeenth century another bard makes the same point regarding the cycle of the year. In August, at the height of the harvest season, he declares, that although officers are absent the robbers do not descend from the mountains.

Ag er maint chwant swyddogion
Nid dar lladron o'r elltydd.[25]

BANDIT REDOUBTS

In Wales in the fifteenth century particular regions became notorious for their disorder. The most lawless areas were those on the Anglo-Welsh border and in central Wales. The Council of the Marches and its Court, established in 1474, was set up primarily to deal with disorder in these areas. I. Bowen writes

> This Court was created for the purpose of establishing and maintaining order in the borderland which had been the scene of so much disturbance and misrule for years. The most turbulent districts within its jurisdiction were those which subsequently formed the counties of Radnor, Montgomery and Denbigh. The following lordships are repeatedly mentioned as the haunts of criminal's, viz: Elvael, Arwystli, Kerry [Ceri] and Caedwen [Cydewain] and Cyfeiliog... The lordships of Chepstow and Gower in South Wales, the lordships of Oswestry and Powys, the shires of Merioneth and Cardigan were noted for their disorder, but the Marcher Lordships of northern and central Wales appear to have been the worst.[26]

Certain localities were notorious as bandit strongholds – Y Graig Lwyd

(Llanymynaich) celebrated by Llywelyn ab y Moel, Cefn Digoll (Long Mountain) near Welshpool, Gwern y gof in Ceri, Y Drum Ddu (the mountain regions of the lordships of Gwerthrynion, Cwmwd Deuddwr and Builth), and the Dugoed forest of Mawddwy.[27] In north east Wales were the disordered lordships of Oswestry and Chirk, and the neighbouring lordship of Bromfield and Yale centred on Holt. Further south were lordships such as Brecon and Maelienydd, which were a by-word for disorder and cattle rustling. In Cardiganshire the Cwmystwyth area was notorious for its outlaws as were the regions of Uwch Aeron and Is Aeron. Dafydd Nanmor in a poem to William Fychan of Rhydhelig, constable of Aberystwyth castle and mayor of the town in the reign of Edward IV, urges him to suppress the robbers of the Uwch Aeron district (*lladron y Blaenau*).[28]

Merionethshire and several adjoining districts, such as Nant Conwy, Eifionydd, Berwyn and Mawddwy became notorious as outlaw haunts. The Berwyn mountains, bordering Merionethshire and the marcher lordships of Powys, had been the heartland of Glyndŵr territory, and contained the sanctuary of Penant Melangell. Between Berwyn and Mawddwy lay Bwlch y Groes (the Pass of the Cross), a pass through the mountains guarded by a Catholic cross, which was supposed to provide immunity for travellers. Berwyn's reputation as an outlaw redoubt was almost certainly influenced by the fact that this was Glyndŵr country, and must have provided a haven for rebels in the decades after the rising. Local folk traditions concerning the outlaws of Berwyn are strong, but there is little surviving information in the historical records and historians have almost all ignored it.

However, the region's reputation as an outlaw redoubt is amply confirmed by the bards. Tudur Aled describes Siôn ap Meredydd of Trefor as a guardian of Ruthin, Hiraethog and Dinmael, and a fortress against the men of Berwyn (*Caer fawr rhag gwyr o Ferwyn*).[29] Guto'r Glyn lamented the death of Siôn ap Madog Pilstwn of Maelor, describing him as the great oak beneath Berwyn (*Dâr fawr is daer Berwyn*).[30] Dafydd Llwyd of Mathafarn in one of his vaticinatory poems anticipates the return of Henry Tudor, whereby order will be imposed on Berwyn.[31] Dafydd Nanmor having fallen out with his patron, Rhys ap Meredydd, the leading magnate in the troubled region of Is Aeron, Cardiganshire, wrote a poem of propitiation in which he threatened to take up the life of an outlaw in Berwyn Forest (*Af ar herw i Goed Berwyn*) where neither man nor beast is safe.[32] Owain ap Llywelyn ab y Moel in requesting two greyhounds from a patron says that they will make short play of the 'stags of Berwyn' (*Chwarae a wnant yn chwyrn ynn, Chwarae byr a cheirw Berwyn*).[33] Berwyn was good hunting ground, but this may also be read as a grim jesting reference to the outlaws of the region, implying that hunting dogs were used to pursue them.

The bandits of Ysbyty Ifan

The Conwy valley was a major battleground between the Yorkists and Lancastrians and the main area of operation of the Lancastrian partisan Dafydd ap Siencyn. Towards the end of the Wars of the Roses it became the haunt of bandits who used the hospice of the Knights of St. John at Ysbyty Ifan in Dolgynwal, as their base. Ysbyty Ifan, situated on the border between Merionethshire, Caernarfonshire and the lordship of Denbigh was well placed to serve as a bandit redoubt. It offered sanctuary to felons at nearby Dinas Noddfa.

The Knights of the Order of St.John, or the Knights Hospitallers, owned various properties in north Wales dating back to the twelfth century. They were administered by the Preceptory at Halston near Oswestry. The hospices were situated on the main pilgrim routes, often in remote and dangerous places.[34] They were at the height of their influence in the thirteenth century. Dafydd Nanmor in the fifteenth century could still sing of its proverbial hospitality, although by this time its fortunes had declined.[35]

The main account of these bandits is provided by Sir John Wynn in his celebrated *History of the Gwydir Family* written early in the seventeenth century:

> From the town of Conway to Bala and from Nan Conway to Denbigh, there was continually fashioned a wasp's nest which troubled the whole country, I mean a lordship (sic) belonging to St. John's of Jerusalem, called Yspytty Jevan, a large thing which had privilege of Sanctuary. This peculiar jurisdiction, not governed by the King's laws became a receptacle of thieves and murtherers, who being safely warranted there thoroughly peopled the place. No spot within twenty miles was safe from their incursions and robberies, and what they got within their limits was their own. They had got their backstay friends and receptors in all the county of Merioneth and Powisland and these helping the former desolations and preying upon their near neighbours, kept most part of the country all waste and without inhabitants.[36]

This vivid description of organised banditry provides an important part of Sir John Wynn's account of the origins of the Gwydir family. Towards the beginning of Henry VII's reign his ancestor Meredydd ap Ifan

purchased Dolwyddelan castle and its land, previously the property of one
Hywel ap Ifan, an outlaw. Meredydd ap Ifan had been compelled to leave
his home amongst his kinsmen in Eifionydd on account of a blood feud.
According to Sir John Wynn there was nothing in Eifionydd 'but killing
and fighting'. His grandfather resolved to move to Nantconwy which was
'swarming with thieves and bondmen'. He determined that 'he had rather
fight with outlaws and thieves than with his own blood and kindred, for if
I live in my own house in Eifionydd I must either kill mine own kinsmen
or be killed by them'. In the Conwy valley he hoped he 'should find elbow
room in that vast country amongst the bondsmen'.

Meredydd ap Ifan established himself at Dolwyddelan castle but owned
also a nearby house called Penanmen. He kept constantly on his guard
against attack. His home was fortified and heavily guarded; he kept
different refuges in the locality, and in his travels he avoided familiar
routes and narrow places, lest he be 'layd for'. He went to church armed
with twenty tall archers, with a look-out posted to oversee his house and to
raise the alarm in case of attack.

According to Sir John Wynn, he assembled an army of a hundred and
forty bowmen from his followers, who were provided with bows, swords,
daggers, steel caps, armolets, horses and 'chasing slaves' who were all to
turn out on being summoned. He chose the tallest and most able men he
could find who were then placed in the empty tenements through the
district. Having consolidated his position, Meredydd ap Ifan moved
against the strongholds of the bandits of Ysbyty Ifan: 'Whereby he grew
so strong that he began to put back and to curb the sanctuary of thieves and
robbers which at times were wont to be above a hundred and fifty well
horsed and well appointed'.[37] Meredydd ap Ifan moved in the early
sixteenth century from Penanmen to Gwydir near Llanrwst where he
enlarged and fortified the house which was to become the family seat. His
descendant were to play a prominent part in the government and administration of north Wales and represented one of the dominant families of
native landowners to emerge in the fifteenth century.[38]

Sir John Wynn's picture of Meredydd ap Ifan as a doughty bandit fighter
is corroborated in a praise poem addressed to him by the bard Lewis Môn:

Llai tyrfay gwylliaid tra fych
Llai o rodiaw lle'rydych,
Llai treisir gywir a gwan
Llai draw nyth lladron weithian;
Llai pryder yn d'amser di,
Llai ar wŷr holl Eryri.[39]

Fewer bandits gather whilst you be,
Fewer loiter where you live,
Fewer oppress the upright and weak,
Fewer inhabit the robber's nest;
Fewer are terrorised in your time,
Fewer oppress the men of Eryri (Snowdon).

In the decades of the early sixteenth century the hospital reverted to its original role. In 1540 the Order of the Knights of St. John was dissolved and its properties, including Ysbyty Ifan, were sold off.

Sir John Wynn's account of the bandits of Ysbyty Ifan is well known and has attracted much commentary. Glyn Williams has offered an interesting 'reading' of this account. He argues that Meredydd ap Ifan was a proto-capitalist engaged in a ruthless policy of estate consolidation, which set him in conflict with other families in the Conwy valley, such as the family of Plas Iolyn. It also set him in conflict with the tenants and bondmen who had held their land by traditional tenure. The opposition to these moves to expropriate the tenantry provided the basis for the so-called 'bandits' who used the traditional sanctuary afforded by Ysbyty Ifan to wage their struggle against this new capitalist interloper.[40]

This interpretation shares a tendency amongst Welsh historians to regard the accounts of Tudor commentators as purely self-serving. It makes assumptions regarding the nature and activities of the 'bandits' of Ysbyty Ifan, as part of a struggle by the dispossessed against an emergent capitalist class, which cannot be substantiated, and which may be somewhat premature. Alternatively it might be argued that Ysbyty Ifan typifies the problem of disorder in remote, inaccessible border regions (*gorwledydd*) which was a common phenomenon in so many parts of Wales and its borders in the fifteenth and sixteenth century.

J. Gwynfor Jones, warning of the exaggerated nature of Sir John Wynn's account of disorder in fifteenth century Wales, writes of the outlaws of Ysbyty Ifan: 'These marauders were not brigands or *banditti* in the normal sense but modest gentry, pressurised by social and political conditions'.[41] In fact we know little about the social composition of the bandits of Ysbyty Ifan. But we might note that for Braudel it was precisely the depressed gentry who provided the base of much bandit activity in sixteenth century Europe.

The raiders of Brecon

One region with a notorious reputation for lawlessness was the lordship of Brecon, held by the powerful duke of Buckingham. The tenants of Brecon evidently regarded cattle stealing as a legitimate source of income. Early in the 1450s complaints were made to the duke concerning their 'great robberies and pillages'. At this time bands of robbers from Brecon were reported to have raided deep into the lordship of Ogmore, a distance of nearly 50 miles. There the auditor's clerk preferred to travel by sea rather than face Welsh bandits in the area.[42]

The following incident is recounted by Rice Merrick (Rhys Amheurig o'r Cotrel) writing around 1584/5. It recalls a battle between the men of Brecon and Glamorgan, which appears to relate to the period of the Wars of the Roses. The murder of one Jenkin Mathew at Cowbridge brought swift retaliation. This Jenkin Mathew was the son of Sir Dafydd Mathew of Llandaf, who died in 1461.

> Within this parish, upon the down called Mynydd Llangeinwyr, [Llangynidr] was fought a great skirmish between Glamorgan and Brecknockshire men. After that the Breconians had slain Jenkin Mathew in Cowbridge and rifled and spoiled Michaelmas fair then kept in Ewenny, being pursued to this place and there overtaken, and after a sharp encounter, a great part of the Breconians were then slain, among whom was one Dafydd Tew Dwrgi [Fat David the Otter], a valiant and mighty man, being their leader, was slain and the rest saved themselves by flight, and one Dafydd ap Jenkin ab Ieuan ap Hywel of Braichycymer, who by his mother side descended out of Brecon carried with his oxen the dead carcasses to Llangeinwyr's [Llangynidir's] churchyard, and there caused them to be buried in a great heap yet to be seen in the north part of the churchyard. Since this time the fair was removed to St. Bride's Down and was not kept since at Ewenny.[43]

This incident, not recorded in any surviving documents of the time, sheds an interesting light on the nature of raiding in this period.

This event may be the inspiration behind a poem of reconciliation between the men of Glamorgan and Brecon (*rwng sir Vorganwg a sir vrychainog*) by the bard Hywel Dafi (who flourished between 1450–80). The details of the conflict in the poem are sparse, but it refers to bitter enmity between the men of these two regions, who it is said, had previously been closely associated with one another. The bard describes the men of both regions as plunderers (*Y ddwywlad yn gribddeilwyr*).

This incident clearly belongs to the tradition of Welsh brigandage alongside Sir John Wynn's account of the outlaws of Ysbyty Ifan. In both cases our knowledge of these events derives from just one source. Without the accounts of Sir John Wynn and Rice Merrick we would not be able to make sense of the limited documentary accounts in the archives and the fleeting references in the poetry of the period.

These accounts, and other related evidence, suggest a number of conclusions. Firstly, it is clear that brigands were often surprisingly mobile and their activities were well organised. Secondly, raids were often carried out over considerable distances, and that brigands relied on extensive networks of contacts is assisting their enterprises in procuring, concealing and disposing of their gains. Thirdly, that such actions very often depended on, or was facilitated by, some form of official protection or collusion with law enforcement officers and court officials. Fourthly, that brigandage involved in some instances virtually a form of inter-communal warfare (Uwch Aeron against Is Aeron; Brecon against Ogmore; Mawddwy against Merioneth).

ASSESSING THE SCALE OF DISORDER

We know almost nothing about the history of the great bandit redoubts of Wales, other than their location and reputation. In other cases we have to make do with the most meagre accounts. In 1484 the stewards of Maelinedd and Buellt and the officers of the earldom of March were commissioned to arrest David ap Ieuan ap Rees and his brother Owen for robbing the king's mills and the king's subjects.[44] The same year a priest, Sir Lewis Deykin, charged with multiple murder and robbery, escaped from Radnor castle goal.[45] We cannot on the basis of this limited information arrive at any real assessment of the significance of these events.

The eminent Welsh historian Professor Glanmor Williams has argued that the view of Wales in the fifteenth century as a country racked by disorder is based largely on the testimony of Tudor commentators who had a vested interest in exaggerating the disorder of the past. The Wars of the Roses, he argues, had only a limited and localised impact. Moreover, the evidence of growing prosperity reflected in church building and repair, does not correspond with a picture of a country devastated by disorder. The century saw the golden age of Welsh poetry, based on generous patronage by the *uchelwyr*.

The poetry of the period taken as a whole, he argues, also supports this picture of relative order.

The life portrayed in the verse of some of the greatest poets of the age – Dafydd ap Edmwnd and Gutun Owain, for example – contain virtually no hint of conflict or struggle, but is one where enjoyment of the delights of love, nature and pleasurable living wholly dominates.

A large part of the work of even the most politically conscious poets, like Guto'r Glyn or Lewys Glyn Cothi, for much of the time suggests little stress or disorder but a great deal of leisured comfort, high spirits and merriment. People of all ranks in society moved freely around the countryside, seemingly without let or hindrance. Poets, pilgrims, friars, students, drovers, tradesmen, craftsmen, harvest workers, and others went about their lawful business unimpeded for most of the time.[46]

Violence, disorder and bloodshed, he argues, were present but were not predominant concerns; this was a society 'which enjoyed a relatively high standard of living and a reasonably secure existence'. The country, he asserts, was geared for peace not war.[47]

Professor Williams in undoubtedly right, this was not a society paralysed by disorder. But human societies demonstrate an extraordinary capacity to adjust to very high levels of disorder. Unquestionably, there is a connection between poverty and lawlessness, but this is by no means a simple relationship. The experience of other societies (e.g. Italy in the fifteenth and sixteenth centuries) demonstrate that serious and prolonged civil disorder can and frequently does coexist with the large scale accumulation of wealth, with extensive patronage of the arts and in displays of public piety reflected in church restoration and building.

There is ample evidence in the poetry of the period, in the legislation passed by parliament and in the account of later chroniclers of a major crisis of public order. The fact that bards such as Gutun Owain and his pupil Dafydd ap Edmwnd largely ignore the problem deserves some explanation. Both were *uchelwyr* who specialised in praise-poetry, addressed to the Welsh magnates of north-east Wales. This poetry is highly wrought and is concerned, more than the work of any other contemporary bards, with an idealised world of generous patrons and powerful magnates versed in the lore of chivalry.[48]

One of Gutun Owain's rare comments on lawlessness in Wales comes in a poem in which he offers a derogatory comparison between the God-ordained destiny of his patron, Siôn Edward of Chirk, and the ill fate of bandits.

Car di yn ieuangk air da
Cywirdeb a vac gwirda
Nid o enill un gwilliad
O ras Duw yr a ystad[49]

As a youth you loved honour
Virtue breeds gentlemen

Which is beyond a bandit's attainment
God's grace ordains our estate.

This conservative outlook legitimises the prevailing social order whilst ignoring its blemishes. Gutun Owain's reticence in dealing with the problem of lawlessness in Wales might be interpreted as prudence, or more bluntly as the indifference of a comfortably placed *uchelwr*. Gutun Owain and Guto'r Glyn sang many praise poems to members of the Trevor and Kyffin families, who were prominent landowners and ecclesiastics in north Wales. Nowhere in these poems in there a hint of the bloody enmity between them, their hiring of assassins and their contribution to lawless-ness, as recorded by Sir John Wynn of Gwydir and hinted at by the bard Lewis Môn.[50]

CONCLUSION

Welsh poetry of the fifteenth century confirms in many ways the English government's view concerning the disordered state of the country. It reveals the strong antipathy of at least some of the Welsh gentry to this lawlessness, and their efforts to stamp it out, and testifies to the important role of the *uchelwyr* as office holders. Leading *uchelwyr* families were celebrated by the bards as bandit-fighters – in north Wales the families of Penrhyn, Gwydir, Lleweni, Chirk and Corsygedol, in south Wales the families of Raglan, Hergest, Glyn Nedd, Penrhys, and Dinefwr. The bards frequently refer to the wildness (*gwylltineb*) of Wales. This was no hyper-bole, but reflected a real problem. This was not a society which revelled in anarchy but one that was deeply perplexed by the chaos and disorder which plagued it.

The testimony of the bards, however, has to be treated with great circumspection. Much of the lawlessness of the age, the organising of cross-border raids, the maintenance of armed retainers, the harbouring of murderers and other felons, was at the behest of marcher lords, their agents and powerful *uchelwyr*. Significantly, but not surprisingly, this does not find its way into the poetry of the period. This reflected the reality of government at local level in the later middle ages. Individuals who were praised by the bards as guardians of order, including Sir William Herbert of Raglan, Gruffydd ap Nicholas of Dinefwr and Watcyn Vaughan of Hergest, were seen by others as perpetrators of gross acts of lawlessness. The terminology employed is significant, presenting as it does a simple duality between the good *uchelwyr* and the evil brigand. There is no room here for subtlety or nuance. There is no requirement to inquire into the causes of such disorder, to question the legitimacy of those who dispense justice, or to inquire into the part which many of the *uchelwyr* themselves played in the perpetration of criminal acts.

7 Cross-Border Raiding

Border regions spawn their own outlaw traditions, but relate common elements: cattle lifting, the seizure and holding of men and goods for ransom and the abduction of women. Dramatic instances of banditry in border regions are provided by the Balkan haiducks, Greek klephts, Indian dacoits and Moroccan rezzous. Rob Roy in Scotland in the early eighteenth century was one of many highland cattle rustlers (herd widdiefows) who preyed on the Lowland farms, robbed cattle drovers, levied protection money (blackmail) and abducted women. The experience of the Anglo-Welsh border invites comparison with the Anglo-Scottish border and its reivers, and with the Anglo-Irish border in the Pale.[1] The Anglo-Welsh border was both a geographic divide, and a cultural divide. It was administratively a fragmented border, dominated by the marcher lordships which had been set up after the Norman conquest as a buffer to protect the English shires. Here the tradition of border raiding was centuries old.

The regulation of the Anglo-Welsh border was entrusted largely to the officers of the English border towns and shires and the constables of the castles. Major towns – Chester, Oswestry, Shrewsbury, Montgomery, Ludlow, Monmouth, Hereford, Worcester, Gloucester, Newport and Chepstow – served as bastions against possible rebellion. This contrasted with the limited defences on the Anglo-Scottish border provided by Carlisle, Alnwick and Berwick. Murage was granted to Shrewsbury in 1417–20, 1420, 1423, 1431 and 1446, and to Hereford in 1418 and 1419–22 on account of their proximity to Wales and the needs to resist the 'enemies of the king'.[2] Within the border towns relations between Welsh settlers and the English inhabitants was often fraught.

The Glyndŵr rebellion had a lasting influence. The dread prospect of a new Welsh revolt and its threat to the stability of the realm is vividly conveyed in *The Libelle of Englyshe Polycye*, written in the mid-1430s

Beware of Walys, Criste Jhesu mutt us kepe,
That it make not oure childeis childe to wepe,
Ne us also, if it goes his waye
By unwareness; seth that many a day
Men have be ferde of her rebellioun
By grete tokenss and ostentacioun.[3]

As well as containing the threat of rebellion or invasion from Wales a prime concern of the English state was the problem posed by Welsh raiders into the border English counties. In controlling such raids, the authorities in the English shires sought cooperation with the authorities in the marcher lordships. Within this system an important role was assigned to local Welsh magnates to regulate the territories under their control. In the Welsh Marches, as on the Anglo-Scottish border, raiding was seasonal, commencing after the ending of the harvest. Then men were freed people from their established occupations, whilst the longer nights provided a cover for raiders. At this time of year the ground was firm, whilst horses and cattle were in good condition and could be driven long distances. After February, as the days lengthened, the incidence of raiding decreased.[4]

THE LEGACY OF THE GLYNDŴR RISING 1410–1440

The Glyndŵr rising enflamed ethnic hatreds. This was particular so in the Marches, which had been subject to repeated rebel incursions. In the following decades, sporadic border raiding remained a major problem.[5] The most vexatious cases of lawlessness in the marches stemmed from a number of causes: 1) border raids by the Welsh, who were often said to have secret accomplices among the Welsh inhabitants of the marcher towns and border counties, 2) the arrest and detention of merchants going into Wales with their goods and merchandise, either by free agents or the officers of the marcher lordships, for ransom, 3) indiscriminate distressing between country and country, reflecting endemic feuds between marcher lords.[6] Disputes arose over a variety of issues; territory, grazing rights, cattle-lifting, abductions, and the repatriation of felons. Cattle stolen on the border may well have been used to further the Welsh cattle trade, a mainstay of the Welsh economy.

The disordered state of the Anglo-Welsh border stemmed not only from problems in Wales, but from the disorder in the English border counties themselves. The county palatine of Cheshire, with its own rights of sanctuary, was notorious as a haven for felons.[7] In the first decade of the century a major problem was posed by Shropshire where crime went largely unpunished.[8] Of just over a hundred Welshmen summoned before the courts of Shropshire, most from Wales and the marches, in the years after 1409 only 3 attended.[9] In July and October 1410 commissions were established in Shropshire to deal with border strife.[10]

Thomas, earl of Arundel, lord of Clun and Oswestry, who had been responsible for protecting the county against Glyndŵr's rebels, was engaged in a bitter feud with John Talbot, Lord Furnival, a powerful landowner. This resulted in a major break down of order. Arundel's men, John Wele, constable of Oswestry, and Richard Lacon, constable of Clun, were accused of carrying out depredations on the neighbouring lordships.[11] A superior eyre, under Chief Justice Hanford, was sent to investigate.[12] In 1414 Wele and Lacon were charged with seizure of provisions, contacts with the Welsh rebels, provisioning the rebels, and levying fines to allow rebels to live unmolested.[13] The disorder in the county appears to have eased with the recruitment of Arundel's men for the Agincourt campaign.[14]

The people of Gloucester, Worcester, Hereford, Bristol and Somerset in 1411 complained to the king of '*les graundes Mischiefs & Damages*' which they suffered at the hands of the rebels and thieves ('*les Rebelx & Larouns*') from the Welsh seigniories. The king's subjects were ambushed, taken into Wales and held to ransom. The crown forbade the officers of the marcher lordships from providing protection, 'safe conduct' or 'trewes' for such rebels and thieves.[15] In November 1412 the earl of Arundel, as sheriff of Hereford, and John Greyndour were commissioned 'to enquire about all congregations and other unlawful conventicles, sieges of castles of the king's subjects, forcible entries into these or other lordships or lands, confederacies, maintenances of quarrels, contempts, misprisons, injuries and other trespasses and evil deeds in the said county and the marches of Wales adjacent'.[16]

An Act passed in 1413 noted that many Welsh rebels continued daily to 'make quarrel', to avenge themselves, and bring actions to recoup their losses. The king's subjects were threatened, kidnapped and held to ransom, whilst others were vexed by 'indictments, accusements or impeachments'. Individuals accused of killing a rebel were sometimes tried by the Welsh practice of assache, whereby 300 men were required to swear to his innocence. The Act declared that former rebels and their adherents should cease such demands on pain of having to pay to the grieved parties treble their costs, and to be imprisoned for two years.[17]

In 1414 another Act asserted that 'many of the rebels of Wales' 'with force and arms in the manner of war' entered the counties of Salop, Hereford, Gloucester and neighbouring areas, hiding in woods and remote places. They seized the king's subjects, holding them in Wales for six months and more until large ransoms were paid 'in like manner as is used in time of war'. The Act empowered the JPs in the English counties 'to inquire, hear and determine all manner of such treasons and felonies'. They were to require that the offenders appear before them, on pain of outlawry. The officers of the lordships, in which the offenders resided, were to be informed of the outlawry and were required to 'do execution upon them' as the law demanded, without invoking the Welsh practice of *arddel*, whereby offenders could buy their freedom through the payment of a fine.[18]

In February 1414 John Bodenham, the sheriff of Hereford, and others were commissioned to inquire into the petition of John Baskerville, knight. On 23 December 1413 Richard de la Beere, esquire, with a force of a hundred men, English and Welsh, invaded Overwelshton (now Upper Welson), in the lordship of Eardisley, broke into Baskerville's house, imprisoned two of his servants and drove off over 80 head of cattle into Wales.[19] In June 1415 the earl of Warwick and others were empowered 'to conserve and govern the marches of Wales adjoining the counties of Hereford and Gloucester against hostilities and invasions of the rebels there'.[20]

Wales also provided a haven for English felons.[21] In 1416 Robert Whittington and his retinue were waylaid in the village of Mordiford in Herefordshire by about thirty men 'armed and arrayed in manner of war', the servants of Richard Oldcastle, a long-standing rival of Whittington. The captives were taken to a mountain named 'Dynmorehill', robbed, and threatened with being carried into Wales as prisoners, unless ransom was paid and sureties given for immunity from retaliation.[22]

The task of curbing lawlessness originating in the March was given to the sheriffs, escheators and officers of the border English counties. In October 1422, one of the first acts of Henry VI's government, commissioned John Talbot, lord Ferrers and others, to ensure that the sheriffs of Salop, Herefordshire, Worcestershire and Gloucestershire enforced the peace in these counties and the adjoining marches.[23]

The situation on the border was complicated by the feuds between marcher lords and the sanctuary afforded by the lordships to fleeing criminals. John Talbot of Goodrich Castle, later earl of Shrewsbury, in 1424, prior to going on the king's service in France, resolved to compensate himself for arrears of salary as constable of Montgomery castle by pillaging the wealthy farmers of Herefordshire. Talbot's retainers in this enterprise included many Welshmen. Men were held to ransom at Goodrich castle as if in wartime. A mass rising in Herefordshire was feared as a result of his actions. On a petition from the county, the king's council appointed a special commission to investigate the affair.[24]

One notable aspect of border relations in this period was the employment of Welshmen in the retinues of English magnates.[25] In November 1422 William Fitzwarin and Sir Richard Laken were recruiting Welshmen for an attack on Whittington castle in Shropshire.[26] The hiring of assassins was another facet of border relations. In one case Alice Mutton, a well to do widow of Shrewsbury hired a number of neer-do-wells from Powys to do her bidding by murdering some of her neighbours.[27]

The disorder even affected transport on the river Severn. Already in November 1409 the crown commissioned John Greyndre and others to issue proclamations in the Forest of Dean and Gloucestershire prohibiting any attempts to prevent the transportation of corn and other victuals by river to Bristol.[28] In 1427 the English border counties petitioned the king in Parliament, complaining of the depredations of Welsh raiders. In 1429 the burgesses of Tewkesbury petitioned parliament concerning attacks on traders on the Severn by armed robbers from the Forest of Dean, Bledisloe and Westbury in Gloucestershire.[29] In 1430–1 the English inhabitants neighbouring the Severn complained to the king of attacks by Welsh raiders on river traffic, the destruction of goods, the killing and black-mailing of merchants and traders.[30] The Forest of Dean retained long after a reputation for lawlessness and as a refuge for felons.[31]

Attacks by Welsh raiders on the English border counties were often highly organised. It was partly inspired by racial animosities, and for some, as illustrated by the work of Llewelyn ab y Moel, it was a continuation, by other means, of the Glyndŵr rebellion.

THE FRONTIER IN TURMOIL 1440–1470

In the 1440s border raiding reached heights unprecedented since the Glyndŵr rebellion. In 1441/2 an Act was passed which criticised the failure of the Act of 1401 to eradicate the problem of cross-border raiding. It ruled that felons from Wales and the Marches who seized goods and chattels, as well as their abettors, were to be judged guilty of 'high treason', and to be sentenced as 'traitors' i.e. to be executed. The property of such felons, once reparations to the offended parties had been made, was to fall to the marcher lord. In 1448/9 the Act was confirmed for another six years.[32]

This Act initiated a harsher policy with regard to Welsh border raiders. In some cases, however, clemency was shown. In August 1440 Bedoe Wyth of Elfael, on account of his services in France, was pardoned for thefts in Herefordshire and freed of any outlawry.[33] In July 1443 pardons were granted to Rhys ap Griffith ap Richard and twelve compatriots from Cantrefselyf, most of who were listed as yeomen, for stealing twenty oxen in a raid on Herefordshire.[34] In April 1444 David ap Griffith Lloyd, gentleman of Ewyas, was pardoned for cattle lifting raids in Herefordshire. He had also taken 200 armed men to Dorstone in the Golden Vale to threaten the local magnate Kynard de la Bere.[35]

In 1444/5 an Act of parliament censured the sheriff of Herefordshire for allowing Welsh outlaws, who had been convicted of felony and treason, to enter the county unhindered, either out of ignorance or 'for favour or amity' or 'doubt of hurt'. Official negligence emboldened outlaws to enter the county to 'slay, burn, rob and to do other offences in the said county, to the perpetual destruction and impoverishment of the commons of the said county'.[36] The Act directed the sheriff to arrest and prosecute such outlaws, and to raise a hue and cry against those who resisted arrest. The Justices of the Peace were to enforce the Act and investigate cases of official negligence.

A further Act of 1449 sought to curb offences in Wales and the Duchy of Lancaster lordships in Wales, whereby various felons seized persons, goods and chattels 'under the colour of distress', and 'feign some actions and quarrels to grieve and destroy the faithful people of the said counties, duchy and seigniories against law, reason and conscience'. Such actions provoked strong resistance – 'great assemblies of people, riots, maims, and murders', with the affect that the people of the said parts 'daily abound and increase in evil government'.[37] Such felonies were to be treated as capital offences. The weakening of central authority and the descent into civil war compounded the problem of border strife.

The Southern March

The disorder was marked in the southern march adjoining Gloucestershire and Herefordshire. In 1433 the corruption and partisanship of the sheriffs in Herefordshire drew the crown's censure.[38] In 1437 there were riots in Tewkesbury involving Welsh settlers.[39] Hereford in the 1440s was riven by conflict between the governing merchant oligarchy and the city's trades-men and craftsmen. The conflict was focused around the elections of the mayor. The city's tradesmen and craftsmen, led by John Weobley, sought to impose their candidate. The rival factions were dubbed 'English' and 'Welsh'. Weobley's faction called on the 'Welsh' in the city to rise in rebellion against the 'English' mayor and his party. The 'Welsh ' faction included many with English names, and settlers from the west of the county with Welsh connections as well as those of Welsh descent.[40]

In the 1450s Sir Walter Devereux, with his ally and son-in-law William Herbert of Raglan, dominated Herefordshire and south east Wales. In 1452 Devereux attempted to consolidate his power in the region on behalf of the Yorkist cause. He extended his patronage by giving livery to thirty-one tradesmen and craftsmen of John Weobley's faction in Hereford. As a result of the ensuing disturbances measures were instituted against William Herbert, but in October 1452 he was pardoned for all offences, outlawries and forfeitures imposed on him.[41]

In March 1456 William Herbert with twenty-one followers from the Welsh gentry seized Hereford for two days. The action was prompted by the murder of Walter Vaughan, one of Herbert's kinsmen. Herbert forced the justice to declare one John Glover and other tradesmen guilty of the murder and to carry out their summary execution.[42] In June 1457 William Herbert and his followers, having been outlawed for this high-handed action, were granted a general pardon.[43] Herbert was knighted in 1461 and became the main prop of Yorkist rule in Wales and the border.

The ambiguous position of Welsh magnates responsible for policing the border is illustrated also by the case of Watcyn Vaughan of Hergest (Herast). Lewis Glyn Cothi urged him with his gauntlet and spear to fell the deceitful (*hocedion*), and with his sword to be a guardian of the innocent and the common people as far as Warwick castle. He called on him to extirpate the robbers, and to restore to the Welsh their ancient rights and laws.

Master Watcyn myn wrth y menyg, a'r ffon;
Lluddiaw hocedion val lladd coedwig.
A'th gledd bydd geidwad yn voneddig...
Ar gwmmin werin hyd gaer Warwig gron,
Ac ar y gwirion o'th gaer geryg...
Myn ddiva'r lladron, vy mhendevig.
Ordeinia i eraill bardwn orig;
Ennyn y gyfraith unig i Gymru.[44]

Watcyn Vaughan's renown as a bandit fighter and guardian of the border was also recounted by Tudur Penllyn and Owain Llywelyn ab y Moel.[45] However, in Herefordshire he entered into local folklore as Black Vaughan, a tyrant whose ghost haunted the neighbourhood after his death at the Battle of Banbury in 1469. His wife, known as Gethen the Terrible, allegedly killed her brother's murderer, by entering an archery contest disguised as a man, and shooting her arrow into her victim's heart. The couple's effigy lies in the Vaughan chapel in Kington church.[46]

Sir Thomas Vaughan of Tretower, one of the most powerful magnates in the southern march, was praised by Lewis Glyn Cothi as a guardian of law and order.

Ni bydd Sir Thomas dra dygasog
Onid i'r lleidr, neu i dra llidiog;
Y dewr cywir ceidw rhag geuog;
A'r anghywir was a yr yn nghrog.[47]

Sir Thomas will not be so ruthless
Except to the robber and those inflamed;
The brave and good he protects from the guilty;
And the lawless lad he takes to be hung.

Other notables are praised in similar vein. The bard effusively praises
Jenkin Winston of Llangarron, Herefordshire. Although of English birth,
he loved the Welsh language and was a patron of bards and minstrels.
Moreover, he was both lock and key upon bandits (*A chlo ac allwydd
uwchlaw gwylliaid*).[48] He described Siôn ab Hywel of Ewyas as the strong-
man of the March and as naked steel through the Marchland (*Dur noeth
drwy'r marsdir, a'i nerth*). He was the protector of Hay (*I'r Gelli dor ac
allwydd*), and a bridle on the haughty of the Golden Vale (*A frwyn i weilch
Dyffryn Aur*).[49] Of Dafydd ap Rhys of Pen Craig (Radnorshire) he noted
that the king Edward had reason to be grateful for him for putting, by force
of arms, this lawless region in order:

Ymddiried y mae Edwart
I ŵr a'i ddwrn ar ei ddart;
O gadw'r wlad, anwastad oedd[50]

Lewis Glyn Cothi expressed particular venom towards the men of the
March. Many of his patrons on the border shared his views. Thomas ap
Rhys of Maelinedd, the bard states, hated the descendants of Rowenna, the
men of the March and the language of the manor

Ni charai enwi un ach i Ronwen,
Na gwŷr y Mars na geiriau men.[51]

Rhys Awbrey and William ab Morgan, the bard declares, would like
lions quickly destroy the fortified houses of the March.

Hwy a dorant ar deirawr
Tai'r Mars gyda'r tyrau mawr.[52]

The records of the king's bench and of the commissions of oyer and
terminer for Herefordshire in 1452 and 1457 show that cattle-rustling and
horse stealing by Welsh raiders was a major problem. The commission in
1457 encountered great difficulty in indicting Welsh offenders. Only
sixteen out of 123 Welshmen indicted (13 per cent) appeared in court in
contrast to 149 out of 274 Englishmen who were charged (54 per cent). In

spite of the Acts of Parliament passed in the previous decade Welsh felons were still able to find shelter in the marcher lordships.[53]

The southern march extended into south Wales as far as the crown controlled county of Carmarthenshire. The town of Carmarthen constituted a strong point for controlling this frontier region. Lewis Glyn Cothi says of Henry ab Thomas of Llanymddyfri that he will protect Carmarthen from the men of the March (*'Na gwyr y Mars i Gaer mwy*).[54]

The hiring of Welsh mercenaries by English magnates persisted for a long time. In Gloucestershire the bitter Berkeley-Talbot feud resulted in the last private battle on English soil, at Nibley Green in 1470. The Berkeley family employed a Welsh squire, Rice Tewe (Rhys Tew or Rhys the Fat), who with twenty armed retainers attacked the strongholds of the rival Talbot family. Thomas Talbot, in challenging William, Lord Berkeley, to single combat, hotly rebutted the latter's charge that he had planned to bring in the detested and fearsome Welshmen to 'destroy and hunt my own nation and country'. Against this charge of treachery he replied 'I let thee wit I was never so disposed nor never will be'.[55]

The Central March

The central march adjoined Shropshire and included the earl of Arundel's lordships of Clun, Oswestry and Whittington, as well as the lordships of Ceri and Cedewain, and the outlaw redoubts of Cefn Digoll, Y Graig Llwyd and Gwern y Gof.

One of the Welsh magnates entrusted with the task of policing the border was Sir Gruffydd Vaughan of Broniarth and Treflydan near Welshpool. He had supported Glyndŵr but thereafter submitted to the English crown. In 1417 he assisted in apprehending Sir John Oldcastle. In the following years he served with the English army in France. He became a favourite of the bards as a doughty champion of Welsh interests on the border.[56] In August 1443, he slew Sir Christopher Talbot, third son of the earl of Shrewsbury, and the champion tilter of England, in an affray at Caus castle. As a result he was outlawed, together with sixteen compatriots from the Welshpool area, and a reward of 500 marks was offered for his capture. Their lands were seized by the crown and granted to Lord Dudley, keeper of Shrawardyn castle in Shropshire.[57]

Sir Gruffydd Vaughan remained an outlaw for four years. In November 1445 a pardon was granted to one Morris ap Evan Gittin of Oswestry. He was accused of having protected Sir Gruffydd Vaughan and of being an accessory of David Lloyd, who was charged with cattle lifting in

Shropshire.[58] In July 1447 Sir Henry Grey, earl of Tancarville, lured Sir Gruffydd Vaughan to Powys castle under the cover of a safe conduct (*secwndid*), where he was immediately seized and beheaded, and the bounty on his head claimed.

The Welsh bards were incensed by this act of English treachery, with elegies being composed by Lewis Glyn Cothi and Dafydd Llwyd. The latter recounted how he had searched for his friend in the outlaw redoubts of mid-Wales, amongst the forests and streams of Cedewain, in the Dugoed forest of Mawddwy, at Cefn Digoll, and how the 'stags' (outlaws) still awaited his return in the Drum Ddu.[59] In December 1448 a general pardon was granted to Reynold and David Lloyd, relatives of Sir Gruffydd Vaughan.[60]

The problem of disorder was exacerbated by the protection which powerful Welsh magnates and marcher lords offered to border raiders. In 1453–4 Roger Corbet, Walter Honton, Ralph Lee and other prominent men of Shropshire complained against Philip ap Howel of Knocklas, in the lordship of Maelienydd, for various losses and damages. They were unable to secure justice since Philip ap Howel was protected by Gruffydd ap Nicholas of Dinefwr. In the summer of 1454 York visited the central march to suppress the disorder. (p. 65 above) In June of that year John, earl of Worcester, was commissioned to make inquisitions in Shropshire, into treasons, insurrections, murders and felonies in the county and in the March of Wales.[61] In 1454 an indictment was made before the justices in Shrewsbury accusing Philip ap Howel and Gruffydd ap Nicholas of felony.[62]

Shrawardyn and Caus castles were two of the key strong points in the central March. In February 1444 on appointing Lord Dudley as keeper of Shrawardyn castle the crown noted 'which is no small burden owing to diverse disturbances in the march of Wales'.[63] The neighbouring country-side around Caus was so badly affected by disorder that in 1454 John Woderton, the receiver, hired a Welsh mercenary 'for keeping my lord's tenants of the said lordship from robbery and pillage'.[64] The situation was made worse by a protracted boundary dispute with the duke of York, whose followers had seized some of Buckingham's tenants and imprisoned them in Montgomery castle.

Lewis Glyn Cothi in a poem to Griffith ab Ieuan ab Madog of Gwenwys, stewart of Caus castle (which the bard describes as being crowded with refugees) seeks to inspire him to wreak vengeance on traitors and other enemies of his country.[65] The bard describes Griffith ab Howell from Churchstoke (Ystog), another stewart of Caus castle, arresting the lawless (*Arestiaw rhai'n yr Ystog*). It was he who made king Edward's writ run in this disorderly region.

A phen, ac arglwydd, a phont,
Y wlad hon a'i Lutenont;
A dwrn, a chleddau, a dart
A throed i Briv-lythyr Edwart.[66]

But the bard also recalls the past humiliations inflicted upon the Welsh by the English. He calls on his patron, 'the great oak' of the March (*gaterwen i dir y Mars draw*), to struggle to free the Welsh 'nation' in Jesus' name from their oppression:

I ryddhau, drwy'r arwydd hwn,
Y dan Iesu dy nasiwn.[67]

One of the targets for cross-border raids, mentioned by Llywelyn ab y Moel, was Ruyton-XI Towns in the earl of Arundel's lordship of Whittington to the north-west of Shrewsbury. The bard Hywel Cilan described Gruffydd Penrhyn ap Llywelyn from Deuddwr, a large land-owner in the Oswestry area, as a giant in the field against outlaws, a mighty fort above the borderland (*Cawr i faes rhag herwyr fydd/Caer i wlad rhag gorwledydd*).[68] His patron, he asserts, was admired by the Welsh and English alike for his efforts in maintaining order, whilst the tenants of Ruyton-XI Towns looked to him as a guardian.

Richard Gough in his *History of Myddle*, written around 1700, describing the marcher lordship of Myddle, neighbouring Ruyton-XI Towns, recounts the measures which had to be taken in the English border region against Welsh raiders:

We have by tradition that there was much enmity between the Britons and Saxons, that the Welshmen accounted all for a lawful prize which they stole from the English. And we have a tradition, that the inhabitants of these neighbouring towns, had in every town, a piece of ground adjoining to their houses, which was moated about with a large ditch, and fenced with a strong ditch fence and pale, therein they kept their cattle every night, with persons to watch them; and that there was a light-horse-man maintained in every town with a good horse, sword and spear, who was always ready, upon the least notice to ride straight to the Platt Bridge, there to meet his companions; and if they found any Welshman on this side the Platt Bridge, and the river of Perry, if they could apprehend him he was sure to be put to death: but if the Welshmen had got over the Bridge with stolen cattle, (then we have an ancient saying that) they would cry 'Ptroove mine own', for the horsemen durst not follow any further; if they were taken beyond the bridge they were straight way hanged.[69]

[Platt Bridge spanned the river Perry half a mile east of Ruyton-XI Towns and four miles west of Myddle]

According to William Gerard the same practice of guarding cattle against Welsh raiders persisted in the English border counties until the 1530s.

The Northern March

The northern march comprised of the county of Flint, and the lordships of Chirk and Oswestry. These two lordships were amongst the most disordered in the March, and were a constant irritant as the base of raiders into Cheshire and Shropshire. Oswestry was regarded by the bards as 'theirs', a substatial, predominatly Welsh town, to which Guto'r Glyn sang an ode of praise. Sieffrai Cyffin, constable of Oswestry under the earl of Arundel, according to the bard, hated oppression, robbery and disorder (*Nid caru nerthu a wnaeth, Na lleidr nac anllywodraeth*).[70]

In this region a key role in policing the border during the Wars of the Roses was shouldered by Siôn Edward of Chirk. Gutun Owain and Guto'r Glyn celebrated his role as both guardian of order, and defender of Welsh interests against the English. He is a rampart protecting his lands against bandits (*Allt serth i wylliaid yw Siôn*); he was related to Glyndŵr (*gwaed Owain Glyn*), but had served under Richard III in England.[71]

For the Yorkist bards there was no contradiction between their allegiance to Edward IV as king, and their allegiance to local Welsh magnates whom they saw as bastions against the power of the English lords of the Marches or the English garrisons and burgess towns in Wales. Guto'r Glyn in his ode on the death of Robert Trefor, describes him as a loyal servant of the king, but also as a tower above the Marches (*Tŵr i'r Mars*) and a check on Denbigh, (*Wrth Ddinbech garw a thanbaid*) whose English garrison and burgesses were an object of particular venom for the Welsh bards. The bard feared the consequences which his death would have for this border region and for the Welsh (*Gwae'r Waun Isaf, gwae'r nasiwn*).[72] Siôn Hanmer is described as a soldier (*ŵr rhyfel*), the 'captain of the March' (*Capten y Mars*), the dragon of Whitchurch and a veritable Arthur restraining the men of Chester.[73]

In north-east Wales relations between the Welsh and the English burgesses of Chester and Flint remained tense.[74] This animosity features in the poems of Lewis Glyn Cothi and the traditions surrounding Rheinallt ap Gruffydd. (pp. 86–7 above) In lighter vein Tudur Penllyn recounts the hostile reception he encountered in a tavern in Flint, where the boorish English clientele preferred the vile bagpipes to his own highly skilled verse. In another poem he relates how his amorous advances were repelled by an Englishwoman, who feared that she would be branded a whore by associating with a Welshman.[75] Dafydd Llwyd in a vitriolic attack on the English boroughs in north Wales and the border implied that if the English burgesses were ejected their property and womenfolk could be seized by the Welsh.[76]

CONCLUSION

The onus of policing the frontier was placed on the marcher lords, the sheriffs in the English border shires, and the Welsh magnates, backed up in periods of emergency by the crown. The solution, however, was flawed and the lordships themselves were a contributory factor in the endemic lawlessness, which vexed the area. Similarly feuds amongst English magnates on the border, who hired into their services Welsh mercenaries and assassins, contruibuted to the disorder. Ethnic animosities, heightened by the Glyndŵr rising, exacerbated the situation. The basis of trust was fragile.

The English Victorian historian Hallam described the Anglo-Welsh border in the fifteenth century as constantly in a state of war, which he attributed to the legal reprisals enacted against the Welsh by Henry IV.[77] The periods of most intense disorder occurred in specific phases. The last three decades of the fourteenth century saw a growth of lawlessness. The Glyndŵr rising turned the border area into a war zone with widespread destruction. The disorders thereafter assumed a more sporadic form, which in the late 1420s required crown intervention. The 1440s saw new heights of disturbance, whilst the Wars of the Roses turned the border area into a major scene of conflict. In the 1470s disturbances in the Marches again required the crown's attention.

8 Yorkist Ascendancy and Lancastrian Triumph 1471–1485

In 1471 Edward IV regained the throne. The second period of his rule proved more stable as the crisis of civil war eased. This new found stability allowed the crown more freedom to address the problems of disorder in the realm. In Wales and the Marches it saw a significant change of policy, through the creation of the Council of Wales and the Marches. The Lancastrian challenge, however, remained alive, focused on Henry Tudor in exile in Brittany. With the death of Edward IV and the accession of Richard III the civil war between York and Lancaster again flared into life. This dynastic struggle, at the heart of which lay the question of legitimate royal authority, held wide implications for the maintenance of order within the realm and its periphery.

The establishment of the Council in the Marches

With the ebbing of the civil war, more effective administration of justice became possible.[1] Even Lancastrian bards, such as Lewis Glyn Cothi, acknowledged the ascendancy of the Yorkists and wrote praise poems to Edward IV, stressing his Welsh connections. Edward IV intended to make his brother, Richard of Gloucester, his strong man in Wales. From 1471 onwards, however, Gloucester was preoccupied with disorder in the north of England. The role of strong man in Wales was temporarily placed on the shoulders of William Herbert, second earl of Pembroke. He proved ineffectual in this work and a new solution was sought. The solution took the form of a greatly strengthened council of the Prince of Wales.

The crown's main concern remained the Anglo-Welsh border, the Welsh Marches. The marcher lordships, established after the Norman conquest, remained as separate entities, although the crown itself was now the main marcher lord. The border region during the Glyndŵr rebellion and during the Wars of the Roses had proved vulnerable to invasion from Wales. It was a region in which ethic relations could easily become inflamed. It remained a region plagued by seasonal incursions by Welsh raiders, who were protected by the marcher lords and by powerful Welsh magnates.

In November 1472 the infant Edward Prince of Wales, was invested with his properties in Wales, Chester and Flint.[2] A Prince's Council was established, headed by John Alcock, bishop of Worcester, and Lord Rivers, the head of the Woodville family. It was given responsibility to manage the prince's estates, and to deal with civil commotions. The Prince took up residence in Ludlow, the former capital of the Mortimer lordship, which became the administrative centre of royal authority within the March. The Council acquired its own Court with the responsibility for enforcing justice. The Council held its sessions in the main English towns adjoining the Marches – Hereford (1473), Chester (1474), Monmouth (1474), Coventry (1474), Wigmore (1478), Haverfordwest (1478), and Worcester (1481).

Sir Thomas More in his *The History of King Richard III* writes of the establishment of the Council of the Marches:

> Which country [Wales] being far off from the law and recourse to justice, was begon to be far out of good will & waxen wild, robbers and rivers [reivers] walking at liberty uncorrected. And for this encheason [reason] the prince was in the life of his father sent thither, to that end that the authority of his presence, should refrain evil disposed parsons from the boldness of their former outrages.[3]

In 1472/3 Lord Rochester, on behalf of the Commons, presented a petition to the crown which complained of the breakdown in the administration of justice in the kingdom, drawing specific attention to the situation on the Welsh border, calling on the king

> To consider the intolerable extortions, oppressions and wrongs, that to your subjects daily been put, and in especial in the parts of this your land adjoining Wales, which by the outrageous demeaning of Welshmen, favoured under such persons as have the keeping of castles and other places of strength there as it is supposed, been wasted and likely utterly to be destroyed.[4]

The king was requested to take resolute measures:

> in the said parts towards Wales, that such direction might be taken by the advice of the Lords Marchers, that your true subjects there inhabitauntes may in like wise live out of the fear and danger of the said Welshmen.[5]

In the spring of 1473 the Council of the Prince of Wales was directed to pacify the Marches. In Herefordshire and Salop complaints were made of serious crimes committed by the men of those counties and men from the Marches. There was no remedy to be had without the king's own presence there. The Queen and the Prince of Wales, together with 'many great Lords Spiritual, and Temporal' leading judges, commissioners and other notables were sent to Hereford to investigate. The commissioners summoned an inquest of eighteen knights and squires of the county to examine the problem. Those summoned attended reluctantly and testified that they dare not give evidence against the wrongdoers, 'considering the great number of the said misdoers, and the great bearers-up of the same'.[6]

The commission investigated various crimes. The most notable was the case of twenty three felons, mostly Welshmen, who were charged with 'murder, ravishments, robberies, extortions' and other crimes. Those charged included three gentlemen (Miles ap Henry, Robert Apye, Robert ap Glun ap Thomas), eight yeomen, eight husbandmen, one butcher, two labourers, and one whose occupation was unspecified. They had been indicted at Hereford, but in spite of strict instructions to the contrary, had been acquitted. The crown quashed the acquittals and ordered a retrial.[7]

In 1473 the Prince of Wales conferred with the marcher lords at Shrewsbury and concluded an agreement with them. These indentures codified current customary and statutory methods of upholding order in the marches and border shires. They stressed the need for the appointment of resident and conscientious officers, and for the proper regulation of relations between the lordships. The king, as earl of March not as sovereign, sealed this agreement, although the king's council was to be the final court of appeal.[8]

The prince's Council strove to bring the area to order. In 1475 Prince Edward instructed the Shrewsbury bailiffs to suppress border raiders:

> Whereas there have been perpetrated great and heinous complaints of robberies, murders, manslaughters, ravishing of women, burning of houses by the inhabitants of the Marches and now of late by the errant thieves and rebellious of Oswestry hundred and Chirkland; for the redress of the same I am commanded to assemble the people to punish the misdoers, and I entrust Thomas, marquis of Dorset, and Richard Grey, knight, to do the same. Therefore all men in your bailiwick between 60 and 16 should array themselves as soon as possible.[9]

In 1478 the Council approved regulations for the better government of Shrewsbury, described as the 'greatest strength and defence that His (the King's) subjects of that shire have against the wildness of Wales and the Marches'.[10]

The Prince's Council was strengthened and accorded further powers. In January 1476 the prince was made justiciary of Wales and granted a general commission of oyer and terminer to hear cases in Shropshire, Herefordshire, Gloucestershire, Worcestershire, the Marches of Wales and the Principality itself, with the power to array archers and men at arms, and to investigate the escape of criminals.[11] In December 1477 the prince's Council took over the administration of the crown's lordships including those of the Duchy of Lancaster.[12]

The king summoned the Council to meet at Ludlow on 24 March 1476 to discuss with the marcher lords the best means to restore order, and to curb the high incidence of murders, robberies, spoilings and oppressions in Wales and the Marches, intimating that he himself would be there after Easter.[13] In March the Prince, or his nominee, was appointed to inquire into the liberties, privileges and franchises of the counties of Salop, Hereford and Gloucester and of the marcher lordships and to deal with the flight of criminals between the shires and the lordships.[14] In December the prince was empowered to appoint judicial commissioners in Wales, the marcher lordships and the four border shires.

Alongside the creation of the prince's Council went a major new innovation, which was intended to compel the marcher lords to ensure effective administration of justice. In 1476 an indenture was concluded between the crown and the lordship of Newport. The inhabitants of the lordship were obliged to give assurances of their future law-abiding conduct on pain of forfeiture of considerable sums if they defaulted. This process of indenture appears to have been applied in other lordships.[15]

The creation of the prince's Council bypassed the crown's erstwhile mainstay in Wales, William Herbert. In February 1474 a commission was given to Lord Rivers, Lord Ferrers and others to 'array the king's lieges' in Herefordshire, Gloucestershire and Shropshire. They were to apprehend William Herbert, and his two bastard sons, and the two sons of Roger Vaughan of Tretower, who had refused to attend the king's council to answer charges of offences committed by them in Wales and the Marches. Instead they had withdrawn to Wales, allegedly intent on stirring up insurrection. The commission was to arrest them and their abettors, and render what assistance was needed to the Prince's Council.[16] However, the order proved to be a dead letter. They were still at large in 1478 when they seized Pembroke castle.[17]

In 1479, however, the king finally required William Herbert to exchange the earldom of Pembroke for that of Huntingdon. The earldom of Pembroke was bestowed on the Prince of Wales, 'for the reformation of the wele public, restful governance and ministration of justice in the said parts of South Wales'. The coup de grace came in 1479 when William Herbert was dismissed as justice and chamberlain of south Wales.[18]

After 1478 the prince's Council in Wales disappears from view, and with the death of Edward IV in 1483 may have ceased to exist.[19]

The reign of Richard III

Edward IV's death created a new political uncertainty, heightened by the still simmering conflict between Yorkists and Lancastrians. The situation was exacerbated by the poor harvests of 1481 and 1482. In 1483 Richard, duke of York, deposed the young Edward V and seized the throne. As Richard III he was supported by powerful magnates, pre-eminent amongst who was Henry Stafford, the second duke of Buckingham. Buckingham, second only to the king, was the most powerful of the marcher lords. He was made the king's plenipotentiary in Wales, and entrusted with pro-consular powers similar to those enjoyed earlier by Sir William Herbert. In May 1483 he was appointed chief justice and chamberlain in north and south Wales, constable of the main castles and steward and receiver general of all the crown lands.[20]

In July 1483 the king appointed Morgan Kidwelly, a Dorset man of Welsh ancestry, as his Attorney General in England and Wales.[21] Within Wales he inherited the administration of Edward IV. He confirmed in office the constables of Conwy, Beaumaris and Harlech.[22] Nicholas Spicer was appointed as the king's auditor in north and south Wales with the task of tightening up control over the collection of revenues from the crown's properties.[23]

Richard III resolved to put Wales in order. An injuction issued at this time noted that no other region beside the principality of Wales, because of its remote position, its distinctive language and culture, required 'separate and immediate rule under us'[24] He appointed his seven-year-old son Edward as Prince of Wales and Earl of Chester in September 1483. Edward's death in April 1484, however, ruled out the option of recreating the Prince's Council, as it had operated under Edward IV.[25]

The dangers of delegating too much power to one magnate had been illustrated in the 1470s with Sir Walter Herbert. In 1483 Buckingham raised an army in Wales with the aim of deposing Richard III and replacing him with the exiled Henry Tudor in Brittany. In October 1483 a commission was issued to Viscount Lovell to resist Buckingham who was proclaimed a rebel and the following month a commission of array was issued to William Herbert, earl of Huntington, and James Tyrrel to the same end.[26]

Buckingham lacked support amongst local families. As soon as he left Brecon the Vaughans of Tretower sacked the castle. According to Polydore

Vergil, Buckingham's army consisted mainly of Welshmen 'whom he, as a sore and hard dealing man, had brought to the field against their wills, and without any lust to fight for him'.[27] The project ended ignominiously, Buckingham was captured and executed in November 1483.

William Herbert, Sir James Tyrrel and others were commissioned to enter all the castles, lands and tenements in Wales and the marches belonging to Buckingham and other traitors. Herbert was appointed chief justice of south Wales, and annuities were granted to a number of prominent Welshmen in south Wales. In north Wales William Griffiths was made chamberlain. Tyrrel, reputedly the man who organised the murder of the princes in the Tower, was appointed to key positions in Wales, as a receiver of revenues for the crown.[28]

Securing these revenues, however, proved more difficult. Richard III in 1484 was required to pardon all arrears due from the tenants of the counties of Caernarfon, Anglesey and Merioneth.[29] The king's officers in Carmarthen, Kidwelly, and Carnewalltan were ordered to ensure that the revenues of the church of Our Lady in Leicester were paid, which had been withheld or misappropriated 'by might and power of evilly disposed persons having rule in those parts and also by other whom they have favoured maintained and supported'.[30]

The Lancastrian project to recapture the throne acquired a new momentum with the maturing of Henry Tudor's plans for the invasion of the kingdom. In June 1485 Richard III issued a vituperative proclamation denouncing 'one Henry Tudor, son of Edmund Tudor, son of Owain Tudor, which of his ambitiousness and insatiable covetousness encroacheth and usurpeth upon him the name and title of royal estate of this Realm of England, where unto he hath no manner interest, right, title or colour, as every man well knoweth'. The rebels on landing, the king warned, intended 'to do the most cruel murders, slaughters and robberies and dissertions that ever was seen in any Christian realm'.[31]

In his address to his confederates in Wales Henry Tudor declared his right to the throne and his intention to remove the usurper; to restore 'the ancient estate, and honour, and property and prosperity ' of England, and of 'this our said principality of Wales and the people of the same to their erst liberties, delivering them of such miserable servitude as they have long piteously stood in'.[32]

Insurgent and outlaw: Henry Tudor

The search for a new 'son of prophecy' (*y mab darogan*), a new 'Owain', after the failure of the Glyndŵr rebellion took various forms. During the

Wars of the Roses some bards attached the title to William Herbert, and even Edward IV. The Lancastrian cause was associated with Owen Tudor, who was executed following the battle of Mortimer's Cross in 1461. Ieuan Gethin ab Ieuan ap Lleison reacted to the news, bewailing 'Woe unto us our prophesying of Owain'.[33] Thereafter the Lancastrian cause was tied to Owen's son Jasper Tudor, and to his gradson (the son of Edmund Tudor) Henry, who were both seen as the new 'Owain'.

With the seizure of power by the Yorkists the Lancastrian leaders were outlawed. In the 1460s Jasper Tudor organised the Lancastrian opposition, particularly in Gwynedd, and from the castle at Harlech waged his campaign against the Yorkist usurpers. Local gentry, most notably Gruffydd Fychan and his brother Elisau of Corsygedol, sustained the Lancastrian cause. Jasper himself was outlawed, and was forced to seek sanctuary finally in Brittany. The Lancastrian bards Lewis Glyn Cothi and Tudur Penllyn recounted in their poems the exploits of Jasper Tudor and his nephew Henry Tudor. For these bards Jasper and Henry were the 'Earls' over the water, the legitimate claimants to the English throne. However, with the fall of Harlech in 1468 some of the Lancastrian captains who had held the castle from 1461 sued for pardon. Dafydd ap Siencyn was pardoned. So also was Gruffydd Fychan of Corsygedol. On his death Guto'r Glyn composed an elegy extolling his services to Edward IV.[34]

There was a great outpouring of vaticinatory verse anticipating Henry Tudor's return from exile in Brittany. Often the bards refer to the mythic 'Owain' as the redeemer and liberator, referring directly to both Jasper and Henry Tudor as the new 'Owain'. For Dafydd Llwyd, Henry Tudor was a second Arthur, the new Owain (*Owain o Rufain yw'r Iôn/Owain fwyn, awen o Fôn*).[35] In his poems to Henry Tudor and his main supporter Rhys ap Thomas the bard anticipates the fulfilment of the ancient prophecies, the wreaking of vengeance on the English, the children of Alis and Rhonwen, the descendants of Hors and Hengist. With venom he anticipates the devastation to be visited upon the English (*Pobl Lloegrwys pawb a lygrir*).[36]

The Tudors' bid for the throne was sometimes directly associated with Owain Glyndŵr's rebellion in 1400. Tudur Penllyn in his poem to Dafydd ap Siencyn recounts his descent from Rhys Gethin, one of Glyndŵr's captains. He recounts that the mother of Gruffydd and Elisau Fychan of Corsygedol was Glyndŵr's niece. Tudur Penllyn speaks of Gruffydd Fychan keeping the door to Gwynedd open for the earl, and the return of the 'black eagle' (*eryr du*).

Henry is presented by the bards as the 'son of prophecy' (*y mab darogan*) who was destined to sit on the English throne.[37] The outstanding prophetic bard (*brudiwr*) of this period was Dafydd Llwyd of Mathafarn, near Machynlleth. His works are full of obscure allusions to individuals, events, omens and armorial symbols. More than any other bard in the fifteenth century Dafydd Llwyd articulated a sense of Welsh national identity, founded on a common language, history, territory, and shared aspirations.[38] It is at this time that he begins to refer to the Welsh as a nation (*nasiwn*). In his 'Poem to the Raven' (*Cywydd i'r Gigfran*) he prophesies a time of great slaughter, when the carrion crows will be sated with human flesh. Gwynedd, like Samson, will pull down the house of Dagon on its head.[39]

Dafydd Llwyd applies the title of *herwr*, which means both 'outlaw' and 'challenger', to his hero, referring to him as 'Harry the Outlaw' (*Harri Herwr*). Henry Tudor is depicted as the noble outlaw, a fugitive or outcast persecuted by those who have illegally seized power. The outlaw waits impatiently but will soon set out on the water and alight on the land like a bird (*Yr herwr i'r dŵr a dynn, A diria yn aderyn*). The outlaw will return from over the water (*Oddi ar y dŵr daw'r herwr hyn*). The brave, long-haired outlaw will return from over the sea (*Y daw'r herwr dewr hirwallt, A'i dai ar hyd y dŵr hallt*). The bard asks the Virgin Mary for patience in awaiting the outlaw's return. Elsewhere the bard describes his hero as an 'insurgent' (*Terfysgwr yw*). In one poem he advises his listeners to sleep not, an insurgent is setting out on the water (*Na chysg, y mae terfysgwr/ Yngod yn dyfod i'r dŵr*).[40]

The bard presents Henry Tudor as a saviour, a noble outlaw, who will rescue the country from lawlessness and extirpate the bandits. Here the term bandits (*gwylliaid*) appears to refer to those in existing positions of authority under Richard III, the Yorkist usurpers, as well as ordinary criminals. Will it be long, the bard asks, before the bandit horde is wasted? (*Yn eu hoes, ni wn ai hir/Haid o'r gwylliaid a gollir*). Henry will punish the bandits and give them woe (*Y gwylliaid drwg a gollir/O chwant da uchenaid hir*). He will cast the bandits into darkness (*Troed wylliaid trwy dywyllwg*). The bandits that are as pervasive as the wind have cause to tremble (*Y gwylliaid a gaid fal gwynt/Anwadal pob un ydynt*). He calls on the handsome bandits from the woods to cease their sport and show restraint (*Y gwylliaid heirdd o'r gelli/Ddichel chwyl, byddwch gall chwi*).[41]

The definition of outlaw is thus neatly reversed. Similarly the bard Gruffydd ap Dafydd Fychan anticipates that the tables will be turned on the usurper Richard III, 'the tall boar', who will be cast into outlawry (*A baedd hir a bydd herwr*). Iorwerth Fynglwyd declared that if Richard III lived long they would all be reduced to the status of outlaws.[42]

Henry Tudor landed in Mill Bay, Dale, Pembrokeshire on 7 August and commenced his famous march to Bosworth, where the death of Richard III brought to an end the rule of the Plantagenets. Having raised his banner, the leading Welsh Lancastrian families rallied to his cause. The most prominent being Sir Rhys ap Thomas of Dinefwr, the grandson of Gruffydd ap Nicholas.

Henry Tudor's route took him through the lawless lordships of mid-Wales, skirting the region of Mawddwy and Berwyn. His army camped near Welshpool at Cefn Digoll (Long Mountain), a famous resort of brigands. The choice of this route was intended primarily to give him time to rally his forces, from north and south Wales, before venturing to give battle to the forces loyal to Richard III. A secondary calculation may have been the aim to sweep up into this campaign the reckless and lawless elements from this region of central Wales, many of who were the descendants of Glyndŵr's die-hard rebels. The vaticinatory poetry of the period, with its invocation of 'Owain', and its depiction of Henry Tudor as the 'Outlaw' might suggests that it was directed particularly at these elements. Whether these brigand elements were mobilised is unclear. It might be noted that Guiseppe Garribaldi in 1860 in his march from Sicily through southern Italy to unify the country succeeded in mobilising a diversity of social groups, including brigand forces, into his army of liberation.

On his march through Wales, Henry stopped at Mathafarn to consult Dafydd Llwyd, the renowned bard and seer, who pronounced the auguries favourable. Dafydd Gorlech looked forward to the English being expelled from the kingdom and the Welsh restored to their patrimony (*a rhoi yr Cymru hu yw r hawl/yn i tiroedd naturiawl*). Llywelyn Fychan looked forward to the end of English oppression, and their removal from office.[43]

The bards rejoiced at Henry Tudor's triumph. Dafydd Llwyd composed a number of praise poems to the new king Henry VII, to his son Prince Arthur and to the king's influential supporters. He also wrote a poem denouncing Richard III's complicity in the murder of the princes in the Tower, as did the bard Huw Pennant.[44] Lewis Glyn Cothi exulted in his death; the cold (cruel) boar had been dispatched to his grave (*A'r baedd oer i'r bedd a aeth*). The importance of the bards as propagandists for the Tudor dynasty in Wales was recognised. Dafydd Llwyd was made Esquire to the Body of the king as his reward. Welsh bards and genealogists, led by Gutun Owain, were commissioned to authenticate his royal line of descent.

CONCLUSION

The consolidation of Edward IV's position after 1470 brought some amelioration of the situation. He attempted to improve administration in the Welsh shires, and to curb the over-mighty subjects such as the Herbert family. He sought to control lawlessness in the marcher lordships through the strengthening crown control through indentures with the marcher lords and by establishing the Council of the Marches with the power of oversight over the region. The effectiveness of these measures is difficult to assess. David Powel, the Welsh historian, in the sixteenth century whilst acknowledging Edward IV's good intentions for the 'reformation of the estate of Wales' believed that the 'troubles and disquietness of his subjects' and the 'shortness of his time' 'sufficed him to do little or nothing in that behalf'.[45] Edward IV's measures to reform the situation in Wales, however, provided a model, which Henry VII after 1485 was to put more vigorously into force.

Although the threat of civil war receded under Edward IV, the problem of disorder remained. The widespread nature of brigandage in this period is illustrated by the powerful traditions connected with the outlaws of Ysbyty Ifan and the raiders of Brecon who came amiss on Llangeinwyr mountain. In contrast to such raiders stood the more real and threatening challenge posed by powerful magnates such as the duke of Buckingham and Henry Tudor. Although Henry Tudor was described by the bards and the authorities as an outlaw and rebel, his position and status accorded him a totally different position to the locally based gangs of raiders and outlaws that infested the remoter parts of the country. He was also seen as the redeemer who would punish the purpetrators of disorder and lawlessness.

9 Wales under the Tudors 1485–1532

The Tudor accession in 1485 inaugurated a new phase in the attempts by the English crown to deal with the problem of lawlessness in Wales and the Marches. The new Tudor dynasty enjoyed unprecedented support in Wales. The civil wars bequeathed a heritage of social disturbance and conflict in Wales. The ushering in of peace provided more conducive conditions for effective government and social order. Henry VII had also before him the precedent set by Edward IV in 1470 of creating the Council of the Prince of Wales as a mechanism for curbing disorder, and through the procedure of concluding indentures with the marcher lords, binding them to enforce the law and uphold justice.

THE CONSOLIDATION OF TUDOR POWER 1485–1514

Under Henry VII, Jasper Tudor, now created earl of Bedford, emerged as the main power in Wales. In December 1485 he was appointed chief justice of south Wales. In March 1486 he was given power to appoint justices to inquire into all treasons and offences committed in Hereford, Gloucester and Worcester in south and west Wales and in the marches adjoining. He acted as deputy to Prince Arthur from 1489 until his death in 1495.[1] Rhys ap Thomas of Carmarthen, the grandson of Gruffydd ap Nicholas of Dinefwr, was appointed chamberlain of south Wales. He became deputy justice of south Wales on the death of Jasper Tudor. William Stanley was appointed chief justice of north Wales. William Griffith was re-appointed chamberlain of north Wales. John Morgan and Edward Vaughan were appointed bishops of St. David's, and Dafydd ap Ieuan became bishop of St. Asaph.[2] Welshmen were increasingly appointed to positions of authority in the shires, albeit under the control of English auditors.[3]

In Wales some leading Yorkists persisted in opposition. Sir Walter Herbert of Raglan was temporarily outlawed for his opposition to the new dynasty.[4] Sir Thomas Vaughan of Tretower in April 1486 raised rebellion at Brecon, Hay and Tretower, and, it was claimed, aimed to kill the king. The rebels seized Brecon castle but the king was able to call on his main ally in south Wales Sir Rhys ap Thomas to put down the rebellion.[5] In February 1487 Thomas Vaughan was pardoned.[6]

In 1486 Henry VII instructed the chamberlains of north Wales, Chester and Flint, and South Wales to ensure the collection of mises and other subsidies to which he was entitled and to ensure payment of arrears.[7] For the crown the withholding of taxes and other dues had been the clearest testimony of its ineffectiveness, particularly in the more lawless regions of Wales.

The disordered state of the central marches at this time is underlined by a commission issued in June 1491 to Richard Pole, knight to the king's body, with the power to pardon all persons inhabiting the lordships of Ceri, Cedewain and Montgomery for all treasons and other offences and to free them of all forfeitures of lands and goods.[8] In November Richard Pole and Sampson Norton, sheriff of Salop, were instructed to enquire into various murders, spoilations and riots in the hundreds of Purslow and Bissoppen on the border, and to commit the offenders to Clun castle and to report to the king's Council on the action taken.[9]

In 1486 the Statute of Livery and Maintenance was introduced in England and Wales. This forbade knights, esquires, gentlemen, yeomen and others from granting liveries and prohibited them from retaining, aiding or comforting any man knowing him to be a murderer, felon or an outlaw. In practice the law proved unenforceable.[10]

In the following years the Tudor monarchy faced various threats. The conspiracy of Perkin Warbeck in 1495 led to the execution of Sir William Stanley, chamberlain of Chester and Flint. Discontent over taxation led to the Yorkshire rebellion of 1489 and the Cornish rebellion of 1497. Wales by contrast, and in sharp contrast to the preceding decades, produced no such challenge to the crown.

The continuing disorder in Gwynedd

Throughout the fifteenth century Gwynedd, and especially the county of Merionethshire, was one of the most disordered regions in Wales. After 1485 the crown attempted to deal with the problem by the more rigorous enforcement of the law, and by attempts to secure unpaid revenues which had been withheld. These policies provoked a strong counter reaction. In May 1498 the deputy-chamberlain of north Wales toured the commotes of Merionethshire with a force of sixty-five soldiers, 'to hold the great turn and to resist rev[b]els and outlaws'. They met with violent resistance at Dolgellau. This turned into a local insurrection, with the insurgents seizing Harlech castle. Rowland Buckley, deputy constable of Beaumaris castle, recaptured the castle. In October 1498 the captured rebels were escorted from Harlech to Caernarfon where the justice's sessions for Merionethshire were held, and fines were imposed. Immediately after the sessions at Caernarfon a force of soldiers went once more to Merioneth and again moved from commote to commote 'to resist and expel rebels and outlaws'. At the sessions for the county held at Caernarfon in July 1499, the community of Merioneth was fined eight hundred marks 'for certain offences and enormities committed by them'.[11] To deal with offences between jurisdictions the traditional *dies marchie* were convened in 1498 between the men of Merioneth and those of Powys at Carnedd Hywel, and between the men of Merioneth and Mawddwy.[12]

The Prince's Council in the Marches of Wales

Henry VII emerged as the most powerful marcher lord. He inherited the Lancastrian lordships in the south (Kidwelly, Monmouth etc). With the overthrow of Richard III the lordships of the Earldom of March, the stronghold of Mortimer power, also fell into Henry's hands. The earldom of Pembroke was granted to Jasper Tudor, duke of Bedford, and following his death to Henry's second son Henry, duke of York. In 1495 the lordships of Holt, Bromfield, Yale and Chirk were forfeited to the crown on account of Sir William Stanley's treason. The lordships of Arwystli and Cyfeiliog were purchased in 1495; others escheated to the crown through the failure of heirs. In addition the crown held the lordships of Brecon, Caus and Newport during the minority of the third duke of Buckingham.

   Under Henry VII new efforts were directed at curbing the disorder in Wales and the Marches, by reviving the Prince of Wales' Council in Wales and the Marches.[13] On 29 November 1489 Arthur, the king's eldest son, was created Prince of Wales and was granted lands, castles and lordships in Wales, including the rights of ambobrage. A prince's council was formed based at Ludlow.[14] The history of the Council in these early years is uncertain. Only in 1501 was it formally established, when Prince Arthur, recently married to Princess Catherine, was sent to Ludlow. Within five months Arthur was dead. The Council's president was John Alcock, bishop of Ely, and from 1494 William Smyth, bishop of Coventry and Lichfield, from 1495 bishop of Lincoln. The Council had its own Court and the president was assisted by prominent lawyers – William Uvedale, Thomas Engelfield, Peter Newton, Richard Pole, Gilbert Taylor and Robert Froste.

   William Gerard in 1575 noted that the Council was established as a check on rebellion in Wales, to curb lawlessness, and relieve the oppression of the poor. Its purpose was also to combat border raiding, in this way 'to terrify and keep under the Welsh and to defend the English counties adjoining from their spoils'.[15] It was thus intended to protect the English shires, with the rivers Severn and Dee providing a natural barrier. The Council's authority exdtended over the border English counties, extending its resources and 'by the means provided the Council to be assisted, upon all sudden events with the power of the said English counties adjoining'.[16]

The indenture of the March

With the establishment of the Council in the Marches the crown sought to regulate disorder in the Marches by binding the marcher lords to ensure the law abiding behaviour of their tenants through the instrument of indentures as had already been adopted under Edward IV.

In March 1490 Henry VII concluded an indenture with Ralph Hakluyt, steward of Clifford, Winforton and Glasbury lordships, 'for the subduing of great robberies, murders and other offences there used before this time and for good rule to be had in the same lordships from henceforth'. The indenture stressed the duties of the officers of the marcher lordships to combat the theft of cattle, their obligation not to aid or abet outlaws or other felons, nor to take fees or levy *cymhorthas*. A schedule attached to the indenture included a list of murderers, outlaws and other felons whom the steward was to apprehend on their entering the lordships. All were to be punished in strict accordance with the laws, except for those who 'will come in to make their fines, as the king hath appointed'.[17]

Similar indentures were concluded between the crown and William Herbert, Jasper Tudor, Sir Rhys ap Thomas and the Duke of Buckingham.[18] After Prince Arthur's death in April 1502 the Council in the Marches recommended to Henry VII 'that all lords marcher be bounden by indenture to the king's grace for the good rule and order of the lordships, according to the good and laudable usage and custom there'.[19] The Council of the Marches also often had direct control over the administration of justice in the crown held lordships.[20]

On the death of Jasper Tudor in 1495 most of his extensive lordships were settled on the king's second son, Henry duke of York, and managed on his behalf by powerful magnates. Sir Charles Somerset became steward of Glamorgan for a high rent. The fiscal burden on the people was consequently substantially increased. To deal with lawlessness in Glamorgan Somerset had to give Henry VII in 1496 a bond for £3,000 as a guarantee that he would do impartial justice, and would not pardon murder, robbery or any other heinous crime, where the accused had once already been pardoned such an offence.[21]

The oppressive rule of the marcher lords evoked strong opposition from the tenantry. In the lordships of Gower and Kilvey the tenants fiercely

resisted attempts by Somerset to hold sessions in eyre and to redeem them
by fine or tallage. The lordships had previously been free of these
impositions and had been administered according to their own charter of
liberties. In 1500 the tenants took their case against their lord to the Privy
Council. The matter remained unresolved and in the following decades a
protracted struggle was fought over this issue.[22]

The granting of charters to the Welsh counties and boroughs

Since Henry IV reign Welshmen were prohibited from owning office or
holding land in the English boroughs in Wales and the adjoining marches.
These provisions were evaded by Welshmen purchasing English denizen-
ships, but they remained a source of resentment. Only twenty years after
his accession did Henry VII turn his attention to the question of re-
examining the legal status and rights of the Welsh.

The king granted a charter of liberties on 22 October 1504 to the
inhabitants of Anglesey, Caernarfonshire and Merionethshire. In its pre-
amble it abrogated the legislation enacted against the Welsh under Henry
IV. Welshmen were granted entry into the boroughs, and were allowed to
hold office. Partible succession (*cyfran*) was abolished so that inheritances
should descend according to the common law of England. Amobr and
other dues were abolished. Priests and beneficed clergy were allowed to
make wills.[23] The policy was enshrined in a series of charters, which Henry
granted to the lordships of Bromfield and Yale (August 1505), Chirk
(1506), Denbigh (1506), Ceri and Cydewain (July 1507), Ruthin (June
1508) and Bala (March 1507).[24]

In March 1507 a second charter of liberties was conferred upon the
communities of Anglesey, Caernarfonshire and Merionethshire. This
annulled Henry IV's laws against the Welsh, and listed grants to the
inhabitants of these counties. They were to be allowed to hold and sell their
lands on the same terms as Englishmen. The bondmen of the crown and
those of the church in north Wales were granted 'a general emancipation
and liberty'. In connection with this the office of rhingyll was abolished as
were the dues formerly levied by this officer. Other dues were abolished
and certain goods removed from toll. The goods of those dying without
wills (intestates) were to revert to heirs and relatives. Welshmen could
henceforth prosecute cases against Englishmen.[25]

These charters were granted in return for substantial fines paid to the
crown. They provoked strong opposition from the English burgesses of
Conwy, Caernarfon and Beaumaris, who protested that they violated the
terms of the charter granted to them by Edward I. The Welsh foreigners

(*forins*), they declared, should be contented with the liberties granted them in the eight other North Wales towns – Rhuddlan, Denbigh, Harlech, Bala, Cricieth, Nefyn and Newburch. These towns, they claimed, were now 'utterly in decay and desolate of wealth or English men'. They demanded also that the constable of Conwy castle a Welshman be replaced by an Englishman:

> for by the Welsh officers the town hath often been destroyed, for it is no more mete for a Welshman to bear any office in Wales, or especially in any of the three English towns, then it is for a Frenchman to be officer in Cal[a]is or a Scot in Barwick.[26]

As a result of these representations the king's council on 20 February 1509 reversed its decision granting liberties and franchises to Welshmen in the principality of north Wales. The burgesses and the Welsh foreigners (*forenses inhabitauntes*) were to appear before the king at a later date when the matter was to be 'discussed and utterly determined according to the law'.[27] The main question at issue concerned the rights of Welshmen in the three towns of Conwy, Caernarfon and Beaumaris. The rights of Welshmen in the other eight towns in north Wales was unaffected. The freeing of the bondmen was also unaffected.

The changing climate

The Tudor ascendancy did not bring fundamental changes in the administration of Wales, but Welsh identification with the new dynasty was strong.[28] The dream of an independent state which Glyndŵr had entertained had passed. Confronted by the power of unified English state such aspiration were relegated to the world of millenarian dreams. Through the conferring of office and grants the Welsh gentry were increasingly bound to the Tudor dynasty.

A contemporary account *The Italian Relation* asserted that 'The Welsh may now be said to have recovered their former independence, for the most wise and fortunate Henry VII is a Welshman'.[29] The influx of Welshmen into the capital, and into administrative and professional positions after 1485 was viewed with irony by some English observers. In the 'Merrie Tales of Skelton' Skelton reports a conversation with a Welshman at court who confided:

> Sir, it is so that many doth come up of my country to the king's court, and some doth get of the king by patent a castle, and some a park, and some a forest, and some one fee and some another, and they do live

like honest men.[30]

However, amongst some of the bards there was a certain disappoint-ment. Tudur Aled, who had enthusiastically welcomed the new dynasty, later reflected some of the disappointment of Welsh Tudor supporters who fell victim to royal persecution. Llywelyn ap Hywel complained that the king favoured Englishmen, the 'Normans', over his own people

Gwell gan Siasper a Harri
Y Gwyr o'r Nordd na gwyr ni.[31]

Nevertheless for many Welshmen Henry VII was a deliverer. The bard Hywel ap Rheinallt saw the Tudor ascendancy as inaugurating a new propitious age for Wales.[32] Siôn Tudur hailed Henry VII as the man who had freed the Welsh from bondage (*Yr un a'n rhoes ninnau'n rhydd*).[33] The historian David Powel in *The History of Cambria* (1584) asserted that Henry VII had delivered the Welsh from their thraldom.[34] These sentiments were echoed by William Salesbury and George Owen.[35]

WALES UNDER HENRY VIII 1509–1532

Henry VIII's accession in 1509 brought no immediate change in govern-ment policy towards Wales. The Council of the Marches, headed by bishop William Smith and from 1512 by Geoffrey Blythe, bishop of Coventry and Lichfield, retained its prominent role in dealing with treasons, insurrections, murderers and serious felonies, and to muster and array the fencible men of those parts.[36]

The governance of north Wales

In north Wales the representative of the crown from 1509 to 1525 was Charles Brandon, duke of Suffolk.[37] Under Brandon the government of north Wales was entrusted to Sir William Griffith of Penrhyn, as chamberlain. He was the third member of his family to hold this office. He served from 1516 as deputy chief justice of north Wales and was deputy sheriff and deputy escheator of Caernarfonshire, and was knighted in 1513.
    The bard Lewys Môn eulogised Sir William Griffith as a doughty upholder of the law, presenting him as one who had tamed the young bandits of the region and left the mountains widowed (*Gwell dofi'r gwylliaid ifanc: Mae'n llai o raid nag yr oedd, Mae'n weddwon y mynyddoedd*).[38] Other contemporaries viewed him in a very different light.

In January 1519 the Council of the Marches, attended by bishop Blythe and Sir Rhys ap Thomas, met at Shrewsbury and heard depositions against Sir William Griffith. Evidence was given by five Caernarfonshire gentlemen and thirteen Anglesey gentlemen, including prominent figures such as John Puleston (sergeant at arms), William Glyn (archdeacon of Merionethshire) and Rhydderch ap Dafydd (a lawyer in the London courts).

Three main charges were levelled at the chamberlain. Firstly, that he had maintained outlaws, robbers and murderers, and procured their release from prison. Secondly, he kept his own armed retinue, estimated by one witness to number 500 men. Thirdly, he used his office for self-enrichment through patronage, extortion and intimidation. He had confiscated the goods of people in Merionethshire on the pretext that they were harbourers of outlaws. He also levied a *cymhortha*, to celebrate his daughters' wedding, of nearly 1,000 head of cattle on Anglesey and Caernarfonshire. The people yielded to these exactions for 'fear of vexation because he was a great officer'. He was accused of failing to suppress banditry in Caernarfonshire and of conspiring to discredit and dismiss the sheriff of Merionethshire.

Sir William Griffith denied all these charges, which, he alleged, were framed by 'the enticement of diverse malicious persons'. One of his accusers, Gruffydd ap Morris, a yeoman of the guard, was allegedly inspired by malice, because the chamberlain had rejected his petition for a farm, on the grounds that his brother was a leader of a gang of eighteen outlaws, who might use the farm as a base.

On 5 June 1519 the king's Council, attended by Suffolk, agreed to place restraints on Sir William Griffith. He was to levy no more *cymhorthas*, and was to hold no office other than that of chamberlain except with the express consent of the king. His standing in north Wales was otherwise undiminished. Measures were taken against some of the complainants, with Gruffydd ap Moris being committed to the Fleet prison. Supervision over the chamberlain's work through the Council of the Marches, particularly over royal revenues, was tightened up.

The charges laid against Sir William Griffith recall the charges laid against Thomas Barneby as chamberlain of north Wales in 1413–14. The fact that one was a Welshmen the other an Englishman appears incidental. It suggests that the office itself, and the way by which political control in the region was maintained, tended to reproduce the same patterns of corruption. Public office became a source of plunder. In both cases collusion with 'rebels' and 'outlaws' appears to have been a means of enforcing control over the country, and intimidating others into submission.

That this was no aberration is confirmed by the case of William Brereton, a member of the king's privy chamber and a dominant figure in Cheshire and north Wales. In July 1527 John Puleston, sergeant of Caernarfon castle, wrote to Brereton about serious disorders in Merionethshire. He complained that John ap Madock ap Howell, deputy sheriff of the county under Sir Hugh Vaughan, had empanelled thieves and wretches, had falsely indicted his (Puleston's) servants, and was responsible for a breakdown of law and order in the county. In the ensuing months Brereton was appointed sheriff of Merionethshire, and John Puleston, for a fee, was appointed his under sheriff.[39]

In October 1527 Puleston reported to Brereton that he had brought 64 persons of 'evil demeanour' to Harlech and Caernarfon castle. Moreover, he requested that the Council in the Marches should require the adjoining lordships of Powys and Cyfeiliog to extradite '24 outlaws and rebellious', so that 'the shire of Merioneth may have rest'. There was acute disorder, with the gentlemen of the county being 'maintainers and comforters' of felons. Appeals to the Council of the Marches were to no avail. Puleston had arrested six or seven of the most heinous thieves and executed four of them. As a consequence he had 'lost the love of the gentlemen of the said county' and incurred much expense.

Brereton was appointed steward of the lordship of Chirk and Chirkland in November 1527.[40] The lordship was plagued by attacks by raiders from Merionethshire and from the lordships of Powys (probably the Berwyn mountains) and Mawddwy. The problem stemmed from the slackening of judicial control following the dismissal of the Duke of Suffolk as chief steward of Chirk in 1525. William Brereton became deputy steward in 1527 and then chief steward. The post of sergeant of the peace (*pencais*) was held by an absentee. A petition from the free tenants of Cynllaith and Mochnant to Brereton complained of the disorder, which threatened a flight of tenants from the lordship.[41]

Brereton became chamberlain of Chester in 1531. His power was much resented and he acquired a reputation for lawlessness. He was charged as steward of Chirk by his deputy John Griffith Eyton with 'diverse articles of maintenance of murderers, thieves and misruled persons and bearing of ill facts and deeds'. Chirk under Brereton became a haven for border cattle thieves, with the cattle being kept in Black Park. Those who attempted to track stolen cattle into the lordship were imprisoned in Chirk castle. Brereton's deputies also organised a raid on the earl of Arundel's tenants of Oswestry, sending the town's inhabitants fleeing to the church for protection. Brereton in November 1533 arranged for the arrest, trial and execution of Eyton, his chief accuser.[42]

Brereton had been appointed to the same posts in the region as Sir

William Stanley in 1485. In spite of the allegations of lawlessness directed against him he remained untouched. He was engaged in bitter feuding with other prominent families, including the Cholmondeleys of Cheshire and the Sneyds of Staffordshire. In 1536 he was beheaded for his alleged liaison with Anne Boleyn, and two days later the queen herself was executed.

Another powerful English magnate with Welsh possessions was Henry Lord Stafford. In the 1530s he sought the support of the Council of the Marches to deal with his recalcitrant tenants, who resisted his attempts to revive ancient dues as a means of boosting his revenues. The lordship of Caus neighboured the Long Mountain (Cefn Digoll), had once been a notorious haunt of outlaws. The Welshry in the lordship objected to the attempt to levy on them *portheant bugail* (shepherd's keeping), since they claimed that this was a fee for a slave cattle-guard. This had been necessary in the days when the hills were infested with thieves and outlaws and payable only when such a guard was provided.[43]

The governance of south Wales

In south Wales Sir Rhys ap Thomas, chamberlain, exercised wide jurisdiction and was responsible for the administration of justice. He used the law for his own ends and to strengthen his family's position in the area at the expense of his tenants and neighbours. Sir Rhys and his son Griffith were also involved in various disturbances. The most serious stemmed from a dispute between Griffith ap Rhys and one West, who had leased to him the commandery of the Knights of St. John at Slebech.[44]

Edward Stafford, third duke of Buckingham, was the most powerful nobleman in England, and owned substantial estates in Wales. Friction between Buckingham and the crown were deep seated, and he had been excluded from the king's council. To recover lost revenues Buckingham in 1500 ordered his council to make a survey of his Welsh lordships and to restore ancestral rights.[45] This produced a situation of seething discontent and a breakdown of order in the south Wales lordships. In 1504 the crown required Buckingham to observe the conditions of his indenture.[46]

In 1518 the duke's tenants in the lordship of Hay and Brecon petitioned the king's Council, protesting against the injustice of the system of redeeming the sessions in eyre, whereby the law-abiding were obliged to pay for the misdemeanours of the lawless. Wolsey and the Council in Star Chamber intervened to impose a settlement between Buckingham and his tenants.[47] The king admonished Buckingham for failing to enforce the condition of the indenture of 1504 to uphold the law and bring felons to justice.[48]

In 1521 Buckingham sought a licence from the king authorising him to visit his Welsh lordships with an armed escort of 300 to 400 men, made up of his officers and tenants, for the purpose of collecting revenue and enforcing justice.[49] The crown took fright at this proposal. The second duke of Buckingham's abortive rebellion against Richard III in 1483 provided an ominous precedent. Buckingham was arrested and in May 1521 was tried and executed.[50] His great estates, including the lordships of Brecon, Caus, Hay, Huntington and Newport, were forfeited. Caus, however, was restored to the duke's son, Henry Stafford, in 1523.

Following Buckingham's execution no attempt was made to hold the Great Sessions in the lordships until 1524. A petition from the tenants in 1525 protested against the exactions made on them. They made it clear that they were prepared to redeem the sessions 'for that time only' but insisted that in future 'all murderers, felons and other offenders may be there duly punished, depressed and corrected for their offences'[51] In 1528 the tenants of Brecknock complained that justice was not upheld in the lordship. A set of royal ordinances were issued, in which the articles of the 1504 indenture were reiterated, and these were again confirmed in a further ordinance of 1535.[52]

In the lordship of Gower and Kilvey Sir Charles Somerset, later earl of Worcester, and his chief agent, Sir Mathew Craddock, met similar opposition. In 1500 the tenants took their lord to the Privy Council, and in 1524 petitioned Star Chamber contesting his right to hold sessions in eyre or to redeem them by a collective fine. On both occasions the rights of the lord were upheld. The resistance in 1524, Sir Mathew Craddock alleged, came from the lesser gentry in the lordships who were aggrieved at the limits which had been set on their own rights to levy *cymhorthas* and aids from their tenants. In 1532 an agreement was reached between the parties restricting the lord's rights over the convening of sessions in eyre, requiring the attendance of the tenants before these sessions for only one day.[53]

Aspects of lawlessness

The effectiveness of the administration of justice in this period is a matter of controversy. The picture was clearly very mixed. In Carmarthen, Cardigan and the marcher lordships of south Wales (excepting Brecon, Hay and Gower) the practice of redeeming the Great Sessions continued. In north Wales the situation was better. Sir John Wynn notes that the courts in Caernarfon under Henry VII were held regularly. The plea rolls of Anglesey between 1509 and 1516 show that despite acts of violence and weaknesses in the work of the courts there was no serious disorder. The

Justice of north Wales, or his deputy, held his sessions and the sheriffs their county courts and great tourns. The ecclesiastical courts continued to operate.[54]

Individual as well as organised gangs of outlaws, however, remained a problem. In 1521 one Griffith ap Evan ap Dafydd, 'a cruel and notable outlaw of Wales', was brought to Shrewsbury, tried, hanged, drawn and quartered. He had turned to outlawry following the theft of his cattle, and waged a bloody vendetta against the kin of those responsible for the theft. The corporation paid a labourer 5d for fixing his head 'upon a post over the town gate towards Wales to the terror and example of other like felons and rebels'.[55]

From 1525 the Lord President of the Council of Wales and the Marches was John Veysey, bishop of Exeter, a compassionate but aged man, whose grip on affairs was weak. Veysey was reluctant to resort to the use of capital punishment. He saw the problem of disorder as stemming at least in part from economic circumstances, and the particularly oppressive exactions to which the Welsh were subjected.[56]

In September 1525 princess Mary was sent to Ludlow. The Princess's Council was given wide powers to deal with lawlessness – to punish those who levied *cymhorthas*, to compound with and pardon outlaws, to issue proclamations of good order, to enforce indentures and to prohibit the practice of redeeming the Great Sessions.[57] However, when Henry VIII divorced Catherine of Aragon in 1528 the Princess's household at Ludlow was broken up, to prevent the formation of a faction around her. Mary was recalled and deprived of her status as Princess.[58]

The revolt of Rhys ap Griffith

In 1525 Sir Rhys ap Thomas, lord of Dinefwr and a stalwart supporter of the Tudor monarch, died. Walter Devereux, Lord Ferrers, was appointed Justice and Chamberlain of south Wales in his place. Sir Rhys' grandson and heir Rhys ap Griffith were aggrieved at not having been appointed as his grandfather's successor in south Wales. He was popular and had extensive family connections amongst the gentry of south west Wales. In the following years tension between Rhys ap Griffith and Lord Ferrers intensified.[59]

The abuse of legal procedure became one issue of contention. Lord Ferrers, in a letter to the Lord President of the Council of the Marches of Wales, complained against the issuing of subpoenas in Carmarthen and Cardigan by Rhys ap Griffith's officers, contrary to Wolsey's instructions. Local feelings were so intense, Ferrers reported, that the populace was threatening to withhold payments, declaring, 'plainly that they would not pay a groat … if any man do appear otherwise than they have been accustomed, but they had liever run into the woods'. In March 1529 Rhys ap Griffith complained to Wolsey that his 'poor tenants and servants' were daily vexed by the malicious and 'light persons' whom Ferrers employed as his deputies. He urged that he be appointed deputy Justice and Chamberlain of south Wales to redress the situation.[60]

When Rhys visited Wales, in 1529, the whole country had turned out to see him. In June 1529, when Ferrers attempted to hold the Great Session in Eyre in Carmarthen, clashes occurred between the retainers and supporters of both men. An attempt was made to release some of Rhys ap Griffith's men who had been imprisoned in Carmarthen castle. Rhys himself was taken and imprisoned. Ferrers complained to Wolsey of the greatest insurrection anyone could remember in Wales.[61] The two parties were summoned to the Star Chamber in Westminster, severely censured by Wolsey and warned of their future conduct.

In November 1531 Rhys was tried before the King's Bench on charges of plotting against the king and in schemes to call on the support of the Scottish king James V. Rhys ap Griffith was found guilty of treason and executed on 4 December 1531.

The execution sent shock waves throughout south Wales, inflamed feelings against Ferrers and brought the region close to rebellion. King Henry's plans to divorce Catherine of Aragon for Anne Boleyn, and the measures against the power of the Catholic church and the monasteries only heightened tensions. The Catholic Queen Catherine was popular in Wales and included a number of Welshmen in her retinue. In August 1534 Martin de Cornoca wrote, 'the whole province is alienated from the king'. Chapuys, the Spanish ambassador, in November 1534, wrote of anger in Wales at the treatment of the Queen, state policy towards religion, and the attempt to deprive the people of their native laws, customs and privileges 'the very thing which they can endure least patiently'. He concluded, 'the people only wait for a chief to take the field'. In 1535 the ambassador reported that the king had been hunting on the border and visiting the principality, 'traversing the country to gain the people'.[62] However, the rebellion failed to materialise.

In 1532 James ap Griffith ap Howel, who had testified against his nephew, was granted a royal pardon on payment of a heavy fine of £526 13s 4d.[63] He returned to Wales, but in 1533 fled to Ireland, and thence to Scotland, gaining an audience with James V with the aim of procuring aid for some scheme in Wales.[64] Thereafter he travelled to Flanders and Germany, moving from court to court, plotting with Reginald Pole and other Welsh exiles. He was outlawed. On the accession of Mary he returned to Wales, living out his days in poverty.[65]

How far Rhys had conspired against the crown is uncertain. Like the duke of Buckingham he appears to have fallen victim to an overly suspicious crown. Rhys was executed on the same spot as Buckingham. Another parallel noted by William Nevill, who had consulted one wizard Jones at Oxford, was 'that the late Duke of Buckingham, young Ryse, and others, had cast themselves away by too much trust in prophecies'.[66]

CONCLUSION

In the first fifteen years of his reign Henry VII paid scant attention to the problem of lawlessness in Wales. The Tudor accession changed the climate of opinion in Wales. It created as new sense of identification with the central government and led to an abatement of the ethnic hatreds which had coloured so much of the fifteenth century. The establishment of a stable central government, and the ending of the inter-dynastic feuds of the Wars of the Roses, contributed to alleviating the crisis of disorder. But the administration of justice was still 'lop-sided', powerful officers and lords administered the law in their own interests, and were themselves major contributors to the disorder which they themselves were supposed to control.

The crown's attempts to reform Wales and the border through the Council of the Marches, by indenture with the marcher lords and recourse to commissions of oyer and terminer failed to provide an adequate means for dealing with the problem. The granting of charters to the boroughs of north Wales represented the main innovation, but its halting realisation underscored how far the crown remained constrained in dealing with the governance of Wales. In the 1520s complaints regarding the disordered state of Wales began to mount. It appears that the situation deteriorated in the first two decades of Henry VIII's reign. In the more peaceful climate of the times opinion became less tolerant of lawlessness, reflected in the protests of tenants and lesser gentry against the abuses perpetrated by the great officers and lords. Government policy towards Wales was caught between making the existing system of government more effective and undertaking fundamental reform. The alleged rebellions attempted by Buckingham and Rhys ap Griffith gave a new impetus to curb the over-mighty subjects and to institute more lasting reform.

10 Union and Reformation 1532–1555

In 1532 Thomas Cromwell replaced Wolsey as Lord Privy Seal. As the king's chief adviser he presided over what the historian G. R. Elton has called the 'Tudor revolution in government'.[1] This involved an unprecedented centralisation of state power, the creation of a 'modern' state, with its bureaucratic governmental and judicial apparatus, and its own mechanisms of concilliary government over its peripheral regions. The state which was forged in these decades was jealous of its own powers and prerogatives, and sought to sweep away the anachronistic survivals of medieval privilege, represented by the independent jurisdictions wielded by the marcher lords, the church and the monastic houses. It sought direct control over its own subjects, unimpeded by such particularistic institutional powers. Associated with these changes went a new intolerance towards the multiple forms of lawlessness, which had earlier characterised medieval society. Through institutions like Star Chamber the central state extended its arm to check, control and intimidate the powerful magnates of the shires.[2] With the Reformation the state's supremacy over the church was decisively asserted and a veritable revolution in the lives of people was carried through.

THE PRESSURE FOR REFORM

From the late 1520s onwards the English crown increasingly recognised that the existing system of administration in Wales and the Marches was no longer tenable and that fundamental reform would have to be undertaken. Already in 1528 proposals were advanced for some of the marcher lordships and their towns to be annexed and joined to the neighbouring English counties. In 1531 Dr. James Denton, Chancellor of the Council in the Marches, proposed to Thomas Howard, Earl of Norfolk, a scheme to shire the Marches. The king had expressed the view that 'it were a gracious deed to reform Wales', although adding that opposition could be expected from the marcher lords, since they and their officers derived profit from pardoning thieves and oppressing the poor.[3]

In 1531 the crown renewed its bonds with the marcher lords, which required the lords to administer impartial justice, prohibited the harbouring of felons and outlaws, and made assemblies (*cymhortha*) unlawful.[4] Within the lordships the opposition of tenants to the payment of tallage for redeeming the Great Sessions remained strong. In 1532 the Earl of Worcester was obliged to come to terms with his tenants in Gower, agreeing that they should be required to attend only the first day of the sessions.[5]

The problem of disorder was not confined to the marches. In March 1531 the King's Commissioners in the shires of north Wales were accused of extortion, concealment of felons and embezzlement of fines. The Privy Council instructed John Pakington, justice of north Wales, to investigate the matter. He reported that the commissioners had fined many 'poor creatures' for 300 marks and more. Those unable to pay their fines were left languishing in castle dungeons. Many inhabitants of north Wales had been indicted and outlawed, and had 'eloigned themselves into strange countries' or had bribed the officials to stay the prosecution.[6]

The first step towards a fundamental overhaul of the administration of justice in Wales and the Marches came in 1532, when the marcher lords and the officers in Wales were instructed to present, secretly and on oath, to the Council in the Marches their views regarding 'not only the great causes of misrule but also the remedy of the same'.[7] The response indicated the depth of concern at the situation particularly amongst the gentry. There was also a remarkable degree of consensus concerning the causes of disorder.

The Earl of Worcester identified perjury, retaining and maintenance by the gentry as the chief problem, together with unlawful assemblies. Edmund Turner, clerk of Glamorgan county court, noted that in Cardiff 'there is much idle people there … that liveth idly and daily haunteth taverns and ale houses'; they had little to maintain themselves, but lived 'by other shifts and ways and those be they that maketh frays and revengeth quarrels of other men'.[8] Thomas Phillips informed Cromwell that Wales was in 'great decay', with cattle lifting widespread. He demanded that officers in Wales be restrained from taking fines for felony and murder and that the system of tracking cattle should be enforced. He urged that the Princess' Council at Ludlow should not delay justice, declaring – 'Desire that such a council be established in the Marches that the best officers in Wales shall quake if found in default'.[9]

The same year T. Engelfield of the Council in the Marches wrote to Cromwell concerning four murders committed in the lordship of Elfael by members of the powerful Vaughan family. He stressed that it was necessary to ensure justice at the forthcoming assizes at Hereford and warned of attempts to petition the king for clemency.[10] John Salusbury, steward of Denbigh, and John Salter, justice of north Wales, wrote to the Council in the Marches protesting at the prevalence of perjury, maintenance and unlawful assemblies. Another correspondent, John Parker, advocated stricter constraints on officers, urging that they be forbidden from pardoning murder or felony in return for a fine, and called for the practice of *cymhortha* to be prohibited.[11]

In 1533 Thomas Holte, member of the Council in the Marches and the king's attorney, in a memorandum noted the 'greatest things that be amiss at this time in Wales' were that murder and cattle stealing often went unpunished, and that the people were oppressed by the levying of *cymhortha*. Juries refused to convict members of the Welsh gentry because of corruption and intimidation, and in the marcher lordships cases rarely came before the courts because of the practice of *arddel*. Holte argued that only 'evil officers' in the lordships and the impoverished gentry would oppose the abolition of these practices. He advocated also the abolition of the Welsh law of inheritance (*cyfran*) to reduce the number of the impoverished Welsh gentry who were the patrons of thieves.[12]

Many of the worst abuses occurred in the marcher lordships controlled by Henry Somerset, Earl of Worcester, who as the king's steward, governed the lordships of Abergavenny, Brecon, Elfael, Ewyas Lacy, Ceri, Magor, Montgomery, Monmouth, Ruthin, Gower, Glamorgan and Morgannwg. Many of these lordships were a byword for tyranny and corruption.[13] Other lords acknowledged their difficulties in maintaining order. Henry, Lord Stafford, who was Lord of Caus and the king's steward at Hay, petitioned Anne Boleyn for financial assistance in repairing his castles, declaring 'if those castles go down there will be no good rule in the king's lordships of the Hay nor in my lordship of Caursland'.[14] Elsewhere the minority of lords, such as Earl Edward, Lord Stanley from 1521 to 1531 created problems in administering justice and collecting revenue.[15] In June 1533 Elizabeth, Lady Worcester, complained to Cromwell of the powerful Stradling family, of whom there were twelve brothers, 'the most part bastards', who lived by extortion and the 'pilling' of the king's subjects.[16]

Increasingly the blame was laid at the door of the Council of Wales and the Marches. In March 1533 Sir Edward Croft, the vice chamberlain of south Wales, wrote to Cromwell, criticising the laxity of Veysey as Lord President:

> Wales is far out of order, and there have been many murders in Oswestry and Powys. No punishment has followed, because the chief of the Council is a spiritual man, and cannot administer punishment of death for felony or murder. Wishes some man to be sent down to

use the sword of justice where he shall see cause throughout the principality; otherwise the Welsh will wax so wild it will not be easy to bring them into order again.[17]

Thomas Croft, his son, complained to Cromwell that since the appointment of Veysey as President of the Council in 1525 more than 100 had been slain in Wales and the Marches 'and not one of them punished'.[18]

In response to these petitions the crown decided to act.[19] In the autumn of 1533 draft bills were prepared for submission to parliament, including measures to strengthen the power of Star Chamber in cases of murder, to increase the powers of the King's Commissioners in the Marches, and to regulate the appointment of Welshmen to offices in Wales.[20]

The king scathingly admonished Veysey for the Council's laxity, which had allowed lawlessness and cattle stealing to thrive. Cromwell insisted that Veysey inquire into extortion and misdemeanours by marcher officials, and embezzlement by crown officials.[21]

Sir Edward Croft complained to Cromwell in July 1534 that despite proclamations by the King's Commissioners in the Marches forbidding the carrying of weapons at markets and fairs a great affray had occurred at Bishop's Castle the previous month with many left maimed.[22] Cromwell arranged for the king to meet the marcher lords at Shrewsbury. There they agreed on a number of ordinances regarding the appointment of reliable officers, preventing the harbouring of felons and ensuring the regular holding of the courts.[23] At this time the crown confirmed all indentures concluded between Henry VII and the late duke of Buckingham and all other marcher lords in south Wales.[24]

Legislative Reform 1534–1536

The appointment of bishop Rowland Lee as Lord President of the Council of Wales in 1534 signalled a more assertive policy. This was accompanied by a series of major reforms concerning the administration of justice in the principality and the marches, which Cromwell played a key role in drafting.[25] In 1534 a series of Acts of Parliament were passed dealing with asspects of lawlessness in Wales, which provide an extraordinary and graphic commentary on the problem.

One Act dealt with the intimidation and subornation of juries in Wales and the Marches by friends, kinsmen and accessories of offenders brought to trial for murder and felony.[26] It established the office of bailiff to safeguard jurors from such threats and pressures. Where juries returned acquittals 'contrary to good and pregnant evidence', they and the officers of the court were to be called before the President and Council of the marches and, where found in default, to be fined or imprisoned.[27]

A second Act confirmed that felonies committed within the Welsh Marches could be tried in the adjoining English counties. An acquittal in the courts of the marcher lords was to be no bar to indictment in the ordinary courts within two years after the offence was committed. The Justices in England could issue process into the marcher lordships against offenders and were to certify outlawries and attainders to their officers, who were to convey the offenders into England.[28]

A third Act prohibiting ferryboats on the Severn from conveying persons, goods, cattle and horses between sun down and sun up. It noted that murders and felonies committed at night in Gloucestershire and Somersetshire by intruders from south Wales posed a serious problem. These felons were able to flee by ferry from Aust, Fremeland, Purton, Arlingham, Newnham, Portishead Point and other places into south Wales and the Forest of Dean. Similarly many robberies and murders were committed on the border adjoining the river 'to the great damage and hurt of the King's Subjects'. Ferrymen were made answerable for observing this law and were required to allow passage only to those whose abode were known to them. The Justices of the Peace in Gloucester and Somerset were to call before them anyone who contravened this order.[29]

A fourth Act provided for the punishment of Welshmen who attempted assault on any of the inhabitants of Herefordshire, Gloucestershire and Shropshire. Felons from Wales who had committed offences in the border counties often fled to their homes to avoid capture. Those who pursued them with the intent of apprehending them and bringing them to the court were frequently ambushed, 'beaten, mayhemed, grievously wounded and some times murdered'. Any person attempting such an assault was to be imprisoned for one year. In 1536 the Act was extended until the next Parliament.[30]

Two further Acts were passed to strengthen the role of the courts. The Bill Concerning Councils in Wales outlined various remedies.[31] All persons dwelling in Wales and the marcher lordships were required to attend the courts when convened. Officials of the marcher lordships who undertook wilful prosecutions or who wrongfully imprisoned individuals as a means of securing exactions were liable to prosecution. The carrying of weapons to court or other places of assembly was forbidden. Courts were to be held in the most peaceable places in the marcher lordships. The old Welsh practices of *cymhortha* and *arddel* were abolished. Justices of the Peace in the neighbouring English counties were empowered to extradite known offenders and outlaws from the Marches.[32] Murder and felony in the marcher lordships were to be inquired of at the sessions in the nearest shire where the King's writ ran. Marcher lords who refused to hand over felons were liable to a fine of £100. Wrongful acquittals by jurors in the marcher courts were to be punished by the Council in the Marches.[33]

The First Act of Union 1536

These laws proved inadequate to deal with the problem. The king and the Privy Council in December 1535 discussed further measures 'to reform the administration of Wales so that peace should be preserved and justice done'.[34] The reorganisation was embodied in a series of laws enacted in 1536 and 1543 which incorporated Wales and the Marches into the same administrative, legal and political framework as England.

Lee and Engelfield in a letter to Cromwell in February 1536 urged that the marcher lords be compelled strictly to enforce the law, rigorously observing the process of 'tracking' stolen cattle; curbing the buying of pardons, and halting the levying of *cymhortha*. Lee anticipated strong opposition from the Earl of Worcester and lord Ferrers, who would 'greatly stick at it', 'for it will touch them most, as they use their offices, for the manifold selling of thieves, is the greatest occasion of the innumerable thieves'.[35]

Welsh petitioners supported radical changes. One petition, variously attributed to Sir Richard Herbert or Sir John Price, craved that the Welsh be 'received and adopted into the same laws and privileges' as were enjoyed by the king's other subjects, and expressed the earnest wish to 'unite ourselves to the greater and better part of the island'.[36] A petition from the burgesses and landowners of Anglesey, Caernarfon, Conwy and Beaumaris, presented to the king by John Puleston, supported the extension of English laws and rights to the inhabitants of the Welsh shires.[37] Petitioners from mid-Wales in 1536 complained to the Council in the Marches against the oppression of their lords and their officers, who relied not on written law, but on custom, which they invariably interpreted to their advantage and profit, 'having little respect or none to any good equity or conscience'.[38]

In 1536 an Act was passed to deal with abuses in the forests of Wales, which belonged to the king and the marcher lords. This allowed free passage through the forests by those on horseback, on foot and those driving cattle. Attempts to impose tolls or fines on those passing through the forests were to be treated as an act of robbery on the king's highway. Heavy fines were to be imposed on foresters who seized stray cattle as their own. Those who had lost cattle could recover them once they had paid for their upkeep whilst in the charge of the foresters. Foresters who attempted to impose traditional exactions, were liable to prosecution, and to be outlawed if they failed to answer charges brought against them in the courts.[39]

Leland in his account of his travels in Wales in 1536–1539 noted that on the Brecon-Llanymddovery road, through the Maiscaro forest, that 'men of late were not wont to pass without toll of money'. He observed also that the infestation of the forests by outlaws was a persistent problem. Concerning the loss of woodland around Strata Florida, he noted that men had 'destroyed the great woods that they should not harbour thieves'.[40]

A major step to bring the administration of justice in Wales in line with England was the Act of 1536, which established the office of Justice of the Peace, Justice of the Quorum and Justice of Gaol-Delivery. These officers were to be appointed by the Lord Chancellor under the king's seal in the counties of Anglesey, Caernarfon, Merioneth, Flint, Cardigan, Carmarthen, Pembroke and Glamorgan. The JPs were to keep the sessions, enforce the law and supervise the work of the sheriffs. The king's Exchequers at Caernarfon, Carmarthen, Pembroke and Cardiff were to receive the sheriff's accounts.[41]

Crown supremacy in the administration of justice in Wales and the marches was underlined by an Act of 1536 which asserted that the king alone, henceforth, had the power and authority to pardon or remit any treasons, murders, manslaughters, felonies, or any accessories to these crimes, or any outlawries stemming from such offences. Moreover, only the king had the authority to appoint justices, and all writs and indictments for treason, felony or trespass should be made in the king's name alone.[42]

In 1536 parliament passed 'An Act for Laws and Justice to be administered in Wales in like form as it is in this Realm'. This, the first of the so-called Acts of Union, declared that 'the Dominion, Principality and Country of Wales' was and ever had been 'incorporated, annexed, united and subject to and under the Imperial Crown of this Realm', with his most Royal Majesty as its 'very Head, King, Lord and Ruler'. In this it asserted that the crown was merely reclaiming its sovereign power over Wales, and eradicating distinctions which had developed under the marcher lords.[43] This was a legal fiction, as the crown had never had power over these territories.[44]

The Act declared that great discord had developed between the king's English and Welsh subjects because of differences in laws and customs of these people, and the discrimination which had been exercised against the Welsh. To remedy this situation it was resolved that Wales should be incorporated with England and that 'all persons born, or to be born' in Wales should have all the liberties, rights, privileges and laws which were enjoyed by the king's English subjects. The reform was inspired, it declared, by the 'singular zeal, love and favour' which the king bore towards his Welsh subjects.[45]

The Act was significant for the proposal for shiring the marcher lordships, through the creation of five new counties: Monmouth, Brecknock, Radnor, Montgomery and Denbigh. The Welsh shires were to be organised on the same lines as the English shires, and were to be divided into hundreds. Each county was to have its own JPs, sheriffs, escheators and coroners. Each county was to elect to Parliament a knight for the shire and a burgess for the shire town (Merioneth being excepted, which was only to return a knight). New Chanceries and Exchequers were to be established at Brecon and Denbigh to complement those already existing in Caernarfon and Carmarthen, and were to oversee the administration of justice.[46]

The language of the courts was to be English and any person who could not use English was to be barred from holding office. The law was predominantly English law, although it was proposed to establish a commission to investigate traditional Welsh legal usage and custom. The neighbouring English counties retained the right to try cases of murder, treason and felony committed in the adjoining marcher lordships. The gathering of *cymhortha* was prohibited, and the Welsh law of inheritance, *cyfran*, was replaced by the English law of primogeniture.

The power of the marcher lords was to be drastically curtailed, but they retained the right to try felons caught on their property or felons who had fled from another jurisdiction (infangenetheof and outfangetheof). They also retained traditional rights, such as mises, the payment made to the lord on his first entry into the lordship. They retained the rights to call courts baron and leet.

Lee fulminated against the proposals to shire the marcher lordships and to establish the office of JP in Wales. In a letter to Cromwell in March 1536 he declared it to be 'not much expedient'. If the statute went forward he warned that the 'bearing of thieves' would become more prevalent, noting that 'the demeanour of Merionethshire and Cardiganshire; for though they are shire ground they are as ill as the worst part of Wales'.[47] The attempt to entrust the administration of justice to the Welsh was vain – 'If one thief shall try another all we have here begun is foredone'. The Welsh gentry, Lee argued, could not be trusted as JPs, and lacked the necessary property qualifications of £20 per annum: 'There be very few Welshmen in Wales above Brecknock that may dispende ten pounds land, and, to say truth, their discretion less than their lands'. He implored Cromwell 'Would God I were with you one hour to declare my mind therein at full'.[48]

In 1537 Lee again informed Cromwell that, like most people, he thought the changes undesirable.[49] Lee's apprehensions were shared by those of the Welsh gentry who feared that they would lose out in the ensuing scramble for office. In a document amongst the State Papers the king was warned in 1538 not to appoint Justices for Anglesey, Caernarfon or Merioneth, for most of the gentlemen were poor and quarrelsome, 'bearers of thieves and misruled persons', and that if appointed to such offices the problems of partiality and extortion would increase.[50]

The Second Act of Union 1543

In 1542 the first Welsh county sheriffs and JPs were appointed, and the first Welsh MPs elected to Parliament. In 1552 Nicholas Heath, a member of the Council, instructed the gentry of Caernarfon to be careful in the choice of their MPs.[51]

The work of the commission on shiring the marcher lordships was not completed until 1542. Lee continued to oppose the project.[52] In 1543 parliament approved the 'Act for certain ordinances in the King's Dominion and Principality of Wales', in effect the second of the Acts of Union, which confirmed the division of Wales into shires.[53] The most radical innovation of the Act was the creation of the King's Court of Great Session in Wales, which was to exercise the same powers as the Court of King's Bench and the Court of Common Pleas in England.[54] Wales was divided up into four circuits each embracing three counties, with two circuits in the North and two in the South:

Anglesey, Caernarfon and Merioneth
Denbigh, Flint and Montgomery
Cardigan, Pembroke and Carmarthen
Brecknock, Radnor and Glamorgan.

Monmouthshire was excluded and added to one of the English court circuits. Each circuit was to be presided over by a Justice. The Courts of Great Sessions were to be held in each county town twice each year, each for six days in the spring and autumn.

The Council of Wales, with its own Court of the Marches, was to oversee the administration of justice by the Court of Great Sessions. Cases tried at the quarter sessions and Court of Great Sessions could be appealed to the Court at Ludlow. The higher courts in Westminster, the Courts of Chancery, Exchequer and Star Chamber, also exercised judicial authority in Wales as in England.[55]

The Act formalised the administration of justice in the shires. Within each shire there were to be appointed a sheriff, eight Justices of the Peace, and one 'custos rotulorum' for the keeping the court records. The Justices of the Peace were appointed by the Lord Chancellor England, on the advice and recommendation of the Council in Wales. Care was also to be taken in the appointment of the sheriffs. The JPs were to organise the Quarter Sessions courts in the shires, to deal with cases of felony, petty lawsuits and misdemeanours. Within each county the sheriff was to hold monthly county courts and his deputies were to conduct the hundred courts every two or three weeks, dealing with matters such as petty debt or trespass. The JPs and sheriffs were to be assisted in their work by escheators, coroners and constables.

The Act established English law as the law in Wales, finally sweeping away the traditional Welsh laws, which had for long been in decay. The Act specified that fines were not to be accepted in cases of murder or other felonies as a means of forestalling the judicial process. Moreover, private agreements between disputant parties concerning murders and felonies were not to be entered into without the consent of the Justices of the Great Sessions. These private agreements, nevertheless, as shall be seen, persisted. One traditional Welsh legal practice that was preserved concerned the tracking of stolen cattle.

The new machinery of justice effectively by-passed the autonomous courts of the marcher lords, although the marcher lords retained the right to summon manorial, leet and courts baron to deal with minor affrays and disputes. Another major reform was that the Act forbade the practice of paying tallage for redeeming the great sessions and sessions in eyre.[56] The marcher lords retained the rights accorded to them in the Act of 1536. The shiring of the marcher lordships eliminated their rights and privileges of sanctuary.[57]

By the two Acts of Union of 1536 and 1543 the border between Wales and England was at last settled. Within Wales the marcher lordships were organised into the new counties of Denbighshire, Montgomeryshire, Radnorshire and Brecknockshire. Flintshire, which had a special jurisdiction under the oversight of the County Palatine of Chester, emerged as an autonomous county. A number of lordships, with large Welsh speaking populations, were annexed to the adjoining English counties; Oswestry, Whittington and Clun were joined to Shropshire, whilst Ewyas Lacy, Ewyas Harold, Wigmore and Archenfield were joined to Herefordshire. These measures, by eliminating separate jurisdictions, were intended to eradicate the problem of border raiding.

THE REFORMATION IN WALES

The Reformation saw the establishment of state supremacy over the church, the severing of the link with Rome, the assumption by the king of his position as head of the church, and the dissolution of the monasteries. These were major step towards the establishment of the 'modern sovereign state'. This involved sweeping away centuries old traditions of Catholic belief and practice, it brought a revolution in the culture life of the people, which had far reaching social and psychological implications. In the case of Wales there is little doubt that this was a revolution from above, directed by the state.[58]

The parlous state of the church and of the monastic houses since the time of the Glyndŵr rising placed them in a vulnerable position. Their financial power had weakened, the support from powerful patrons diminished. The church and the monasteries often fell prey to the ambitions of powerful local magnates. Contenders for church and monastic office themselves resorted to force to settle the issue. The sanctuary provided by the church, abbeys and the monasteries lay them open to widespread abuse. The privileges associated with benefit of clergy served to bring the church into disrepute. The problem of lawlessness extended into the church and the monastic houses, with priors and abbots themselves being brought before the courts for various misdemeanours.[59]

A 'breviat' of murders and misdemeanours committed in Wales under Henry VIII drew attention to riots and affrays at Margam abbey caused by the enmity between two of its leading tenants, John Loughor and Christopher Turberville, each with a great company of men, as a result of which Loughor was killed.[60] In 1535 Robert Salusbury, abbot of Valle Crusis, was found guilty of a series of armed highway robberies with a band of acquaintances in Oxfordshire. The 'bandit abbott' was imprisoned without being able to plead right of clergy. At this time also a monk of Strata Florida was accused on conspiracy to forge coins.[61]

The lax or compliant attitude of individual priests to lawlessness in Wales was noted by Sir Thomas More in his *A Dialogue Concerning Heresies*. Irish and Welsh felons and raiders, he alleged, sought and obtained the blessing of priests before embarking on their exploits. 'And commonly in the wild Irish and some in Wales too, as men say, when they go forth in robbing they bless them and pray God send them good speed that they may meet with a good purse and do harm and take none'.[62] In bandit infested regions, such as southern Italy in the nineteenth century, collusion between the church and bandit gangs was common, with the Catholic church blessing felons and celebrating, what were termed, 'brigand masses', with monks and priests themselves involved in murder and extortion.[63] For Wales in the fifteenth and sixteenth century we have substantial evidence of monks and priests engaged in crime, with abbots relying on armed force to settle their disputes.

The Reformation undermined clerical privileges. In 1529 parliament, despite the opposition of the church, prohibited the payment of mortuary fees to the clergy, whereby fees were claimed for burial, including the apparel and property of the deceased.[64] In 1534 benefit of clergy, already severely restricted in England in 1515, was abolished in Wales for cases of petty treason, wilful murder, robbing of churches and chapels, house breaking, highway robbery and arson. Only senior churchmen were excluded from the ruling.[65]

Cromwell's stated objective was the 'utter destruction of seyntuaries' throughout the realm, especially ecclesiastical sanctuaries.[66] In August 1533 Thomas Crofte complained to Cromwell of the lordship of Wigmore: 'there is no worse rule kept within England nor Wales than is there kept'. The blame was placed on the abbot, who allowed the abbey's right of sanctuary to be abused by felons.[67] In February 1536 Lee wrote to Cromwell to 'please help the reformation of the club sanctuaries of Wigmore and Bewdley, as they have no privilege. Not a few thieves are received there'.[68] In January 1537 he reported to Cromwell that he had at Wigmore and elsewhere 'a great number of petty felons' whom he could not dispatch 'until we know the king's grace's pleasure for shiregrounds'.[69]

The commissioners who visited the monastic houses used evidence of disorder to justify their closure. At Monmouth Priory one of the investigating commissioners, Vaughan, expressed the intention to suppress it 'for it is the voice of the country that whilst you have monks there you shall have neither good rule nor good order'.[70] He also reported that other houses, including Tintern Abbey, were greatly abused. How far these charges were justified is difficult to determine.

The Welsh monasteries were already in a parlous state. The monasteries in the 1530s were systematically closed – Tintern, Whitland, Strata Florida, Aberconwy, Valle Crusis, Basingwerk, Margam, Neath, Cwm Hir, Ystrad Marchell and Cymer – their lands leased by the crown through the Court of Augmentation or sold off to local landowners.[71] In abolishing the monastic houses the crown was automatically removing their rights of sanctuary.[72]

The attack on traditional Catholic practices, shrines and pilgrimages was intense, with a prominent role in their destruction played by Richard Devereaux, bishop of Dover. In south Wales bishop Barlow of St. David's waged a ruthless campaign against 'Popish pageants'. In a letter to Cromwell in 1538, Barlow proposed that the see be transferred from St. David's to

Carmarthen. St. David's, he argued, was too remote, rarely visited except by 'vagabond pilgrims' and moreover 'evil disposed persons, unwilling to do good, may lurk there at liberty in secret without restraint' – indicating the problem associated with the abuse of sanctuary. St. David's he argued was too immersed in Popish tradition to be easily reformed. He doubted that St. David was ever in fact a historical personage. By transferring the see to a more populous centre he argued 'the Welsh rudeness would be soon framed to English civility'.[73]

Under Barlow's 'civilising' influence enormous damage was done to the fabric of the cathedral and its library was largely destroyed. The diocese reached its low point under his chosen successor, bishop Robert Farrar, who was burnt at the stake in Carmarthen in 1555 for gross abuses and heresy. Ellis Price, the Red Doctor, accompanied by his child concubine, toured north Wales destroying Catholic relics.[74] He was responsible for the removal of one of the most famous relics, the image of the warrior-saint Dervel Gadarn, from the church of Llandderfel, near Bala and, significantly, in the shadow of the bandit infested Berwyn mountains. Price asserted that the common people who visited the image in great multitudes, believed the relic could save them from damnation. The image was taken to London and burnt. A poem attached to the image prior to its burning declared that Welshmen believed that the image had 'Fetched outlaws out of hell'.[75]

CONCLUSION

The Acts of Union of 1536 and 1543 created a fundamentally new political, judicial and administrative framework for the governance of Wales. The integration of Wales into the English state transformed its status from a semi-colonial frontier zone into a province of the kingdom. In 1543, through the Subsidy Act, Wales was subject to central government taxation. The old divisions between shireground, palatine and marcher lands were ended. For T. B. Pugh the Acts of Union marked 'the ending of the Middle Ages in Welsh government'.[76] These measures were enacted from above as part of a fundamental recasting of the Tudor state. The reform commanded strong assent amongst sections of the Welsh gentry. This represented a major step to granting of full rights and equal citizenship to the Welsh as those enjoyed by the English.[77] In entrusting local government to the hands of the Welsh gentry Cromwell was acknowledging the changing balance of power in Wales and the demise of the marcher lords and the English burgesses. At the same time the policy, as Lee had warned, was fraught with difficulties.

If the Acts of Union commanded considerable support amongst the Welsh gentry, there is evidence of strong opposition to the attack on Catholicism and the destruction of the monasteries. The Reformation destroyed the position of the Catholic priests and the monks, who had served as two of the main leaders of medieval Welsh society. This was part of a 'revolution from above' which was also a 'cultural revolution' imposed from outside. It involved plunder and cultural vandalism on a vast scale, carried through by ecclesiastical gangsters such as Lee, Barlow, Farrar and Price in the name of the new state Protestant religion.

Here we might recall St.Augustine's wry distinction between a kingdom and a gang of bandits, or Chaucer's distinction between an outlaw and a tyrant. The great Florentine thinker Machiavelli, who died in 1527, so much admired by Thomas Cromwell, in his *Prince* declared that for the foundation of new states or the reform of existing states the most extreme methods may have to be countenanced. But he also noted that actions carried out on a large enough scale and with courage and audacity, cease to be judged as crimes, but come to be considered great acts of state, great political acts, to which normal moral judgement cannot be applied.[78]

11 Rowland Lee and the Council of the Marches

The major constitutional and legislative reforms introduced between 1536 and 1543, were accompanied by a ruthless policy to suppress lawlessness. This was instituted by bishop Rowland Lee, president of the Council of Wales and the Marches. Lee's correspondence with Cromwell, concerning the conduct and objectives of this campaign, although incomplete and patchy, provide a unique insight into the way the authorities perceived the problem. The campaign, which was unprecedented in its scope and intensity, extended through the Welsh Marches and the neighbouring English counties. What emerges is a picture of a society in which lawlessness is endemic, where the weakening of state authority produces an upsurge in disorder and violence. Lawlessness is presented in its many facets, in which representatives of all social classes were involved, where local magnates often protected and sponsored criminal acts.

Bishop Rowland Lee

In May 1534 Lee replaced Veysey as Lord President of the Council of Wales and the Marches. In June he was elected bishop of Coventry and Lichfield, which encompassed also the diocese of Chester. The son of the receiver-general in Berwick, Northumberland, he was educated at Cambridge, before making his career in the church. From 1528 onwards, under the patronage of Wolsey and Cromwell, he was active in suppressing many monasteries and priories. He was one of the first three bishops to take the new oath of consecration which recognised the king as the supreme head of the Church of England. He assisted in arranging the king's divorce in 1533, and officiated at his marriage to Anne Boleyn.[1]

Lee was a political bishop, who, until his appointment, had never preached from a pulpit. One of Cromwell's agents, Stephen Vaughan, wrote to his master denouncing Lee's appointment as bishop, describing him as 'an earthly beast, a mole, and an enemy of all godly learning … a papist, an idolater, and a fleshly priest'.[2] Cromwell, however, knew his man and was to employ Lee for his own purposes in putting Wales in order.

Under Lee the Council of the Marches was greatly strengthened and closely linked with the Privy Council as part of the system of 'conciliar government' so characteristic of the Tudor era. It sat permanently at Ludlow, which became the effective administrative capital of Wales. It also held sessions at Hereford, Bewdley, Shrewsbury, Worcester, Gloucester, Tewkesbury, Hartlebury, Bridgnorth, Oswestry and Wrexham. The Council had its own Court, which was responsible for overseeing the administration of justice, dealing with breaches of the peace and hearing civil actions.[3] The Council was also a co-ordinating military authority, responsible for putting the castles in order, maintaining coastal defences, organising musters and suppressing piracy.[4]

Lee's leading assistant was Sir Thomas Engelfield, Chief Justice of Chester, who had served on the Council since Henry VII's time. He was a more moderate and judicious figure than Lee, but Lee relied heavily on him. Writing to Cromwell in November 1535 he requested that Engelfield be commanded to return to his post at Ludlow, which he was loath to do on account of his poor health, the poor conditions and the dangers. Lee complained that, without his help, he was overwhelmed with work. In another letter he asked for a license for Engelfield to be allowed to carry a crossbow for his own security.[5]

Many prominent administrators and judges, a number with connections with the English border shires, were drafted on to the Council in this period. On his death Engelfield was replaced as Chief Justice of Chester and member of the council by Sir George Bromley. He in turn was succeeded by Sir Nicholas Hare. Other prominent judges appointed to the Council at this time were Sir William Sulyard and Roger Wigeston.[6] Thomas Holte, the king's attorney, played a prominent part in the work of the Council. Another of Cromwell's proteges Richard Rich, appointed Attorney General for Wales and the counties of Chester and Flint in May 1532, also played a key role in this campaign.[7]

Lee insisted on having disinterested individuals on the Council. In December 1536 he requested that Cromwell exclude John Scudamore from the commission, since he was 'a gentleman dwelling nigh the Welshery and kinned and allied in the same; through the bearing and bolstering of such gentlemen Wales was brought to that point that I found it in', adding 'he is unfit for this room'.[8] Lee encountered considerable obstacles in obtaining convictions of notorious felons, as royal and manorial officials flouted their duties and protected criminals; whilst the privilege of sanctuary was abused with the connivance of church authorities. Lack of cooperation between different lordships compounded the problem, with Lee himself, in one instance, having to intervene to extradite various sheep stealers and arsonists between Chirk and Powys.[9]

Lee's Campaign to Suppress Disorder

The campaign, entrusted to Lee, was at its most intense from 1534 to 1537. He travelled extensively through the marches, apprehending felons and holding cour. In December 1534 he recounted to Cromwell his experiences in Radnor and Presteign, and his plans to resume his campaign the following spring.

> I have been in Wales, at Presteign, where I was right heartily welcomed with all the honest of that parties [those parts], as Sir James Baskerville and many others, without any spears or other fashion as heretofore hath been used, as at large this bearer shall inform you. Which journey was thought much dangerous to some; but, God willing, I intend after Easter to lie one month at Presteign, even amongst the thickest of the thieves, to do my master such service as the strongest of them shall be afraid to do as heretofore, God willing. And from thence to Hereford, Monmouth, and Chepstow, for this summer, which will be costly. Wherefore, if the king's highness will have this country reformed, which is nigh at a point, his grace may not stick to spend one hundred pounds more or less for the same.[10]

Lee pursued a policy of judicial terror. Unlike Veysey he did not hesitate to use the death penalty.[11] He confronted directly the lawless elements on their own ground, freely using the gibbet, employing spies and informers, intimidating witnesses and using torture to exact confessions.[12] He was determined to demonstrate that there was now no area in Wales or the marches where the king's writ did not run, nor any subject, however mighty, who was above the law. Soon after his appointment Lee wrote to Cromwell triumphantly 'I hope you understand the good order begun in Wales so that thieves are afraid'.[13]

Lee in July 1534 wrote 'The Welshmen above Shrewsbury be very busy and as I am informed do burn diverse houses and do great displeasure which cannot be without the consent of some heads whose heads if I may know justly the truth I shall make ache'.[14] In November 1535 he reported that he and Engelfield had brought the 'parties [parts] about Shrewsbury into a reasonable stay touching such robberies and other malefacts as were there used'.[15]

The execution of large numbers of arrested felons had its effect. Lee reported to Cromwell, in June 1535, on 'the multitude of outlaws who are submitting themselves voluntarily without safe-conduct, which has not been heretofore'.[16] He declared:

Daily the outlaws submit themselves, or be taken. If he be taken he playeth his pageant. If he come and submit himself, I take him to God's mercy and the King's grace upon his fine.[17]

Engelfield informed Cromwell at this time:

Wales is very well amended, and, in comparison, there is very little thieving of cattle, chiefly because no one will buy them if they are suspected of being stolen. We are harder on the thieves than before, and compelled by policy to take the outlaws, so they now come in fast by themselves, desiring pardon, and we are obliged to take means to prevent them.[18]

Lee sought advice regarding the policy which should be adopted with murderers and rapists who surrendered themselves, noting that some of them 'have offered to take other thieves for their pardon, and for eight years to be of good disposition'.[19]

In the summer, after five weeks in Gloucester, Lee and Engelfield intended visiting Worcester and Bewdley and then moving to Shrewsbury 'to be nearer Wales, for though they are well reformed for the time, they will be sure to return to their unhappy demeanour except for fear'.[20] He was reluctant to absent himself from Wales to attend Parliament, 'considering the frailty of the inhabitants and their love of novelty'.[21]

One of the outlaws who surrendered himself at Bewdley in September 1535 was Robert Stradling of the powerful south Wales family of that name. In a dispute over the ownership of land, he had hired two Welsh murderers and thieves (Griffith and Lewes), and had himself killed one Guto Jenkins. Having been outlawed, he seized a balinger from Padstowe near Neath Abbey, and forced the mariners to set to sea for three weeks. He made his way to Milford Haven and then to Waterford, but returned to Wales on hearing of the proclamations against him. Lee advised that he be pardoned, for he was a 'proper man and a good archer and willing to pay a reasonable fine'.[22]

The ability of powerful figures to evade the law was illustrated also by the case of George Mathew, a gentleman of south Wales, who had received a licence exempting him from the statute prohibiting the levying of *cymhortha*. This licence, Lee estimated, would be worth a thousand marks to him. If such concessions were granted, Lee warned, the law would be rendered null and void.[23]

The protection and harbouring of felons by powerful patrons was a major problem. These patrons were referred to as 'resetters' (i.e.

receptors), although the term resetters was also applied to the felons thus protected. On the 6 January 1536 Lee requested that Cromwell send him the 'great rebel and outlaw' David Lloyd of Y Plas, Machynlleth, and his fellow John ap Richard Hocklington who had fled Wales, to escape 'my persecution' and sought sanctuary in Westminster. Lloyd had left sanctuary and had since 'stolen, burned and killed without mercy'. On his testimony Lee hoped to be able to hang another twenty 'resetters' who had similarly broken sanctuary. In this way Lee intended to 'end the maliciousness of these parts'. He also requested that Richard ap Howell, alias Sumner, who had murdered a man in Monmouth, be sent to him. He also protested against a commission of inquiry into the case of Thomas ap Griffith, who had been tried and sentenced by the Court at Ludlow:

> He has been a great resetter, and his two cousins are in the wood, and he has been admonished by me and the Council to bring in the thieves, his kinsmen. If the laws are to be stopped on the bare assertion of other thieves who are his kin, that he is a true man, when there is not a true man in that country, it will be folly in me to attempt reformation.[24]

In his next letter to Cromwell, dated 19 January, Lee acknowledged the receipt of David Lloyd, John ap Richard Hocklington and the murderer Richard ap Howell (Sumner). The two former they had 'sent to their trial according to Justice which tomorrow they shall receive' ('God pardon their souls'). Lee reported with relish the dipatch of four other prominent outlaws:

> … whereof three were alive and one slain brought in a sack trussed upon a horse, whom we have cause to be hanged upon the gallows here for a sign. Would God you had seen the fashion thereof. It chanced the same day to be market day here, by reason whereof three hundred people followed to see the said carriage of the said thief in a sack, the manner whereof had not been seen heretofore.[25]

As a result, Lee reported, 'all the thieves in Wales quake for fear'. There remained at large only one major outlaw, Hugh Durrant. In an important insight on popular attitudes to these felons, Lee added 'The takers of these outlaws were my Lord of Richmond's tenants of Cyfeiliog and Arwstli, most part for fear and money, and part of to have thanks, and partly to have some of their kindred discharged'.[26] Lee requested additional help in his work. The hatred that Lee's work had generated was acknowledged.

'Though the thieves have hanged me in imagination, I trust to be even with them shortly in very deed'.[27]

A number of individual cases caught Lee's attention. In March 1536 he reported to Cromwell that John Trevor, a gentleman of Oswestry, summoned to the Council for burning a man's house in Chirkland, had 'gone into the woods' with Robert ap Maurice, who had been condemned for 'resetting' David Lloyd o'r Plas.[28] The same year he indignantly complained that a certain Richard Lloyd of Welshpool, 'a gentlemen and a thief and a receiver of thieves' had attended a cattle sale dressed in a crimson doublet of velvet or satin – 'which does not become a thief'. The hanging of such a thief would cause another forty to beware. Lee requested that Lloyd, who had fled to London and sought sanctuary in St Martin's, should be returned to face trial, before the Court of the Marches.[29]

Ecclesiastical sanctuary posed a continuing problem for law enforcement. Lee and Engelfield wrote to Cromwell in 1536 regarding the murder of John ap David Griffith by John ap Morice Lloyd, whilst serving a letter from the Council on the latter. The murderer had sought sanctuary in Westminster and his friends were petitioning the king for a pardon.[30] The flight of felons to London to seek sanctuary suggests that they were often surprisingly mobile.

The maintenance of hired killers by powerful notables was an additional source of complaint. In October 1535 Lee reported to Cromwell that certain murderers, wearing the Duke of Richmond's livery, namely David, Edward and Morgan ap Dafydd ap Robert ap Jankyn, and Robert ap Dafydd Vaughan, were resident at Holt castle. He insisted that the matter be dealt with speedily.[31] Another case in 1540, concerned the murder of one Richard Johns of Elfael by David ap Howell, a hired killer. Lee noted the need in such cases 'if the law "cast" them, to make a spectacle to all others'. He proposed that the murderer's goods be used to pay for the repair of Ludlow castle, once relief for the widow was agreed.[32]

The lordship of Magor became a haven for murderers and robbers, protected by Walter Herbert (probably a bastard son of Sir Walter Herbert of Raglan) who was the Earl of Worcester's deputy in his capacity as the king's steward. Lee complained that the small lordship harboured twenty-three murderers (of whom three were members of the Herbert family and ten more were Walter Herbert's servants) and twenty-five notorious thieves, outlaws and robbers. They included Walter Herbert's friend, Miles Mathew of Llandaff, who allegedly had committed sacrilege by robbing Llandaff cathedral. In February 1533 the Herberts and their retainers sought to overawe and take over the town of Newport. This followed the seizure by the king's deputy-sheriff of the goods and chattels of one of

Walter Herbert's servants, John Sisyllt, who had murdered a man and then found a safe haven at Magor. In another incident Herbert's men had seized a Breton ship in the Severn estuary.[33]

Lee reported to Cromwell in October 1537 that 'Welshmen of the evil sort' regarded himself and the late Engelfield as veritable devils.[34] He advocated drastic measures, arguing that he should not be constrained by legal niceties. In a letter to Cromwell in July 1538 he declared 'if we should do nothing but as the common law will, these things so far out of order will never be redressed'. Lee's advice was approved. Cromwell, however, stressed that 'indifferent justice must be ministered to the poor and rich alike according to their demerits'. In this, Cromwell claimed, he wished to protect Lee from accusations of 'straightness and hard dealing'.[35]

Irked by these criticisms Lee replied 'I hear it noised in the Court that many poor thieves are executed here but no gentlemen thieves'. The impression, he argued, was mistaken; at one quarter session, in the presence of the Earl of Worcester and Lord Ferrers, he had hanged 'four of the best blood in the county of Shropshire'.[36]

In a rare reference to social and economic conditions that fostered lawlessness, Lee in November 1535 wrote to Cromwell that the scarceness of grain became daily more acute and caused more robberies.[37] One aspect of the problem of lawlessness referred to by Cromwell in a letter to Lee concerned the gypsies (commonly known as Egyptians or gupcians). The gipsies arrived in England early in the sixteenth century and many had located themselves in the Marches. Cromwell instructed Lee to take measures for their forcible deportation.[38] Lee's attentions were also drawn to the forging of coin on a large scale in the neighbourhood of Abergavenny.[39]

Lee put the Act of 1534 against the subornation of juries into effect. Sir Edward Grey writing to Cromwell in February 1536, concerning a case of murder noted the difficulty of finding an impartial and independent jury, adding that 'affection leads my countrymen many times to say more than the truth is'.[40]

In Cheshire the problem of lawlessness was compounded by factional struggles, such as the Cholmodleye-Mainwaringe feud. Within the county palatine and its borders over a two-year period more murders and manslaughters had been committed than in the whole of Wales.[41] In 1538 Lee informed Cromwell that a Cheshire grand jury 'had found murders to be man-slaughters and riots to be misbehaviours', for this 'lightness' its members had been imprisoned.

A Gloucestershire jury was 'ceessed good fines' for acquittal in a Welsh abduction case.[42] This involved one Roger Morgan of Wales, who with a great number of his company, had abducted a widow against her will from church. This was a crime common in Wales and the acquittal set a bad example. Lee warned 'if this be not looked upon, farewell all good rule'.[43]

Major trouble spots

In May 1537 Lee reported serious disturbances and a number of armed assemblies and that 'there was never more rioting in Wales than now'.[44] He noted that 'In Glamorganshire they ride daily' but the most serious disturbances had occurred in mid-Wales and in Denbigh, and involved some of the most eminent men in the districts, in open defiance of the instructions of the crown and of the Council of the Marches.[45]

'At Denbigh', Lee reported to Sir Thomas Engelfield in May 1537, 'an assembly none like many a years', which resulted from the attempt to enforce the new law prohibiting the bearing of arms at markets and fairs. William Jeordan, the king's messenger, served an order on John Salusbury of Llewenni, squire and steward of Denbigh, to enforce the order and to redress matters between the mainly English burgesses of the town and the Welsh 'foreigners'.[46] Salusbury reacted indignantly to this attempt to interfere in what he regarded as his jurisdiction, drawing his dagger at the king's messenger. The following day, three hundred Welshmen assembled at the market cross where their spokesman, wearing a hood, 'made their proclamation that the Welshmen were as free as Englishmen and that they should pay no stallage there'.[47] Those who were armed were taken prisoner to the castle. Otherwise the incident seems to have had no serious repercussions.

By the Act of 1536 the lordship of Mold and Hawarden was attached to the new county of Denbighshire. Mold, however, was too far from Denbigh and Ruthin and was rarely visited by the sheriff. The town became a haven for felons, with lawbreakers fleeing there from Flintshire to escape the sheriff of that county. In 1538 one Edward ap Rice with six companions seized the manor, which was the property of Lord Stanley, proclaiming 'I am heir of Moldesdale and of all Wales'. In 1542 the lordship of Mold and Hawarden were transferred from Denbighshire to Flintshire, in order to ensure more effective rule.[48]

A second trouble spot was mid-Wales, and the lordships of Arwystli, Cyfeiliog, Ceri, Cedewain and Clun. These former independent marcher lordships, now under crown control, gained an unrivalled reputation for disorder. Arwystli and Cyfeiliog were districts in which James ap Griffith ap Howell, the uncle of the executed Rhys ap Griffith, had influence. There is no proof of James ap Griffith's complicity in inciting the turmoil. Nevertheless, much of the disorder was directed at Lord Ferrers who had played a part in the downfall of Rhys ap Griffith. There may also have been contacts between James ap Griffith ap Howell and David Lloyd of Y Plas, Machynlleth, 'the great rebel and outlaw', who was executed in January 1536.[49]

From Monmouth, in June 1536, Lee complained that in Arwystli there had gathered together 'a certain cluster or company of thieves and murderers'.[50] In May 1537 he wrote to Cromwell explaining that 'The cause of disobedience in Arwystli is that my lords of Worcester and Ferrers do not agree on the stewardship there; no courts are kept nor commands of this house served'. The 'great sort of gentlemen of Arwystli' had met in unlawful assemblies to prevent Lord Ferrers from keeping the court. Many of these gentlemen had been brought before the Council and 'put in hold' with the porter. Cromwell instructed Lee to put Arwystli and Cyfeiliog in order, and certain 'dread letters' were sent by the king to the Earl of Worcester and Lord Ferrers to resolve their dispute.[51]

In May the Earl of Worcester and Lord Ferrers met the Lord President and the King's Commissioners and jointly undertook to restore peace and order in Arwystli and Cyfeiliog.[52] The Council determined that Lord Ferrers should hold the stewardship of the two lordships during the Earl of Worcester's life. However, disagreement again quickly erupted. Lee reported to Cromwell that the Earl had dismissed Lord Ferrers as steward and had removed his deputies, with the result that no courts were held. The Earl of Worcester's servants had broken into the gaol at Llanidloes.[53] Ferrers petitioned Cromwell to be restored to the stewardship.[54]

In December 1537 Lee assured Cromwell that Lord Ferrers would obey the order of the Council of Wales and the Marches.[55] The same month he acknowledged that there had been an improvement, but that there was a limit to what could be expected in this district:

> All in good order here (Shrewsbury) saving now and then a little conveying amongst themselves for a fat sheep or a bullock in Ceri, Cedewain, Arwystli and Cyfeiliog, which is impossible to be amended; for thieves I found them, and thieves I shall leave them.[56]

The problems in this district persisted. In October 1539 Lee reported that John Thomas ap Rice of Cedewain, one of Lord Ferrers' men, had committed manslaughter and fled. He urged Cromwell to stop any suit to the king for his pardon on the ground that to hang such a gentleman for such an offence would save twenty men's lives and do more good than to hang a hundred petty wretches.[57]

In other areas feuding families sought to gain advantage out of the new order. In north-west Wales the feud between Sir Richard Bulkeley on the one hand and Edward Gruffydd of Penrhyn and Dr William Glyn reached new heights. Bulkeley begged Cromwell to stop the Lord Chancellor from appointing any Justices of the Peace in north Wales' three shires on the ground that his rivals would give large sums for the office.[58] The feud led to a riot in Bangor cathedral during the holding of a consistory court. In February 1537 Bulkeley requested from Cromwell a king's letter forbidding the wearing of armour by Welshmen, except the king's officers, adding, 'without speedy remedy the King will have as much to do in Wales as ever he had in Ireland'.[59]

In spite of these local problems progress in quelling the disorders in Wales proceeded. In January 1537 Lee confidently reported that the Welsh were of 'as good towardness to do the king's grace service with as good intent as any of his subjects living'.[60] The birth of Prince Edward, in October of that year, Lee reported, occasioned an outburst of Welsh rejoicing. Lee, however, feared that the prospect of an amnesty for criminals might exacerbate the problem of lawlessness, remarking that 'a little the thieves begin to steal, trusting to white books by the birth of a Prince'. Nevertheless, Lee and Judge Sir John Pakington, Justice of north Wales, assured Cromwell that Wales and the Marches were never in better order.[61]

In the winter of 1537/8 Lee repeatedly assured Cromwell that the situation was calm; faction fights restricted; stealing, murders and riots few in number.[62] In September 1538 he reported 'In the marches and in Wales in the wild parts where I have been, is order and quiet such as is now in England'.[63] In 1539 he reported to Cromwell from Wigmore: 'All is quiet here, and never better'.[64] The situation in Cheshire and Gloucestershire, he reported, had also improved.[65]

Bandit fighters

William Gerard, a prominent member of the Council in Elizabeth's reign, described how Lee and his assistants, Engelfield, Bromley, Holt and others, traversed the marches and the Welsh borderland in this campaign to impose order:

(They) spent their whole time in travelling yearly either through Wales or a great part of the same, in causes touching civil government, and by that travel knew the people and found their disposition, favoured and preferred to office in their counties such, how mean of living soever they were, as they found diligent and willing to serve in discovering and trying out of offence and offenders. They likewise deforced and discountenanced others, of how great calling and possessions soever they were, being of contrary disposition … this stout bishop's dealing and the terror that the virtue or learning worketh in the subject when he perceiveth that he is governed under a learned Magistrate within three or four years generally so terrified them, as the very fear of punishment rather than the desire or love that the people had to change their Welshery wrought first in them the obedience they now be grown into. Then was this Council and their proceedings as much feared, reverenced and had in estimation of the Welsh as at this day the Star Chamber of the English.[66]

Gerard described Lee as 'stout of nature, ready witted, rough in speech, not affable to any of the Welshry, an extreme severe punisher of offenders, desirous to gain (as indeed he did) credit with the King and commendation for his service'.[67]

J. A. Froude, the Victorian historian, described Lee as 'The last survivor of the old martial prelates, fitter for harness than for bishop's robes, for a court of justice than a court of theology; more at home at the head of his troopers, chasing cattle stealers in the gorges of Llangollen, than hunting heretics to the stake, or chasing in the arduous defiles of controversy'.[68]

The work took its toll. Following the death of Justice Engelfield in September 1537 Lee wrote to Cromwell requesting assistance of 'Someone of learning and experience', promising 'to do my part while my rude carcass shall endure', but warning that without such help the 'commonwealth of these parts … will decay again'.[69] Sir Richard Herbert of Chirbury died on 23 March 1539. Lee lamented him as 'the best of his name that I know. I have as great loss of him as though I had lost one of my arms, in governing Powes, Kerry, Kedewen and Cloones land'.[70] His great grandson Lord Herbert of Chirbury described him as using wide powers in 'the East, West and North Wales' for the ruthless but 'just and conscionable' suppression of 'rebels, thieves and outlaws'.[71] Sir William Sulyard and Justice Porter both died the following year. Lee requested learned men to replace them, complaining that the burden of hearing cases daily for three parts of the year had 'brought many honest men to their death'.[72]

Lee himself died on 24 January 1543 at Shrewsbury and was buried at St. Chad's church. Of his manor house at Shotton, near Shrewsbury, it was said that the tradition of 'Bishop Rowland's summary justice long clung'.[73] Lee, according to a later chronicler, was the man 'who brought Wales being at his first coming very wild in good civility before he died who said he would make the white sheep keep the black'.[74]

The full scale of Lee's campaign against lawlessness can only be guessed at. A contemporary, the Welsh soldier-chronicler Ellis Griffiths, reported 'it is said that over five thousand men were hanged within the space of six years, among whom were certain men of the guard with the King's liveries on their backs'.[75] Although historians have expressed scepticism regarding this high figure, it should be borne in mind that Henry VIII's reign saw the use of capital punishment on an unprecedented scale.[76]

Lee's successors 1543–1558

In 1543 bishop Sampson of Lichfield succeeded bishop Lee as Lord President of the Council of Wales, and he was briefly followed by the Earl of Warwick. For the next fifteen years few documents survive concerning the Council's work.[77] The years 1549–1550 saw major public disorder in the west of England, prompted by widespread popular opposition to the attack on the power of the church, and exacerbated by economic hardships. Robert Ferrar, bishop of St. David's, warned of rebellion spreading from Cornwall and Devon to Wales, and urged that the laws against Catholics should not be too rigorously enforced 'for fear of tumult'.[78] In Shrewsbury the court term of Trinity was postponed until Michelmas 'because the gentlemen should tarry at home to keep the people in quiet from commotions'.[79]

The crisis allowed the Earl of Warwick to consolidate his position at Court, supplanting his rival Somerset. In 1549 Warwick employed two of his proteges, William Herbert and Lord Russell, to put down the rebels in the West Country. Herbert, with a force of one thousand Welsh soldiers, was involved in securing Exeter and in mopping up operations against the rebels. The Privy Council also dispatched him to Wales to 'prevent the inconstant dispositions of the commons'. In 1551 the Spanish ambassador reported, although his grasp of geography may have been at fault, on the successful crushing of peasant rebellions in England, near Windsor (?), and in Wales, which had been caused by food shortages and the debasement of the coinage.[80]

From 1550 to 1558, under Warwick's patronage, William Herbert served as Lord President of the Council of Wales, the first Welshman to hold the post. In 1551 he was made first Earl of Pembroke and rewarded with extensive estates in Wales and the West Country.[81] Of Pembroke it was said that he knew only Welsh well. A bony, red haired man with a sharp eye and a stern look he served under four monarchs. He had assisted in the suppression of the monasteries, and played a key role in the high politics of the time. His fellow countryman and protege, Sir John Price, held the secretaryship from 1540 to 1555.

Herbert in 1554 participated in putting down the Wyatt rebellion against Queen Mary, and was temporarily replaced as President of the Council of Wales by Nicholas Heath, bishop of Worcester.[82] In 1555 he was re-appointed Lord President of the Council of the Marches but was again removed in 1558 when the Queen insisted that his absence from the Marches was allowing disorder to increase. The post was then briefly occupied by Gilbert Bourne, bishop of Bath and Worcester, and by Lord Williams of Thame.[83]

In the 1550s a new wave of repression was instituted, with the Privy Council issuing instructions to the Council of Wales for the apprehension of murderers and felons.[84] This campaign appears to have been at its height in 1554–5. In 1555 the Privy Council issued instructions to the Council outlining what appears to be a programme for the execution, rather than the imprisonment, of felons on a mass scale. It declared: 'and as touching their motion to have 3,000 of such notable outlaws and felons as they complain of to be otherwise bestowed in the King and Queen's service, they are willed to root them out according to justice, for as much as the Queen's Majesty hath no occasion elsewhere to place them'.[85]

Sir Hugh Paulet, Vice President of the Council under Lord Thame, waged a vigorous campaign against crime and disorder, the intensity of which was only exceeded by that instituted by Lee. In a memorandum he lamented that crime was going unchecked, that *arddel* and *cymhortha* were still practiced. He singled out Monmouthshire as a cause of particular concern, because of the empanelling of partial juries. He sought permission for the Council itself to try murderers and felons from the county.[86]

CONCLUSION

Lee's policies were applied in Wales and the border English counties with equal severity. He was under pressure from Cromwell to apply the policy impartially to rich and poor alike. To assist him in this work he sought the support of local notables and gentry, and thus was able to bind them to the central government. These measures were not applied to Wales and the Marches uniquely. In 1539 special commissions were dispatched to Hampshire, Wiltshire, Somerset, Devon and Cornwall to enforce order through a ruthless policy of execution of felons.[87] The policy was to eliminate the most prominent wrong doers, cow others into submission and to identify the government with the interests of the law abiding. For Lee the policies were justified as part of a campaign to tame these wilder regions, and to impose what was construed as 'civility'.

Lee's campaign demonstrated the dramatically increased power of the

Council of Wales and the Marches, and its ability to pursue a policy of judicial terror, backed up by its own courts, prisons and its own armed forces. This underlined the seriousness with which the authorities regarded the problem of lawlessness in Wales. The public reaction in Wales to this policy is more difficult to assess. Lee's own comments on the attitude of the tenants of Arwystli and Cyfeiliog may be symptomatic of the mixed and sometimes ambivalent attitude to both the law-breakers and to the law-enforcers. In the following decades demands were renewed for a return to these methods in governing Wales and the marches. The administrative model of the Council and the methods that Lee employed were seen as having wider application on the Anglo-Scottish border and in Ireland.

12 Conduct and Consciousness

Through the sixteenth century Welsh society underwent major changes. The new structures of government at the level of the shires created unprecedented opportunities for office holding. The struggle for precedence, economic power and office amongst the gentry was intensified and constituted a dominant feature of Welsh life throughout the Elizabeth age. New economic opportunities brought changes in employment and aspirations. The Renaissance and the new learning brought its liberating but corrosive influence to bear on Welsh culture. The Reformation brought also profound changes, and an attempt to extirpate the Catholic faith. Amongst the population at large older attitudes and traditions proved more resilient. Here we shall examine these contradictory processes and their significance for the way in which the problem of law and order was perceived.

Some contemporaries sought to identify the social and economic causes of lawlessness and disorder in England, which had also some bearing on the situation in Wales. Sir Thomas More in *Utopia*, written in 1516, identified as a prime cause of lawlessness, the large numbers of 'idle retainers' maintained by the nobility, and the large number of disbanded soldiers who were left destitute and without profession. Public disorder was further exacerbated by the growing divide between rich and poor, accelerated by enclosures, with sheep devouring men, with the expulsion of peasants off the land now turned into sheep-walks, and the creation of a rootless multitude of vagabonds.[1] Holinshed the Elizabethan chronicler believed that the persistent offenders were often 'rogues', that is to say able-bodied men without employment. He identified two other categories of offenders: the 'young shifting gentlemen which oftentimes do bear more port than they are able to maintain' and the 'serving-men whose wages cannot suffice so much as to find them breeches'.[2]

THE SOCIAL ORDER

By the second half of the sixteenth century the main structure of medieval Welsh society had been transformed. The Acts of Union clipped the powers of the Marcher lords. Under the Tudors the new Welsh gentry came into its own, consolidating its land holdings, benefiting from the sale and lease of former monastic and crown property. Money made in London in trade, commerce, political service, the Church and the professions was used to enlarge family estates. The Elizabethan age saw the entry of the descendants of this strata into the highest levels of English social, economic and cultural life (Robert Cecil, Hugh Middleton, Roger Williams, John Dee, Thomas Traherne, George Herbert). This was the class which dominated local politics and administration as MPs, sheriffs and JPs. Below were the lesser squires and tenant farmers. At the base of the pyramid lay the landless labourers. Bond labour effectively disappeared.[3]

Although a very large number of Welsh families claimed gentry rank, very few of them commanded the wealth of their English equivalents. The gentry still jealously guarded social pedigree, although it was increasingly penetrated by new families. Good background (*o dras bonheddig*) still counted, but the style of the gentry changed. The mark of nobility (*boneddigeiddrwydd*) became more a matter of 'courtesy, humanity and civility', whilst the older codes of behaviour, based on ancient lineage and martial valour declined. The replacement of *cyfran* (partible inheritance) by primogeniture provided the basis for the consolidation of landholding. It also forced the younger sons of the gentry into seeking employment elsewhere. The impoverished gentry were seen as a major source of disorder. Whilst some found occupations in trade, commerce and the professions, others continued to find employment in the retinues of Welsh and English magnates.

The transforming effect of education on public attitudes, particularly that of the gentry, and its role in creating public servants fitted for administration was widely stressed by contemporaries.[4] For the sociologist Norbert Elias the growing concern with 'civility' and 'gentility' of this age in Europe generally reflected the development of important social codes and manners of self-restraint. The checks to lawlessness were not just those imposed by the law, but derived also from these new codes of social behaviour and of individual self-regulation.[5]

This new concern with personal conduct, manners and etiquette was reflected in the enormous influence of the work of the Italian courtier, diplomat and writer Castiglione, *Il Cortegiano* (The Courtier). Published in Venice in 1528 it was translated into various European languages, including the English traslation by Sir Thomas Hoby *The Courtyer* in 1561.

Elias' depiction of the growth of 'civility' as regards to Wales must, however, be qualified. Despite the frequent protestations concerning the advance of 'civility' and 'gentility', these ideals were far from universally realised. Traditional values of obligation to kin and community were undermined. How far this led to groups and communities developing a respect for the rights and properties of neighbouring groups and communities, whether English or Welsh, is more difficult to determine.

But the concept of 'civility' has itself to be handled with caution. The terms itself was politically loaded. The term 'civility' often implied as its opposite not 'incivility', but rather implied an opposition between civilisation and barbarism, with the English depicted as civilised and the Welsh as barbarous. With the revolution in the religious life of the people Puritanism was equated with civilisation and learning and Catholicism with barbarism and superstition. From the standpoint of educated Welsh Catholics this was a distinction which was pregnant with political significance. Given the destruction wrought on Catholic culture and learning in Wales, and the unbridled rapacity of the new Tudor gentry the very notion of 'civility' was highly debatable.

Humphrey Llwyd noted a new application to learning amongst the Welsh through the universities and Inns of Court as a means to secure office and social advancement.[6] Richard Vaughan, bishop of Chester, petitioned St. John's College, Cambridge, for a scholarship for his son John in order 'that he may prove fit for civil company and for some purpose in the commonweal...'[7] Sir John Wynn' noted how the north Wales towns had prospered since his grandfather's time, and how in Caernarfon 'Civility and learning' had flourished. Sir John also stressed how he was counselled as a young man to bridle his hot temper, which had been the occasion of heated conflicts.[8]

William Harrison suggested that the Welsh were more addicted to litigation than anyone else.[9] A contemporary Welsh poem, 'The poem of the Hen and the Awl' (*Cywydd yr Iâr ar Mynawyd*) satirised the senselessness of pursuing litigation even in petty disputes.[10] In this period 'feuds took refuge within the law'. Morus Kyffin wrote of the need to propagandise the gospel amidst the Welsh, so as to diminish the hatred, jealousy, treachery and wicked intentions so prevalent amongst them. He condemned the widespread attempts, through litigation, and false accusations, to seize the property and land of others.[11]

Richard Davies, bishop of St. David's, scathingly criticised the new social order in Wales. There was nothing but 'Crime, theft, disunity, deceit, falseness and oppression' (*Trais, a lladrad, anundon, dichell, ffalster a ttraha*). Wales was engulfed by a wave of self-seeking, whereby public office became a means of self-enrichment and of despoiling one's neighbour, where learning and knowledge of the law was a means to plunder others, where gentlemen's halls were turned into sanctuaries of thieves (*ceir neuadd y gwr bonheddig yn noddfa lladron*).[12]

The first elected Welsh MPs took their seats in 1542. In Parliament the Welsh members played an undistinguished role, suggesting how far the principality lacked any coherence or clear political self-identity.[13] The rapacity of the Welsh gentry at home contrasted markedly with their docility in national politics. Elections provided a further field of conflict between rival families in the localities. In the remoter, economically backward regions gentry backwoodsmen found it difficult to adapt to the new age. The depressed gentry provided in these regions the focus of much criminal activity. Even in relatively prosperous regions, such as the south west of Wales, the gentry were distinguished by a certain inertia.[14]

Wales' political incorporation into England was linked also to its economic incorporation, through the development of the cattle trade and the cloth industry.[15] The emergent capitalist economic order deepened class divisions. The gentry, enriched through the plunder of monastic lands, enclosure and estate consolidation, and the perks of public office, were increasingly isolated from the common mass of the people, for whom impoverishment, and vagabondage became a common experience. The new social order was legitimised by the new state religion, but had to be bound together by ever more repressive social legislation.

From 1485 onwards Wales passed increasingly from a system of military-political control, to one of administrative-political governance. This was reflected particularly in the decline and abandonment of the castle. Leland's *Itinerary* for the 1530s provides clear evidence of this trend. Out of 72 castles in south and east Wales, twenty-seven (37.5 per cent) remained in normal use, roughly the same proportion as in the south-east of England. Glamorgan, Powys and Shropshire headed the list for all counties in England and Wales for the highest number of abandonments. The castles at Hereford and Shrewsbury were in poor repair. The castles in north Wales were also in decline. Garrisons ceased to be maintained in them in the early seventeenth century.[16] Alongside the decline of the castle went the neglect of the walled fortifications of the towns.

The Reformation encountered no organised resistance in Wales, although it provoked much resentment. A strong attachment to the Catholic faith persisted. One bard equated Protestantism with English religion. Others embraced the new religion and wrote verses lauding the translators of the Bible into Welsh – the Protestant churchmen such as William Morgan, Richard Davies and Thomas Davies. Selections from the Bible were published as early as 1551 in *Kynniver Llith a Ban*. St.John chapter 10, verse 7, on Jesus as the Good Shepherd, in which all earlier false prophets are compared to bandits and thieves, must have had a special resonance.[17]

Notwithstanding the enormous effort undertaken by the state to uproot and destroy the Catholic faith, and to intimidate the populace into conforming, the old faith in Wales proved remarkably tenancious. In a report from the 1570s the Welsh were described as 'very devout', frequenting pilgrimages and attending the holy wells, still strongly conscious of their own history, proud of their past and their country, still much influenced by the bards.[18]

The survival of 'popish heresy' in Wales remained a cause of concern, with accusations of religious ignorance and superstition, and the people framing their lives in 'looseness, licentiousness, contention and other such like'. The poor quality of the clergy was in part held responsible. In Wales the holding of fairs on Sundays remained widespread, a practice long since banned in England.[19] For Welsh Puritans, like John Penry, Wales was a country in need of urgent missionary work.

Puritan zealots regarded the Welsh as sunk in ignorance, and in as much need of salvation as the 'savages' of the New World. In 1622 the Puritan educational theorist John Brinsley counted the Welsh with the Irish, Virginians and Bermudans as ignorant and in need of more schooling in English, Latin and 'other tongues':

> the more easily thereby to reduce them to a loving civility with loyal and faithful obedience to our Sovereign, and good law, and to prepare a way to pull them from the power and service of Satan that they may jointly submit themselves to Jesus Christ.[20]

The persecution of Welsh Catholic recusants, and particularly of the Welsh seminary priests who fled to the Continent, saw the full power of the state being deployed against potential subversives. Leading Welsh Catholic ecclesiastics and intellectuals such as Morus Clynnog, Gruffydd Roberts and Siôn Dafydd Rees found a congenial spiritual home in Italy. The execution of Richard White in October 1584 marked the most dramatic part of this campaign. The number of martyrs in Wales was small, indicating a willingness to bend before the power of the state.[21]

Thieves, assassins, serving men and soldiers

Wales's reputation for lawlessness fostered the stereotyped picture of the Welsh as querulous, quick tempered, haughty, proud of their pedigrees, indolent, poor and dishonest. A Venetian diplomat in 1531 noted 'The Welshman is sturdy, poor, adaptable to war and sociable'.[22] In 1551 another foreign observer noted that the Welsh were little inclined to cultivate their lands, but were much given to theft (*a deiti ai latroncinii*).[23] Polydore Vergil in his *History of England* in 1551 repeated the accusation, noting that young Welshmen went 'roving abroad and wandering, molest as well their own natives as also other with their theft and robberies'.[24]

Andrew Boorde, the popular poet, described the Welsh as loving, kind hearted, faithful and virtuous, but noted also 'there be many of them the which be light fingered and loveth a purse'. A view underlined in his doggerel verse:

I am a Welshman a do dwell in Wales
I have loved to serche boudgets and looke in males;
I love not to labour not to delve nor to dyg;
My fingers be lymed lyke a lyme twyg;
And whereby ryches I do not greatly set,
Syth all hys fysshe that commeth to the net.[25]

Welshmen continued to find employment as liveried retainers in the households of English magnates. In 1539 Sir John Huddlestone complained that his servant had been murdered in Cheltenham by the liveried followers of Sir John Bridges, declaring that it was common practice for men like Bridges to bring 'lyeth' (light) fellows out of Wales to commit such acts.[26] Sir John Wynn of Gwydir stated that Sir Edmund Knivett, of Buckname castle, Norfolk 'retained a great many of our country gentlemen, on whom it was thought he did most rely for his safety'.[27]

Humphrey Llwyd, with characteristic exaggeration, described his compatriots thus:

They be somewhat impatient of labour, and overmuch boasting of the nobility of their stock, applying themselves rather to the service of noblemen than giving themselves to the learning of handicrafts. So that you shall find but few noblemen in England but that the greater part of their retinue are Welshmen born.[28]

The life of a liveried serving man are captured in a poem '*Carol 'Duwke Hunfrey*'' by Hugh Gryfie, describing a life of indolence, carousing in London's taverns, wenching, play-going at Bank Side, purse-cutting and highway robbery.[29]

As in the preceding century large numbers of Welsh soldiers were recruited to serve in the English army in France. In September 1515 Mountjoy, one of the captains in Calais, warned Wolsey that if the many thieves amongst the English and Welsh soldiery were not pardoned they might go over to the enemy.[30] In the 1520s further serious disturbances amongst the Welsh soldiers, involving conflicts with the local inhabitants, riots and threats of mutiny, resulted in demands that the worst offenders be executed.[31] In 1585/6 a contingent of Welsh soldiers, together with some of the leading gentry of north Wales, served in the earl of Leicester's campaign in the Low Countries.[32] The exploits of Sir Thomas Morgan and Sir Roger Williams in these conflicts were widely celebrated. Between 1594 and 1602 2.9 per cent of the estimated population of Wales were called up for service in Ireland. The musters of this period provided ample opportunity for local notables for extortion. It provided an opportunity also to empty the gaols.[33] In 1598 complaints were voiced that some of the Welsh soldiers in Ireland were unreliable and that some had defected to the Earl of Tyrone.[34]

The masculine and martial qualities were still lauded. The bard Thomas Prys revelled in his exploits as a pirate and he sang the praises of soldiers and men of action such as Thomas Owen and Ellis Vychan.[35] Edwart Konwy wrote his poem 'In Praise of War' (*Canmol Rhyfel*), recounting how he preferred to follow the trumpet and drum on the continent rather than languish at home listening to the plaintive strains of the harp.[36] Other poems recount the difficulties of the life of the destitute serving man and soldier.[37]

The decline of the bardic profession

In the sixteenth century the bardic order was thrown into crisis. The old Welsh culture struggled to fend off the challenge posed by English culture. Increasingly defensive, the bards attempted to protect their position. The Caerwys Eisteddfod of 1525 sought to tighten the conditions of admission into the bardic profession and to lay down strict rules on versification and metre. These measures failed to arrest the decline.

The patronage provided by the church declined, and the dissolution of the monasteries in the 1530s was a serious blow, with Lleision Caradoc, Owain Gwynedd and Siôn Brwynog lamenting their loss.[38] Gentry patronage of the bards also declined, drawing strong protests from bards such as Siôn Mawddwy and Siôn Tudur.[39] Notwithstanding these reverses the popular verse and ballads of the sixteenth and seventeenth century are distinguished often by vibrancy, wit and creativity. The picaresque themes are developed particularly by bards such as Richard Hughes and Thomas Prys of Plas Iolyn, with their delight in the underside of society and its rough humour.

In 1567 the Council in the Marches authorised another eisteddfod at

Caerwys to put the bardic profession in order. The bards allegedly constituted an 'intolerable multitude within the principality of north Wales' and were the cause of 'shameless disorders'.[40] The eisteddfod was to licence the bards, excluding from their number 'vagrant and idle persons naming themselves minstrels, rhymers and bards', with the aim 'to return to some honest labour and due exercise … upon pain to be taken as sturdy and idle vagabonds'. These complaints reflected not so much a concern about protecting the bardic profession, as a concern regarding the potentially subversive influence of the bards. In 1594, at a time of acute social crisis, the complaint was again made that 'bad, unsober, undiscreet and unhonest persons' had entered the profession.[41]

Office holding

The Acts of Union greatly enlarged opportunities for office holding amongst the Welsh gentry. This itself divided opinion amongst the bards. One current condemned the new passion amongst the *uchelwyr* for office. Tudur Aled lauded the valour and sagacity of Meredydd ap Ieuan ap Robert of Dolwyddelan and praised him for not holding office. In a famous admonitory poem to Hwnffre ap Hywel of Ynys y Maengwyn, in which he tried to reconcile him and his kinsman, he lamented the dishonesty of the age, the craving of office and the ensuing hatreds and jealousies:

Mae, oes heddyw, am swyddau,
Megis hyn, in ymgashau.[42]

The bard William Cynwal repeatedly inveighs against office holding, since it bred abuses and oppressions and led to the *uchelwyr* losing the respect of their community, whilst the true office of notables was to serve God. Lewys Môn and Siôn Brwynog echoed these sentiments. Edmwnd Prys in the next century denounced the 'lawlessness of the mighty' (*anllywodraeth y cedyrn*) who used office for self-enrichment, through enforced taxes, *cymhorthas*, enclosure, peculation and nepotism.

Nevertheless, the Acts of Union in opening up offices to the Welsh *uchelwyr* led to a scramble for public office, prompting one commentator to note

For the nature of a Welsh man is for to bear office and to be in authority. He will not let to run through the fire of hell to sell and give all that he can make of his own and of his friends for the same, and also they be very tycle of themselves.[43]

The poetry of the second half of the sixteenth century, however, reflects a new emphasis on the importance of public office, and the duties and obligations of public life. It is rich in its references to the *uchelwyr* as office holders, as justices of the peace (*iustus hedd*), sheriffs, custos rotulorum etc. The bards present an idealised picture of the strong, resolute governors, incorruptibles, who cherish those in their care. They are the wise justices, dispensing the law, golden pillars against rebellion (*aur biler rhag rebeliwns*) and defenders of the country from foreign invasion.[44]

The new political conformism of the gentry was reflected in what J. Gwynfor Jones has called the 'cult of royal sovereignty', as seen in the Welsh poems addressed to Elizabeth I as 'Sidanen'.[45] Siôn Tudur lauds her as the powerful ruler of the realm, its protector from foreign foes, a staunch guardian and defender of the Protestant faith, and the embodiment of just rule and order. He advises her to use the sword of justice against outlaws and traitors, against whom no mercy should be shown.

Troi'r cledd a'i rinwedd oedd raid
At herwr, neu draeturiaid;
Os bradwyr ynys Brydain
Na by rhwydd i neb o'r rhain.[46]

BARDS, GENTRY AND BANDITS

The high expectations which the bards had entertained of the new Tudor monarchy were not fulfilled, and this sense of disappointment found expression in their poetry. Lewis Glyn Cothi in a poem to Richard Herbert, constable of Aberystwyth castle, pictured the continuing miseries of his country:

Mae bywyd trist, mae byd trwm
Meibion a gweision oedd gaeth
Myned weithion maent waethwaeth.[47]

Life is sad, the world is burdensome
Men and their followers were enslaved
Things have become ever worse.

He called upon Herbert to follow his father's course and with his sword to tame the restless land and to restore law and order throughout Wales. Lewis Môn praised the resolve of Sir Richard Herbert in fighting bandits, imploring him to search them out with his axe, to vent his fury on the outlaws and to bring them to justice before the duke (*Dwys i herwyr dy soriant; Dwg hwy i'r iawn, i'n duc yr ant*).[48] Tudur Aled stressed his ferocious dealing with bandits, depicting him as a mighty wolf (*blaidd cadarn*) who stood with the might of the law (*Wrth rym y gyfraith yr oedd*).[49]

Iorwerth Fynglwyd from Glamorganshire celebrated Sir Walter Herbert as a ruthless suppressor of outlaws, who strung up those captured from tall trees (*Oged herwyr dan goed hirion*). He praised the late Morgan Mathau as a canny fighter of bandits, noting that he had died but not at their hands (*Ni bu o'r gwylliaid wynebwr gallach: Ef air heb wylliaid i feirw bellach*). Sir William Bawdrem hated deceit and gave no peace to the robbers. The bard received the news of Ieuan Gethin's death by an outlaw's spear as though the shaft had pierced his own ears (*Gwae herwr ddwyn gwayw hiraeth: Gloes drwy fy nau glust yr aeth*). The bard himself was once imprisoned by Mathew Craddock of Swansea but was protected by Rhys ap Siôn of Glyn Nedd. He lauded Rhys' work in protecting the virtuous and in pursuing thieves from their haunts. (*Y cywir a gaiff hirwg. A'r lleidr a droir o'r lle drwg*).[50]

Another Glamorganshire bard, Rhisiart ap Rhys, in an elegy to Siôn Stradling of Merthyr Mawr, noted his ruthless suppression of banditry:

Maneg las a min ei gledd
A dynn wylliaid dan allwedd. [51]

Blue gauntlet at sword's point
He places bandits under lock.

The bard also paid tribute to the charity shown by his subject to the weak and defenceless.

Lewis Môn, the Anglesey bard, specialised in praise-poems to the gentry of north Wales. Of Tomas Salbri of Lleweni, who was knighted in 1497, he says, that he was the only one who could rule Ruthin. Whereas in the past it was impossible to gain a day's respite, he could now traverse north Wales from the Dee with his purse on a pole without fearing molestation by outlaws. He praised Thomas ap Rhys of Newtown for pursuing outlaws like a thunderbolt, and restraing those easily corrupted (*Ymlid herwyr mal taran,/A 'mogel rhoi magl ar wan*).[52] Lewis Môn stressed the success of the campaigns against bandits and urged his patrons to pursue them with still greater determination. He advised Edward Gray, Lord of Powys, on his coming of age, to surround himself with strong men who spoke the native tongue, and who were ready to deal with bandits and

fugitives.[53] Lewis Môn's testimony concerning the virtues of his patrons
has to be treated with much circumspection, as witnessed by his lavish
praise of the notorious Sir William Griffiths, chamberlain of north Wales.
(pp. 139–9 above)

Tudur Aled, the last outstanding Welsh bard of the middle ages, was a
pillar of the bardic establishment and was closely tied to the *uchelwyr*. He
welcomed the peace brought by the Tudor dynasty but feared it might be
transient. In one of his poem he describes human history as a wheel in
which Peace, Wealth, War and Poverty succeed one another in an endless
cycle.[54] The role of his patrons in fighting lawlessness is a recurrent theme
in his poetry. He praised Robert Salbri the elder, of Llanrwst, neighbouring
Ysbyty Ifan, for his part in taming the 'wild land' (*y tir gwyllt*) around
Ruthin.:

Bid heddwch. Heb oed dyddiaw
Blinder oedd, yn y blaen, draw;
Y tir gwyllt, natur gwalltan
Heddychol yw heddyw, achlân;
Holl Ruthun, hyll yr athoedd
Nes dy gael, anosteg oedd;
Od egyr drws dy gaer draw,
Nid rhaid i'r gweiniaid gwynaw.[55]

There is peace. Not long since
Tiresome it was in the valley yonder;
The wild land, the fiery temperament.
Today it is peaceful, be praised;
All of Ruthin, it was hideous
Until you came, all was disorder;
But whilst your castle door is open
The weak need not complain

He lamented the death of Dafydd ap Hywell ap Gruffydd ap Ednyfed to
the fight against banditry.

Caewyd wybr y coed obry
Colled fawr rhag gwylliaid fu;
Doed herwyr hyd y tiroedd,
Yn i oes ef, anos oedd;
Pob siwrnai, pawb sy arnun
E fu ddydd na feiddia un![56]

The forest sky is closed above him
A great loss in the fight against bandits;
Outlaws infested the lands,
In his age, it was more difficult,
Every journey, everybody is on the lands
There were days no one would dare.

Many of Tudur Aled's patrons and subjects of his praise poems had won
renown as bandit-fighters. They were hated by the bandits but received the
praise of the bards. Lewys Môn and Guto'r Glyn praised Sir Thomas Salbri
of Lleweni as a bandit-fighter as did Tudur Aled who recounts the joy of
outlaws and lawless magnates at the news of his death:

Llawen yw cedeirn llawn hocediaeth
O'i rym y dygynt rwymedigaeth;
A llawer eraill, o'u herwriaeth,
A gyrchai o'r coed i garchar caeth.[57]

Happy are the mighty ones full of deceit
Through his power they were in bondage
And many more from outlawry
He took from the woods to a secure gaol.

In his praise poem to William ap Siôn Edward of Chirk Castle (Y Waun)
Tudur Aled recounts his prowess as a bandit-fighter, just as Guto'r Glyn
and Gutun Owain sang the praise of his father Siôn Edward.

Caterwen, lle caut aros
Carcharu wnaut cyrchwyr nos
....
Cur ladron, câr lywodraeth;
Cadw o Geiriawg hyd Gorwen
Curas a dart, corsed wen.[58]

Mighty oak, which afforded us shelter
You imprisoned the night stalkers
....
Beat the robbers, love the law;
Protect the lands from Ceiriog to Corwen
With curiass, javelin and white corselet.

The district from Corwen to Ceiriog, Edernion, it might be noted, was precisely that region bordering onto the Berwyn mountains. Tudur Aled tells how Siôn ap Meredudd of Trefor seized traitors and took them to the Prince of Wales' court at Ludlow to be tried and topped (*Dwyn bradwyr, dyn brau ydoedd. At y prins, a'u topio'r oedd*). He was a 'hawk', a ruthless suppressor of lawlessness who stood with the might of the law (*Wrth rym y gyfraith yr oedd*).[59]

Even with Tudur Aled, whose attitude towards bandits is quite clear, there are poems which present difficulties. In a poem 'Where a Death-Thief climbed' (*Lle Dringodd Lleidr o Angau*) he depicts the death of Hywel ap Siencyn ab Ierweth, who evidently led a bandit existence, as an adventurer and man of action whose death was grieved in his native region of Dolgellau. He depict the grove where outlaws (foresters) found shelter:

Llwyn oeddim mwn lle neu ddau
Lle dringodd lleidr o angau
Fforestwyr a choedwyr chwyrn
A gur coed, a gwŷr cedyrn.[60]

A grove which afforded me a hiding place
Where a dying thief sought shelter
Ferocious foresters and woodmen
Who strike down trees and great men.

In such untamed localities such adventurers could still be seen as heroes. Gruffydd Hiraethog, the bard of the Mostyn family of Flintshire, rejoiced in the beauty and tranquillity of his native Tegaingl, whose groves did not breed or shelter robbers (*Ni feidr fagu lleidr mewn llwyn*). His antipathy to the English was strong. He complemented his patrons who were not tainted with English blood (*Nid oes isel waed Saeson/Na deifr waed o fewn dy fron*) He celebrates the role of his patrons in preserving order. Edward Stanley, constable of Harlech castle, is noted for suppressing banditry (*curo gwylliaid*). Siôn Prys of Eglwyseg is a fighter of bandits (*Herw wylliad swrth hir llid Siôn*). Cadwaladyr Morys of Foelas is celebrated as a pure Welshman (*Kymro gloyw*) who hates and seeks out the robbers (*Kas wr lladron ai kessiaw*). Howel Fychan is a doughty hunter of outlaws (*helfab herwyr*). Cadwaladr ap Rhobert of Rhiwlas defends the true and upright (*gwir a chowir*) but strings up the robbers from the trees (*lladron llowerion preiffion ymhen pob prynn*). In spite of the efforts of such individuals he noted that disorder sometimes went out of control (*Aeth anhrefn weithian rhyfawr*).[61]

These praise-poems to members of the Welsh gentry as fighters against the lawless could be repeated almost endlessly.[62] However, even those bards who sang the praise of the new generation of *uchelwyr* office-holders could voice reservations concerning the way the society was evolving. Bards lamented how the calls of office and the opportunities of life in England drew many of the *uchelwyr* away from their own native communities, leaving communities bereft of effective leadership and protection.

One of the most critically minded bards of this period was Siôn Tudur who in poems such as 'The Bustle of the World' (*Bustle y Byd*) deplores the corruption of his age. He censured the corrupt officials, the usurers, gamblers and the persecutors of the poor, all of whom, he asserted, would be denied entry into heaven. In his 'Poem to the Officials' (*Cywydd i'r Swyddogion*) he denounced the *uchelwyr* who were too cowardly to follow a military career and sought office instead. He attacked the grasping, corrupt officials (*aflan swyddwyr*) who oppress the poor. He railed at the hypocrites who presented themselves as upright upholders of the law but who were the first to break it themselves for personal gain (*Cyfraith rhont, caf warth i'r rhain/A honni'i thorri'u hunain*).[63]

Siôn Tudur, like Siôn Cent a century earlier, severely censured his fellows bards (*Cywydd i'r Beirdd*) who demeaned themselves by flattering in their verse the unworthy and unscrupulous. He lamented the degeneration of the language, the decline of patronage and the loss of cultural vitality. Whilst the *uchelwyr* scrambled after office, the 'office' of the bard had lost its status and dignity (*Swydd y bardd y sydd heb urddas*).[64] Siôn Tudur attributes the faults of the world to irreligion and the failure of the church. In his 'Poem to the World' (*Cywydd i'r Byd*) he lamented how people had become materialistic and corrupt:

Llawn beiau oll yw'n bywyd
Llawn bai yw pob lle'n y byd.[65]

(Our lives are full of sin
Corruption fills the whole world).

Siôn Tudur describes with humour how he might retire from the world, and buy a cottage amongst the mountain robbers (*Kael tyddyn yn y mynydd/ Y mysg lladron y gwledydd*) but fears that they will despoil him of all his livestock, property and clothing

Ar karn lladron ar gwylliaid
Yn dwyn fy wyn am defaid

Dwyn yr ŷd or stakie
A dwyn yr iâr ar gwydde
A dwyn fynhrys am siaked
A dwyn y karth or pared.

Underlying the humour, however, is a sharp critique of the prevailing social order, where the law has outlawed Perfect Love (*A bod Cariad Perffaith/Yn outlaw drwy'r gyfraith*).[66]

Rhys Llwyd, from Llanharan, spoke of the distrust and fear of aliens, liars and outlaws

Na choll dy genedl medd yr hen ddynion
Os gwell yw gwegil câr nac wyneb Estron
Gwagel gelwyddur a Herwr o goed
Os drwg oedd y ddau ŵr hynny erioed. [67]

Lose not your kinsmen, said the elders,
For better is a kinsman's back than an Alien's face,
The back of a liar or an Outlaw from the woods,
For Wicked were those two gentlemen ever.

In a more radical vein in 'The Dream of Rhisiart Fychan' (*Breuddwyd Rhisiart Fychan*) composed probably at the beginning of the seventeenth century, the bard recalls how in a dream he saw the country beset by ungodliness and corruption. Landowners, the clergy, officials, commissioners, the professions and tradesmen all conspired to oppress the common people. The wolves had become the shepherds (*Fleiddiad yn fugeiliaid*), and the only salvation was that they be unmasked and exposed (*Tynnu y crwyn oddi am danyn, Ac yno pawb a'u hedwyn*). In this dream he presents a picture of anarchy and lawlessness:

bydde yno rai yn byw yn dda
wrth herwa a lladrata
dwyn y gwartheg ar defed
a ffob math ar aneifelied
rhai yn kerdded llann a thre
yn unig i dorri pyrsse
eraill yn waeth no rheini
yn byw wrth ladd a llosgi
Rhai yn byw wrth dorri teie
eraill yn ysbelio yn ole

rhai yn aros mewn kyfle
yn restio pob un a bassie.[68]

There, others lived well
through outlawry and robbery
stealing cattle and sheep
and all kinds of livestock
some walked country and town
only to cut purses
others worse than these
lived by killing and arson
Some lived by house breaking
others plundered in daylight
whilst others waited their chance
to ambush all who passed their way

CONCLUSION

From the Acts of Union onwards Wales was incorporated into the English
state. The relations between the Welsh and the English underwent a profound change. The discriminatory legislation of Henry V became a dead
letter as the Welsh were granted the same rights as the English. More
complex lines of cleavage, which also highlighted the divisions in Welsh
society itself, replaced the central ethnic divide between the Welsh and the
English. These divisions reflected the bitter struggles for power, wealth
and social precedence amongst the gentry itself, made possible by the new
economic opportunities, and the prospects of public office. Bonds of
kinship were weakened, the relations between gentry and tenantry were
transformed, as social interests were increasingly based on instrumental
calculations rather than on traditionalist bonds of allegiance. The effect of
these changes was to draw Wales more closely to English patterns of social
organisation, whilst also deepening the gulf between social classes in
Wales.

   These changes occurred within the framework created by the Tudor
dynasty and the established power of the Protestant church. Church and
state reinforced one another. The new emphasis on gentility and civility
reflected a change in attitude but its impact on the behaviour of the gentry
is more questionable. The state was the benefactor of the gentry, and relied
upon them as its agents in the localities, in maintaining public order, in
securing the defences of the realm from invasion. In suppressing Catholic
recusants and dealing with the problem of vagabondage and the associated

threat of civil disturbance the Tudor state and the Welsh gentry found a bond of mutual self-interest. At the same time the notion of 'civility' sought to draw an aspiring gentry into the orbit of what was essentially Puritan English manners and culture, in opposition too what was increasingly defined as a barbarous native Welsh Catholic culture that required fundamental reformation.

13 Rule of Law 1555–1603

The Acts of Union created a new political framework within which the problem of lawlessness in Wales was to be addressed. They standardised the way in which the country was governed, through the shires, and eliminated the particularistic powers of the marcher lords and of the church. The Acts of Union sought to reorder the way Wales was governed in a more fundamental sense. It sought to create a system of rule which no longer depended on powerful local magnates, with their own clients, with their private retinues and their protection and sponsorship of freelance criminal elements for gain and for the intimidation of others. It sought to strengthen the control of the state at local level. At the same time it sought to dispense with private retinues, to restrict the opportunities for corruption, and to penalise collusion between local magnates and public officials with criminals. The Court of Star Chamber, the Council of the Marches, the Court of Great Sessions and the county courts assumed a growing role in dealing with the more significant manifestations of lawlessness in this period. But they were also required to exercise control over the gentry itself which was entrusted with dispensing justice at local level.[1]

The Council in the Marches

In 1560 Sir Henry Sidney became Lord President of the Council in Wales. A trained lawyer, he was one of the outstanding political administrators of Elizabeth's reign, as well as being a great patron of learning and literature. During the quarter century of his rule Sidney was absent from Ludlow for extended periods. In 1565 he became Lord Deputy of Ireland. In his absence leadership of the Council was entrusted to the vice president – William Gerard (Justice of South Wales), Sir John Throckmorton (Chief Justice of Chester), Sir Hugh Cholmondeley, and John Whitgift (bishop of Worcester).

The factional struggles at court between Leicester and Lord Burghley were reflected in rivalry to control the Council and local offices in the Principality. Sir Henry Sidney enjoyed Leicester's patronage, and his appointment to the two key offices in Wales and Ireland was a source of jealousy. The opposition faction allied to Burghley, comprised John Whitgift, Sir James Croft, Fabian Phillips and John Scory (bishop of

Hereford). Sidney's opponents criticised his weakness and demanded a return to the methods of Rowland Lee to suppress disorder.[2]

In 1567 Nicholas Robinson, bishop of Bangor, expressed satisfaction with the enforcement of law in the shires of north Wales, under the chief justice George Bromley. At the same time he deplored the irreligious state of the people, who were in 'the dregs of superstition', chiefly owing to the 'blindness of the clergy', with pilgrimages, altars and other images much frequented.[3]

The Privy Council in 1570 instituted an inquiry into the work of the Council and issued new instructions regarding its work. Sidney and Gerard strenuously defended the Council, advancing proposals to improve its efficiency, and fighting off their critics.[4] Sidney insisted that as a result of the Council's work all parts of Wales had been 'brought from their disobedient, barbarous, and (as may be termed) lawless incivility, to the civil and obedient estate they now remain'.[5]

Early in 1572 Sir Henry Sidney on returning to Ludlow from Ireland reported that he had 'found the Country in reasonable good State, saving only the County of Monmouth'.[6] Sidney himself visited Monmouth, to rectify the situation, to ensure that sheriffs and JPs upheld the law, that cases were promptly examined, punishment dispensed and the law upheld without favour.

In March 1573 the Council instructed sheriffs and JPs to reduce the excessive number of alehouses in Wales, always considered a source of dissoluteness and subversion, which were often run by dubious characters and were a factor contributing to lawlessness:

> And as by this felonies are increased, thieves, murderers and women of light conversation are harboured, rogues and vagabonds maintained, whoredom, filthy and detestable life much frequented, unlawful games as tables, dice, cards, bowls, kayles, quoits and such like commonly exercised, bows and arrows left aside to the great decay of artillery and emboldening and encouragement of the foreign enemy.[7]

The JPs were to secure speedy enforcement of justice, ensure the implementation of the statutes for the relief of the poor and for the suppression of vagabonds. The problem of absentee JPs and sheriffs had to be ended:

> The use hath been to make strangers, that hath neither lands nor goods in the country, sheriffs in Wales, and they lie in ale-houses and live off the spoil of the country, or else take £100 of a polling under-sheriff for the office and never come there.[8]

A continuing problem was the maintenance of armed retainers. The crown again in 1572 issued a proclamation for the enforcement of laws against the maintenance of 'unlawful retainers' and the Council in the Marches directed the sheriffs in the Welsh counties to enforce the law.[9] The prohibition on the maintenance of armed liveried retainers proved ineffective, as illustrated by an order against the Herberts in 1581 following a riot in Abergavenny.[10]

The levying of *cymhortha*, outlawed in 1534, continued as a form of illegal taxation imposed by the Welsh *uchelwyr* on their own tenants. This highlighted the weakness of the central government, and demonstrated the often brutally exploitative relations between classes in Welsh society. A Bill presented to Parliament in 1571 to prohibit *cymhorthas* failed after the first reading.[11] In 1572 and 1577 the Council of Wales again instructed sheriffs and JPs to stamp out these illegal *cymhorthas*.[12]

One distinct sub-category of cases handled by Star Chamber concerned the property of wives and heiresses. During Elizabeth's reign there were 26 actions, which involved the abduction of women and forced marriages, in many instances involving girls as young as 12 years of age. These forced marriages were often intended to secure the property of young heiresses. In one case a marriage was concluded as a means of reconciling two warring families; the failure of the marriage precipitating renewed conflicts.[13]

Complaints regarding cattle stealing in Wales persisted.[14] In 1570 the Council in the Marches again approved regulations concerning the tracking of stolen cattle. It noted the difficulty of tracking beasts along much-frequented routes, and the problem of rustlers participating in the tracking to misdirect the search.[15] One case brought before Star Chamber in 1597 concerned a cattle-thieving riot at Ffestiniog in 1597, when the owner and his men were attacked when tracking stolen cattle. One of the defendants was Edmund Price, Archdeacon of Merioneth.[16]

In about 1573 there was a dramatic deterioration in the situation, with a dramatic upsurge in public disorder. In January 1575 Richard Price, a gentleman of Brecknock, complained to Lord Burghley of the 'great disorders which do very grievously annoy the common-wealth of this poor Country of Wales and the good subjects of the same'. The Council of Wales failed to enforce the outlawing of *cymhortha*, which 'lewd officers', 'unruly gentlemen' and criminals used to exact tribute. Price also complained of the large number of different courts, those of the shires and those of marcher lords, and the courrption of court officials.[17]

In January 1576 David Lewis, a native of Abergavenny, who became Judge of the High Court of Admiralty, and first principle of Jesus College,

Oxford, in a letter to Walsingham delivered a severe indictment of Sidney's presidency of the council, and harkened back to the period of Lee's administration.

> My country is so far out of order at this time as do the require severe remedy and in every commonwealth severity used with indifference of justice to all men is more commended than levity ... And in my country this medicine hath been tried in bishop Rowlands and Mr Eglefeldes (sic) time, and since in that little time that Sir Hugh Powlett was there, and seeing experience is counted best mistress in my opinion she is to be followed.[18]

Lee's rule over the Welsh he compared to that of Joseph over the Egyptians.

Lewis mentioned the 'late inordinate and unlawful assembly in Glamorganshire' and the problem of retainers, which if not checked would spread a bad example to the rest of the country.

> The great disorders in Wales, specially in South Wales have grown much of late days by retainers of gentlemen, whom they must after the manner of the country bear out in all actions be they never too bad. They have also foster brothers, loitering and idle kinsmen and others hangers-on, that do nothing else but play at cards and dice and pick and steal and kill or hurt any man when they will have them, and yet they themselves will wash their hands thereof when the ill fact is done. These idle loiterers when they have offended will be shifted off to some friends of theirs in any other quarter, so as they will not be found to be punished when time shall require, and in the meanwhile the gentlemen will practice an agreement with the parties grieved, and then because the loiterers have nothing of their own the gentlemen must help them to a comortha to satisfy the parties dampnifyed.[19]

Lawlessness thrived because of the low calibre of men appointed as sheriffs and JPs, many of whom lived by 'polling and pylling'. The authority of the Council in the March was undermined by the reluctance of sheriffs, JPs, mayors, bailiffs and other officers to apprehend those who had powerful friends or masters. Instead they 'play bo-peep seest me and seest me not' with the result that crimes were committed with impunity. Lewis urged that gentlemen should be held responsible for the acts of their retainers. *Cymhorthas*, except by special permission, should be utterly forbidden. Council members should be carefully selected, excluding anyone who was in 'fee with any gentleman within the limits of their Commission'.[20]

Lewis' account of the protection of criminals by the gentry echoes the account provided by Sir John Wynn of the conduct of the Trefor and Cyffin families in the fifteenth century (ch.3). These were the men who acted as the bodyguards and enforcers of their patrons against rival gentry, and who also ensured by intimidation that others were kept in their place.

As a result of these criticisms Gerard, Sidney's acting deputy on the Council, was summoned to the Privy Council and accused of laxity. Sir John Throckmorton was summoned by Walsingham to be questioned by Burghley, in the presence of Sir James Croft, the leading opponent of the Sidney-faction on the Council, and accused of failing to attend the meetings of the Council and of embezzling fines.[21]

William Gerard initially strongly defended the Council's record, declaring: 'At this day, it is to be affirmed, that in Wales universally, are as civil people and obedient to law, as are in England'.[22] This, he asserted, stood in marked contrast to the period before 1540 when the people of Wales and of the adjoining English counties 'lived as in a country of war and not as in a country governed by law'. Under pressure from his critics, however, he was forced into a volte-face. In a letter to Walsingham he presented a far more critical assessment of the council's work and the low calibre of its officials.

> At this day, to be plain, the Council and Court are neither reverenced, feared, or their proceedings esteemed. There is not neither hath been sithens the Queens reign any of the Council appointed to continual attendance of such profound judgement as the place requireth, or that may be termed profound, learned, comparable with those meanest of these that served as Justice sythens Engelfelds.[23]

The Council had lost the ability to inspire dread. The porter's lodge at Ludlow, which supervised the castle gaol, 'was in Bishop Rowlands time such a strait place of punishment as the common people termed it a hell; and now is grown to no terror of punishment of the body but a gulph through fees to suck up a mean man'.

Gerard lamented the number of trivial suits brought before the court at Ludlow, which stemmed from the inclination of the Welsh for litigation. At the same time it demonstrated that the 'simpler sort' no longer felt the 'terror of the oppressor' and could bring their grievances to court. It was necessary to strengthen the Court with qualified men, with one of the Justices being familiar with Welsh. Moreover, the Court should travel more in Wales, as in Lee's time, to bring justice closer to the people. Only through a strong Council and Court could lawlessness be curbed.

> You poor Welsh Creatures, it is not you, but those appointed to govern you who be the causers of your beggary; the establishment is to devise for your wealth that which your malicious and wilful dispositions cannot procure to yourself.[24]

The weakness of the courts at local level encouraged litigants to take their cases to higher courts where they hoped to find a more impartial judgement. Lord St. John in a letter to Sir Edward Stradling in 1574 requested the former to use his influence.

> And for that I have seen the disposition of your country before this hath been much led by affection rather than equity of law, which maketh me to trouble you and others of my friends and kinsmen for the procuring of an indifferent wise jury...[25]

As a result the Court of Great Sessions was deluged with work. In 1576 it was enacted that the four circuits of the Court of Great Sessions should be presided over by two instead of one justice. It was asserted that as a result of the work of the Court of Great Sessions and its 'good administration of justice' Wales and the County Palatine of Chester were reduced 'to great obedience of Her Majesty's laws and the same greatly inhabited, manned, and peopled'.[26]

In 1575/6 the Privy Council protested to the vice-president of the Council of Wales of the 'great disorder' in Wales.[27] In Glamorgan there had been serious riots precipitated by feuds over the election of coroners.[28] In October 1575 the Council censured the failure of the sheriff and JPs in Radnor to apprehend vagabonds and sturdy beggars who were allowed to wander freely, committing robberies and other felonies. Officials had also failed to regulate the licensing of alehouses. In November the Council issued commissions for the counties of Merioneth and Montgomery to apprehend offenders.[29] An order of the Privy Council in 1576 noted the 'great and sundry abuses and disorders are crept into the Court of the Marches of Wales'.[30] In October 1576 the Council of Wales established commissions for each of the counties of Wales and the neighbouring English counties, with wide ranging powers to enquire into abuses and to ensure the rigorous upholding of the law.[31]

Sir Henry Sidney in November 1576 in a letter to the Privy Council argued strongly against the abolition of the Council and the Court. The court, he argued, was convenient for plaintiffs, and without it the poor subjects of the country would either have to 'rest with their harms at home' or seek redress at the Courts of Chancery or Requests at Westminster. Moreover, the Court at Ludlow did help to suppress lawlessness through 'the Terror, which the long continued Severity of that House, holdeth the base people of that Country in, in restraining them from robbing and killing one another'. Unless, he declared, the 'regiment of the whole realm' were to be slackened the Court had to be retained. However, it needed to be staffed with resolute and qualified men, who would 'severely rebuke and punish the proudest' following the example set earlier by bishop Rowland Lee.[32]

In 1577 bishop John Whitgift, and a strong advocate of sterner measures, particularly concerning recusants, was appointed vice-president of the Council during Sidney's absence and following the transfer of Gerard as Lord Chancellor in Ireland. The Privy Council requested a report on the state of Wales and the Marches, and issued an order for the reform of the Court at Ludlow. The Privy Council in 1577–8 instructed the Council to take measures to apprehend various 'notorious felons'. The same year it instructed the Council to check the licensing of *cymhorthas*, which allowed local notables and their deputies to 'disorderly vex and molest the people to their great discontentacion'.[33] In spite of the rulings of the Council of Wales and of Star Chamber the levying of *cymhorthas* continued unchecked.[34]

In October 1577 the Council issued an order which presented a grim picture of the situation and censured the 'negligence' of law officers to apprehend offenders. It enjoined all sheriffs and JPs to report to the Council within twenty days of any robberies or felonies by bands of three or more men, and to do their utmost to apprehend them.[35]

In his funeral sermon to the Earl of Essex in Carmarthen in 1577 Richard Davies, bishop of St David's, castigated the corruption of the gentry appointed as JPs and sheriffs.

> They have altogether applied their authority and office to pyll and poll the country and to beggar their poor neighbours; to perform that which Isaiah the prophet says, 'You dress your house with the goods of the poor'. How think you what it is to commit authority to such men? Is it any better than to commit a sword to a madman's hand? Would to God the manners and conditions of all justices of the peace and sheriffs in Wales were as well-known to her Highness's Council as they be in the country amongst their neighbours.[36]

From 1582 to 1587 the situation with regard to lawlessness in Wales appears to have eased. Despite strong criticisms of the situation in Wales Sir Henry Sidney continued to take a sanguine view, as related in a letter to Walsingham in March 1583. 'A happy place of government it is, for a better people to govern or better subjects to their sovereign Europe holdeth not'.[37] Sidney's view was sharply at variance with that of his critics, who accused him of dangerous complacency.

In 1585, after serving two years in the Privy Council, Sidney was again sent to Ludlow to head the Council. In his absence reports had been made to the queen and her Privy Council regarding 'many outrageous offences and misdemeanours' committed within the Council's jurisdiction, especially in south Wales, without action or punishment, the 'which had been imputed by Her Majesty to the said Lord President as a great fault'. Sidney blamed the disorder on the prevalence of factional fights between contending parties, and the failure of sheriffs and JPs to apprehend the offenders or to inform the Lord President and the Council of these events.[38]

The Council admitted that individuals taking cases to higher courts in Westminster were bypassing it. It added: for 'such is the malice of the people, that rather than make complaint or information to this Council they will revenge their supposed injuries and prosecute one another by extreme expense and travail out of the limits of this court being specially appointed to redress the same'. It was proposed to improve the effectiveness of the Court and Council, obliging JPs and other officers to submit monthly reports to the Council documenting serious offences, and requiring the sheriffs to appoint subordinates to take charge of particular hundreds, and redouble their efforts to apprehend wrong doers.[39]

The Court at Ludlow, Star Chamber and the Courts of Great Session had to address themselves constantly to the corruption of the lower courts and empanelling of partial juries in Wales.[40] The problem of petty and malicious suits brought before the Court remained a problem. George Owen, in his Dialogue, noted the continuing problem of the low calibre of men appointed to the bench, as a result of the waiving of the property qualifications and the use by sheriffs of hundred courts for extortion.[41] As a consequence the Council was 'the very place of refuge for the poor oppressed of this country of Wales to fly unto', providing 'the best cheap Court in England for fees' and ensuring speedy resolution of matters.[42]

Sir Henry Sidney died in May 1586. He was replaced as Lord President of the Council by his son-in-law Henry Herbert, Second Earl of Pembroke, son of William Herbert, the First Earl of Pembroke who had held the office in 1550–55. Pembroke was closely connected to the Leicester faction, and like his predecessor was constantly under attack in the Council from the rival supporters of Burghley. He was described by Thomas Williams of Trefriw as 'the eye of all Wales' (*llygad holl Cymru*). He was a ruthless individual and far from universally admired. In 1559 on becoming lord of

Glamorgan he demanded mises and sought to levy tallage for redeeming the Great Sessions in the county, which the crown had outlawed in 1536. This provoked the ire of the local gentry, who in a petition protested to the crown.[43]

Star Chamber

The proceedings of the Star Chamber provide an insight into the state of disorder in Wales during the sixteenth century. In the listing of Welsh cases before the Star Chamber, compiled by Ifan ab Owen Edwards, a total of 1,234 cases are given from 1509 to 1603. During the reign of Henry VIII (1509–1547) there were 166 cases, 3 per annum; Edward VI (1547–1553) 17 cases, 3 per annum; Philip and Mary (1553–1558) 17 cases, 3 per annum; Elizabeth (1558–1603) 1034 cases, 30 cases per annum. A more detailed analysis of the cases brought during Elizabeth's reign, when the Star Chamber came into its own, provides a number of important indicators.

The geographical distribution of the cases provides an indication of the most lawless counties in this period. In the table below is provided a breakdown of the number of cases per county, the percentage of cases for each county, and finally the number of cases per head of population of each country. These figures need to be treated with caution particularly the estimates of crimes per head of population.[44]

County	Number of cases	% of cases	Population	Cases per 1,000 inhabitants
Anglesey	23	2.2	9,770	2.3
Brecon	67	6.4	21,190	3.2
Caernarfon	66	6.3	14,920	4.4
Cardigan	30	2.9	17,320	1.7
Carmarthen	89	8.6	34,375	2.6
Denbigh	142	13.7	22,482	6.3
Flint	42	4.1	12,570	3.3
Glamorgan	119	11.5	29,493	4.0
Merioneth	50	4.8	10,470	4.8
Monmouth	193	18.6	26,080	7.4
Montgomery	122	11.8	18,972	6.4
Pembroke	41	3.9	20,079	2.0
Radnor	50	4.8	14,185	3.5
Total	1034	100.0	251,906	4.1

In terms of the number of cases, four counties stand out as being particularly lawless: Denbigh, Glamorgan, Monmouth and Montgomery. Populous Carmarthen, and Brecon return surprisingly low figures. Sparsely populated counties, notably Merioneth and Caernarfon, register above average figures. By contrast Cardigan, Pembroke, Flint, Radnor and Anglesey appear, perhaps misleadingly, havens of social tranquillity.

If we break down the cases brought before Star Chamber during Elizabeth's reign into five yearly periods the following pattern emerges.

Period	Number of cases	Number per annum
1558–1562	12	2.4
1563–1567	24	4.8
1568–1572	43	8.6
1573–1577	104	20.8
1578–1582	107	21.4
1583–1587	76	15.2
1588–1592	172	34.4
1593–1597	276	55.2
1598–1603	154	30.8

This provides a crude barometer of disorder. The reign can be neatly divided into three fifteen year periods – the first (1558–72) when the number of cases was small, corresponding to the pattern of the preceding fifty years; the second (1573–87) showing a marked rise in the number of cases; the third (1588–1603) showing a dramatic leap. In terms of individual years 1592/3 and 1593/4 were peak years with 72 and 68 cases respectively. There had been a small peak earlier in 1573/4 and 1574/5 with 29 cases each.

A high proportion of the cases involved an element of violence, with 490 cases (47.2%) falling into this category. It is possible to sub-divide these cases according to their seriousness. Here two principle categories are employed: 1. riot (often overlapping with cases of assault) and including outrages; 2. organised use of force by armed bands of men – listed variously as 'armed assembly', 'riotous assembly', 'unlawful assembly', 'warlike assembly' and other cases, which in terms of seriousness fall within this sphere.

County	Cases of riot	Cases of assembly	Riot/Assembly
Anglesey	2	0	2
Brecon	8	3	11
Caernarfon	13	0	13
Cardigan	3	1	4
Carmarthen	11	4	15
Denbigh	17	8	25
Flint	1	1	2
Glamorgan	26	3	29
Merioneth	5	7	12
Monmouth	19	10	29
Montgomery	17	2	19
Pembroke	5	2	7
Radnor	7	0	7
Miscellaneous	4		
Total	136	33	169

Glamorganshire, Denbighshire and Monmouthshire together accounted for 83, half of all cases of riot and assembly in Wales. The cases of assault in Monmouth were so numerous in 1563/4 that the JPs could not cope with them.[45]

The dramatic deterioration in the last nine years of Elizabeth's reign, compared to the preceding thirty six years, is reflected in the number of cases brought before Star Chamber, particularly those cases involving riot and assembly:

	All cases	Riot	Assembly	Riot/Assembly
1558–1594	538	59	15	74
1594–1603	430	71	24	95
Total	968	130	39	169

In the first thirty-five years of the reign there were 15.3 cases per annum, whilst in the last nine years 47.7 cases, a three fold increase. Over the same period the number of cases of riot increased from 1.7 per annum to 7.9 per annum, a fourfold increase. The number of cases of assembly increased from 0.4 per annum to 2.7 per annum, a 6 fold increase. In each year from 1594 to 1603 there were on average 10.5 cases of riot or assembly in Wales. This may reflect the growing effectiveness of the organs of justice, but it is difficult to avoid the conclusion that it reflected in the main a growing problem of lawlessness in the final decades of the sixteenth century.

Whilst in the first year of Elizabeth's reign there were only two cases brought before Star Chamber from Wales, in the last year there were 48. This represented an average of 3.7 cases from each of the thirteen Welsh shires, in comparison with 17 from each of the English shires.[46] The Council in the Marches relieved Star Chamber of many cases that might otherwise have burdened it.

The evidence of a growing crisis in lawlessness in Wales in the last two decades of Elizabeth's reign appears to mirror general trends. Joel Samaha in a study of Elizabeth Essex identifies a marked deterioration in public order in this period, with the 1590 revealing a clear correspondence between harvest failure and increased incidence of crime.[47] J. S. Cockburn using data from Sussex, Essex and Hertfordshire argues that in every decade from 1559 until 1600 there was a marked rise in the incidence of crime, but that the two following decades showed a decline.[48]

Economic hardship and lawlessness

Whilst the sixteenth century was an age of economic growth, it was marked also by pressures of population growth and acute price inflation and a growing gulf between rich and poor. The labour shortage of the previous century, which had kept wages high, disappeared. For the lower social classes the sixteenth century was economically more oppressive than the fifteenth. The population of Wales rose from an estimated 278,000 in 1536 to an estimated 405,000 in 1630.[49]

In 1563 the Statute of Artificers was passed which compelled the unemployed to enter into service as agricultural labourers at wages set by the local JPs.[50] In 1572 draconian measures were introduced to deal with the problem of vagabondage, with the imposition of the death sentence in cases of a second offence, unless employment could be found, with death sentences mandatory for third offences.

From 1570 onwards acute economic distress heightened social tensions. The Earl of Worcester in 1570 expressed fears of open conflict between rich and poor 'partly through the wilful disobedience of the meaner sort towards their superiors, and partly also by the wealthier sort meaning to oppress their inferiors by ravine (rapine)'.[51] Thomas Mansell of Margam in a letter to Sir Edward Stradling requested that the latter take charge of his affairs in his absence, to manage his lands and assume responsibility for 'the protection of my poor neighbours and friends, in preventing that the rich shall not oppress the poor, and that the poor injure not the wealthy'.[52]

In these years economic conditions in Wales sharply deteriorated. The cloth trade suffered in the face of growing English competition, and disruption of the export trade with Spain and France. There was a series of disastrous harvests in 1576, 1585/6, 1594–1597, and again in 1602, which resulted in famine. The Privy Council ordered the Council of Wales and the Marches to compel corn merchants who were hoarding grain to bring it to the market for the relief of the poor.[53] Cases of petty theft, particularly of food, increased sharply but, as Glanmor Williams notes, it was by no means only the poor who were convicted of theft.[54] These problems were exacerbated by upward leaps in prices in the 1540s, 1550s and 1590s. The enclosure of common land, particularly in the regions of arable farming, contributed further to social distress. As well as the deteriorating economic situation an additional burden was placed on the Welsh economy by the war in Ireland.[55]

The large growth of the vagabond population in Elizabethan society caused intense concern.[56] Recorder Fleetwood of London noted that of a large haul of rogues apprehended in 1582 many were from Wales.[57] The Welsh were to form an important element in the low life of the capital, as testified by their prominence in the street ballads of the time. In a contemporary discussion of different categories of vagabonds the Welsh were said to predominate as palliards – beggars who covered their bodies with artificial sores, and as dummerers – beggars who feigned dumbness.[58] English border towns, like Worcester and Shrewsbury, were another destination for the destitute population of Wales.[59] The Poor Law Act of 1598 provided for relief for the 'deserving poor' whilst 'rogues and vagabonds' were to be harried and punished and returned to their place of residence.[60]

The regard for justice in the shires

No Welsh county nor any of the bordering English counties were free of the factional struggles between powerful families. It was Games against Awbrey in Brecknock, Vaughan against Price in Radnor, Herbert against Vaughan in Montgomery, Salusbery against Trevor and later against Myddleton in Denbigh, Morgan against Herbert in Monmouth.[61] On a local scale the same rivalries reproduced themselves – Aberystwyth, Bersham, Llanfyllin, Dolgellau all had their contending factions.[62]

The dangers of armed assault made protection a necessity. Henry Salesbury of Lleweni was reproved by a friend for riding without an escort to protect him from attack by Sir Robert Cholmondeley's retainers.[63] Thomas Prys, of Plas Iolyn, Denbighshire, petitioned Star Chamber against Henry Holland, bailiff of Conwy, who it was alleged had, with a company of 40 men in 'riotous and warlike array', attempted to waylay and assault him as he crossed via the ferry to the town in May 1601.[64]

The concern with lawlessness in the second half of the sixteenth century changed in some important respects. The concern with recusants was a quite new issue. With the extension of landed estates, and growing population pressures on the land disputes over the enclosure of common land became a growing issue of conflict. In north Wales the enclosure of the forest of Snowdonia led to bitter disputes between Essex's faction and local notables.

The growing number of cases brought before the Court of the Marches and Star Chamber during Elizabeth's reign testify to the growing power of the centre and to the development of a system of rational legal authority. As Penry Williams, notes this indicated a readiness to turn from violent to legal methods to redress disputes. The growth of the courts' powers meant that there was little open violence which did not come to the notice of the courts and it was increasingly difficult for lawbreakers to go unpunished.[65]

George Owen provides a graphic assessment of the situation in the individual counties. Anglesey people were 'quiet and civil, little or no theft', of Caernarfonshire he noted 'the country is well governed and little or no theft'; Merionethshire possessed 'tall men, well governed, and theft hated'; in Flintshire 'the gentlemen are very discreet and well inclined' and the 'People very civil'; whilst Pembrokeshire people were 'most of them seamen and mariners, quiet for government, little theft or other oppressions'.[66]

In sharp contrast stood those counties with a reputation for serious disorder. Of Monmouthshire he asserted 'The people well governed, but many recusants and theft too common in most parts'. Glamorganshire was one of the most lawless of the Welsh counties, possessing 'many gentlemen of great livings' but its people 'impatient of injuries, and therefore often quarrels with great outrages: thefts in some parts too common; great groups of retainers follow every gentleman'. Carmarthenshire people were 'unruly, many recusants lately sprung up, theft much nourished, often brawls and other disorders'. Of Carmarthen, he noted, the 'largest town in Wales, fair and in good state', with 'many unruly and querulous people there'. Radnorshire's population were 'for the generality poor, tall and personable, unruly, spotted with oppressions, idle life and excesses in gaming, government and good order neglected, much theft and little thrift'. Brecknockshire folk were 'not eritche [rich] in general, unruly, theft abounding: and too many retainers'. Cardiganshire people were 'quiet in government, but abounding in theft'. The description of Denbighshire is accidentally omitted but Owen says of Denbigh 'a good town but much given to quarrelling and suites in law'. Of Montgomeryshire, he noted, 'much theft and other unruliness with troubles among themselves'.[67]

Wales in the 1590s

The last two decades of Elizabeth's reign saw a sharp deterioration in public order, compounded by mounting concern over the succession, the intensification of inter-gentry quarrels, and deteriorating economic conditions. The problem of disorder in Wales was heightened by factional struggle. Following the death of Leicester in 1588 Robert Devereux, Earl of Essex, dominated Welsh politics. Essex's main base of support was in south-west Wales, where eleven JPs were said to be 'serving men in livery' belonging to the Earl, and where in 1593 four out of seven MPs were said to be his followers.[68]

Sir Gelly Meyrick, the organiser of the Essex faction in Wales, ruthlessly assisted in promoting his supporters into positions of power. Attempts by the Earl of Pembroke to limit the build up of the Essex faction in Radnorshire were derisively brushed aside by Essex.[69] Susan Morgan of Whitland wrote that Essex's men were insatiable for office – 'everything is fish that comes to their net'. They exercised oppressive rule – 'so with their offices and brags they oppress all her Highness' poor subjects'. In 1595 an order was issued to remove many of Essex's followers from the posts as commissioners of the peace. The rivalry between Pembroke and Essex intensified.

Essex's bid to seize power in London in February 1601 collapsed.[70] His Welsh support proved fragile. Sir Richard Lewkenor informed Robert Cecil of the reaction in Wales: the 'fall of the earl in those parts where he was greatest is not grieved at … Sir Gelly Meyrick himself lived by such oppression and overruling them that they do not only rejoice at his fall but curse him bitterly'.[71]

Pembroke as lord president of the Council of Wales, after 1588 increasingly absented himself from Ludlow, on grounds of ill health. His handling of the work of the Council in 1589 was strongly criticised by Sir James Croft.[72] In January 1601 Pembroke died and was replaced by Edward Lord Zouch, one of Burghley's proteges. Zouch was remembered primarily for his haughtiness and contempt for his subjects, as Chamberlain writes: 'Lord Zouch plays rex in Wales and takes upon him comme un Milord d'Angleterre both with the counsails and justices as also with the poor Welshmen'.[73] In 1607 Zouch was succeeded by Ralph, Lord Eure, who, like his father and grandfather, had served as Lord Warden of the Middle March on the Anglo-Scottish border.

Notwithstanding the centre's growing power, great difficulties were still encountered in controlling local officials and in curbing collusion between them and criminals. During Elizabeth's reign the Star Chamber heard seven cases regarding the maintaining of murderers in Wales by leading gentry families. Breconshire had a notorious reputation in this regard, particularly relating to murders and crimes committed in Herefordshire.[74]

The problem is most graphically illustrated by a document drawn up on behalf of Sir Thomas Myddleton of Chirk Castle in 1599. This lists 17 murders committed in the county of Denbighshire in the preceding eight years, in which cases Sir John Salesbury of Lleweni had protected or interceded to ensure their acquittal or to effect a settlement. Many of these murderers were committed by Salesbury's servants, followers or near neighbours. The county at this time was riven by factional rivalry between the two families, with clashes between their retainers. Salesbury in 1586 was tried for treason and the fortunes of Lleweni fell into eclipse. The emergence of Myddleton as a real power in the county was confirmed in 1595 when he purchased Chirk Castle.[75]

CONCLUSION

The Acts of Union placed responsibility for the administration of justice in the Welsh shires on ther shoulders of the gentry. With the consolidation of the gentry's power the relations between it and other social classes in Wales became more strained. The expansion of office holding increased the opportunities for corruption, and intensified the rivalries between contending gentry families and their followers for precedence in the counties. The peculiar nature of the problem in Wales was reflected in the battery of judicial and administrative controls that were established with the Privy Council, Star Chamber, the Council of the Marches and the Courts of Great Sessions having power to try local officials. More effective enforcement of the law, the threat of prosecution, or the threat of more punitive measures, on the model provided by Roland Lee, may have had some restraining influence. Some of the wilder excesses of lawlessness in Wales were curbed – cross-border raiding, the kidnapping of people for ransom, the harassment of English travellers in Wales, and the harbouring of criminals in the marcher lordships and ecclesiastical sanctuaries. The power of the state at central and local level was strengthened.

The threat of political rebellion from Wales had long since disappeared. At the same time the problem of public order remained acute, and was compounded by economic hardships in the final decades of Elizabeth's reign. In spite of the government's repeated injuctions, various practices persisted: the levying of *cymhortha*, the maintenance of armed retinues, the harbouring of murderers and felons, and the conclusions of private settlements to offset legal proceedings in the courts. These survivals, which reflected traditions derived from an older kin-based society proved extremely tenacious and difficult to eradicate.

14 Outlaw and Bandit Traditions

We have already examined (pp. 101–5 above) two important traditions concerning Welsh outlaw and bandit from the fifteenth century, the bandits of Ysbyty Ifan and the Brecon raiders. In this chapter we shall examine other traditions from the second half of sixteenth century, namely those relating to the Red Bandits of Mawddwy, and the bandits of Cardiganshire and Montgomeryshire. The genesis of these traditions, their survival and development over time need to be studied critically and closely related to the actual historical records which survive. These traditions shed light on the nature of brigandage in Wales in this period, but it should be noted that these fragmentary accounts are chance survivals of what was a more widespread phenomenon.

There are various categories of organised criminal activity in Wales in this period which can be distinguished. Firstly, forms of guerrilla warfare, related to regionally based rebellion and dynastic struggles for power, as witnessed during the Glyndŵr rising, and during the Wars of the Roses. In such periods when the legitimacy of the crown was itself disputed, that which was lawful was a matter of contention. In such periods outlawry became a badge of honour. This category of 'outlaw' hero so evident during the fifteenth century disappears from the poetry of the bards after 1485.

Secondly, were those organised criminal activities which was supported, protected and licensed by the gentry. Such activities might be associated with the kind of dynastic struggles noted above, but they might also have no overt political significance. In the fifteenth century powerful Welsh magnates such as Gruffydd ap Nicholas of Dinefwr, and William Herbert of Raglan sponsored such forms of criminal action amongst their own retainers and amongst their own tenantry, often as part of a struggle with rival magnates. In the sixteenth century there are innumerable cases of gentry protection of such lawlessness; the protection of murderers and felons in the lordship of Magor, the reported protection of murderers by Salusberry of Lleweni.

Thirdly, were those criminal activities undertaken by subordinate social classes, which may represent a form of resistance to oppressive seignorial exactions. This corresponds to Hobsbawm's category of 'social bandits'.

Examples of this are more difficult to find. There are hints at this phenomenon in the poems of the fifteenth century which advocate the despoiling
of the wealthy. We have considerable evidence of resistance by the
tenantry to excessive exactions by the gentry and the crown, which took
the form of withholding dues, legal petitions or flight.

Fourthly, were those criminal enterprises that cut across class lines, and
were in some sense self-sustaining. Some of the examples of the border-
raiders of the fifteenth century, drawn from a cross-section of Welsh
society, organised for particular raids, fit into this grouping. We have also
the evidence of the great bandit redoubts of Wales in the fifteenth century
such as Ysbyty Ifan.

Fifthly, particular regions acquired a reputation for brigandage which
persisted over generations. These were remote, mountainous regions,
whose inhabitants engaged in raiding as a seasonal occupation, with
particular families and their allies regularly involved. These were sometimes loosely referred to as the "mountain thieves" or "*lladron yr elltydd*".
In this category we might include the region of Berwyn and Mawddwy.

These categories are not rigid, and often categories overlap and merge
into one another. The evidence which we have regarding these forms of
organised criminal activities also needs to be treated with caution. This is
especially the case with the poetry of the period and the family histories of
leading gentry families. In these sources the *uchelwyr* are invariably
presented as firm upholders of the rule of law, the suppressers of evil and
lawlessness, the defenders of the weak and innocent. Their struggle against
those labelled as criminals and brigands is used to legitimise their position
in society. How such outlaws and bandits were viewed by the wider society
is much more difficult to determine, and here rather than drawing fixed
conclusions it is necessary to retain an open-mind.

Y Gwylliaid Cochion

The tradition of the Gwylliaid Cochion of Mawddwy or Gwylliad y
Dugoed – the Red Bandits of Mawddwy (named after their red hair) or the
Bandits of the Black Wood (named after the Dugoed forest in the
Mawddwy valley) – is one of the most famous in Wales. The notoriety of
the Gwylliaid Cochion stemmed from the murder of Lewis Owen, sheriff
of Merionethshire and Baron of the Exchequer of North Wales in 1555.
Legal documentation concerning this affair has proved extremely elusive,
and our knowledge is based mainly on an account written some time after
the event, and must therefore be treated with some circumspection.

Merionethshire, one of the original Welsh shires established after the

Edwardian conquest was the least populous and one of the poorest of the Welsh counties.[1] Leland in his 'Itinerary', written between 1536 and 1539, noted that the towns such as Harlech, Dolgellau and Bala were little more than villages with poor markets.[2] In the sixteenth century a number of modest gentry families, Nannau, Owens of Llwyn, Salusberies of Rug, Lloyds of Rhiwedog, Prices of Plas Iolyn and Rhiwlas, and Vaughans of Corsygedol, struggled for predominance.[3]

The county had a notorious reputation for lawlessness, with constant raiding between it and the neighbouring lordships of Powys.[4] The county bordered the ancient lordship of Mawddwy. In the fifteenth century Guto'r Glyn wrote praise-poems to Sir John Burroughs, Lord of Mawddwy, who died in 1471, describing him as a loyal official of the king (*Swyddawg breiniawg i'r brenin*) suggesting that the lordship of Mawddwy was a stewardship of the crown. He praises his protection of the weak and upright and his suppression of the false and deceitful (*Holi ffals a'i heli a ffon*). Dafydd Llwyd of nearby Mathafarn wrote an ode to St Tudecho, the local saint, in which he notes the problem of night raiders. Tudur Penllyn in his humorous ode to the robber Deicws Chwith depicts the scoundrel storming through Dinas Mawddwy.

In the folk memory of the region, Mawddwy is depicted as sharing the same tradition of raiding as the neighbouring Berwyn mountains, with strong connections between the families of the two regions that were involved in these activities. We have already noted the persistent references by the bards to Berwyn's reputation as a haunt of outlaws (ch. 6). Through the fifteenth and sixteenth century we have a wealth of references to raiding between Merionethshire and the lordships of Powys. We also have evidence that raiders from Mawddwy and Berwyn carried their raids as far as the lordship of Chirk.[5]

The lordship of Mawddwy passed at the beginning of the sixteenth century, either through marriage or royal decree, to the Myttons, a family of wealthy Shrewsbury burghers. By the 1530s the lordship was in the hands of Richard Mytton, who was an absentee lord. Leland refers to 'Mitton, called lord of Mothey' but thought he was the king's steward there. He lived at 'Cotton a quarter of a mile out of Shrewsbury'.[6] Rowland Lee, president of the Council of Wales and the Marches, in 1541 suggested his nomination as MP for Merionethshire. In 1542 he was elected MP for Shrewsbury. In 1544 he was sheriff of Shropshire and in 1547 and 1554 was sheriff of Merionethshire.[7]

In a law passed in 1534 provision was made for serious offences committed in any of the Welsh counties to be tried in the nearest adjoining English county. This was to deal with the widespread problem of corrupt juries and the intimidation of law officers. Exceptionally it ruled that serious offences committed in Merionethshire could be tried before the courts in Shropshire, or heard before the King's Justice of North Wales, or his deputy in Anglesey and Caernarfonshire. The act repealing the law in 1566 noted that this had been 'much to the discredit of the inhabitants of the said county of Merioneth'.[8]

In 1535, with the shiring of the marcher lordships, it was decreed that 'the lordship town and parish of Mouthway' should be 'guildable forever'. It was granted a mayor and corporation, which it retained until 1688. The decree ended Mawddwy's existence as an independent lordship declaring that it should be 'united annexed and joined to and with the County of Merioneth'.[9] Merioneth's sheriff and law officers were given direct power in Mawddwy. In 1535 the practice of *arddel* was specifically forbidden for its effect in corrupting the judicial process.[10] Sir John Wynn in his *History of the Gwydir Family* refers to *arddel* as 'this damnable custom used in those days in the lordship marchers which was used also in Mowddwy until the new ordinance of Wales made in the twenty sixth year of Henry the eight'.[11]

Lewis Owen's public career benefited from the patronage of the powerful Puleston family in North Wales. He married Margaret, the niece of the influential Sir John Puleston. He was appointed deputy sheriff of Merionethshire in 1537 and 1538, when Sir John Puleston was sheriff.[12] Sir John served as baron of the Exchequer and vice-chamberlain of North Wales and from 1547 until his death in 1551 was chamberlain of North Wales.

Lewis Owen was sheriff of Merionethshire in 1545–46 and 1554–55. Significantly no Welshman had served in this capacity between 1400 and 1540.[13] He represented Merionethshire as its knight in the Parliaments of 1547, the spring of 1553 and 1554. He was appointed vice-chamberlain of North Wales and baron of the Exchequer at Caernarfon, from which he derived his familiar title. The Exchequer was responsible for the leasing of crown lands, overseeing their management, and collecting revenues.[14] The Welsh JPs Act of 1536 ruled that the JPs of Anglesey, Caernarfonshire and Merionethshire were to make returns of fines to the Exchequer and the Chamberlain.

At the time of his death in 1555 Lewis Owen was at the height of his power, one of the most influential men in North Wales. He was the son of Owen ap Hywel ap Llywelyn of Llwyn, Dolgellau.[15] He lived at Cwrt Plas yn Dre, Dolgellau.[16] The Owen family were bitter rivals of the more established families of Nannau and Rug who had dominated the area in the past.[17] Lewis Owen leased crown properties, as well as confiscated monastic property from the Court of Augmentation. His son John Lewis Owen renewed some of these leases in 1571.[18]

In 1554/5, during his second term as sheriff of Merionethshire, Lewis Owen oversaw a vigorous drive against law breakers, which appears to be part of a concerted campaign directed by the Council of Wales and the Marches. In the Great Sessions for the county in 1554–55 almost 300 men from Merioneth were brought before the court and thirty before the Council in the Marches. Nine of them were hanged for cattle stealing and a further three hanged for protecting felons.[19]

The antiquarian Robert Vaughan of Hengwrt, Dolgellau who lived from 1592 to 1667, provides the main account of these bandits. His account appears in a manuscript account of the circumstances of the murder of his great grandfather, the baron Lewis Owen, which is presented as his martyrdom in the struggle to bring order to the society.[20]

> Lewis Owen, esquire: vice chamberlain and Baron of the Exchequer of North Wales, lived in great credit and authority in the time of King Henry VIII, Edward VI, and Queen Mary, as it appeareth by their letters under their sign manual directed to him and John Wynn ap Meredith of Gwydir esquire touching matters that concerned the peace and quiet government of the country, as the apprehending of and punishment of felons and outlaws (which from the civil wars between York and Lancaster abounded in the country, and never left robbing, burning of houses, and murdering of people, in so much that being very numerous they did often drive great droves of cattle sometimes to the number of a hundred and more from one country to another at middle day, as in the time of war without fear, shame, pity or punishment to the utter undoing of the poorer sort;). And they in performance of the dutie required by some of these letters, (being authorised to call to their aid the power of the counties, and also to keep sessions of gaol delivery when occasion required) raised a great company of tall and lusty men, and on a Christmas eve took above 80 felons and outlaws, whom they punished according to the nature of their delinquencies... Afterwards the said Lewis Owen being high sheriff of the county of Merioneth, and having occasion to go to Montgomeryshire assizes to treat with the lord of Mawddwy, about a marriage to be had between John Owen, his son and heir and the daughter of the said Lord of Mawddwy, was in his return met by a damned crew of thieves and outlaws, who in the thick woods of Mawddwy lay in wait for his coming, and had cut down long trees to cross the way and hinder his passage, and being come to the place,

they let fly at him a shower of arrows, whereof one lighted in his face, the which he took out with his hand and broke it, then they fell upon him with their bills and javelins and killed him – his men upon the first assault fled and left him only accompanied with his son in law John Lloyd of Ceiswyn esquire who defended him till he fell down to the ground as dead, where he was found having above 30 bloody wounds in his body. This cruel murder was committed about allhallowtide in the year of our Lord 1555. And the murderers soon after were for the most part taken and executed, some few fled the land and never returned. And so, with the loss of his life, he purchased peace and quietness to his country, the which God be praised we enjoy even to our days.[21]

Robert Vaughan asserted that his account was based on the testimony of Sir John Wynn of Gwydir, grandson of John Wynn ap Meredydd. He adds further that he himself had seen the commission granted to Lewis Owen and John Wynn ap Meredydd, which at that time was extant and kept at Gwydir. John Wynn was MP for Caernarfonshire in 1542 and deputised for the deceased member, John Puleston, in 1553. He was reputed an indefatigable fighter of lawlessness. His father, Meredydd ap Ifan, was famed for his campaign against the bandits of Ysbyty Ifan in the reign of Henry VII.[22] John Lloyd of Ceiswyn, served as sheriff of the county in 1550, 1558 and 1562 , and variously served as a JP.[23]

The murder occurred on 12 October 1555. The site of the muder at Bwlch y Fedwen, close by the Dugoed forest, is still known as Llidiart y Barwn (the baron's gate). Lewis Owen's body was buried in the church of Llanfair Brynmeurig in Dolgellau. A cross was erected to commemorate the site of the murder; the nearby hill still bears the name Ffridd y Groes (Cross Hill).[24] Following the murder Sir John Salesbury, Chamberlain and Receiver-General of North Wales, dispatched one Simon Thelwall to Dolgellau to put the deceased's affairs in order. Thelwall also made an inventory of the baron's meagre possessions left at the Exchequer at Caernarfon.[25]

The assassins were apprehended and brought before the courts. Eight men were charged with the murder; Gruffydd Wyn ap Dafydd ap Gutun, yeoman of Brithdir; Ellis ap Tudur, yeoman of Nannau; John Goch ap Gruffydd ap Huw, yeoman of Mawddwy; Robert ap Rhys ap Hywel, yeoman of Mawddwy; Jenkyn ap Einion; Dafydd Gwyn ap Gruffydd ap Huw, yeoman of Mawddwy; Morris Goch, yeoman of Cemais, Montgomeryshire; and Ieuan Thomas, yeoman of Llanwddyn.They were sentenced and hanged. The individual who killed the sheriff was one John Goch ap Gruffudd ap

Huw, and it may be that it was a brother of his, Dafydd Goch, who was amongst those executed by the courts in 1554–55.[26] Evidence regarding the bandits of Mawddwy is slim.[27] As yeomen farmers they stood in contrast to other types of brigands; the lawless gangs of the gentry and their retainers; the loose associations of outlaws who set up temporary bases such as those associated with Yspyty Ifan at the end of the fifteenth century.

Five bards sang elegies to the dead baron. The family bard, Owain Gwynedd, composed one (*Cywydd marwnad Lewis ab Owen y Barwn*). Lewis Owen is depicted as a man of mature years, white headed, short of stature but manly and vigorous. His supposed noble lineage from Bradwen and the princes of South Wales is alluded to. The bard stresses the baron's role as a persecutor of robbers and outlaws (*Cadw'r oedd acw...Rhag herwyr, y cywiriaid... A bwrw'i lawr beiau'r wlad*), who sought to wrest the country from the rule of robbers (*llywodraeth lladron*). The bard calls on God's aid to bring the guilty to justice. The Dugoed forest, he asserts, will forever be notorious for this foul act. The assassins may rejoice over the murder but it will be of no profit to them. As the baron is laid to rest the assassins must hide in the hollows, awaiting the retribution that is inevitable.[28]

Gruffudd Hiraethog, the bard of the Mostyn family, wrote another elegy. The same bard also composed an elegy to Sir John Wynn ap Meredydd of Gwydir, who died in 1559 at the age of 67. The bard pays effusive praise to Sir John's efforts in suppressing lawlessness.[29] By contrast, it might be added that few members of the Welsh gentry of the age attracted the opprobrium, which Sir John Wynn attracted for his ruthlessness and self-aggrandisement.

For some the story of the Red Bandits came to symbolise resistance to alien rule by the English and their Welsh agents. A poem by an anonymous bard from Glamorgan sometime in the sixteenth century makes an enigmatic reference to the story. The poem laments the despoliation of Glyn Cynon by English entrepreneurs felling timber for charcoal to feed the new iron works and descends into a virulent piece of anti-English invective. The destruction of the forest, the bard says, has caused the red stags (i.e the red outlaws) to flee the valley and seek sanctuary in Mawddwy.

Clywais ddoedyd ar fy llw
Fod haid o'r ceirw cochion
Yn oer eu lle'n ymado a'u plwy
I ddugoed Mowddwy'r aethon.[30]

The men of Mawddwy long afterwards retained a reputation for corrupt legal practices. At the end of the sixteenth century Thomas Prys in a prophetic poem predicts wonderful manifestations, which will appear once certain conditions, are fulfilled: when an impartial inquest of Mawddwy *uchelwyr* is convened, when her lands are free of robbers, when Edeirnion is free of robbers and fighting, when Shrewsbury has lost its officials.[31]

Lewis Owen was twice married. From his marriage to Margaret Puleston there issued seven sons and four daughters.[32] The family bard, Owain Gwynedd, wrote an ode praising the virtues of the seven sons.[33] The eldest son John Lewis Owen played an important part in the life of the county. He was knight for Merionethshire in the Parliament of 1572 and was also sheriff of the county in 1565–66, 1572–73 and 1589–90. In 1589 John Lewis Owen and Cadwaladr Price of Rhiwlas were appointed as Deputy Lieutenants of the shire on the recommendation of the earl of Pembroke, Lord President of the Council in the Marches.[34]

The bards presented the descendants of Lewis Owen as honourable gentlemen who exemplified all the virtues of that rank in a manner characteristic of the poetry of the age.[35] Owain Gwynedd, the Owen family bard, eulogised John Lewis Owen as the 'Eagle of Meirion'.[36] The renowned bard Wiliam Llŷn in 1559 also wrote a tribute to him in which he extolled the virtues of his slain father.[37] Siôn Mawddwy described John Lewis Owen as a guardian of law and order and as the son of the pure, upright baron (*mab barwn per*). He executed robbers without mercy, but loved the upright and struck terror in the mighty but lawless.[38] Siôn Tudur describes him as the heir of the brave baron (*Aer barwn glew*).[39] Gruffydd Hiraethog also paid lavish tribute to him as the branch sprung from the mighty baron (*Irbren braisg o'r barwn brau*).[40]

The history of the period casts John Lewis Owen and his sons in a less flattering light. In 1597–8 and 1599–1600 one Price Lloyd of Dolau indicted John Lewis Owen and Cadwallader Price of Rhiwlas before the Star Chamber. They were charged with embezzling £1,000 worth of armour from Harlech Castle, which was in their guardianship; illegally taxing the people to conceal the loss; imprisoning some three hundred people who refused to pay the tax; organising musters of forces for their own enrichment; forcing the election of John Vaughan, Caergai, a kinsman, as MP; bribery and corruption as JPs.[41] In 1594 John Lewis Owen was brought before Star Chamber by Gruffydd Nanney accused of armed assemblies and riots concerning the enclosure of a tenement.[42]

His son Lewis Owen, who served as sheriff of the county in 1597, was brought before Star Chamber with a number of other defendants, charged with assault, jury packing and the intimidation of witnesses.[43] In this period the rivalry between the Owen and Nannau families came to a head over the question of erecting a family pew in the church at Dolgellau. The case was brought before Star Chamber.[44] Inquiries by the Privy Council revealed that John Lewis Owen was a poor man, and depended on the deputy-lieutenancy for his living. Two years later Star Chamber gave its verdict: Price and Owen were outlawed. The Privy Council removed both from office and appointed two new deputy lieutenants.[45]

In this manner, using lawful and more questionable means, the Owen family consolidated its power. Even at the end of the nineteenth century many of the leading families of the area traced their descent from Lewis Owen.[46] The Wynnes of Peniarth and the Vaughans of Nannau provided a great many of the MPs, Lord Lieutenants and JPs of the county. Some of the most notable figures from the area were descended from him, such as the antiquarian Robert Vaughan of Hengwrt, John Owen the Independent Puritan divine of the seventeenth century; Lewis Owen (1572–1629) of Talybont the anti-Catholic propagandist; Robert Owen (died 1685) a leading Parliamentarian in North Wales; Hugh Owen (1639–1700) of Bronclydwr, Independent Puritan minister and 'apostle of Merioneth'.[47]

Notwithstanding the efforts made to eradicate brigandage from the region it persisted as a problem in the succeeding decades. The Council of the Marches in January 1570 noted the practice of felons fleeing from Merioneth into the counties of Cardigan and Montgomery to escape the sheriff and avoid punishment. It empowered the sheriff, Owen Wyn, to adopt a policy of hot pursuit into those counties 'to make diligent search for all outlaws, murderers, felons and suspects to felony and to apprehend and examine them', to commit them to goal in Merioneth and to bring them before the courts.[48]

In November 1575 the Council censured the failure of the authorities in Merioneth and Montgomery to apprehend and punish those guilty of felonies, thefts and spoils, and noted that the offenders 'wander in secret places in those counties and may easily be apprehended'. The Council commissioned Ellis Price, Richard Mytton, John Salusbury of Rug, John Lewis Owen, Ievan Lloyd ap David, and the sheriff of the county to search and apprehend these offenders in the two counties. A similar commission was issued for Montgomeryshire.[49]

At this time the Council of the Marches instructed the sheriff of Merionethshire regarding the suppression of crime, particularly cattle stealing. It required the appointment of an overseer for each parish with wide ranging powers. He was to summon the heads of all households and ascertain their means of support. The needy and the unemployed were to be put to work. He was to visit suspect families at least twice a week to investigate robberies, identify strangers in the parish and to control the killing, movement, ear marking and sale of livestock. The overseer was to report to the JP every three weeks.[50]

The noted Welsh antiquarian Edward Lhuyd in his *Parochialia*, written around 1700, was the first in print to use the name of the 'Gwilhiaid Kochion' in connection with the murder of Baron Owen.[51] In 1769 Ellis Roberts (Ellis y Cowper) published an interlude in the form of a discourse between Grace and Nature which refers briefly to the Gwilliaid Cochion.[52] In 1796 a Welsh translation was published of the work of the Puritan divine John Owen (1616–1683) – *Of the Mortification of Sin in Believers* (first published in 1668). The introduction by Hugh Jones (Maesglasau) mentions John Owen's great grandfather, the Baron Owen, and recounts the circumstances of his murder at the hands of the Gwylliaid Cochion.[53]

In his celebrated *Tours in Wales*, first published in 1784, Thomas Pennant recounted the story of the red haired bandits of Mawddwy. This account was based on Robert Vaughan's manuscript, with some romantic embellishments.[54] Pennant's work generated considerable interest amongst local historians and antiquarians.[55]

Montgomeryshire bandits

In the fifteenth and sixteenth centuries the lordships of Arwystli, Cyfeiliog, Cedewain and Ceri were amongst the most violent and lawless in Wales. Under Rowland Lee the Council of the Marches assumed a major role in the administration of these lordships. Lee relied heavily on the support of Sir Richard Herbert, the founder of the famous Chirbury family. A ruthless individual in advancing his own interests, he was accused of 'gathering goods by extortion and polling … of poor tenants in those parts for his own proper lucre and advantage'.[56]

In the new county of Montgomeryshire power was placed in the hands of the local gentry. As a consequence, as in other counties, there ensued a furious struggle for precedence between contending families and their allies, and the use of office to gain advantage over rivals and for self-enrichment. The Council of the Marches sought with only limited success to control these factional feuds. Problems persisted in Arwystli and Cyfeiliog with conflicts between lords, freeholders and tenants over rights to the commons.[57] From the examination of cases brought before Star Chamber during Elizabeth's reign it is clear that Montgomeryshire was amongst the most disordered of the Welsh counties.

Sir Richard Herbert's eldest son Edward Herbert was a prominent figure at court and served as squire to the body of Queen Elizabeth. Edward

Herbert's son Richard Herbert succeeded him, and served as MP for the county in 1586.[58] The influence of the Herbert family in Montgomeryshire was fiercely contested by John Owen Vaughan of Llwydiarth. From 1584 to 1602 a series of cases were brought before Star Chamber which were part of the ongoing feud between these two families and their factions. Accusations were made of assault, abuse of office, and the harbouring of felons and murderers.[59] In 1602 Vaughan brought charges against Richard Herbert of having secured illegally his appointment as JP; of levying taxes for armour and appropriating the funds for his own use; accepting bribes as JP for the commutation of sentences. In 1603 John Owen Vaughan's sons, Owen and Cadwalader, as JPs were charged with allowing misdemeanours to accumulate 'whereby insolences, outrages and disorders, in that part of Wales do more abound than in any other part of her Majesty's kingdom'.[60]

Edward Herbert's drive against the outlaws of mid-Wales is recounted by his grandson in his autobiography, which provides an account of his family's rise to prominence

> Noted to be a great enemy of the outlaws and thieves of his time, who robbed in great numbers in the mountains of Montgomeryshire, for the suppressing of whom he went both day and night to those places where they were… Some outlaws being lodged in an alehouse upon the hills of Llandinam, my grandfather and a few servants coming to apprehend them, the principal outlaw shot an arrow against my grandfather, which struck in the pummel of his saddle, and taking him prisoner, he showed him the said arrow bidding him to look what he had done, whereof the outlaw was no further sensible than to say he was sorry that he left his better bow at home, which he conceived would have carried his shot to his body, but the outlaw being brought to justice suffered for it.[61]

Cardiganshire bandits

In the fifteenth century Cardiganshire witnessed acute disorder, with a state of virtual war existing at one time between the men of Uwch and Is Aeron. The Aeron and Yswyth valleys were notorious as haunts of outlaws. In the sixteenth century the records of the court of Star Chamber testify to bitter feuding between the main families in the county. In 1583 Maurice Phillips of Llanbadarn Fawr was indicted for 'the maintenance of thieves and robbers'.[62] In 1599 the court referred to the great malice between the men of Cardiganshire.[63]

In 1594 George Owen, in his 'Dialogue on the Government of Wales', noted the continuing problem of brigandage in Cardiganshire:

I was put in great fear how I should pass the upper part of Cardiganshire, for it was told me that I must pass a place called Cwm Ystwyth, where many thieves that lived as outlaws, and some not outlawed indeed, made their abode, and that they lived by open robbing… The place itself is very wild and desolate full of great and wild mountains and few inhabitants and thereabouts joineth the three shires of Cardigan, Montgomery and Radnor together being three shires in three several circuits ruled by three several justices of assizes, which you cannot find in all Wales besides. And there were such ill people if they be pursued by one good sheriff of one of the three shires they hoped to be favoured of another, these two causes, as I think maketh them to draw together into that place above the rest of Wales.[64]

George Owen lay responsibility for this state of affairs at the door of negligent sheriffs and JPs who wilfully turned a blind eye to these brigands and their harbourers, who 'supported and winked' at offences, or connived with them in the breaking of the law:

I have heard it said that diverse of these gentlemen do not lose by those kind of spoilers and that it is very common that those thieves and outlaws do yearly compound and agree with those sheriffs as soon as they come into office and reward them largely that they should not prosecute them eagerly for that year and in this sort they live in companies and will often times come to the church and to fairs and markets and nothing said unto them. Those live upon the spoil of the poor and honest labouring people.[65]

Another bandit tradition from Cardiganshire concerns a band of outlaws known as Plant Mat or Mat's Children. The outlaws are associated with the Cwm Ystwyth area with a cave near Devil's Bridge as their habitation. From there they raided the neighbouring countryside until they were eventually hunted down, taken and executed.[66] One of the crimes attributed to Plant Mat was the murder of a judge at Rhayader, as a result of which it was ordered that the court of Great Sessions should henceforth be transferred from Rhayader to Presteign. In 1542 Parliament did in fact rule that the county court of Radnor be held alternately at New Radnor and Presteign and should never more be held at Rhayader.[67]

The tradition of brigandage in Cardiganshire is also connected with the name of Thomas Jones (Twm Siôn Cati) of Fountain Gate, near Tregaron, Cardiganshire who lived from 1530 to 1609.[68] In 1559 he was listed amongst a hundred names of those amnestied by Elizabeth I. He appears to have led the life of an outlaw in his early life. The tradition resurfaced in the eighteenth century. In these tales Twm Sion Catti is presented as the lovable rogue, and prankster who though wit and guile is able to outwit those who represent wealth and authority.[69] These naive and maudlin tales, which reflected more the taste of their time than the real history of Wales in the sixteenth century, proved extremely popular and were republished many times in the nineteenth century.[70]

CONCLUSION

The bandit tradition examined in this chapter all relate to the same period, the 1540s–1560s, with the account of the bandits of Cwm Ystwyth related by George Owen belonging to the 1590s. They mark the end of the age of organised banditry in Wales. These traditions belong to the remoter, inaccesible parts of the country, into which the arm of the law was increasingly extending its hold. The accounts which we have of these bandits is limited, often based on one account, or based simply on the traditions of folklore. It is therefore difficult to provide any systematic analysis of these traditions. None of the groups examined could fit into the category of 'social bandits', although as we have seen there were some who viewed the gwylliaid cochion with admiration.

The legends examined point to banditry as a form of self-sustaining activity, sometimes in collusion with corrupt law officers, possibly protected by gentry families. At the same time we need to regard with care some of these accounts; the account of chroniclers are often more highly coloured than is suggested by the limited archival evidence which survives. What emerges is a picture of communities in remoter parts of the country (those sometimes referred to as the mountain thieves – *lladron yr elltydd*) the members of which would engaged in predatory brigandage on nearby communities. In so far as we can guess what public attitudes to these bandits was, we might suggest a degree of ambivalence, but that the attitude towards the upholders of law, the representatives of the rapacious Welsh gentry, was itself equally ambivalent. This reflected the realities of life: there was no real prospect of the existing social order being fundamental transformed or effectively challenged.

Many of these bandit traditions were first recorded by contemporaries in the poetry of the period, in family histories or accounts by chroniclers. They are less about the bandits than about the bandit fighters who sought to suppress them. In the main they were intended to glorify the role of individual gentry families in bringing order to their society, and thus to legitimise their position. At the end of the eighteenth and at the beginning of the nineteenth centuries, associated with the Romantic movement, these Welsh bandit traditions were rediscovered, with the publication of Sir John Wynn's *The History of the Gwydir Family* in 1770, the publication of Pennant's *Tours in Wales* in 1784.

Conclusion

Tudor policy towards Wales as an experiment in state building and constitutional reform, provided a subject for much reflection for contemporaries and later generations of historians. Here we shall examine the way they were viewed by contemporary Welsh chroniclers, and the lessons that were learnt from this experience by government officials concerned with the government of the Anglo-Scottish border and Ireland. In a sense these represent the views of members of the Welsh gentry and of 'official' Tudor and Stuart administrators. We shall also examine the way in which Welsh historians have viewed the issue.

The testimony of Welsh chroniclers

For Tudor commentators the Acts of Union marked the watershed in the establishment of law and order in Wales. They were introduced in Wales with no evident opposition, and commanded considerable support. Rice Merrick (Rhys Meurig Y Cotrel) in *A Booke of Glamorganshire Antiquities*, written between 1578 and 1584, celebrated the benefits of the Acts of Union.

> Now, since Wales was thus, by gracious King Henry VIII, enabled with the laws of England, and thereby united to the same, and so brought to monarchy, which is the most sure, stable and best regiment, they (the Welsh) are exempted from the dangers before remembered: for now life and death, lands and goods rest in the monarch, and not in the pleasure of the subject. Laws whereby they are governed are written, and therefore more certain to be truly and indifferently administered. What was then justifiable by might, although not by right, is now to receive condign punishment by law. The discord between England and Wales then procured slaughters, invasions enmities, burning, poverty and such like fruits of war. This unity engendered friendship, amity, love, alliance, unistance, wealth and quietness. God preserve and increase it.[1]

Rice Merrick declared the 'alteration of government' to be 'worthy of remembrance' in that Wales had attained a state of 'singular commodity' with England 'as the commonwealth universally'.[2]

George Owen of Henllys, the Elizabethan antiquarian, in his 'Dialogue on the Government of Wales', praised the benevolent paternalism of the Tudors. He noted the change which constitutional reform had wrought in the attitudes and consciousness of the people:

> No country in England so flourished in one hundred years as Wales hath done, sithence the government of Henry VII to this time, in so much that if our fathers were now living they would think it some strange country inhabited with a foreign nation, so altered is the countrymen, the people changed in heart within and the land altered in hue without from evil to good and from bad to better... Surely these laws have brought Wales to great civility from that evil government that was here in old time: for it is as safe travelling for a stranger here in Wales as in any part of Christendom, whereas in old time it is said robberies and murders were very common.[3]

He paid tribute to the Council of the Marches 'which at the beginning brought Wales to that civility and quietness that you now see it, from that wild and outrageous state'.[4] Moreover 'the gentlemen and people of Wales', he noted had 'greatly increased in learning and civility'.

The views of Rhys Meurig and George Owen are echoed also in the accounts given by Sir John Wynn, Lord Herbert, Sir John Price and William Salesbury and by bards such as Siôn Tudur and Lewis Mogannwg.[5] It is reflected in the writings of those officers who served in the Council of Wales, such as Sir Henry Sidney and William Gerard. Although dissenting voices were raised, particularly in the 1570s, regarding the prevailing disorder in Wales, there was a strong consensus that a major change had occurred since the 1530s. The testimony of such commentators deserves serious consideration.

The taming of the border

In the decades after the Acts of Union the border was tamed. Sir Henry Sidney, Lord President of the Marches of Wales, noted that since the legislation of Henry VIII Wales had been reduced to a state of tranquillity to the benefit of the adjoining English counties. In the past he observed

> And all the English counties, bordering thereon, brought to be afraid from such Spoils and Felonies, as the Welsh, before that Time, usually by invading their borders, annoyed them with.[6]

William Gerard, his deputy, in a memorandum of 1577, probably
addressed to the Privy Council, confirmed this assessment

> Before the 26th year of King Henry the Eighth (1535), who was he of
> the English counties that bordered upon the skirts of the mountains of
> Montgomery, Radnor, Brecknock, or Monmouth, that in towns nightly
> kept not their cattle in folds, and the fear of the mountain thieves
> caused it.[7]

The problem, Gerard noted, had not been wholly eliminated, in that
'yearly be given to the Council in the Marches in the beginning of
November, when the nights grow long, of several felonies in manner in
every mountain country, notwithstanding they be civilly governed'.[8]

Sidney and Gerard had a vested interest in stressing the improvement in
the Marches under their stewardship. Nevertheless, cross-border raiding does
appear to have greatly diminished. Significantly few cases concerning cross-
border assaults were brought before Star Chamber during Elizabeth's reign.

The border region was not entirely free of conflict. In 1575 an attempt
was made by various unknown felons to ambush the Shrewsbury drapers
on their way to purchase Welsh cloth at the Oswestry market.[9] The affair
led to a Star Chamber suit. One of the depositions records a warning given
to the deponent; 'beware of outlaws, for I hear say there be many in these
parts'.[10]

In the early years of the seventeenth century there was a dispute between
the men of Flintshire and those of Chester regarding the mills and causeways on the river Dee. The Welshmen appointed a commission which
decreed that the mills and causeways be destroyed 'whereby the Welsh
people are so encouraged as to threaten to come very speedily to Chester,
with great multitudes, to put the said decree in execution. So that the
memory of that ancient enmity and hostility which was sometimes betwixt
the English and the Welsh is revived, and the minds of the peaceably
affected much disquieted'.[11]

The danger of rebellion in Wales threatening the stability of the English
shires had long passed, but the tradition of Welsh depredations in the
English border counties, however, was long remembered.[12] But border
raiding declined dramatically. This was in part the result of more effective
administration of the border. But this was part of a broader cultural change,
a change in attitudes and perceptions produced by increased intercourse
between the Welsh and the English. These changes were also made
possible by a new political climate which fostered trust between
communities, and which allayed ancient fears and animosities.

As the problem of disorder receded so the English border counties (Cheshire, Shropshire, Herefordshire, Gloucestershire and Worcestershire) and towns expressed growing dissatisfaction with their subordination to the Council of the Marches and its court at Ludlow. In 1562 Bristol succeeded in being exempted from the jurisdiction of the Council. In 1569 Cheshire was freed from the Council's authority. But Worcester in 1574 and Gloucester in the 1590s failed to gain exemption.[13]

After 1604 a prolonged battle was waged in Parliament, led by Sir Roger Owen of Shropshire and Sir Herbert Croft of Herefordshire, to gain exemption for the shires of Salop, Hereford, Gloucester and Worcester. The campaign finally succeeded in 1624.[14] The original intention behind the inclusion of the shires within the Council's jurisdiction, one Welsh MP noted, had been so that 'the President might have Englishmen to subdue the rudeness of the Welshmen, if they rebelled'.[15]

The Welsh, Scottish and Irish Frontiers

The Anglo-Welsh border provides an interesting contrast with England's two other frontier zones, with Scotland and Ireland. The Welsh border was the first to be tamed. In the Elizabethan period the Anglo-Welsh border had in effect disappeared as a political issue, in contrast to the continuous warfare and armed incursions on the Scottish border and in Ireland.[16]

On the Anglo-Scottish border, inter-state rivalry compounded the prevailing disorder. A buffer zone comprised of the west, middle and east marches on either side, with each headed by its warden, appointed by their respective crowns. On the English side the marches were controlled by the Privy Council and the Council of the North, which was remodelled in the 1537 along the lines of the Council of Wales and the Marches.[17] Treaties concluded between the two states regulated the affairs of the border.

The Anglo-Scottish border was notorious for its outlaws, especially Teviotdale, Liddesdale, Tynedale and Redesdale. Family feuds, such as the Maxwell-Johnson feud, persisted for decades and claimed many lives. Outlaws were an integral part of this society, variously referred to as reivers, broken men, rank riders or men who had been put to the horn. The protection or receting of outlaws was widespread amongst the gentry, who resided in highly fortified tower-houses.[18]

Contemporaries saw the success of Henry VIII's policy in taming the Welsh border in the 1530s as a model for dealing with Scotland and Ireland. The Irish and Scots, like the Welsh, were seen by one commentator as 'contending for their liberty'.[19] One writer in 1560/1 wrote of the Scottish border

The frontier are easy to be reformed if the Queen chooses some diligent servant to be President in these parts as Bishop Lee was in Wales, and send with him such a discreet counsellor as Sir William Inglefield was.[20]

In 1574 the President of the Council of the North, Lord Huntingdon, was instructed to apply measures of 'speedy severity' against notable felons, since mildness emboldened the evilly inclined and that force would achieve what gentleness could not attain, with the observation that 'good quiet having ensued by this means in Wales'.[21] Only with the joining of the two kingdoms under James I in 1603 was the problem effectively tackled, when a new administrative system was established both sides of the border and a sustained campaign, lasting seven years, was waged to extirpate the border reivers.

With regard to English policy in Ireland contemporaries drew direct parallels with the Edwardian conquest of Wales in the thirteenth century, emphasising the need to establish strongholds from which to subjugate the county, plant English boroughs, transfer peoples and colonise the country.[22] The policy of the English government in Wales in the sixteenth century was also seen as having direct relevance. In 1565 Sir Thomas Smith wrote to Cecil as follows

Henry VIII did much in Wales when he took the authority of 'hault justice' from the Lords Marchers, and reduced the country into English shires. But Ireland has remained in that barbarous state that Richard II left it in.[23]

In 1565 Sir Henry Sidney was sent to Ireland as Lord Deputy with warrant to 'have like authority for hearing and determining of causes, as the President and Council have here in England in the marches of Wales'.[24] The council, which he established in Munster, was modelled on the council at Ludlow.

William Gerard, Sidney's vice-president of the Council of Wales, was appointed in 1576 Lord Chancellor of Ireland under Sidney. On reforming Ireland, Gerard advised the English Privy Council that there was no 'better precedent' than to 'imitate the course that reformed Wales'.[25] Gerard drew a parallel between the problem of cattle lifting in the two countries by 'the mountain thieves'. These thieves in Ireland carried their raids into the environs of Dublin itself. The chief cause of disorder in Wales, he asserted, had been 'the privilege and custom, which lord marchers had to agree and redeem felons'.[26] The same situation held in Ireland. The Court of Great

Sessions in Wales, which visited the shires, provided a precedent:

> Besides sitting terms at Dublin, there must be itinerant circuiting sessions throughout the Pale twice every year, to administer justice with severity. By that means your people in Wales were brought to civility.[27]

The Lord President's deputy should pass through the strongholds of the rebels and thieves dispensing justice as had been done in Wales.[28]

Other leading figures of the Council of Wales and the Marches who also served in Ireland were Sir William Herbert and Sir James Croft. Both of them drew lessons from the policy of the Tudor government in subjugating Wales.[29] Sir William Herbert saw the problem of lawlessness as rooted in the existing system of land tenure in Ireland and proposed the introduction of primogeniture as a means of reducing the number of impoverished gentry who were the harbourers of thieves. This, he argued, had played a vital role in reducing Wales to 'perfect obedience'[30]

In Ireland the struggle to establish English dominance was protracted. Major rebellions erupted through the sixteenth century, culminating in the rebellion of Hugh O'Neil, earl of Tyrone 1595–1603. Confronted by Irish intransigence, English statesmen still at the end of the sixteenth century saw the solution in military conquest on the model of the Edwardian conquest of Wales.[31]

Another writer comparing the situation in Wales and Ireland urged the application of Lee's repressive policies to subdue the Irish

> Yet Wales was exceeding wild until Bishop Rowland's time, who being Lord President of the Marches, maintained so many spials (spies) ... and had so good intelligence who were the maintainers of the thieves and doing justice upon them without partiality.[32]

The Privy Council was not afraid to trust men from Wales with governmental responsibility elsewhere. Sir John Perrott served as Lord Deputy of Ireland 1584–1588, when Dublin Castle became the home of many Welsh administrators.[33]

James I's Attorney General in Ireland, Sir John Davies, a Wiltshire man of remote Welsh ancestry, in discussing the failures of English policy in Ireland drew attention to Henry VIII's policy in Wales as an alternative:

> For he united the dominion of Wales to the Crown of England and divided it into shires ... enabled them to send Knights and Burgesses

to the Parliament ... made all the laws and statutes of England in force
there ... by means whereof the entire country in a short time was
securely settled in peace and obedience, and hath attained to that
civility of manners and plenty of all things as now we find it not
inferior to the best parts of England.[34]

The eminent lawyer Sir John Dodridge praised Henry VIII's annexation
of Wales to England for the peace and civility it brought the Welsh, and
also 'because in some respects it may serve as a project & precedent of
some other union and annexation by your Majesty of as much or more
consequence and importance'.[35]

The significance of the incorporation of Wales into the English polity as
a constitutional precedent was widely accepted. Edmund Burke in March
1775 addressing the House of Commons on a resolution for the
conciliation of the American colonists cited the union of England and
Wales, commending the precedent set by Henry VIII

Henry VIII gave to the Welsh all the rights and privileges of English
subjects. A political order was established; the military power gave
way to the civil; the Marches were turned into counties ... a complete
and not ill-proportioned representation of the counties and boroughs
was bestowed upon Wales. From that moment, as by a charm, the
tumults subsided; obedience was restored; peace, order and civilisation followed in the train of liberty. When the day star of the English
constitution had arisen in their hearts all was harmony within and
without.[36]

The perspective of historians

From the lofty detachment of Victorian Britain the eminent historian J. A.
Froude applauded the efforts of Rowland Lee to 'tame into civility' the
lawless Welsh. In the Elizabethan age the Welsh accommodated themselves to the new order:

They had ceased to maintain, like the Irish, a feeling of national
hostility. They were suffering now from the intermediate disorders
which intervene when a smaller race is merging into a stronger and
larger; when traditional customs are falling into desuetude, and the
laws designed to take their place have not yet actively grown into
operation.[37]

In the twentieth century Welsh historians have been divided on the significance of the Acts of Union. W. Llywelyn Williams in his book *The Making of Modern Wales* (1919) underscored the benefits of the settlement, reflecting a common liberal view of the time that it released Wales from subjugation and set it on a course towards becoming a nation in the modern world.[38] T. Gwynn Jones, from a nationalist perspective, argued that Welsh society prior to the Acts of Union was dynamic, the disorder of the age reflected a struggle against oppression, and that the Acts of Union cut off the trajectory of development of the society, reducing Wales to a province of England, and incorporating the gentry into that process.[39]

Other Welsh historians such as William Rees, emphasise that the Acts of Union successfully coopted the Welsh gentry into the new system of administration. They shared in the spoils of office, became progressively anglicised, abandoned their own language and their obligations as patron of the native culture.[40] Peter Roberts argues that the Welsh gentry were the principal beneficiaries of the Acts of Union. The decline of the native language and culture, he argues, was not part of a deliberate policy of the Tudor state, but reflected rather longer term economic, social and cultural processes.[41]

The Tudor revolution in government of the 1530s had far reaching implications.[42] The state's supremacy over the church was firmly established. The new absolutist state established its monopoly over the means of warfare, over the administration of justice, and sought to impose its monopoly over taxation. The process of state formation had a direct bearing on the administration of the frontier zones.[43] Wales was transformed from a semi-colonial appendage of the English state to becoming a province. The legislation introduced under Henry IV against the Welsh became effectively a dead letter, although these laws remained on the statute book and were not rescinded until an Act, introduced by Sir James Perrot of Pembrokeshire, was passed in 1624. This conferred on the Welsh the same legal equality as that enjoyed by the English, and which had been conferred on the Scots already in 1607.[44]

The checks to lawlessness were not just those imposed by the law, but by the development of new codes of behaviour, codes of individual self-regulation. This was part of an European trend, reflecting what Norbert Elias has described as the new concern for 'civility'.[45] Despite the frequent protestations concerning the advance of 'civility' and 'gentility' in Wales in the sixteenth century, these ideals were far from universally realised. The concept of civility was also used to define what was culturally acceptable, and in this traditional Welsh culture, language and Catholicism were defined as part of a backward and barbaric world which needed to be transformed.

This 'cultural revolution' swept away the Catholic past and erected a new Protestant state religion.[46] The process of cultural revolution in Elizabethan England saw the new learning of science and letters harnessed to the state's use, in which fear of Catholic Spain consolidated a sense of identity. This served to legitimise not just the power of a particular dynasty but also the new emergent social order. The old order in Wales proved incapable of resisting these forces.

The *uchelwyr* rapaciously enriched themselves and consolidated their position. Their preoccupations were essentially local and they proved incapable of developing a broader conception of national politics.[47] They exercised power at local level within a framework of political, administrative and judicial control directed from the centre. Through these mechanisms some of the worst abuses could be mitigated. Even powerful magnates were brought to account before the Court of the Marches, Star Chamber and the Courts of Great Session. These structures assisted in tempering feuds, and creating a growing respect for the majesty of the law and for the institutions of justice. This was a slow process marked by frequent resort to traditional methods of settling problems – vendetta, the private settlement for homicides

The fundamental social cleavage, the ethnic divide between Welsh and English, which had provided the basis for large scale social mobilisation during the Glyndŵr revolt, remained the most significant political divide through most of the fifteenth century. In the sixteenth century it receded in importance. Other lines of cleavage emerged as of growing importance, the divisions between the gentry themselves and the growing divide between the gentry and other social classes.

In the fifteenth century Wales had been the base of a major revolt against the crown, the base for contending dynasties during the Wars of the Roses, and the bridgehead for the seizure of the throne in 1485. In the sixteenth century the main revolts – the Pilgrimage of Grace of 1536, the western Prayer Book rebellion of 1549, Kett's rebellion in 1549, Wight's rebellion of 1554, and the revolt of the northern earls in 1569[48] – occurred in the south-west and the north of England, fuelled by Catholic opposition to the Reformation and by general economic grievances. Wales provided nothing comparable. The revolts of Buckingham and of Rhys ap Gruffydd were largely figments of an over anxious government's imagination.

Whilst the evidence for mass violence in this period is missing, there is abundant evidence of widespread lawlessness. It is clear that the generalisations offered by MacFarlane[49] for the low level of violence in English society in the sixteenth and seventeenth century cannot be applied to Wales, although Wales was certainly less disordered than other areas under the English crown – the Anglo-Scottish border and Ireland. Conflicts between town and country, yeomen against yeomen, or, more frequently, between individual gentlemen and their factions were common. Riots, as Glanmor Williams notes, were frequent but often orderly and ritualised – intended to proclaim the rights of the community against an aggressor, as in protests against commons enclosures or market forestallers.[50] In a European context, England in the sixteenth century was relatively quiescent compared to France where peasant, urban and provincial revolts proliferated, or Germany which saw the dramatic peasant war of 1525.

The problems of lawlessness in Wales were transformed in a number of ways, with the 1530s marking a watershed, with some forms of lawlessness receding. Firstly, Wales, which since the Glyndŵr rebellion onwards had been seen as a potential source of rebellion, no longer posed such a threat to the crown. It no longer served as a recruiting ground for the armies of dynastic families engaged in war. Secondly, in the 1530s the separate jurisdictions of the marcher lordships and the ecclesiastical courts, was severely curtailed, and as a result the problem of armed confrontation, or private wars, between powerful secular and ecclesiastical magnates disappeared. Thirdly, the reorganisation of the administration of Wales in the 1530s, assisted by the easing of ethnic relations, solved the problem of raiding into the neighbouring English counties. Fourthly, the establishment of a uniform system of justice eliminated the separate jurisdictions where criminals could find safe havens; the system of sanctuary, with its attendant abuses, was curbed, and the onerous forest laws were abolished. Fifthly, conflict between the Welsh and the English in the boroughs diminished. Sixthly, raiding as a form of inter-communal warfare in Wales disappeared.

The concern with lawlessness was refracted through the prism of a Puritan worldview. In the Elizabethan age new issues of public order arose, the suppression of Catholic recusants, the maintenance of public order, defending the country from attack, and curbing the wilder excesses of lawlessness such as piracy on the coast.

Tudor commentators, such as Sir Thomas More, Sir John Wynn, Dr. David Powel, George Owen, William Gerard and Edward Hall reflected the change. This is not to say that the Elizabethan period was free from disorder, far from it, but the nature of the disorder changed. The change was recognised by contemporaries in Wales. The improvement with regard to the maintenance of law and order explains why the union with England was so widely welcomed by the Welsh gentry. This underlines the inability of the Welsh gentry on its own to deal with the crisis. It explains also how this bound the gentry to the Tudor state, and how each sought to justify their position as guardians of order and prosperity.

However, this view cannot be taken wholly at face value. Widespread disorder remained a feature of Welsh life. What emerged under the Elizabethan state was a more ruthless and organised system of social exploitation than had existed previously, in which the power of the *uchelwyr* was now backed up by the power of the state, in which a more ruthless capitalist, market economy, worked towards the dispossession of the lower stratum of society. Bond labour may have disappeared but in its place emerged the phenomenon of mass vagabondage, and the deepening social divide between rich and poor. In the 1580s and 1590s, there was a marked deterioration in public order. This was a European wide phenomena associated with bad harvests and a problem of overpopulation. Insecurity regarding the future succession added to the problem. However, the political significance of lawlessness had changed. Whilst lawlessness was high it was not perceived as a threat to the central government, nor as part of a national revolt, nor a serious threat to the prevailing social order.

Notes

INTRODUCTION

1. St. Augustine, *The City of God Against the Pagans*, Book iv, iv.
2. Geoffrey Chaucer, *The Canterbury Tales* (edited from the Hengwrt Manuscripts by N. F. Blake) (London, 1980) p. 588, lines 223–34.
3. *The Complete Works of John Gower*, ed G. C. Macaulay (Oxford, 1899–1902) vol. iii, p. 317.
4. William of Ockham, *A Short Discourse on the Tyrannical Government* (edited by Arthur Stephen McGrade) (Cambridge, 1992).
5. P. Zagorin, *Rebels and Rulers 1500–1660* (Cambridge, 1982) vol. 1, p. 41.
6. J. Bellamy, *Crime and Public Order in England in the Later Middle Ages* (London, 1973) pp. 70–3, 82–3.
7. M. Keen, *English Society in the Later Middle Ages 1348–1500* (London, 1990) ch. 8. 'Aristocratic Violence: From Civil Strife to Forcible Entry'.
8. L. O. Pike, *A History of Crime in England* (London, 1876) vol. i, p. 297.
9. B. A. Hanwalt, *Crime and Conflict in English Communities 1300–1348* (Harvard, 1979); J. Bellamy, *Crime and Public Order in England in the Later Middle Ages* (London, 1973); A. Fletcher and J. Stevenson, *Order and Disorder in Early Modern England* (Cambridge, 1985).
10. Jessie Crosland, *Outlaws in Fact and Fiction* (London, 1959) p. 9–12; T. Jones, *Chaucer's Knight* (London, 1980) pp. 274–5.
11. F. Braudel, *The Mediterranean* (London, 1973) vol. II, p. 744.
12. E. J. Hobsbawm, *Primitive Rebels* (Manchester, 1963); E. J. Hobsbawm, *Bandits* (London, 1969) a revised edition was published in London, 2000 with a survey of the debate on the 'social bandit'. On the concept of 'primitive rebels' see G. A. Williams, *The Welsh in their History* (London, 1982) pp. 1–12.
13. F. Braudel, *The Mediterranean* (London, 1973) vol. II.
14. See the fascinating account in Count Maffei, *Brigand Life in Italy* (London, 1865) 2 vols. Renato Mammucari, *I Briganti* (Edimond,

Citta di Castello, 2000) provides a richly illustrated acount of brigands in Italian history, literature and art. The classic account of the mafia is Norman Lewis, *The Honoured Society* (London, 1964). See also D. Dolci, *The Bandits of Partinicio* (London, 1960) which highlights the role of the poor and uneducated, cowherds, day labourers and shepherds in Sicilian banditry in the twentieth century.

15. W. Gaunt, *Bandits in a Landscape* (London, 1937).
16. J. Brooks, *When Russia Learned to Read: Literacy and Popular Literature, 1861–1917* (Princeton, 1985) ch. v 'Bandits, Ideas of Freedom and Order'. In his discussion of banditry in nineteenth century Russia Brooks argues that peasants commonly did not consider the seizure of property from the church, the state, the landlords or other communities as theft, since they recognised no obligations towards them.
17. A. D. Carr, *Owen of Wales: The End of the House of Gwynedd* (Cardiff, 1991).
18. For an interesting account of the role of the Norman barons see J. Meisel, *Barons of the Welsh Frontier: The Corbet, Pantulf and Fitzwarin Families, 1066–1272* (Lincoln, Nebraska, 1980).
19. Rees Davies, 'Frontier Arrangements in Fragmented Societies' in Robert Bartlett and Angus MacKay (eds) *Medieval Frontier Societies* (Oxford, 1989) pp. 77–100.
20. A. D. Carr, *Owen of Wales*, p. 76.
21. R. R. Davies, *Domination and Conquest: The Experience of Ireland, Scotland and Wales 1100–1300* (Cambridge, 1990) ch. 6.
22. J. R. Kenyon (ed) *Castles in Wales and the Marches* (Cardiff, 1987); S. C. Stanford, *The Archaeology of the Welsh Marches* (London, 1980) ch. 9.
23. W. R. Jones, 'England Against the Celtic Fringe: A Study in Cultural Stereotypes', *Journal of World History*, vol. xiii (1971) pp. 155–71.
24. M. Salmon, *A Source-Book of Welsh History* (Oxford, 1927) pp. 136, 140, 148, 188. Around 1300 the inhabitants of Malpas, Cheshire appealed to the church authorities that burials and baptisms should be held not at Malpas church but in Cholmondeley Chapel on the grounds 'that the dead in time of war are buried in the fields, because the church of Malpas is so near to Wales that part of the parish belongs to the Welsh and part to the English. Wherefore the English dare not go with their dead to the said church of Malpas in time of war. And likewise at one time it happened that no Englishman dared to come to the said parish church on Easter Day to receive the Body of Christ for fear of the Welsh'. The appeal was

rejected. T. M. Rylands, *An Illustrated History of St. Oswald's Malpas* (Malpas, 1985).

25. R. R. Davies, 'Race Relations in Post-Conquest Wales: Confrontation and Compromise', *THSC*, 1974–5, pp. 32–56; G. Roberts, *Aspects of Welsh History* (Cardiff, 1969) ch. xii 'Wales and England, Antipathy and Sympathy 1282–1485'. See also R. A. Griffiths, 'Medieval Severnside; The Welsh Connection' in R. R. Davies (ed) *Welsh Society and Nationhood* (Cardiff, 1984) pp. 70–89.

26. A. D. Carr, *Owen of Wales*, pp. 78–9.

27. J. Goronwy Edwards, *Calendar of Ancient Correspondence Concerning Wales* (Cardiff, 1935) pp. 227–35. James Given, *State and Society in Medieval Europe: Gwynedd and Languedoc under Outside Rule* (Ithaca and London, 1990) pp. 209–211.

28. *Ibid.*, pp. 230–1.

29. T. Wright, *The History of Ludlow and its Neighbourhood* (London, 1825) p. 236, cites *Foedera*, vol. iii, pp. 869, 901, 1075.

30. *Ibid.*, p. 229, cites *Foedera*, vol. iii, pp. 81, 139, 201, 280.

31. J. J. Jussurand, *English Wayfaring Life in the Middle Ages* (London, 1950) pp. 149, 153–4.

32. *Rot.Parl.*, ii, p. 352 (173).

33. W. Rees (ed), *Calendar of Ancient Petitions relating to Wales* (Cardiff, 1975) pp. 166–167.

34. An early case is cited in *CCR*, 1330–1334, pp. 571–2.

35. *Rot.Parl.*, iii, p. 45.

36. *CPR*, 1385–1389, p. 19.

37. *Rot.Parl.*, iii, p. 272 (1389).

38. *Rot.Parl.*, ii, pp. 259, 358; iii, p. 45 (1378), p. 272 (1389).

39. *Rot.Parl.*, iii, p. 391.

40. E. A. Lewis, 'The Development of Industry and Commerce in Wales during the Middle Ages', *TRHS*, vol. xvii (1903) p. 172.

41. *DHST*, vol. 30, p. 115.

42. Cited in G. R. Elton, *The Tudor Constitution* (Cambridge, 1982) p. 15.

43. G. R. Elton, *The Tudor Revolution in Government* (Cambridge, 1953). G. R. Elton, *The Tudor Constitution* (Cambridge, 1982).

44. Steven G. Ellis and Sarah Barber (eds) *Conquest and Union: Fashioning a British State 1485–1725* (London and New York, 1995).

45. P. Corrigan & D. Sayer, *The Great Arch: English State Formation as Cultural Revolution* (Oxford, 1985).

46.   See N. Elias, *The Civilising Process*, and *The History of Manners* (Oxford, 1982). For a further discussion of the concept of 'civility' see John Hale, *The Civilization of Europe in the Renaissance* (London, 1993).
47.   M. Schipa, *Masaniello* (Bari, 1925) p. 177, cited in G. Zagorin, *Rebels and Rulers*, vol. 1, pp. 252–3.
48.   Niccolo Machiavelli, *The Prince* (Penguin edition, 1986). In the celebated chapter 26 of this work Machiavelli exhorts Lorenzo the Magnifient to use all political guile and force of arms to unify Italy and to expel the 'barbarians'.

CHAPTER 1: THE GLYNDŴR RISING 1400–1412

1.   For a fuller account of the Glyndŵr revolt see R. R. Davies, *The Revolt of Owain Glyndŵr* (Oxford, 1995), J. E. Lloyd, *Owen Glendower/Owain Glyndŵr* (Oxford, 1931); A. G. Bradley, *Owen Glyndŵr and the last struggle for Welsh independence* (London, 1901). See also the entry by T. F. Tout on Glendower in *DNB*, vol. viii, pp. 1308–1313. Glanmor Williams, *Owain Glyndŵr* (Cardiff, 1993). Glanmor Williams, *The Welsh Church from Conquest to Reformation* (Cardiff, 1976) ch. vi 'Glyndŵr and the Church'.
2.   James Given, *State and Society in Medieval Europe: Gwynedd and Languedoc under Outside Rule* (Ithaca and London, 1990 ch. 8 'Resistance and Rebellion'. R. R. Davies, *The Age of Conquest: Wales 1063–1415* (Oxford, 1987).
3.   B. Evans, 'Owain Glyn Dŵr's Raid on Ruthin', *DHST*, vol. 10, 1961, p. 239, *CPR*, 1399–1401, pp. 19, 26.
4.   *CPR*, 1399–1401, p. 26.
5.   *CPR*, 1399–1401, p. 555.
6.   *CPR*, 1399–1401, pp. 415, 360.
7.   *CPR*, 1399–1401, pp. 370, 386, 242.
8.   *CPR*, 1399–1401, p. 392.
9.   *CPR*, 1399–1401, p. 396, 466.
10.   B. Evans, 'Owain Glyn Dŵr's Raid on Ruthin', pp. 239–41.
11.   Sir H. Ellis (ed) *Original Letters Illustrative of English History* (London, 1824) vol. 1, pp. 13–14.
12.   *Ibid*, pp. 4, 13–4, 20.
13.   *CPR*, 1399–1401, p. 451.
14.   *CPR*, 1399–1401, pp. 470, 475.
15.   *CPR*, 1399–1401, pp. 518, 520.

16. *CPR*, 1399–1401, p. 447.
17. *CPR*, 1399–1401, p. 371.
18. J. E. Lloyd, *Owen Glendower*, pp. 39, 150–1.
19. *CPR*, 1399–1401, pp. 421–2, 469–70.
20. *CPR*, 1399–1401, pp. 554; *CPR*, 1401–1405, p. 68.
21. *DNB*, vol. viii, p. 1310.
22. *CPR*, 1401–1405, pp. 155, 171.
23. *CPR*, 1401–1405, pp. 58, 61.
24. *CPR*, 1401–1405, pp. 54, 55.
25. *CPR*, 1401–1405, p. 574.
26. Ellis (ed) *Original Letters*, pp. 24–9.
27. *Rot.Parl.*, iii, p. 457.
28. R. A. Griffiths, 'Some partisans of Owain Glyndŵr at Oxford', *BBCS*, vol. 1962–64, pp. 282–92. *CPR*, 1401–1405, pp. 132, 133. See also Ellis (ed) *Original Letters*, pp. 8–9.
29. *CPR*, 1399–1402, p. 492. *CPR*, 1401–1405, pp. 492–3, 554.
30. *CPR*, 1401–1405, pp. 138, 139, 140, 91.
31. *CPR*, 1401–1405, p. 120.
32. I. Bowen (ed) *The Statutes of Wales* (London, 1908) pp. 31–32: *Rot.Parl.*, iii, p. 474.
33. *Ibid.*, p. 31: *Rot.Parl.*, iii, pp. 472, 476.
34. *Ibid.*, pp. 31–34. See also *CPR*, 1399–1401, pp. 469–70.
35. *Ibid.*, pp. 32–33: *Rot.Parl.*, iii, p. 476. See M. C. Jones, *The Feudal Barons of Powys* (London, 1868) p. 28.
36. J. Gwynfor Jones, 'Government and the Welsh Community: The North-East Borderland in the Fifteenth Century' in H. Hearder and H. R. Loyn (eds) *British Government and Administration* (Cardiff, 1974) p. 58 cites *The Record of Caernarvon* ed H. Ellis (London, 1838) pp. 239–240.
37. Bowen, *Statutes of Wales*, pp. 34–6.
38. *CPR*, 1399–1401, pp. 328, 440. M. C. Jones, *The Feudal Barons of Powys*, pp. 30–31. D. Pratt, 'Medieval Holt', *DHST*, vol. 14, 1965, p. 32.
39. G. Williams, Recovery, *Reorientation and Reformation: Wales c 1415–1642* (Oxford, 1987) p. 12.
40. *CPR*, 1401–1405, pp. 216, 280, 135, 512; CCR, 1402–05, p. 72.
41. *CPR*, 1405–1408, pp. 140, 169, 215, 289, 299, 445.
42. Ellis (ed) *Original Letters*, pp. 10–13.
43. *Ordin. of the Privy Council*, ii, 63.
44. Ellis (ed) *Original Letters*, pp. 15–6, 22–3.
45. F. C. Hingeston (ed) *Royal and Historical Letters during the reign*

of Henry IV (London, 1860) pp. 140, 142, 143. See also Ellis (ed) *Original Letters*, vol. 1, pp. 13–6, 17–20 – these undated letters may refer to this period.

46. *Ibid.*, pp. 138–162. In 1406 John Bodenham, former sheriff of Hereford, was given grants for 'resisting the malice of the Welsh rebels and especially in rescuing the castle and town of Brecon besieged by them' – *CPR*, 1405–1408, p. 281.

47. *CPR*, 1401–1405, p. 297.

48. *CPR*, 1401–1405, p. 293.

49. *CPR*, 1401–1405, p. 299. See also J. E. Messham, 'The County of Flint and the Rebellion of Owen Glyndŵr in the records of the Earldom of Chester', *FHSP*, 1967–8, vol. 23, pp. 9, 14–15.

50. *CPR*, 1401–1405, pp. 253, 353, 365; *CCR*, 1402–5, p. 333.

51. *CPR*, 1401–1405, pp. 330, 412.

52. *CPR*, 1401–1405, p. 294.

53. *CPR*, 1401–1405, p. 285.

54. T. Rymer, *Foedera*, iv, pt II, 54–55. *CPR*, 1401–1405, pp. 186, 111, 293, 313, 109, 285–6, 294, 295, 296–7, 292. *CCR*, 1402–05, p. 111.

55. *CPR*, 1401–1405, pp. 438, 439.

56. *CPR*, 1401–1405, pp. 225, 322, 328, 438.

57. *Ibid.*, pp. 22–4.

58. *Ibid.*, pp. 15–17.

59. Ellis (ed) *Original Letters*, pp. 30–8.

60. *CPR*, 1401–1405, pp. 354, 365, 380–1, 417.

61. *CPR*, 1402–1405, p. 308; *CCR*, 1402–5, p. 308.

62. Hingeston, *Royal and Historical Letters*, vol. II, pp. 76–9.

63. *CPR*, 1401–1405, pp. 504, 510; *CPR*, 1405–1408, pp. 147, 149.

64. *CPR*, 1401–1405, p. 440.

65. *CPR*, 1401–1405, pp. 407, 416, 418.

66. *CPR*, 1401–1405, pp. 398, 441, 472; *CPR*, 1405–08, p. 49; *CCR*, 1402–5, p. 395.

67. Hingeston, *Royal and Historical Letters*, vol II, pp. 18–20.

68. Ellis (ed) *Original Letters*, vol. i, p. 27.

69. *Ibid.*, vol. i, pp. 38–41.

70. *CPR*, 1405–1408, p. 25.

71. *CPR*, 1405–1408, p. 61.

72. *CPR*, 1405–1408, p. 61; *CCR*, 1402–5, pp. 527–8.

73. *CPR*, 1401–1405, p. 529; *CCR*, 1402–5, p. 460.

74. Ellis (ed) *Original Letters*, p. 43.

75. *DNB*, vol. viii, p. 1312.

76. *Ibid.*

77.   *CPR*, 1405–1408, pp. 92, 93.
78.   *CPR*, 1405–1408, p. 156.
79.   *CPR*, 1405–1408, p. 229.
80.   *DNB*, vol. viii, p. 1312.
81.   *CPR*, 1405–1408, pp. 286, 359, 361–2.
82.   *DNB*, vol. viii, p. 1314.
83.   Bowen, *Statutes*, p. 37.
84.   *CPR*, 1405–1408, p. 264.
85.   *CPR*, 1405–1408, pp. 192, 414, 479, 469.
86.   *Foedera*, viii, p. 611.
87.   J. E. Messham, *op.cit.*, p. 27.
88.   J. E. Lloyd, *Owen Glendower*, p. 140, cites *Rot.Parl.*, iii, p. 612, and
      Foedera iv, i, 154.
89.   J. Beverley Smith, 'The Last phase of the Glyndŵr Rebellion',
      BBCS, 1966–68, pp. 250–60; Ellis (ed) *Original Letters*, pp. 4–7.
90.   J. E. Lloyd, *Owen Glendower*, p. 142.
91.   *CPR*, 1408–1413, pp. 179, 202.
92.   J. E. Lloyd, *Owen Glendower*, p. 142, cites *Proceedings of the Privy
      Council* ii, 14, 18, 35, 38, 146–7, 158, 179.
93.   *Ordinances of the Privy Council*, ii, 18.
94.   *DNB.*, vol. viii., pp. 1312–3.
95.   *CPR*, 1399–1401, pp. 187, 444; 1402–1405, pp. 164, 375, 473;
      1405–1408, p. 118, 159, 388; 1408–1413, p. 165.
96.   *CPR*, 1405–1408, p. 192.
97.   *CPR*, 1405–1408, pp. 189, 190, 199, 208, 284.
98.   *CPR*, 1401–1405, pp. 8, 10, 11, 14, 17, 20, 22, 38, 51, 52, 54, 55, 57,
      86, 241, 331, 347, 352, 369. See also W. Rees (ed) *Calendar of
      Ancient petitions Relating to Wales* (Cardiff, 1975) pp. 73, 381.
99.   *CCR*, 1402–5, pp. 265, 348.
100. *CCR*, 1402–5, p. 252; *CPR*, 1401–1405, pp. 434, 504; 1408–1413,
      pp. 5, 29, 148, 157, 160.
101. Hingeston, *Royal and Historical Letters*, vol. 1, p. 153. *CPR*,
      1405–1408, p. 160. *CPR*, 1405–1408, pp. 27, 42, 80, 181. *CCR*, p. 20
      (c); J. E. Lloyd, *Owen Glendower*, p. 137.
102. *CPR*, 1408–1413, p. 406. *Foedera,* viii, 753.
103. *CPR*, 1401–1405, pp. 294, 298, 299, 311, 326, 438, 439. *CPR*,
      1405–1408, pp. 64, 65.
104. *Foedera*, viii, 436–7.
105. *CPR*, 1405–1408, p. 164.
106. *CPR*, 1405–1408, p. 203.
107. J. E. Lloyd, *Owen Glendower*, p. 129.

108. R. A. Griffiths, 'The Glyn Dŵr Rebellion in North Wales through the eyes of an Englishman', *BBCS*, 1964–66, pp. 162–3.

109. J. E. Messham, *op.cit.*, pp. 21–2, 23–4, 26.

110. G. Roberts, 'The Anglesey Submissions of 1406', *BBCS*, vol. 15, 1952–54, pp. 39–61.

111. *CPR*, 1405–1408, p. 356.

112. *CPR*, 1405–08, pp. 356, 320, 337, 325, 378, 365, 376, 384; On Powys see *Mont.Coll.*, iv, pp. 325–44.

113. E. Powell, *Kingship, Law and Society: Criminal Justice in the Reign of Henry V* (Oxford, 1989) p. 198.

114. *CPR*, 1405–1408, pp. 390, 411, 412, 393; *CPR*, 1408–1413, pp. 30, 54, 166–167.

115. *CPR*, 1405–1408, pp. 325, 378, 385, 390, 411, *CPR*, 1408–1413, pp. 28, 45, 30, 138.

116. *CPR*, 1408–1413, pp. 82, 141.

117. *CPR*, 1408–1413, pp. 171, 216, 283, 284, 303, 305, 295, 307, 304, 364, 413.

118. *Leland's Itinerary in Wales* (ed. L. T. Smith) (London, 1906); See also Sir H. Ellis (ed) *Original Letters*, p. 42. See also the views of a seventeenth century chronicler quoted in D. J. Davies, *Economic History of South Wales Prior to 1800* (Cardiff, 1933) p. 41.

119. G. Pennar Griffiths, *Rhyddiaith Gymreig o'r Mabinogion hyd Heddiw* (Caernarfon, 1911) vol. 1, p. 46

120. *CPR*, 1399–1401, p. 555.

121. *CPR*, 1399–1401, p. 418.

122. *CPR*, 1401–1405, pp. 367, 378, 397, 455, 473. *CPR*, 1405–1408, pp. 53, 22, 65, 90, 93, 187, 192, 306.

123. R. Holinshed, *Holinshed's Chronicle* (Oxford, 1923) p. 36; W. Shakespeare, *Henry IV, Part One*, Act. 1, sc. 1.

124. D. H. Evans, 'An Incident on the Dee during the Glyn Dŵr Rebellion?', *DHST*, vol. 37, 1988, pp. 5–40.

125. M. Salmon, *A Source Book of Welsh History*, p. 203.

126. J. E. Lloyd, *Owen Glendower*, p. 150. *DNB*, vol. viii, p. 1308.

127. G. A. Williams, 'Glyn Dŵr' in A. J. Roderick, *Wales through the Ages*, vol. i, pp. 176–83.

128. R. R. Davies 'Owain Glyn Dŵr and the Welsh Squirearchy', *THSC*, 1968, pp. 168.

129. R. R. Davies, *The Revolt of Owain Glyndŵr*, ch. 11.

130. J. E. Lloyd, *Owen Glendower*, pp. 2–4, 146.

131. P. Zagorin, *Rebels and Rulers 1500–1660*, vol. 1, p. 41. A. Sorokin

in his *Social and Cultural Dynamics* vol i–iv, (New York, 1937–41) assesses the Glyndŵr rebellion as being of greater magnitude than the English peasant's revolt of 1381. This is disputed by Zagorin, but he is under the misapprehension that the former was merely 'an insurrection in North Wales' in 1408. P. Zagorin, *op.cit.*, p. 34.

132. G. Owen, *Pembrokeshire*, vol. iii, p. 123.
133. *Ibid.*, p. 37.
134. *The History of Cambria* (by Caradoc of Llancarvan, Englished by Dr. Powell and augmented by W. Wynne) (London, 1774) pp. 319–20.

CHAPTER 2: A TURBULENT LAND 1413–1450

1. *CCR.*, 1413–1421, pp. 67–68.
2. E. Powell, *Kingship, Law and Society: Criminal Justice in the Reign of Henry V* (Oxford, 1989) pp. 135–6.
3. E. Powell, 'The Restoration of Law and Order', in G. L. Harriss, *Henry V: The Practice of Kingship* (Oxford, 1991) p. 61. *CPR*, 1413–16, pp. 112–13, 114, 179.
4. Powell, *Kingship, Law and Society*, p. 197. *CPR*, 1413–1416, pp. 112–4, 179.
5. *CPR*, 1416–1422, p. 101; *CPR*, 1413–1416, p. 103.
6. *CPR*, 1413–1416, pp. 19, 29; *CPR*, 1416–1422, p. 66.
7. *CPR*, 1413–1416, pp. 11, 19, 29, 22, 26, 44.
8. Powell, *Kingship, Law and Society*, pp. 197–8.
9. R. R. Davies, 'Owain Glyn Dŵr and the Welsh Squirearchy', *THSC*, 1968, p. 167.
10. *CCR*, 1413–1421, p. 89, 110; *CPR*, 1413–1416, pp. 122–125, 128.
11. I. Bowen (ed) *The Statutes of Wales* (London, 1908) pp. 37–39.
12. *CPR*, 1416–1422, pp. 64, 66, 339.
13. R. A. Griffiths, 'The Glyn Dŵr Rebellion in North Wales through the eyes of an Englishman', *BBCS*, 1964–66, pp. 152–3.
14. G. Williams, *Recovery, Reorientation and Reformation: Wales c 1415–1642* (Oxford, 1987) p. 29.
15. *Ibid.*, p. 24.
16. Powell, *Kingship, Law and Society*, p. 198.
17. *CPR*, 1413–1416, pp. 137, 195.
18. *Ibid.*, p. 153. Powell, *Kingship, Law and Society*, p. 197.

19. Griffiths 'The Glyn Dŵr Rebellion', p. 167. *CPR*, 1413–1416, pp. 137, 195.
20. Powell, *Kingship, Law and Society*, pp. 198–9.
21. J. Beverley Smith, 'The Last Phase of the Glyn Dŵr rebellion', *BBCS*, 22 (1966–8) p. 254; T. B. Pugh, *The Marcher Lordships of South Wales, 1415–1536* (Cardiff, 1963) p. 42.
22. Griffiths, 'The Glyn Dŵr Rebellion', p. 154.
23. *Ibid.*, pp. 151–68. Powell, *Kingship, Law and Society*, p. 199; *CPR*, 1413–1416, pp. 231, 271.
24. *CPR*, 1413–1416, p. 229.
25. Powell, *Kingship, Law and Society*, p. 199.
26. *CPR*, 1413–1416, p. 93, pardon to the constable of Chester castle; *CPR*, 1413–1416, p. 100, pardon to Edward de Charleton, lord of Powys; *CPR*, 1416–1422, p. 67, pardon to the constable of Rhuddlan castle.
27. *CPR*, 1413–1416, p. 278. Griffiths, 'The Glyn Dŵr Rebellion' p. 167
28. *CPR*, 1413–1416, pp. 139, 228, 247, 269, 385.
29. *CPR*, 1413– 1416, p. 344.
30. *CPR*, 1413–1416, pp. 21, 182, 258.
31. *CPR*, 1413–1416, p. 308.
32. H. R. Davies, *The Conway and Menai Ferries* (Cardiff, 1966) p. 33.
33. J. Goronwy Edwards, *Calendar of Ancient Correspondence Concerning Wales* (Cardiff, 1935) p. 261.
34. W. Rees, *South Wales and the March, 1282–1415* (Oxford, 1924) p. 275, cites *Min.Acc.* 615/9841, Monmouth (1 H.IV).
35. *Ibid.*, p. 280, cites *Min.Acc.* 1222/12.
36. *Ibid.*, p. 280, cites *Rot.Parl.*, iii, pp. 615, 616.
37. *CPR*, 1413–1416, p. 89.
38. T. B. Pugh, *The Marcher Lordships of South Wales 1415–1536*, pp. 11, 15, 16, 61, 62, 67 Proceedings of the Great Sessions in Chepstow in 1415.
39. J. E. Lloyd, *Owen Glendower* (Oxford, 1966) p. 154.
40. Elissa R. Henken, *National Redeemer: Owain Glyndŵr in Welsh Tradition* (Cardiff, 1996).
41. *CPR*, 1413–1416, pp. 342, 404; *CPR*, 1416–22, p. 89.
42. J. H. Wylie, *The Reign of Henry V* (Cambridge, 1914) vol. 1, p. 456.
43. *DNB*, vol. viii, p. 1313.
44. *CPR*, 1413–1416, p. 395.
45. *CPR*, 1413–1416, pp. 75, 76.
46. *CPR*, 1416–1422, pp. 235, 389.

47. J. Beverley Smith, *op.cit.*, pp. 254–56.

48. H. Ellis (ed) *Original Letters Illustrative of English History* (London, 1824) vol. 1, p. 8.

49. J. Beverley Smith, *op.cit.*, p. 254.

50. Wylie, *The Reign of Henry V*, pp. 277–8; *CPR*, 1416–1422, pp. 145, 372.

51. *Ibid.*, pp. 253–254.

52. *CPR*, 1416–1422, pp. 254, 335.

53. *CPR*, 1416–1422, p. 294. See also *CPR*, 1416–1422, p. 22, commission to Lord Abergavenny to receive the rebels Thomas Vaughan and William ap Thomas.

54. T. Phillips, *The History and Antiquities of Shrewsbury* (Shrewsbury, 1779) p. 205. See also S. Meeson Morris, 'The Obsolete Punishments of Shropshire', *The Shropshire Archaeological Society*, 1889, p. 418.

55. *Rot.Parl.*, iv, pp. 170, 169, 174–5; *CCR*, 1422–30, p. 41; *Foedera*, IV, iv, 81–2.

56. R. A. Griffiths, *The Reign of Henry VI* (London, 1981), p. 149, n. 25.

57. J. Bellamy, *Crime and Public Order in England in the Later Middle Ages* (London, 1973) pp. 8–9.

58. Williams, *Recovery*, p. 175.

59. Griffiths, *Henry VI*, p. 206.

60. *CPR*, 1422–1429, pp. 218, 424.

61. *CPR*, 1413–1416, p. 341. In 1415 Adam Banastre a burgess of Conwy was returned to his franchises and liberties on the order of the crown, having earlier being deprived of them as he had married a Welsh woman. D. Pratt, 'A Holt Petition c. 1429', *DHST*, vol. 26, pp. 153–5. The attempt in 1429 by the burgesses of Holt to prevent Robert Trevor becoming receiver of Bromfield and Yale, because of his grandfather's role in the siege of Holt castle in 1401.

62. *CPR*, 1422–1429, pp. 358, 459, 451.

63. W. Rees (ed) *Calendar of Ancient Petitions relating to Wales* (Cardiff, 1975) pp. 328–9.

64. *Ibid.*, pp. 181–2; Bowen, *Statutes of Wales*, pp. 40–41.

65. *Rot.Parl.*, iv, pp. 377–8, 440–1. Griffiths, *Henry VI*, p. 97.

66. *CPR*, 1461–1467, p. 150.

67. *CPR*, 1429–1436, pp. 130, 200.

68. Bellamy, *op.cit.*, pp. 8–9. Griffiths, *Henry VI*, pp. 144–6.

69. R. A. Griffiths, 'Wales and the Marches', in S. B. Chrimes, C. D. Ross and R. A. Griffiths (eds) *Fifteenth Century England 1399–1509* (Manchester, 1972) p. 155.

70. *CPR*, 1422–1429, pp. 446–7. Griffiths, *Henry VI*, pp. 143–44.

71. *Rot.Parl.*, iv, p. 358.
72. K. Williams-Jones, 'A Mawddwy Court Roll 1415–16', *BBCS*, May 1970, pp. 329–45.
73. J. Beverley Smith, 'The Regulation of the Frontier of Meirionydd in the Fifteenth Century', *JMHRS*, vol. 5, 1965–6, pp. 105–11.
74. *Rot.Parl.*, iv, p. 495.
75. Williams, *Recovery*, p. 175.
76. Griffiths, *Henry VI*, p. 343.
77. *Ibid.*, pp. 342, 783, 310; 833, n.66, n.77; 834, n.79, 820.
78. *Ibid.*, p. 344.
79. *CPR*, 1436–1441, pp. 452, 536.
80. *CPR*, 1446–1452, p. 5.
81. *CPR*, 1441–1446, pp. 222, 365.
82. R. L. Storey, *The End of the House of Lancaster* (London, 1966) p. 135.
83. Griffiths, *Henry VI*, pp. 496–7.
84. Williams, *Recovery*, p. 175.
85. *Ibid.*, p. 259.
86. E. A. Lewis, *The Medieval Boroughs of Snowdonia* (London, 1912) p. 264.
87. *Proceedings and Ordinances of the Privy Council*, vol.5, pp. cxx–cxxi, 211, 213, 215.
88. *Rot.Parl.*, v, pp. 10, 105, 155. See J. Gwynfor Jones, 'Government and the Welsh Community: The North-East Borderland in the Fifteenth Century' in H. Hearder and H. R. Lyon (eds) *British Government and Administration* (Cardiff, 1974) p. 62.
89. *CPR*, 1441–1446, p. 426.
90. W. Rees (ed) *Calendar of Ancient Petitions relating to Wales*, pp. 38–39.
91. *Ibid.*, pp. 248–49.
92. Bowen, *Statutes of Wales*, p. 45: *Rot.Parl.*, v, pp. 138–39.
93. *Rot.Parl.*, v, p. 154.
94. Griffiths, *Henry VI*, p. 411.
95. G. Williams, *The Welsh Church from Conquest to Reformation* (Cardiff, 1976) pp. 228–233.
96. *CPR*, 1413–1416, pp. 152, 201, 234, 246; *CPR*, 1416–1422, p. 179.
108. J. Goronwy Edwards, *Calendar of Ancient Correspondence Concerning Wales*, pp. 257–58.
98. W. de G. Birch, *A History of Margam Abbey* (London, 1897) pp. 340–1. Clark, *Cartae*, iv, 1500–1.
99. Griffiths, *Henry VI*, p. 133.

100. David H. Williams, *The Welsh Cistercians* (Tenby, 1984) vol. 1, ch. 4.

101. R. W. Hays, *The History of the Abbey of Aberconway 1186–1537* (Cardiff, 1963) pp. 132–33. See also W. de G. Birch, *A History of Margam Abbey* (London, 1897) pp. 344–45. For the text of the petition to the king see Stephen W. Williams, *The Cistercian Abbey of Strata Florida* (London, 1889) pp. xxxix–xli.

102. *CPR*, 1429–1436, pp. 69, 194, 106.

103. *CCR*, 1429–1435, p. 364.

104. *CPR*, 1441–1445, pp. 151–2. See W. de G. Birch, *op.cit.*, pp. 344–5.

105. *CPR*, 1441–1446, p. 164.

106. A. J. Taylor, *Raglan Castle, Monmouthshire* (HMSO, London, 1951) p. 8. Graham, *Journal of the Archeological Association*, xxxv, 118–9.

107. *Rot.Parl.*, v, p. 43.

108. *CPR*, 1441–1446, p. 42.

109. *CPR*, 1422–1429, pp. 218, 424.

110. *Acts of the Privy Council*, V, 244, 233.

111. R. A. Griffiths, 'Gruffydd ap Nicholas and the rise of the House of Dinefwr', *NLWJ*, xiii (1964) pp. 260–263.

112. R. A. Griffiths, 'Wales and the Marches', pp. 153–4.

CHAPTER 3: STATE, LAW AND SOCIETY

1. R. A. Griffiths, 'Wales and the Marches', in S. B. Chrimes, C. D. Ross and R. A. Griffiths (eds) *Fifteenth Century England 1399–1509* (Manchester, 1972) p. 146.

2. W. A. Morris, *The Medieval English Sheriff to 1300* (Manchester, 1927) pp. 175–6: I. Gladwin, *The Sheriff: The Man and his Office* (Manchester, 1936) pp. 391–3.

3. R. Stewart-Brown, *The Sarjeants of the Peace in Medieval England and Wales* (Manchester, 1936) pp. 33–46.

4. W. Llywelyn Williams, 'The King's Court of Great Sessions in Wales', *Y Cymmrodor*, xxvi (1912) pp. 4–5.

5. G. Williams, *Recovery, Reorientation and Reformation: Wales c 1415–1642* (Oxford, 1987) p. 36; A. C. Reeves, *The Marcher Lords* (Llandybie, 1983) p. 11. R. R. Davies lists 36 'Anglo-Norman' lordship in the fourteenth century. This excludes some Welsh lordships, and some of the lordships bordering the English shires R. R. Davies, *Conquest, Coexistence and Change: Wales 1063–1415* (Oxford, 1987) appendix.

6. R. Somerville, *History of the Duchy of Lancaster, 1265–1603* (London, 1953) vol. 1.

7. Thomas Roberts, *Gwaith Tudur Penllyn ac Ieuan ap Tudur Penllyn* (Cardiff, 1958) p. 19.

8. I. Williams and J. Ll. Williams (eds) *Gwaith Guto'r Glyn* (Cardiff, 1939) p. 146.

9. W. Rees, *South Wales and the March 1284–1415* (Oxford, 1924) pp. 72–73, 69, 103–109.

10. Williams, *Recovery*, p. 90.

11. W. Ogwen Williams, 'The Social Order in Tudor Wales', *THSC*, 1968, pp. 167–178; W. Rees, *South Wales and the March*, ch. 11. R. R. Davies and J. Beverley Smith, 'The Social Structure of Medieval Glamorgan' in T. B. Pugh (ed) *Glamorgan County History, vol. iii: The Middle Ages* (Cardiff, 1971).

12. Griffiths, 'Wales and the Marches', p. 150.

13. I. Tegid & W. Davies (eds), *Gwaith Lewys Glyn Cothi* (Oxford, 1837) p. 85.

14. I. Williams (ed) *Gwaith Ieuan Deulwyn* (Bangor, 1909) p. 55.

15. On the question of denizenship see H. T. Evans, *Wales and the Wars of the Roses* (Cambridge, 1915) p. 20; W. Rees (ed) *Calendar of Ancient Petitions relating to Wales* (Cardiff, 1975) pp. 38, 135, 136, 144, 146–7, 148, 162, 207, 220.

16. R. A. Griffiths, *The Principality of Wales in the Later Middle Ages I: South Wales 1277–1536* (Cardiff, 1972) pp. 143–5; *Rot.Parl.*, iv, p. 6.

17. Evans, *Wales and the Wars of the Roses*, p. 29.

18. T. Roberts, *Gwaith Tudur Penllyn ac Ieuan ap Tudur Penllyn*, p. 9.

19. W. J. Gruffydd, *Y Flodeugerdd Newydd* (Cardiff, 1909) pp. 37–38 'Cywydd i'r Byd'. See also Saunders Lewis, *Meistri a'u Crefft* (Cardiff, 1981) pp. 158–9.

20. *Ibid.*, pp. 42–47 'Cywydd y Farn'.

21. *Ibid.*, p. 78.

22. Saunders Lewis perceptively compares the Welsh uchelwyr of the fifteenth century with the image of the Milanese gentry of the seventeenth century in Manzoni's novel 'The Betrothed' (*I Promessi Sposi*). Saunders Lewis, *Meistri a'u Crefft* (Cardiff, 1981) pp. 158–9.

23. Griffiths, *Henry VI*, p. 108.

24. C. Ross, *Edward IV* (London, 1974) p. 383.

25. A. Jones (ed), *Flintshire Ministers' Accounts 1301–1328* (Prestatyn, 1913).

26. *Ibid.*, pp. xviii–xx; *CPR*, 1429–1436, pp. 24, 35, 59, 191, 196, 121, 449. *CPR*, 1436–1441, pp. 378, 177; *CPR*, 1441–46, pp. 22–3, 375; *CPR*, 1446–1452, p. 470; *CPR*, 1452–61, pp. 75, 229, 543, 567; *CPR*, 1477–85, p. 455. *Harleian Manuscripts*, vol. I, pp. 108, 119, 286.

27. On the development of *cymhortha* in the Middle Ages see W. Rees, *South Wales and the March 1284–1415*, pp. 229–234.

28. On the Sessions in Eyre in the marcher lordships, see T. B. Pugh, *The Marcher Lordships of South Wales, 1415–1536* (Cardiff, 1963) pp. 7, 36, 42–43, 45, 47, 133, 135, 140.

29. Griffiths, 'Wales and the Marches', p. 153: T. B. Pugh, 'The Ending of the Middle Ages', pp. 578–579: Williams, *Recovery*, pp. 41–42.

30. *Ibid.*, p. 153.

31. *Ibid.*, p. 152. R. A. Griffiths, 'Gruffydd ap Nicholas and the Rise of the House of Dinefwr', *NLWJ*, xiii (1964); R. A. Griffiths, 'Gruffydd ap Nicholas and the Fall of the House of Lancaster', *WHR*, i (1964–1965) pp. 213–231: R. A. Griffiths, *The Principality of Wales in the Later Middle Ages*, 22ff.

32. *CPR*, 1422–1429, p. 332.

33. W. de Gray Birch, *Penrice and Margam Abbey Manuscripts* (London, 1895) vol. 3, pp. 24, 1175.

34. *Rot.Parl.*, iv, pp. 10, 329.

35. Williams, *Recovery*, p. 14.

36. W. Rees, *South Wales and the March*, p. 56. *CPR*, 1413–1416, p. 308.

37. R. R. Davies, 'The Twilight of Welsh Law 1284– 1536', *History*, vol. li. (1966).

38. J. Bellamy, *Crime and Public Order in England in the Later Middle Ages* (London, 1973) p. 133. On the history of trial by ordeal, introduced into Wales by the Normans, and on trial by battle see R. Bartlett, *Trial by Fire and Water* (Oxford, 1988) pp. 47–9, 103–126.

39. Griffiths, 'Gruffydd ap Nicholas and the Fall of the House of Lancaster', p. 213.

40. E. Powell, 'Arbitration and the law in England in the later Middle Ages', *TRHS*, vol. 33 (1983). See the case of the murdered Walter ap Gwilym of Archenfield in 1495. E. Owen (ed) *Catalogue of Manuscripts relating to Wales in the British Museum* (London, 1903) vol. 2, pp. 458–9. See also Ailsa Herbert, 'Herefordshire 1413–61: Some Aspects of Society and Public Order' in R. A. Griffiths (ed) *Patronage, The Crown and the Provinces in Later Medieval England* (Gloucester, 1981) p. 121, f 76.

41. A. C. Reeves, *The Marcher Lords*, p. 19.

42.   J. Beverley Smith, 'The Regulation of the Frontier of Meirionnydd in the Fifteenth Century', *JMHS*, vol. 5 (1965–6), pp. 105–11, J. Beverley Smith, 'Cydfodau o'r Bymthegfed Ganrif', *BBCS*, vol. xxi (1966) pp. 309–324. See also W. Rees, *South Wales and the March*, pp. 45–46, n. 3, and T. B. Pugh, *The Marcher Lordships of South Wales*, p. 30, n. 3.

43.   J. Conway Davies, 'Felony in Edwardian Wales', *THSC*, 1916–1917, pp. 182, 168.

44.   Halsbury's *Laws of England* (Hailsham Edition) vol. ix, pp. 262–263: Pollock and Maitland, *History of English Law*, vol. 1; M. Hastings, *The Court of Common Pleas* (New York, 1947) ch. xii; Jessie Crosland, *Outlaws in Fact and Fiction* (London, 1959) pp. 9–12.

45.   Bellamy, *op.cit*, pp. 104–105, 157–159.

46.   W. Rees (ed) *Calendar of Ancient Petitions Relating to Wales* (Cardiff, 1975) pp. 431–2, see also pp. 120, 183, 205, 341, 366, 532.

47.   Pugh, *The Marcher Lordships of South Wales*, pp. 23–25, 91–92.

48.   Pugh, 'The Ending of the Middle Ages', p. 3.

49.   D. Pratt, 'Medieval Holt', *DHST*, vol. 14, 1965, p. 27.

50.   Pugh, *The Marcher Lordships of South Wales*, p. 41.

51.   *Ibid.*, pp. 254, 268, 271, 272.

52.   A Compton-Reeves, 'The Great Sessions in the Lordship of Newport in 1503', *BBCS*, vol. xxvi, part III, November 1975, pp. 326–27.

53.   *Bewdley in its Golden Age*, Bewdley Historical Research Group (Bewdley, 1991) pp. 5–6.

54.   I. D. Thornley, 'The Destruction of Sanctuary', in R. W. Seton-Watson (ed) *Tudor Studies* (London, 1924) pp. 182–207; Bellamy, *op.cit.*, pp. 106–11.

55.   W. Rees, *South Wales and the March*, p. 179: J. Conway Davies, *op.cit.*, p. 172: A. N. Palmer and E. Owen, *A History of Ancient Tenures of Land in Wales and the Marches* (1910), pp. 137, 163, 184–190.

56.   Robert Richards, *Cymru'r Oesau Canol* (Wrexham, 1933) pp. 343–344; *Y Cymmrodor*, vol. xxv, pp. 97–99. W. Rees, *The Order of St. John in Wales* (Cardiff, 1947) p. 38.

57.   David H.Williams, *The Welsh Cistercians* (Tenby, 1984) vol. 1, p. 176.

58.   *CPL.*, ix, pp. 454–5, 501–3.

59.   Bellamy, *op.cit.*, pp. 111–114: *L.&P. F&D, Henry VIII*, vol. 4, pt. 2, p. 2002. The case of Owen Griffiths of Powys, required to abjure the realm but pardoned in 1528. See the case of the felon Ieuan Glas

cited in de Birch, *A History of Margam Abbey* (London, 1897) p. 349.

60. In the diocese of Hereford 'Gitto Glane' was convicted of rape and robbery in 1475, and William ap Hugyn was similarly accused in 1488. A. T. Bannister, *Registrum Thomae Myllyng* (Cant. and York Society, 1920) pp. 14–16, 52–53, 151. G. Williams, *The Welsh Church*, p. 336. *The Episcopal Registers of the Diocese of St. David's*, vol. II, pp. 527–9.

61. D. Pratt, 'Grant of Office of Keeper of Parks in Bromfield and Yale 1461', *DHST*, vol. 24, 1975, pp. 203–5.

62. *CPR*, 1405–1408, p. 245; *CPR*, 1413–1416, pp. 361, 326; *CPR*, 1422–1429, p. 348; *CPR*, 1429–1436, pp. 450, 466; *CPR*, 1436–1441, pp. 20, 40, 94, 194, 161; *CPR*, 1441–1446, p. 428; *CPR*, 1446–1452, p. 219; *CPR*, 1452–1461, p. 646; *Harleian Manuscripts*, vol. I, p. 286.

63. *CPR*, 1461–1467, pp. 526–7.

64. *CPR*, 1476–1485, pp. 349–50.

65. *Harleian Manuscripts*, vol. I, p. 107; vol. II, pp. 104, 190, 198, 153.

66. I. Williams (ed) *Gwaith Guto'r Glyn*, pp. 210–212, for Guto'r Glyn's poem requesting a woodknife from Gruffydd ap Rhys, forester of Yale, with its frightening description of the woodknife itself.

67. *Harleian Manuscripts*, vol. I, p. 161.

68. R. R. Davies, 'The Survival of the Blood feud in Medieval Wales', *History,* vol. liv, 1969, pp. 338–357; R. R. Davies, 'The Twilight of Welsh Law', p. 154; T. Jones Pierce, *Medieval Welsh Society*, 1972 (ed. J. Beverley Smith) ch. x; T. Lewis, *A Glossary of Medieval Welsh Law* (Cardiff, 1913) p. 151; J. Conway Davies, 'Felony in Edwardian Wales' *THSC*, 1916–1917, pp. 150, 154.

69. William Salesbury, *Oll Synnwyr Pen Kembero yngyd* (ed. J. Gwenogvryn Davies) (Bangor, 1902).

70. I. Tegid & W. Davies (eds) *Gwaith Lewys Glyn Cothi*, p. 475.

71. Meic Stephens, *The Oxford Companion to the Literature of Wales* (Oxford, 1986) p. 556.

72. Sir John Wynn, *The History of the Gwydir Family* (Cardiff, 1927) pp. 29, 30, 38–39, 46.

73. *Ibid.*, p. 41. See also p. 43 for a further example of how families protected assassins.

74. Thomas Roberts, *Gwaith Tudur Penllyn*, pp. 50, 84.

75. J. E. Morris, *The Welsh Wars of Edward I* (Oxford, 1901) p. 280.

76. A. D. Carr, 'Welshmen and the Hundred Years War', *WHR.*, iv

(1968–69) p. 35. M. Siddons, 'Welshmen in the Service of France', *BBCS*, vol. xxxvi, 1989, pp. 160–183.

77. H. J. Hewitt, *The Organization of War under Edward III 1338–1362* (Manchester, 1966) p. 30.

78. A. D. Carr, 'Welshmen and the Hundred Years War', *WHR*, iv (1968–69); H. T. Evans, *Wales and the Wars of the Roses* (Cambridge, 1915); Williams, *Recovery*, ch. 7.

79. H. Lewis *et.al.* (eds) Cywyddau Iolo Goch ac Eraill (Cardiff, 1937) pp. xxxviii–liii, 312. *Rot.Parl.*, iv, p. 6.

CHAPTER 4: THE WARS OF THE ROSES, 1450–1471

1. *Rot.Parl.*, v, p. 200.

2. For a fuller examination of the Wars of the Roses in Wales see H. T. Evans, *Wales and the Wars of the Roses* (Cambridge, 1915); G. Williams, *Recovery, Reorientation and Reformation: Wales c 1415–1642* (Oxford, 1987): Ioan Tegid & W. Davies (eds) *Gwaith Lewis Glyn Cothi* (Oxford, 1837) vol. 1, Introduction 'Historical Sketch of the Wars between the Rival Roses' by Ioan Tegid, pp. iii–xxxviii.

3. P. Anderson, *Lineages of the Absolutist State* (London, 1974) p. 118.

4. *Rot.Parl.*, v, pp. 211–213. See also R. I. Jack, *The Grey of Ruthin Valor* (Sydney, 1965) p. 74. For William Tresham see *DNB*, vol. xix, pp. 1132–3.

5. *Ibid.*, p. 213.

6. *Ibid.*, p. 113.

7. C. Rawcliffe, *The Staffords, Earls of Stafford and Dukes of Buckingham 1394–1521* (Cambridge, 1978) pp. 50, 16.

8. R. L. Storey, *The End of the House of Lancaster* (London, 1966) pp. 101–2.

9. R. A. Griffiths, *The Reign of Henry VI* (London, 1981) p. 257.

10. *Ibid.*, p. 735.

11. *Ibid*, pp. 735, 738, 764 n. 117.

12. Griffiths, *Henry VI*, p. 264.

13. *Ibid.*, p. 779.

14. *Rot.Parl.*, v, p. 279; R. A. Griffiths, 'Wales and the Marches', in S. B. Chrimes, C. D. Ross and R. A. Griffiths (eds) *Fifteenth Century England 1399–1509* (Manchester, 1972) p. 157.

15. Storey, *op.cit.*, p. 179.

16. *Ibid.*, pp. 344–5.

17. *CPR*, 1452–1461, pp. 36, 570.

18. *CPR*, 1446–1452, p. 581.

19. *CPR*, 1452–1461, p. 124.
20. Griffiths, 'Wales and the Marches', p. 157.
21. Griffiths, *Henry VI*, p. 836, n. 108.
22. *Ibid.*, p. 179, fn. 13.
23. *Ibid.*, p. 780; *CPR*, 1452–1461, p. 326.
24. A. J. Taylor, *Raglan Castle, Monmouthshire* (London, 1951) p. 9.
25. *CPR*, 1452–1461, pp. 360, 367.
26. A. J. Taylor, *op.cit.*, p. 9.
27. Griffiths, *Henry VI*, pp. 783, 788.
28. *Ibid.*, p. 822.
29. *CPR*, 1452–1461, p. 557.
30. J. Bellamy, *Crime and Public Order in England in the Later Middle Ages* (London, 1973) p. 9.
31. Griffiths, *Henry VI*, pp. 828–9.
32. *CPR*, 1452–1461, pp. 564–5.
33. *Proceedings and Ordinances of the Privy Council*, vol. 16, pp. lxxxv, 302–305.
34. W & E. L. C. P. Hardy (eds.) Jehan de Waurin, *Recueil des Croniques et anchiennes Istories de la Grant Bretagne* (Rolls Series 1864–91) pp. 311–2.
35. Griffiths, *Henry VI*, p. 869.
36. *Ibid.*, p. 871.
37. H. Lewis et.al., (eds) *Cywyddau Iolo Goch ac Eraill* (Cardiff, 1937) p. 235.
38. W. J. Gruffudd, *Llenyddiaeth Cymru, 1450–1600* (Liverpool, 1922) p. 32.
39. C. Ross, *Edward IV* (London, 1974) p. 76.
40. *Ibid.*, pp. 17, 71, 437.
41. *Ibid.*, pp. 76–7, 81.
42. *CPR*, 1461–1467, pp. 45, 77.
43. *CPR*, 1461–1467, pp. 38, 65.
44. *CPR*, 1461–1467, pp. 98–100.
45. J. H. Gairdiner, (ed) *The Paston Letters* (New York, 1965) vol III, pp. 300, 302, 307.
46. H. Ellis (ed) *Original Letters Illustrative of English History* (London, 1824) vol. I, pp. 15–16.
47. Gardiner *The Paston Letters*, vol. v, p. 312.
48. *CPR*, 1461–1467, p. 100.
49. J. M. Lewis, *Carreg Cennen Castle* (HMSO, London, 1977) p. 10.
50. Williams, *Recovery*, p. 192.
51. *CPR*, 1461–1467, pp. 271, 352.

52. Williams, *Recovery*, p. 200.
53. Gardiner, *The Paston Letters*, vol. iv, p. 96.
54. Edward Hall, *The Union of the Two Noble and Illustre Famelies of York and Lancaster* (London, 1809) p. 261.
55. *Calendar of Papal Registers*, ed J. A. Twemlow (London, 1921) vol. xi, pp. 648–9.
56. Williams, *Recovery*, pp. 193–4, 200; *CPR*, 1466–1477, p. 54.
57. *Rot.Parl.*, vol. vi, pp. 511–12.
58. *CPR*, 1461–1467, p. 529.
59. H. T. Evans, *Wales and the Wars of the Roses*, pp. 165–6; *CPR*, 1461–67, p. 62.
60. Williams, *Recovery*, p. 201.
61. *CPR*, 1466–1477, p. 41.
62. Sir John Wynn, *The History of the Gwydir Family* (ed. J. Ballinger) (Cardiff, 1927) pp. 29, 34.
63. Ross, *Edward IV*, pp. 371–2.
64. I. Williams (ed) *Gwaith Guto'r Glyn* (Cardiff, 1961) pp. 130–1.
65. E. Owen (ed) *A Catalogue of the Manuscripts relating to Wales in the British Museum* (London, 1900) vol. i, pp. 26–27.
66. I. Williams (ed) *Gwaith Guto'r Glyn*, p. 135.
67. Williams, *Recovery*, p. 202.
68. *Ingulph's Chronicle of the Abbey of Croyland*, trans H. T. Riley (London, 1854) p. 446; H. T. Evans, 'William Herbert, Earl of Pembroke', *THSC*, 1909–10, pp. 173–4.
69. Williams, *Recovery*, pp. 204–8.
70. I. Williams (ed) *Gwaith Guto'r Glyn*, pp. 150–52. W. J. Gruffudd, *Llenyddiaeth Cymru, 1450–1600* (Liverpool, 1922) pp. 28–9.
71. Ioan Tegid and W. Davies (eds) *Gwaith Lewis Glyn Cothi*, pp. 26, 46.
72. *CPR*, 1466–1477, p. 165.
73. *CPR*, 1467–1477, pp. 179–180, 275.
74. *CPR*, 1467–1477, p. 172.
75. *CPR*, 1467–1477, pp. 180–181.
76. *CPR*, 1467–1477, p. 172; Ross, *Edward IV*, p. 134.
77. *CPR*, 1467–1477, p. 252.
78. G. M. Trevelyan, *History of England*, p. 259.
79. G. Williams, *The Welsh Church from Conquest to Reformation* (Cardiff, 1976) ch. vii; Williams, *Recovery*, p. 181.

CHAPTER 5: BARDS AND REBELS

1. E. J. Hobsbawm, *Primitive Rebels* (Manchester, 1963); E. J.

Hobsbawm, *Bandits* (London, 1969).

2. Saunders Lewis, *Meistri a'u Crefft* (Cardiff, 1981) pp. 107–123 'Gyrfa Filwrol Guto'r Glyn'.

3. T. Parry (translated by H. I. Bell) *A History of Welsh Literature* (Oxford, 1955); G. Williams, *An Introduction to Welsh Poetry* (London, 1953); T. Gwynn Jones 'Bardism and Romance', *THSC*, 1913–14.

4. W. G. Lewis, 'Herbertiaid Rhaglan Fel Noddwyr Beirddd yn y Bymthegfed Ganrif a Dechrau'r Unfed Ganrif ar Bymtheg', *THSC*, 1986, pp. 33–60.

5. Major Francis Jones, 'An Approach to Welsh Genealogy', *THSC*, 1948.

6. Geoffrey of Monmouth, *Life of Merlin (Vita Merlini)*, ed. Basil Clarke (Cardiff, 1973).

7. M. E. Griffiths, *Early Vaticination in Welsh with English Parallels* (Cardiff, 1937). R. Wallis Evans, 'Prophetic Poetry' in A. O. H. Jarman and Gwilym Rees, *A Guide to Welsh Literature* (Swansea, 1979) vol. 2, pp. 278–89.

8. H. Ellis (ed) *Original Letters Illustrative of English History* (London, 1824) vol. 1, p. 23.

9. *Calendar of State Papers: Spanish*, vol. 1, p. 206.

10. H. E. Lewis, 'Welsh Catholic Poetry of the Fifteenth Century', *THSC*, 1911–1912.

11. D. Johnston, *Medieval Welsh Erotic Poetry* (Cardiff, 1991).

12. H. Lewis et.al (eds) *Cywyddau Iolo Goch ac Eraill* (Cardiff, 1937); see also D. H. Evans, 'An Incident on the Dee during the Glyn Dŵr Rebellion?', *DHST*, vol. 37, 1988, pp. 5–40.

13. Ifor Williams and Thomas Roberts (eds) *Cywyddau Dafydd ap Gwilym a'i Cyfoeswyr* (Cardiff, 1935) pp. xc–c, 147–8, 237. The dates given for Gruffydd Grug (1357–1370) imply that he could not possibly have composed the poem. D. J. Bowen argues that this *cywydd marwnad* was in fact composed whilst Rhys ap Tudur was alive, and thus pre-dated the rebellion: see *Llên Cymru*, viii, II, no. 91.

14. Sir John Wynn, *The History of the Gwydir Family* (ed. J. Ballinger) (Cardiff, 1927) pp. 22–3.

15. C. Ashton, *Gweithiau Iolo Goch* (Oswestry, 1896) p. 144.

16. C. Lloyd Morgan, 'Prophecy and Welsh Nationhood in the Fifteenth Century', *THSC*, 1985, pp. 9–26.

17. T. Gwynn Jones, *Llenyddiaeth y Cymry* (Denbigh, 1915) vol. 1, p. 74.

18.   Elissa R. Henken, *National Redeemer: Owain Glyndŵr in Welsh Tradition* (Cardiff, 1996). H. Lewis, 'Rhai Cywyddau Brud', *BBCS*, vol. i, 1922, pp. 240–55.

19.   E. D. Jones (ed) *Gwaith Lewis Glyn Cothi* (Cardiff, 1953) p. 72.

20.   T. Roberts (ed) *Gwaith Tudur Penllyn ac Ieuan ap Tudur Penllyn* (Cardiff, 1958) p. 21. On the romance of the Lady of the Lake see R. L. Thomson (ed) *Owein* (Dublin, 1986).

21.   Norman Cohn, *The Pursuit of the Millennium* (London, 1957) esp ch. v; Keith Thomas, *Religion and the Decline of Magic* (London, 1971).

22.   E. J. Hobsbawm, *Bandits*.

23.   Glanmor Williams, *Religion, Language and Nationality in Wales* (Cardiff, 1979) ch. 3.

24.   Glanmor Williams, 'Prophecy, poetry and politics in medieval and Tudor Wales', in H. Hearder and H. R. Lyon (eds) *British Government and Administration* (Cardiff, 1974) pp. 104–12; Glanmor Williams, 'Proffwydoliaeth, prydyddiaeth a pholitics yn yr Oeseodd Canol' *Taliesin*, i (1968) pp. 31–8.

25.   *CPR*, 1446–1452, p. 262.

26.   T. Parry (ed) *Gwaith Dafydd ap Gwilym* (Cardiff, 1952) pp. 276, 269.

27.   T. Parry, *The Oxford Book of Welsh Verse* (Oxford, 1962) p. 107. See also 'Cywydd y Dail' in J. Fisher (ed) *Cefn Coch MSS* (Liverpool, 1898) p. 264. See also the poem by Gruffydd ab Adda ap Dafydd 'The Thief of Love' (*Lleidr Serch*) in Ifor Williams and Thomas Roberts (eds) *Cywyddau Dafydd ap Gwilym a'i Cyfoeswyr* (Cardiff, 1936) pp. 115–116.

28.   I. Williams (ed) *Gwaith Guto'r Glyn* (Cardiff, 1961) pp. 22,33, 190.

29.   T. Gwynn Jones (ed), *Gwaith Tudur Aled* (Cardiff, 1926) vol. 1, p. liii. The theme of the bard as outlaw, and the impossibility of a Welshman gaining justice from a jury of English burgesses, is taken up in a second poem

Dyn a las wyf dan law Sais,
Ar ferdyd a roi fwrdais,
Gwylliad ym mraint i golli,
Heb awr yn hwy onis barn hi.

I am a man who killed, under the Saxon's hand,
Awaiting the verdict of the burgesses

A bandit who will lose his rights
Within the hour but for her judgement.

30. P. J. Donovan (ed) *Cywyddau Serch y Tri Bedo* (Cardiff, 1982) pp. 2, 50.
31. J. Fisher (ed) *The Cefn Coch Manuscripts*, p. 65.
32. J. M. Williams, *The Works of Some Fifteenth Century Glamorgan Bards* (University of Wales, unpublished M.A. dissertation, 1923) p. 4n.
33. See E. Roberts, '*Uchelwyr y Beirdd*', *DHST*, vol. 24, 1975, pp. 72–3.
34. H. Lewis et.al. (eds) *Cywyddau Iolo Goch ac Eraill* (Bangor, 1925) pp. 198–9.
35. *Ibid.*, pp. 195–197.
36. *Ibid.*, pp. 191–192.
37. *Ibid.*, pp. 324–326.
38. I. Williams (ed) *Gwaith Guto'r Glyn*, pp. 14–15.
39. I. Tegid & W. Davies (eds) *Gwaith Lewis Glyn Cothi* (Oxford, 1837)
40. *Ibid.*, p. 139.
41. *Ibid.*, p. 139.
42. *Ibid.*, p. 468.
43. T. Pennant, *Tours in Wales*, vol. 1, p. 339; See also *Arch. Cambr.*, 1846, p. 59; G. Ormerod & Helsby, *The History of the County Palatine and City of Chester* (London, 1875) vol. 1, p. 233.
44. I. Tegid & W. Davies, *Gwaith Lewis Glyn Cothi*, pp. 385–388.
45. E. Bachellery, *L'oeuvre poetique de Gutun Owain*, vol. 1, pp. 104–107.
46. T. Roberts (ed) *Gwaith Tudur Penllyn ac Ieuan ap Tudur Penllyn*, pp. 19–22.
47. Islwyn Jones (ed) *Gwaith Hywel Cilan* (Cardiff, 1963) pp. 13–16, xii–xiii.
48. T. Roberts (ed) *Gwaith Tudur Penllyn*, pp. 88–89. *Arch. Cambr.*, 1846, p. 60.
49. Sir John Wynn, *The History of the Gwydir Family* (Cardiff, 1927) p. 30.
50. *Ibid.*, pp. 33–34.
51. *Ibid.*, pp. 52, 44.
52. *Ibid.*, pp. 52–53.
53. T. Roberts (ed) *Gwaith Tudur Penllyn*, pp. 3–4.
54. T. Gwynn Jones (ed) *Gwaith Tudur Aled*, vol. I, p. li.
55. W. Gaunt, *Bandits in a Landscape* (London, 1937) p. 32.

56. M. Keen, *The Outlaws of Medieval Legend* (London, 1977). Jessie Crosland, *Outlaws in Fact and Fiction* (London, 1959).

57. T. Gwynn Jones (ed) *Gwaith Tudur Aled*, vol. 1, p. l.

58. On the controversy concerning the Robin Hood ballads see M. Keen, *The Outlaw in Medieval Legend* (particularly Keen's introduction); J. C. Holt, *Robin Hood* (London, 1982); R. H. Hilton (ed) *Peasants, Knights and Heretics* (Cambridge, 1981); J. Bellamy, *Robin Hood: An Historical Inquiry* (London, 1985).

59. T. Gwynn Jones, 'Cultural Bases: A Study of the Tudor Period in Wales', *Y Cymmrodor*, 1920, pp. 181–3; T. Gwynn Jones, *Gwaith Tudur Aled*, vol. 1, p. li.

CHAPTER SIX: BANDIT AND BANDIT REDOUBTS.

1. On the erosion of chivalry in the fourteenth century see T. Jones, *Chaucer's Knight* (London, 1980).

2. I. Williams (ed) *Gwaith Guto'r Glyn* (collected by J. Ll. Williams) (Cardiff, 1961) pp. 173–5.

3. The term *gwibiad* is used by Tudur Penllyn, see Thomas Roberts (ed), *Gwaith Tudur Penllyn ac Ieuan ap Tudur Penllyn* (Cardiff, 1958) p. 50. *Sglentwyr* is used by Lewys Môn, see E. I. Rowlands (ed) *Gwaith Lewys Môn* (Cardiff, 1975) p. 511.

4. E. I. Rowlands (ed) *Gwaith Rhys Brydydd a Rhisiart ap Rhys* (Cardiff, 1976) p. 3.

5. J. Fisher (ed) *The Cefn Coch MSS* (Liverpool, 1898) p. 28. The poem is attributed in some manuscripts to Dafydd Trevor.

6. W. Leslie Richards (ed), *Gwaith Dafydd Llwyd o Fathafarn* (Cardiff, 1964) p. 131.

7. *Ibid*, p. 156.

8. T. Lewis, *Beirdd a Bardd-Rin Cymru Fu* (Aberystwyth, 1929) pp. 40–47, see also I. Williams, *BBCS*, vol. 1, pp. 229–34.

9. Ioan Tegid & W. Davies (eds) *Gwaith Lewys Glyn Cothi* (Oxford, 1837) vol, p. 66. (Hereafter *GLGC*).

10. *GLGC*, p. 180.

11. *GLGC*, p. 183.

12. *GLGC*, p. 174.

13. I. Williams (ed) *Gwaith Guto'r Glyn* (collected by J. Ll. Williams) (Cardiff, 1961) pp. 268, 271, 187, 41, 160. See also the poem addressed to Ievan ap Einion, attributed to Guto'r Glyn in J. Fisher (ed) *The Cefn Coch MSS*, p. 240.

14. *Ibid.*, pp. 104–6, 71, 110, 112–4, 121.
15. *Ibid.*, pp. 145–6.
16. *Ibid.*, pp. 158–9.
17. T. Roberts (ed) *Gwaith Tudur Penllyn*, p. 16.
18. *Ibid.*, pp. 58–9, 60–1.
19. *Ibid.*, p. 58.
20. *Ibid.*, pp. 49–51. On the funeral practices with thieves see *ibid.*, p. 129.
21. Leslie Harries (ed) *Gwaith Huw Cae Llwyd ac Eraill* (Cardiff, 1953) pp. 36, 38, 58–9.
22. E. Rolant (ed) *Gwaith Owain ap Llywelyn ab y Moel* (Cardiff, 1984) p. 6.
23. D. L. W. Tough, *The Last Years of a Frontier: A History of the Borders during the reign of Elizabeth* (Oxford, 1928) pp. 47–49. G. McDonald-Fraser, *The Steel Bonnets: The Story of the Anglo-Scottish Border Reivers* (London, 1974).
24. Kenneth Jackson, *Early Welsh Gnomic Poems* (Cardiff, 1961) pp. 37–42; T. H. Parry-Williams (ed) *Canu Rhydd Cynnar* (Cardiff, 1932) pp. 244–52.
25. T. H. Parry-Williams (ed) *Canu Rhydd Cynnar*, p. 226, 'Prognosticasiwn Twm Hwsmon'.
26. I. Bowen (ed) *Statutes of Wales* (London, 1908) p. lxxi.
27. E. Roberts, *Dafydd Llwyd o Fathafarn* (Caernarfon, 1981) p. 9.
28. T. Roberts (ed) *The Poetical Works of Dafydd Nanmor*, pp. 11, 59.
29. T. Gwynn Jones, (ed) *Gwaith Tudur Aled* (Cardiff, 1926) vol. ii, pp. 325–6.
30. I. Williams (ed) *Gwaith Guto'r Glyn*, p. 62.
31. W. Leslie Richards (ed) *Gwaith Dafydd Llwyd o Fathafarn*, p. 169.
32. T. Roberts (ed) *The Poetical Works of Dafydd Nanmor* (revised by Ifor Wiliams) (Cardiff, 1923) p. 11.
33. E. Rolant, *Gwaith Owain ap Llywelyn ab y Moel*, p. 33.
34. T. Pennant, *Tours in Wales* (Caernarfon, 1883) vol. 3, p. 183, notes the location of the hospital of the Knights of St. John in Carno in mid-Wales, in a region infested with 'lawless banditti'.
35. W. Rees, *A History of the Order of St.John of Jerusalem in Wales and the Border* (Cardiff, 1947) pp. 63–7. G. Hartwell Jones, *Celtic Britain and the Pilgrim Movement* (London, 1912) pp. 140–142; W. Ogwen Williams, 'A Note on the History of Ysbyty Ifan', *TCHS*, vol. 15, 1954, pp. 8–14.
36. Sir John Wynn, *The History of the Gwydir Family* (Cardiff, 1927) p. 53.

37.　*Ibid.*, p. 60.

38.　On the rise of the Wynn's of Gwydir see *Clenennau Letters and Papers* (Aberystwyth, 1947) introduction by T. Jones Pierce, pp. viii–xiv.

39.　E. I. Rowlands (ed) *Gwaith Lewys Môn*, p. 173.

40.　Glyn Williams, *Y Gwylliaid* (Plas Tan y Bryn, 1989).

41.　*The History of the Gwydir Family and Memoirs*, Sir John Wynn (ed. J. Gwynfor Jones) (Gomer Press, 1990) pp. 159–60. E. Roberts, *Dafydd Llwyd o Fathafarn*, p. 11.

42.　C. Rawcliffe, *The Staffords, Earls of Stafford and Dukes of Buckingham 1394–1521* (Cambridge, 1978) pp. 50, 16; R. R. Davies, 'The Lordship of Ogmore', *Glamorgan County History; The Middle Ages*, vol. III (Cardiff,1971) p. 304.

43.　Dafydd Evans, 'Ysgarmes ar Fynydd Llangeinwyr', *The National Library of Wales Journal*, vol. xxv, 1987–88, pp. 44–52.

44.　E. Owen (ed) *A Catalogue of the Manuscripts relating to Wales in the British Museum* (London,1903) vol. ii, p. 150.

45.　*Ibid.*, p. 150. *Harleian Manuscripts*, vol. II, pp. 209–10.

46.　Williams, *Recovery*, p. 5.

47.　*Ibid*, pp. 50–1, 181.

48.　On Dafydd ap Edmwnd and Gutun Owain see Saunders Lewis, *Meistri a'u Crefft* (Cardiff, 1981) pp. 124–148.

49.　E. Bachellery, *L'oeuvre poetique de Gutun Owain* (Paris, 1950) p. 287.

50.　Sir John Wynn, *The History of the Gwydir Family*, p. 41. On the rivalry between the Kyffins and Trevors (Plas Newydd, Chirk) see Glanmor Williams, *The Welsh Church from Conquest to Reformation* (Cardiff, 1976) pp. 260, 406.

CHAPTER SEVEN: CROSS-BORDER RAIDING

1.　For comparison with the Anglo-Scottish border see D. L. W. Tough, *The Last Years of A Frontier: A History of the Borders during the reign of Elizabeth* (Oxford, 1928). G. McDonald-Fraser, *The Steel Bonnets: The Story of the Anglo-Scottish Border Reivers* (London, 1974). On the Rob Roy legend see Sir. W. Scott, *Rob Roy* (London, 1893). See also J. W. Baggally, *Greek Historical Folk Songs: The Klephtic Ballads* (Chicago, 1968); F. Braudel, *The Mediterranean* (London, 1973) vol. II, p. 752.

2.　*CPR*, 1413–1416, p. 106; 1416–1422, pp. 124, 133, 235, 308; 1422–1429, p. 140; 1429–1436, p. 180; 1441–1446, p. 411.

3.　T. Wright (ed), *Political Poems and Songs* (London, 1861) vol. ii, p.

190; *The Libelle of Englyshe Polycye: A Poem on the Use of Seapower,* ed. Sir George Warner (Oxford, 1926) p. 40.

4. Tough, *op.cit.,* esp. ch. viii; MacDonald-Fraser, *op.cit.,* ch. 12.
5. T. Wright, *The History of Ludlow and its Neighbourhood* (London, 1852) p. 267.
6. E. A. Lewis, 'The Development of Industry and Commerce in Wales during the Middle Ages', *TRHS,* vol. xvii (1903) pp. 171–2.
7. I. D. Thornley, 'The Destruction of Sanctuary' in R. W. Seton-Watson (ed) *Tudor Studies* (London, 1924) pp. 185–6.
8. E. G. Kimball (ed) *The Shropshire Peace Rolls 1400–1414* (Shrewsbury, 1959) pp. 41–42, 45.
9. E. Powell, Kingship, *Law and Society: Criminal Justice in the Reign of Henry V* (Oxford, 1989) p. 185.
10. *CPR,* 1408–1413, pp. 226, 309.
11. E. Powell, *Kingship, Law and Society,* p. 123.
12. E. Powell, 'The Restoration of Law and Order' in G. L. Harriss (ed) *Henry V: The Practice of Kingship* (Oxford, 1991) pp. 68–9.
13. J. Beverley Smith, 'The Last Phase of the Glyn Dŵr Rebellion', *BBCS,* 1966–68, p. 252. E. Powell, *Kingship, Law and Society,* pp. 216–221.
14. E. Powell, 'The Restoration of Law and Order', pp. 64–5, 68–72.
15. *Rot.Parl.,* iii, pp. 663–4.
16. *CPR,* 1408–1413, p. 476.
17. I. Bowen (ed) *The Statutes of Wales* (London, 1908) pp. 37–8.
18. *Ibid.,* pp. 38–9; *Rot.Parl.,* iv, p. 52. The Act is quoted also in W. Gerard, 'Discourse', *Y Cymmrodor,* 1899, vol. xiii, pp. 143–144.
19. *CPR,* 1413–1416, p. 176: J. H. Wylie, *The Reign of Henry V* (Cambridge, 1914) vol. 1, p. 277, fn. 2.
20. *CPR,* 1413–16, p. 347.
21. *CPR,* 1408–1413, p. 260, case of Thomas Moulde of Frome in Selewode who broke into the house of Isabel Barnabe at Berkeley by Frome, 'assaulted her and would have ravished her and taken her to Wales if she had not resisted'.
22. *Rot.Parl.,* vol. iv, p. 99.
23. *CPR,* 1422–1429, p. 35, *Foedera,* IV, iv, 81.
24. G. Williams, *Recovery, Reorientation and Reformation: Wales c 1415–1642* (Oxford, 1987) p. 173. R. A. Griffiths, *The Reign of Henry VI* (London, 1981) p. 131. *Rot.Parl.,* iv, pp. 253–60.
25. C. Rawcliffe, *The Staffords, Earl's of Stafford and Dukes of Buckingham 1394–1521* (Cambridge, 1978) p. 48.
26. *Rot.Parl.,* iv, p. 192.
27. Williams, *Recovery,* p. 173.

28. *CPR*, 1408–1413, p. 175.
29. *Rot.Parl.*, iv, pp. 345–6.
30. *Rot.Parl.*, iv, pp. 332–333 (1427), 351 (1429), 379 (1431); W. Rees (ed), *Calendar of Ancient Petitions Relating to Wales* (Cardiff, 1975) p. 37; R. A. Griffiths, 'Wales and the Marches', *op.cit.*, p. 155.
31. W. Camden, *Britannia* (facsimile of 1695 edition, Newton Abbot, 1971), p. 232. See also M. Keen, *English Society in the Later Middle Ages* (Harmondsworth, 1990) p. 213.
32. Bowen, *Statutes of Wales*, pp. 41–3, 45–6.
33. *CPR*, 1436–1441, pp. 439, 453.
34. *CPR*, 1441–1446, p. 196.
35. *CPR*, 1441–1446, pp. 261–262.
36. Bowen, *Statutes of Wales*, pp. 44–45.
37. *Ibid.*, pp. 46–47; See also W. Rees (ed) *Calendar of Ancient Petitions relating to Wales* (Cardiff, 1975) pp. 39, 192.
38. R. A. Griffiths, *Henry VI*, p. 146.
39. *CPR*, 1436–41, p. 226.
40. Ailsa Herbert, 'Herefordshire 1413–1461: Some Aspects of Society and Public Order' in R. A. Griffiths (ed) *Patronage, The Crown and the Provinces in Later Medieval England* (Gloucester, 1981) pp. 110–111. See also R. L. Storey, *The End of the House of Lancaster* (London, 1966) appendix 5, 'The Civil Disputes in Hereford'.
41. *CPR*, 1452–1461, p. 17.
42. Williams, *Recovery*, p. 47.
43. *CPR*, 1452–1461, pp. 360, 367.
44. Ioan Tegid & W. Davies (eds) *Gwaith Lewis Glyn Cothi* (Oxford, 1837) (Hereafter *GLGC*) p. 35.
45. T. Roberts, *Gwaith Tudur Penllyn ac Ieuan ap Tudur Penllyn* (Cardiff, 1958) pp. 18–19; E. Rolant (ed) *Gwaith Owain ap Llywelyn ab y Moel* (Cardiff, 1984) p. 47.
46. *Folklore Myths and Legends of Britain* (Readers Digest Publication, 1973) pp. 320–1.
47. *GLGC*, pp. 49–50.
48. *GLGC*, pp. 183, 89.
49. *GLGC*, pp. 92–3.
50. *GLGC*, p. 235.
51. *GLGC*, p. 244.
52. *GLGC*, p. 309.
53. Ailsa Herbert, *op.cit.*, pp. 108–109.
54. *GLGC*, pp. 92–3.
55. J. Blow, 'Nibley Green, 1470.' *History Today*, II (1952) pp. 608: See

also V. J. Scattergood, *Politics and Poetry in the Fifteenth Century* (London, 1971) pp. 318–319.

56. *Dictionary of Welsh National Biography*, pp. 1002–3.
57. *CPR*, 1441–1446, pp. 281.
58. *CPR*, 1441–1446, pp. 397–8.
59. T. Gwynn Jones, *Llenyddiaeth y Cymry* (Denbigh, 1915) vol. 1, p. 79.
60. *CPR*, 1446–1452, p. 205.
61. *CPR*, 1452–1461, p. 120.
62. See The Biography of Sir Rice ap Thomas in *The Cambrian Registry*, 1795, pp. 61–2.
63. *CPR*, 1441–1446, p. 240.
64. C. Rawcliffe, *op.cit.*, p. 48.
65. *GLGC*, pp. 423–25.
66. *GLGC*, p. 269.
67. *GLGC*, p. 270.
68. Islwyn Jones (ed) *Gwaith Hywel Cilan* (Cardiff, 1963) pp. 11–13.
69. R. Gough, *The History of Myddle* (Penguin books, Harmondworth, 1981) p. 54.
70. I. Williams (ed) *Gwaith Guto'r Glyn* (collected by J. Ll. Williams) (Cardiff, 1961) pp. 271, 187.
71. *Ibid*, p. 187.
72. *Ibid.*, pp. 49–50.
73. *Ibid.*, pp. 168–9. See also Guto'r Glyn's praise poems to Sir Roger Kinaston of Knockin near Oswestry and to Dafydd Llwyd of Abertanad – *ibid.*, pp. 148, 197.
74. J. Gwynfor Jones, 'Government and the Welsh Community: the North-east Borderland in the Fifteenth Century' in H. Hearder and H. R. Loyn (eds) *British Government and Administration: Studies Presented to S. B. Chrimes* (Cardiff, 1974) pp. 62–63.
75. *Ibid.*, p. 63.
76. *Ibid.*, p. 62.
77. H. Hallam, *View of the State of Europe in the Middle Ages* (London, 1869) p. 561, n. 2.

CHAPTER 8: YORKIST ASCENDANCY AND LANCASTRIAN TRIUMPH 1471–1485

1. J. Bellamy, *Crime and Public Order in England in the Later Middle Ages* (London, 1973) p. 9.
2. *CPR*, 1467–1477, p. 361.

3. R. S. Sylvester (ed) *The Complete Works of St. Thomas More* (London, 1963) vol. 2, p. 14. More's assessment was echoed by Edward Hall, the Elizabethan historian: Edward Hall, *Chronicles* (1809), vol. 2, p. 347.

4. *Rot.Parl.*, vol. vi, p. 8.

5. *Ibid.*

6. *Rot.Parl.*, vol. vi, p. 160. *CPR*, 1467–1477, p. 366; C. A. J. Skeel, *The Council in the Marches of Wales* (London 1904) p. 24; H. T. Evans, *Wales and the Wars of the Roses* (Cambridge, 1915) pp. 198–199.

7. *Rot.Parl.*, vol. vi, p. 160.

8. D. E. Lowe, 'The Council of the Prince of Wales and the Decline of the Herbert Family during the Second Reign of Edward IV (1471–1483)', *BBCS*, vol. xxvii, part II, May, 1977, pp. 278–297.

9. H. Owen & J. B. Blakeway, *A History of Shrewsbury* (London, 1825) vol. 1, p. 252. Evans, *Wales and the Wars of the Roses*, p. 200.

10. P. Williams, *Life in Tudor England* (London, 1964) p. 9.

11. *CPR*, 1466–1477, p. 574; *CPR*, 1476–1485, p. 5.

12. G. Williams, *Recovery, Reorientation and Reformation: Wales c 1415–1642* (Oxford, 1987) p. 52.

13. *CPR*, 1466–1477, p. 574.

14. *CPR*, 1466–1477, p. 605; Skeel, *op.cit.*, pp. 26–27; Evans, *op.cit.*, p. 201.

15. Williams, *Recovery*, p. 53.

16. *CPR*, 1466–1477, pp. 54, 429, 561. See also Evans, *op.cit.*, p. 200; Skeel, *op.cit.*, p. 252; J. H. Gardiner (ed), *Paston Letters*, vol. VIII, p. 107.

17. C. Ross, *Edward IV* (London, 1974) pp. 407–8.

18. Evans, *Wales and the Wars of the Roses*, pp. 198–199.

19. P. Williams, *The Council in the Marches of Wales under Elizabeth I* (Cardiff, 1958) p. 9.

20. *CPR*, 1476–1485, pp. 349–50, 361. See also C. Rawcliffe, *The Staffords, Earls of Stafford and Dukes of Buckingham* (Cambridge, 1978) pp. 29–34. *Harleian Manuscripts*, vol. I, pp. 13–5, 16–7, 28–9, 30–1, 32, 33, 70–1, 72.

21. *CPR*, 1476–1485, p. 463.

22. *CPR*, 1476–1485, pp. 368, 369,408. A new constable was appointed to Beaumaris in February 1485, *Ibid.*, p. 509.

23. *Harleian Manuscripts*, vol. II, pp. 37–8, 160.

24. *Ibid*, vol. I, p. 82.

25. R. A. Griffiths, *The Reign of Henry VI* (London, 1981) p. 424.

26. *CPR*, 1476–1485, p. 370.

27. *Three Books of Polydore Vergil's English History*, ed Sir Henry Ellis (Camden Series, 1844) p. 199.
28. *Harleian Manuscripts*, vol I, pp. 94–5, 160, 208–9; vol. II, p. 31–2, 90, 114.
29. *Ibid*, vol. I, p. 205.
30. *Ibid*, vol. II, p. 93.
31. A. Makinson, 'The Road to Bosworth Field', *History Today*, xiii, 1963, p. 242.
32. Sir John Wynn, *The History of the Gwydir Family*, pp. 27–8.
33. G. A. Williams, 'The Bardic Road to Bosworth: A Welsh View of Henry Tudor', *THSC*, 1986, p. 20.
34. I. Williams (ed) *Gwaith Guto'r Glyn* (Cardiff, 1961) p. 259.
35. W. Leslie Richards (ed) *Gwaith Dafydd Llwyd o Fathafarn* (Cardiff, 1964) pp. 169, 53, 27, 38, 40, 45, 52.
36. *Ibid.*, p. 36.
37. W. Garmon Jones, 'Welsh Nationalism and Henry Tudor', *THSC*, 1917–1918, pp. 1–59; G. Williams, 'Henry Tudor: Mab Darogan (Son of Prophecy) *The Carmarthenshire Antiquary*, vol. xxi, pp. 3–9. G. A. Williams, 'The Bardic road to Bosworth', pp. 7–15.
38. R. M. Jones, 'Y Ddraig Lwyd', in J. E. Caerwyn Williams, *Ysgrifau Beirniadol*, vol. xviii (Denbigh, 1992).
39. W. J. Gruffudd, *Llenyddiaeth Cymru, 1450–1600* (Liverpool, 1922) pp. 38–9.
40. W. Leslie Richards (ed) *Gwaith Dafydd Llwyd o Fathafarn*, pp. 30, 52, 61, 76, 86, 93, 54, 169.
41. *Ibid.*, pp. 25, 36, 92, 100, 169.
42. H. Ll. Jones and E. I. Rowlands (eds) *Gwaith Iorwerth Fynglwyd* (Cardiff, 1975) p. 27.
43. G. A. Williams, 'The Bardic Road to Bosworth', pp. 24–5.
44. W. Garmon Jones, 'Welsh Nationalism and Henry Tudor', *THSC*, 1917–1918, pp. 1–59; G. Williams, 'Henry Tudor: Mab Darogan', pp. 3–9.
45. W. Ll. Williams, *The Making of Modern Wales* (London, 1919) p. 43; D. Powell, *The Historie of Cambria* (Shrewsbury, 1774) p. 245.

CHAPTER 9: WALES UNDER THE TUDORS 1485–1532

1. *CPR*, 1485–1494, pp. 64, 84, 200; See T. B. Pugh, 'The Ending of the Middle Ages 1485–1536' in *Glamorgan County History* (Cardiff 1971) vol iii, pp. 556–557.

2.   *CPR*, 1494–1509, p. 131.
3.   W. Ogwen Williams, *Tudor Gwynedd* (Caernarfon, 1958).
4.   A. J. Taylor, *Raglan Castle, Monmouthshire* (HMSO, London, 1951) p. 12.
5.   Glanmor Williams, *Recovery, Reorientation and Reformation: Wales c 1415–1642* (Oxford, 1987) p. 228.
6.   *CPR*, 1485–1494, p. 177.
7.   J. Goronwy Edwards, *Calendar of Ancient Correspondence Concerning Wales* (Cardiff, 1935) pp. 257–8.
8.   *CPR*, 1485–1494, p. 359.
9.   *CPR*, 1485–1494, p. 393.
10.   J. Bellamy, *Crime and Public Order in England in the Later Middle Ages* (London, 1973) p. 115: Williams, *Recovery*, p. 235.
11.   J. Beverley Smith, 'Crown and Community in the Principality of North Wales in the reign of Henry Tudor, *WHR*, vol. 3, No. 2, December 1966, pp. 166–67.
12.   J. Beverley Smith, 'The Regulation of the Frontier of Meirionydd in the Fifteenth Century', *JHMS*, vol. 5 (1965–66) pp. 105–11.
13.   C. A. J. Skeel, *The Council of the Marches of Wales* (London, 1904) pp. 28–29.
14.   *CPR*, 1485–1494, p. 453: W. Campbell (ed) *Materials for a History of the Reign of Henry VII* (London,1873) pp. 544–45.
15.   D. Lleufer Thomas, 'Further Notes on the Court of the Marches,' *Y Cymmrodor*, xii (1900) pp. 144–45.
16.   *Ibid.*, pp. 145–6.
17.   T. B. Pugh, *The Marcher Lordships of South Wales 1415–1536* (Cardiff, 1963) pp. 279, 257, 279–81.
18.   *Ibid.*, pp. 29–30; Keith Williams-Jones, 'Another "Indenture of the Marches", 1 March 1490', *BBCS*, vol. xxiv, November 1970, part 1, pp. 93–94. T. B. Pugh, 'The Indenture of the Marches between Henry VII and Edward Stafford (1477–1521) Duke of Buckingham', *English History Review*, vol. lxxi, 1956, pp. 436–41.
19.   *Ibid.*, pp. 29–30; R. A. Griffiths, 'Wales and the Marches', in p. 165.
20.   *CPR*, 1494–1509, p.592.
21.   Pugh, 'The Ending of the Middle Ages', pp. 555–61.
22.   T. B. Pugh & W. R. B. Robinson, 'Session in Eyre in a Marcher Lordship', *SWMRS*, iv, 1957, pp. 113–22.
23.   J. Beverley Smith, 'Crown and Community', pp. 157–8.
24.   *Ibid.*, p.169. For the charter granted to Bromfield and Yale, Chirk see A. Palmer, 'Two Charters of Henry VII', *Y Cymmrodor*, vol. xix (1906) pp. 51–67. For the charter granted to Chirk see M. Mahler, *A*

History of Chirk Castle and Chirkland (London, 1912) pp. 109–114. For the charter granteed to Bala see E. A. Lewis, *Medieval Boroughs of Snowdonia* (London, 1912) p. 299. See also *CPR*, 1494–1509, p. 434 (Bromfield and Yale), pp. 464–5 (Chirk and Chirkland), p. 471 (Denbighland), pp. 586–87 (Ruthin).

25. *Ibid.*, p.157. *CPR*, 1494–1509, pp. 534–535. On the manumission of bondmen in North Wales see Diarmid MacCulloch, 'Bondmen under the Tudors' in Claire Cross (ed) *Law and Government under the Tudors* (Cambridge, 1988) pp. 96, 97, 100.

26. R. Williams, *The History and the Antiquities of the Town of Aberconway and its Neighbourhood* (Denbigh, 1835) pp. 43–51. The petition is mistakenly dated to the beginning of Henry VII's reign.

27. *Ibid.*, pp. 170–171.

28. P. R. Roberts, 'The Union with England and the Identity of "Anglican" Wales', *TRHS*, xxii (1972).

29. C. A. J. Skeel, 'Wales under Henry VII', in R. W. Seton-Watson (ed) *Tudor Studies* (London, 1924) p. 22.

30. 'Merrie Tales of Skelton' in W. Carew Hazlitt (ed) *Shakespeare Jest Books* (London, 1881) vol. ii, p. 7.

31. J. M. Williams, 'The Works of Some Fifteenth Century Glamorgan Bards' (University of Wales, unpublished M.A. dissertation, 1923) p. 223.

32. Williams, *Recovery*, p. 245.

33. R. R. Davies, 'The Twilight of Welsh Law', *History*, li, p.153.

34. David Powel, *The Historie of Cambria* (Shrewsbury, 1774) p. 326 states that king Henry VII 'granted to the Welsh a charter of liberty and immunity, whereby they were released from the cruel oppression, which since their subjection to the English government they had most cruelly sustained'. Henry VIII, according to him, continued 'a plenary reformation' of Wales which his father had begun.

35. William Salesbury, *A Dictionary of Englyshe and Welshe* (1547). George Owen, 'The Dialogue of the Government of Wales' in The *Description of Pembrokeshire* (ed. H. Owen) vol. III, pp. 36–7, 56–7.

36. *L&P*, I, i, pp. 195, 534, 606; I, ii, p. 932.

37. S. J. Gunn, 'The Regime of Charles, Duke of Suffolk, in North Wales and the Reform of Welsh Government', *WHR*, 1985, vol. 12, no. 4, pp. 461–92. The following section is based largely on this account.

38. E. I. Rowlands (ed) *Gwaith Lewys Môn* (Cardiff, 1975) p. 138.

39. E. Owen (ed) *A Catalogue of the Manuscripts relating to Wales in*

the British Museum (London, 1922) vol. iv, pp. 819–20. See also E. Ives (ed) 'Letters and Accounts of William Brereton of Malpas', *The Record Society of Lancashire and Cheshire*, 1976, vol. cxvi, pp. 79–80.

40. S. J. Gunn, *op.cit.*, p. 486.
41. E. Owen (ed) *A Catalogue of the Manuscripts relating to Wales in the British Museum*, vol. iv, p. 820: M. Mahler, *A History of Chirk Castle and Chirkland* (London, 1912) pp. 114–15.
42. E. Ives, 'Court and County Palatine in the Reign of Henry VIII: the Career of William Brereton of Malpas', *Transactions of the Historical Society of Lancashire and Cheshire* (1973) vol 123, pp. 28–30: E. W. Ives (ed) 'Letters and Accounts of William Brereton of Malpas', pp. 36–42.
43. A. H. Anderson, 'Henry, Lord Stafford (1501–1563) and the Lordship of Caus', *WHR*, 1972–73, vol. 6, p. 9, ft. 37.
44. Williams, *The Welsh Church*, p. 406.
45. C. Rawcliffe, *The Staffords, Earls of Stafford and Dukes of Buckingham* (Cambridge, 1978) pp. 154, 170.
46. Pugh, 'The Indenture of the Marches', p. 438.
47. *Ibid.*, p. 438.
48. *Ibid.*, p. 438.
49. Rawcliffe, *op.cit.*, p. 100. See also Pugh, *The Marcher Lordships of South Wales 1415–1536*, pp. 239–61.
50. For the trial of Buckingham see *L&P*, III, i, pp. 490–95.
51. Williams, *Recovery*, p. 423, cites Pugh, *The Marcher Lordships of South Wales*, p. 9: Pugh, 'The Ending of the Middle Ages', p. 578.
52. Pugh, 'The Indenture of the Marches', p. 439; *L&P*, IV, ii, no. 5098.
53. Pugh, 'The Ending of the Middle Ages', p. 578.
54. Williams, *Recovery*, pp. 50–1.
55. W. A. Leighton (ed), 'Early Chronicles of Shrewsbury 1372–1603', *Transactions of the Shropshire Archaeological and Natural History Society*, vol. III, 1880, p. 253. S. Meeson Morris, 'The Obsolete Punishments of Shropshire', *The Shropshire Archaeological Society*, 1889, pp. 418–9.
56. *L&P*, IV, ii, no. 3780.
57. P. R. Roberts, 'The Union with England and the identity of "anglican" Wales', p. 59: Pugh, 'The Indenture of the Marches', pp. 438–9: See also *L&P*, vol. iv (i) p. 1044.
58. D. Lleufer Thomas, 'Further Notes on the Court of the Marches', *Y Cymmrodor*, vol. xiii, 1900, p. 105. *L&P*, IV, iii, p. 2558.
59. W. Ll. Williams, 'A Welsh Insurrection', *Y Cymmrodor*, vol. xvi,

1902, pp. 1–93. R. A. Griffiths, *Sir Rhys ap Thomas and his Family* (Cardiff, 1993) ch. 4.

60.   *L&P*, IV, iii, p. 2356.

61.   *L&P*, IV, iii, p. 2519.

62.   *L&P*, IX, 58; *Calendar of State Papers: Spanish*, vol. 1, pt. 1, pp. 235, 529.

63.   W. Ll. Williams, 'A Welsh Insurrection', p. 196.

64.   *Calendar of State Papers: Spanish*, vol. 1, pt. 1, p. 263: *L&P*, VI, 649.

65.   *Acts of the Privy Council*, vol. 2, p. 224.

66.   *L&P*, V, p. 1106.

CHAPTER 10: UNION AND REFORMATION 1532–1545

1.   G. R. Elton, *The Tudor Revolution in Government* (Cambridge, 1953).

2.   Steven G. Ellis and Sarah Barber, *Conquest and Union: Fashioning a British State 1485–1725* (London and New York, 1995)

3.   T. B. Pugh, 'The Ending of the Middle Ages 1485–1536', *Glamorgan County History* (Cardiff, 1971) vol. iii, p. 567.

4.   *Ibid.*, pp. 561, 568.

5.   *Ibid.*, p. 578.

6.   *L&P*, V, 61, 301.

7.   Pugh, 'The Ending of the Middle Ages', p. 566.

8.   *Ibid.*, p. 566.

9.   L.&P, V, p. 462 (no. 991)

10.   *L&P*, V, pp. 378–9.

11.   G. Williams, *Recovery, Reorientation and Reformation: Wales c 1415–1642* (Oxford, 1987) p. 258.

12.   Pugh, 'The Ending of the Middle Ages', pp. 565–7.

13.   Williams, *Recovery*, p. 46.

14.   A. H. Anderson, 'Henry, Lord Stafford (1503–63) and the Lordship of Caus', *WHR*, vol. vi, no. 1, June 1972, p. 7.

15.   B. Coward, 'The Stanleys, Lord Stanley and the Earls of Derby 1385–1672', *Chetham Society*, Manchester, 1983, pp. 21–22.

16.   E. Owen (ed) *A Catalogue of Manuscripts relating to Wales in the British Museum* (London, 1900) vol. 1, p. 27.

17.   *L&P*, VI, p. 95.

18.   *L&P*, VI, p. 411 (no. 946)

19.   *L&P*, VI, pp. 550, 600.

20.   *L&P*, VI, p. 549.

21. Pugh, 'The Ending of the Middle Ages ', p. 563; *L&P*, VI, p. 32. W. R. B. Robinson, 'The Marcher Lords of Wales 1525–1531', *BBCS*, vol. xxvi, part III, Nov., 1975, p. 342: cites *L&P*, V, p. 193.

22. *L&P*, VII, no.949.

23. Williams, *Recovery*, p. 259; *L&P*, IX, no. 58.

24. T. B. Pugh, 'The Indenture of the Marches between Henry VII and Edward Stafford (1477–1521), Duke of Buckingham', *English History Review*, vol. lxxi, 1956, p. 436.

25. P. Williams, *The Council in the Marches of Wales under Elizabeth I* (Cardiff, 1958) p. 23.

26. I. Bowen (ed) *The Statutes of Wales* (London, 1908) pp. lii–liii, 51–2.

27. D. Lewis, 'The Court of the Council of Wales and the Marches', *Y Cymmrodor*, 1897, p. 48, f 2.

28. Bowen, *Statutes of Wales*, p. lv.

29. *Ibid.*, pp. 52–54.

30. *Ibid.*, pp. 63, 94–5.

31. *Ibid.*, p. 54.

32. *Ibid.*, pp. 54–62

33. I. D. Thornley, 'The Destruction of Sanctuary' in R. W. Seton-Watson (ed) *Tudor Studies* (London, 1924) pp. 201–2.

34. For the motives behind the Acts of Union see Edward Lord Herbert of Chirbury, *Autobiography and History of England under Henry VIII* (London, 1886) pp. 556–62: W. Ogwen Williams, *Tudor Gwynedd* (Caernarfon, 1958) pp. 7–9, 17: Williams, *Recovery*, p. 257.

35. *L&P*, X, p. 330.

36. W. Rees, 'The Union of England and Wales', *THSC*, 1937, p. 54: Edward Lord Herbert of Chirbury, *Autobiography and History of England under Henry VIII*, p. 559.

37. W. Rees (ed) *Calendar of Ancient Petitions relating to Wales* (Cardiff, 1975) pp. 186–7.

38. Pugh, 'The Ending of the Middle Ages', p. 579: See also *Mont. Coll.*, vol. vii, pp. 168–72.

39. Bowen, *Statutes of Wales*, pp. 69–72.

40. J. Leland, *The Itinerary in Wales* (ed. Lucy Tomlinson Smith) (London, 1906) pp. 112, 118. Compare this with Count Maffei, *Brigand Life in Italy* (London, 1865) vol. ii, p. 186.

41. Bowen, *Statutes of Wales*, pp. 67–69. On the origin of the office of JP in Wales see T. H. Lewis, 'The Justice of the Peace in Wales', *THSC*, 1943–4, pp. 120–32.

42. *Ibid*, pp. 73–75.
43. *Ibid.*, pp. 75–93.
44. See P. R. Roberts, 'The Union with England and the Identity of 'Anglican' Wales', *TRHS*, xxii (1972)
45. *Ibid.*
46. Bowen, *Statutes of Wales*, p. 62.
47. *L&P*, X, no. 245, pp. 88–9.
48. *L&P*, X, no. 245, p. 90.
49. *L&P Addenda*, i, no. 1193: See also *L&P*, XII, i, 93.
50. *L&P*, X, 245.
51. *Calendar of the Wynn Papers* (Aberystwyth, 1926) p. 3, no. 19. On the appointment of sheriffs see D. Mathews, "Some Elizabethan Documents', *BBCS* (1930/1) vi, pp. 70–4.
52. *L&P*, XV, p. 494: *DNB*, vol. xi, pp. 816–17.
53. Bowen, *Statutes of Wales*, pp. 96–7.
54. *Ibid.*, p. 101: See also W. Llywelyn Williams, 'The King's Court of Great Sessions in Wales', *Y Cymmrodor*, vol. xxvl, 1916, pp. 4–5.
55. W. Llywelyn Williams, 'The King's Court of Great Session in Wales', pp. 63–4. P. Williams, *The Council in the Marches of Wales under Elizabeth I* (Cardiff, 1958) p. 312.
56. Pugh, 'The Ending of the Middle Ages', p. 578.
57. I. D. Thornley, *op.cit.*, pp. 202–3.
58. P. Corrigan and D. Sayer, *The Great Arch: English State Formation as Cultural Revolution* (Oxford, 1985).
59. G. Williams, *The Welsh Church from Conquest to Reformation* (Cardiff, 1976) p. 400. E. J. Newell, *The Welsh Church* (London, 1895) p. 375, cites Godwin, *De Praesulibus*, p. 132.
60. *Ibid.*, p. 406.
61. *Ibid.*, pp. 338–9, 400–1; G. Williams, *Recovery*, pp. 133, 136. See also the two letters concerning Robert Salusbury – E. Owen (ed) *A Catalogue of Manuscripts relating to Wales in the British Museum* (London, 1922) vol. iv, pp. 818–9.
62. *The Complete Works of St. Thomas More* (ed. Thomas M. C. Lawler *et.al.*,) (London, 1981) vol. 6, part 1, p. 236.
63. Count Maffei, *Brigand Life in Italy* (London, 1865) vol. II, p. 67. See also Norman Lewis, *The Honoured Society* (London, 1964) which documents extraordinary cases of monks involved in extortion and murder in Sicily in the twentieth century.
64. Bowen, *Statutes of Wales*, p. 50.
65. *Ibid.*, pp. 64–66.
66. *Ibid.*, p. 182.

67. *L&P*, VI, p. 411 (no. 946)
68. *L&P, Henry VIII*, v, no. 364 (i) and iv, no. 2331.
69. E. Owen (ed) *A Catalogue of the Manuscripts relating to Wales*, vol. i, pp. 39–40.
70. *L&P*, x, 160.
71. Madeline Gray, 'Change and Continuity: The Gentry and the Property of the Church in South East Wales and the Marches' in J. Gwynfor Jones (ed) *Class, Community and Culture in Tudor Wales*, pp. 1–38. Williams, *Recovery*, pp. 291–2.
72. D. Thornley, 'The Destruction of Sanctuary', pp. 182–207.
73. Edward Yardley, *Menevia Sacra* (ed Francis Green) (London, 1927) pp. 91–4.
74. *L&P*, ix, 841, 843.
75. 'Letters relating to the suppression of the monasteries', *Camden Society*, pp. 190–1. The poem is quoted in E. Hall, *The Union of the Two Noble and Illustre Famelies of York and Lancaster*, ed H. Ellis (London, 1809) p. 826.
76. *Ibid.*, p. 577.
77. W. Ogwen Williams, *Calendar of the Caernarvonshire Quarter Sessions Records* (Caernarfon, 1956) vol. 1, 1554–1558, p. lviii.
78. Niccolo Machiavelli, *The Prince* (Penguin edition, Harmondsworth, 1986) ch. viii.

CHAPTER 11: ROWLAND LEE AND THE COUNCIL OF THE MARCHES

1. *DNB*, vol. xi, pp. 814–18.
2. *L&P*, VI, no. 1385.
3. P. Williams, *The Council in the Marches of Wales under Elizabeth I* (Cardiff, 1958) pp. 26–31.
4. C. A. J. Skeel, *The Council in the Marches of Wales* (London, 1904) pp. 70–72.
5. D. Lewis, 'The Court of the Council of Wales and the Marches', *Y Cymmrodor*, 1897, pp. 39–40.
6. *Select Cases in Star Chamber 1509–1544*, vol. II, Seldon Society, vol. 25, 1910, pp. 31, 313.
7. *L&P*, V, no. 484.
8. *L&P*, XI, no. 1255: Skeel, *op.cit.*, p. 64.
9. *L&P*, X, no. 258: Skeel, *op.cit.*, pp. 61–64.
10. *L&P*, VII, 1571: T. Wright, *The History of Ludlow* (London, 1852) p. 380.

11. *DNB*, vol. xi, p. 816.
12. *Calendar of State Papers: Ireland 1601–1603*, p. 254, *L&P*, vol. x, no. 31.
13. *L&P*, VII, no. 1151.
14. *L&P*, VII, no. 940. See Lewis, 'The Court of the Council of Wales and the Marches', pp. 38–39.
15. *L&P*, VII, no. 1393; Lewis, *op.cit.*, p. 38.
16. *L&P*, VIII, 861.
17. J. A. Froude, *History of England* (London, 1875) vol. iii, p. 232.
18. *L&P*, VIII, 947.
19. *L&P*, VIII, 923.
20. *L&P*, VIII, 1058; cf. IX, no. 712, XIII, ii, no. 533.
21. Skeel, *op.cit.*, p. 63.
22. *L&P*, IX, pp. 67, 126, 465, 510.
23. Lewis, 'The Court of the Council of Wales and the Marches', pp. 42–43.
24. *L&P*, X, 30.
25. *Ibid.*
26. *L&P*, X, p. 130: Wright, *The History of Ludlow*, pp. 382–3. The names of the outlaws were Dikin ap Howell Dio Bach; Howell ap Howell Dio Bach alias Howell Bannor (deceased); Howell ap David Vain; John Dee Truydio alias John ap Meredith.
27. *L&P*, X, 129. Wright, *op.cit.*, p. 378.
28. *L&P*, X, 453.
29. *L&P*, X, p. 204.
30. Skeel, *op.cit.*, pp. 63–64.
31. *L&P*, IX, 510.
32. *L&P*, XV, 398, 557, 562.
33. *Ibid.*, pp. 383–5 (Appendix c): T. B. Pugh, 'The Ending of the Middle Ages 1485–1536', *Glamorgan County History* (Cardiff, 1971) vol. iii, pp. 563–4.
34. *L&P*, XII, ii, 896.
35. *DNB*, vol. xi, p. 816.
36. *L&P*, XIII, i, 152.
37. *L&P*, IX, p. 841.
38. Wright, *The History of Ludlow*, pp. 389–392; Skeel, *op.cit.*, pp. 66–7.
39. *Ibid*, p. 383.
40. *L&P*, X, 331.
41. *L&P*, XIII, i, no. 371, 519, 624, 675, 824, 1042, 1411.
42. *L&P*, XIII, i, nos 519, 624, 1042, 1411.
43. *L&P*, XIII, i, pp. 371, 519: Skeel, *op.cit.*, p. 67: Wright, *op.cit.*, pp.

387–9.

44. W. Rees, 'The Union of England and Wales', *THSC*, 1937, p. 50.
45. *L&P*, XII, 1148.
46. *L&P*, XII, 1148, 1183.
47. *L&P*, XII, 1183.
48. B. Coward, 'The Stanleys, Lord Stanley and the Earls of Derby 1385–1672', *Chetham Society*, Manchester, 1983, p. 26: *L&P*, XII, i, no. 624: C. R. Williams (ed) *The History of Flintshire* (Denbigh, 1961) vol. 1, p. 162.
49. W. Ll. Williams, 'A Welsh Insurrection, (1902) *Y Cymmrodor*, vol. xvi, p. 78.
50. *L&P*, X, no. 543, p. 182.
51. *L&P*, XII, ii, 1183, 1148.
52. *L&P*, XII, i, 1272.
53. *L&P*, XII, ii, 896.
54. *L&P*, XII, ii, 897.
55. *L&P*, XII, ii, 1237.
56. *L&P*, XII, ii, 1199.
57. *L&P*, XIV, ii, 384.
58. *L&P*, XI, p. 525.
59. *L&P*, IV, 5533: VIII, 644: XII, i, 507, 655.
60. E. Owen (ed) *A Catalogue of Manuscripts relating to Wales* (London, 1900) vol. 1, p. 39.
61. *L&P*, XII, no. 985.
62. *L&P*, XII, ii, no. 1199; *L&P*, XIII, i, no. 53; ii, no. 222.
63. *L&P*, XIII, ii, no. 276.
64. *L&P*, XIV, ii, no. 49.
65. *L&P*, XIV, ii, no. 1289; XV, no. 308.
66. *State Papers Domestic: Elizabeth*, cvii, no. 10: W. Gerard, 'Discourse', *Y Cymmrodor*, vol. xiii, p. 160.
67. W. Gerard, 'Discourse', *Y Cymmrodor*, vol. xiii, p. 159.
68. Froude, *History of England*, vol. iii, p. 229.
69. *L&P*, XV, p. 398; Skeel, *op.cit.*, pp. 63, 65, 69: Wright, *The History of Ludlow*, pp. 394–5.
70. Skeel, *op.cit.*, p. 68.
71. Lord Herbert, *History of England under Henry VIII*, (London, 1870) p. 322.
72. *L&P*, XV, p. 398.
73. Owen & Blakeway, *History of Shrewsbury*, vol. i, p. 311.
74. W. A. Leighton (ed) 'Early Chronicles of Shrewsbury 1372–1603', *Trans. Shropshire Archaeological and Natural History Society*,

1880, vol. iii, p. 257.

75. *Historical Commission Reports on MSS in the Welsh Language*, vol. 1 1898. Mostyn MSS., No. 158, Preface p. ix (translation).
76. G. Rusche & O. Kirchheimer, *Punishment and Social Structure* (New York, 1939) p. 19.
77. P. R. Roberts, 'The Acts of Union in Welsh History', p. 71.
78. John Foxe, *Acts and Monuments*, ed Cattley and Townshend, 1837–1841, vol. vii, p. 13.
79. W. A. Leighton (ed), 'Early Chronicles of Shrewsbury, ' p. 260.
80. *Calendar of State Papers: Spanish*, vol. x, p. 368.
81. P. Williams, *The Council in the Marches of Wales*, pp. 36–38; *Acts of the Privy Council*, vol. 3, p. 6: Williams, *Recovery*, p. 301.
82. A. Fletcher, *Tudor Rebellions* (London, 1968) pp. 83–4.
83. P. Williams, *The Council in the Marches of Wales*, p. 37
84. *Acts of the Privy Council*, vol. 1, p. 520; vol. 4, p. 154; vol. 5, p. 252; vol. 6, pp. 6, 175, 183, 201.
85. *Acts of the Privy Council*, vol. 5, p. 164.
86. P. Williams, *The Council in the Marches of Wales*, pp. 231, 239–40.
87. Froude, *History of England*, iii, p. 233.

CHAPTER 12: CONDUCT AND CONSCIOUSNESS

1. Thomas More, *Utopia* (trans. P. Turner) (Harmondsworth, 1965) pp. 44–7.
2. R. Holinshed, *Chronicles of England, Scotland and Ireland* (London, 1807) vol. i, p. 313.
3. W. Ogwen Williams 'The Social Order in Tudor Wales', *THSC*, 1967 (ii).
4. William P. Griffiths, 'Schooling and Society' in J. Gwynfor Jones, (ed) *Class, Community and Culture in Tudor Wales* (Cardiff, 1989) pp. 79–119.
5. Norbert Elias, *The Civilizing Process: The History of Manners* (Oxford, 1978) pp. 191–205 'On Changes in Aggressiveness'.
6. E. G. R. Taylor, *Tudor Geography 1485–1583* (London, 1930) p. 75.
7. R. F. Scott (ed) 'Notes from the College Records' *The Eagle*, Magazine of St. John's College, Cambridge, xxi (1900) pp. 153–4, cited by William P. Griffiths 'Schooling and Society' p. 82.
8. Sir John Wynn, *The History of the Gwydir Family* (Cardiff, 1927) p. 50.
9. W. Harrison, *A Description of England* (ed. L. Withington) p. 53.

10. J. Fisher (ed) *Cefn Coch MSS* (Liverpool, 1898) pp. 232–6.

11. G. Pennar Griffiths, *Rhyddiaith Gymreig*, vol. 1 (Caernarfon, 1911) p. 80. Morus Kyffin wrote:'Ag yna ni bydde gymaint cas, cenfigen, brad a bwriad drwg yn eu mysc nhwy; lle nid oes yr owr'on, soweth, ddim cyffredinach (medd pawb) nog ymdrechu ymgyfreithio ag ymgrafangu, drwy gam, trowsedd a dygasedd, I ddwyn o ddaiar pawb ei eiddo'.

12. W. J. Gruffydd, *Llenyddiaeth Cymru: Rhyddiaith o 1546 hyd 1660* (Wrexham, 1926) p. 52.

13. G. R. Elton, 'Wales in Parliament, 1542–1581', in R. R. Davies (ed) *Welsh Society and Nationhood* (Cardiff, 1984) pp. 115–116.

14. H. A. Lloyd, *The Gentry of South West Wales 1540–1640* (Cardiff, 1968).

15. T. C. Mendenhall, *The Shrewsbury Drapers and the Welsh Wool Trade in the XVI and XVII Centuries* (London, 1953); I. Bowen (ed) *The Statutes of Wales* (London, 1908) p. lxv. C. A. J. Skeel, 'The Cattle Trade Between England and Wales from the Fifteenth to the Nineteenth Centuries', *TRHS*, 1926, pp. 135–58.

16. M. W. Thompson, *The Decline of the Castle* (Cambridge, 1987) pp. 106–7 and Appendix 2; M. W. Thompson, 'The abandonment of the castle in Wales and the Marches' in J. R. Kenyon and R. Advent *Castles in Wales and the Marches* (Cardiff, 1987) pp. 205–15.

17. John Fisher (ed) *Kynniver Llith a Ban* (Cardiff, 1931) p. 100. The author has taken the liberty to adapt the transcription. 'Yn wir, yn wir mi a ddywedaf i chwi, Myfi yw drws y defaid. Pawb (cynniver a ddaethant om blaen i) gwylliaid ynt a lladron, eithyr y defaid ny wrandawson arnynt. Myfi yw'r drws: trywo fi y daw neb i mewn, a fydd cadwedig, ac fe ddaw i mewn ac allan, ac a gaiff porfa. Y gwylliad ni ddaw ond i wyllianta, i ladd ac i ddistrywio'.

18. H. Ellis (ed) *Original Letters Illustrative of English History* (London, 1827) vol. III, p. 49, cites 'The State of North Wales, touching Religion' in the Landsdowne Collection, art. 4.

19. *Ibid.*, p. 50.

20. William P. Griffiths, 'Schooling and Society', p. 108. Parallels between the unchristian and uncivilised ways of the Welsh and the North American Indians were drawn by other commentators – see C. Hill, 'Puritans and the Dark Corners of the Land', *TRHS*, v, xiii (1963) pp. 96–7.

21. D. Aneurin Thomas, *The Welsh Elizabethan Catholic Martyrs* (Cardiff, 1971).

22. *Calendar of State Papers: Venetian*, vol. iv, p. 294.

23. *Ibid.*, vol. v, p. 354.
24. Polydore Vergil, *Three Books of Polydore Vergil*, (ed) H. Ellis (Camden Society, 1844) vol. 1, p. 13.
25. E. V. Evans, 'Andrew Boorde and the Welsh People', *Y Cymmrodor*, xxix (1919) pp. 49–52. R. W. Seton-Watson (ed) *Tudor Studies*, p. 23, Andrew Boorde, 'The Fyrst Boke of the Introduction of Knowledge.
26. *L&P*, xiv, i, no. 977.
27. Enid Roberts, 'Everyday Life in the Homes of the Gentry' in J. Gwynfor Jones (ed) *Class, Community and Culture in Tudor Wales*, p. 66.
28. E. G. R. Taylor, *Tudor Geography 1485–1583*, p. 75.
29. T. H. Parry-Williams, *Canu Rhydd Cynnar* (Cardiff, 1932) pp. 180–3.
30. *L&P*, II, i, p. 244.
31. T. Jones, 'A Welsh Chronicler in Tudor England', *WHR*, vol. i, 1960, no. 1, pp. 8–9: E. Hall, *The Union of the Two Noble and Illustre Famelies York and Lancaster*, pp. 644–46, 662.
32. S. L. Adams, 'The Gentry of North Wales and the earl of Leicester's Expedition to the Netherlands, 1585–1586', *WHR*, vii (no 11) 1974, pp. 132–7.
33. J. J. N. McGurk, 'A Survey of the demands made on the Welsh shires to supply soldiers for the Irish War, 1594–1602', *WHR*, pp. 56–68.
34. *Calendar of State Papers: Ireland, 1509–1573*, p. 462.
35. J. Fisher (ed), *The Cefn Coch Manuscripts*, pp. 71, 120.
36. T. H. Parry-Williams, *Canu Rhydd Cynnar*, pp. 394–6.
37. *Ibid.*, pp. 10–13 (Richard Hughes), 415–6 (Siôn Tudur). Nesta Lloyd, *Ffwtman Hoff: Cerddi Richard Hughes, Cefnllanfair* (Barddas, 1998) pp. 23–26.
38. L. J. Hopkin-James & T. C. Evans, *Hen Gwindidau, Carolau a Chywyddau* (Bangor, 1910) pp. xx–xxi.
39. Williams, *Recovery*, p. 443.
40. *Ibid*, p. 443.
41. *H.M.C. Report on MSS in the Welsh Language* (London, 1898) vol. 1, pp. 291–2, 293–4: See also P. Williams, *The Council in the Marches of Wales* (Cardiff, 1958) pp. 110–11.
42. T. Gwynn Jones, *Gwaith Tudur Aled* (Cardiff, 1926) vol. i, p. 266.
43. E. Owen (ed), *A Catalogue of the Manuscripts relating to Wales in the British Museum*, vol. II, p. 125.
44. J. Gwynfor Jones, 'Awdurdod Cyfreithiol a Gweinyddol Lleol yng Nogledd Cymru yn y Cyfnod 1540–1640 Yn ol Tystiolaeth y Beirdd', *Llên Cymru*, vol. xii Jan–Feb 1973, no. 3–4, pp. 154–215;. J. Gwynfor

Jones, 'Rhai Agweddau ar y Consept o Uchelwriaeth yn Nheuluoedd Bonheddig Cymru yn yr Unfed a'r Ail Ganrif ar Bymtheg' in J. E. Caerwyn Williams (ed) *Ysgrifau Beirniadol*, vol. xii (Denbigh, 1982); J. Gwynfor Jones 'Concepts of Order and Gentility' in J. Gwynfor Jones (ed) Class, *Community and Culture in Tudor Wales*, pp. 121–57.

45.   *Ibid.*, pp. 373–80.

46.   J. Gwynfor Jones, 'Rhai agweddau', p. 244.

47.   *Gwaith Lewis Glyn Cothi*, (Oxford, 1937) pp. 70–72.

48.   E. I. Rowlands (ed) *Gwaith Lewys Môn*, (Cardiff, 1975) p. 309.

49.   T. Gwynn Jones (ed) *Gwaith Tudur Aled*, vol. i, pp. 325–6.

50.   H. Ll. Jones & E. I. Rowlands, *Gwaith Iorwerth Fynglwyd* (Cardiff, 1975) pp. 37, 63, 68, 70, 13.

51.   E. I. Rowlands (ed) *Gwaith Rhys Brydydd a Rhisiart ap Rhys* (Cardiff, 1976) p. 34.

52.   E. I. Rowlands (ed) *Gwaith Lewys Môn*, pp. 193, 173, 285.

53.   *Ibid.*, pp. 302.

54.   W. J. Gruffudd, *Llenyddiaeth Cymru 1450–1600* (Liverpool, 1922) p. 32.

55.   T. Gwynn Jones (ed) *Gwaith Tudur Aled*, vol. i, p. 96.

56.   *Ibid.*, vol ii, pp. 357–58.

57.   *Ibid.*, vol. i, p. 55.

58.   *Ibid.*, p. lvi.

59.   *Ibid.*, pp. 325–6.

60.   *Ibid.*, p. 329.

61.   W. Richards, *The Works of Gruffudd Hiraethog* (University of Wales unpublished M.A. dissertation, 1923) pp. 195, 175, 58, 80, 121, 296, 208.

62.   See the poems addressed to Humphrey Huws of Werclas, Merionethshire in J. Fisher (ed) *The Cefn Coch Maunscripts*, pp. 174–92.

63.   E. Roberts, *Gwaith Siôn Tudur* (Cardiff, 1980) vol. i, pp. 602–3.

64.   *Ibid.*, p. 606.

65.   *Ibid.*, p. 615.

66.   T. H. Parry-Williams, *Canu Rhydd Cynnar*, pp. 419–20.

67.   L. J. Hopkin-James & T. C. Evans, *Hen Gwindidau, Carolau a Chywyddau*, p. 194.

68.   T. H. Parry-Williams, *Canu Rhydd Cynnar*, p. 430.

CHAPTER 13: RULE OF LAW 1558–1603

1.   K. O. Fox, 'An Edited Calendar of the First Brecknockshire Plea Roll', *NLWJ*, xiv, 1965–6, pp. 469–84; E. J. Sherrington, 'The Plea

Rolls of the Courts of Great Session', *NLWJ*, xiii, 1964, pp. 363–73; W. Ogwen Williams, *Calendar of the Caernarvonshire Quarter Session Records I* (Caernarfon, 1956); Nia M. W. Powell, 'Crime and Community in Denbighshire during the 1590s' in J. Gwynfor Jones (ed) *Class, Community and Culture in Tudor Wales* (Cardiff, 1989) pp. 237–94.

2. P. Williams, *The Council in the Marches of Wales* (Cardiff, 1958) ch xii.

3. *Ibid.*, p. 274; 'Some Elizabethan Documents' *BBCS*, pp. 77–78.

4. D. Lleufer Thomas, 'Further Notes on the Court of the Marches', *Y Cymmrodor*, 1900, p. 120. See Gerard's proposals to improve the work of the Council – pp. 154–58.

5. A. Collins (ed) *Letters and Memorials ... by Sir Henry Sidney* (London, 1746) p. 1.

6. *Ibid.*, p. 59.

7. R. Flenley (ed), *A Calendar of the Register of the Queen's Majesty's Council in the Marches of Wales, 1569–91* (London, 1916) p. 103.

8. H. A. Lloyd, *The Gentry of South West Wales 1540–1640* (Cardifff, 1968) p. 143, cites PRO S.P. 12/235/18.

9. R. Flenley (ed) *Calendar*, pp. 96–7: See also Dyson, *Elizabethan Proclamations*, pp. 149–50.

10. *Acts of the Privy Council, 1581–2*, pp. 115: see also *Acts of the Privy Council, 1590*, p. 136: *Acts of the Privy Council, 1591–2*, p. 541.

11. G. R. Elton, 'Wales in Parliament 1542–1581' in R.R. Davies (ed) *Welsh Society and Nationhood* (Cardiff, 1984) pp. 115–16.

12. R. Flenley (ed) *Calendar*, pp. 98, 178.

13. Ifan ab Owen Edwards, *A Catalogue of Star Chamber Proceedings relating to Wales* (Cardiff, 1954). For disputes over marriage portion – see *Ibid.*, pp. 25, 45, 48, 66, 106, 118, 124, 125, 125. For cases of abduction and forced marriage – *Ibid.*, pp. 27, 32, 32, 44, 48, 50, 59, 62, 63, 66, 76, 84, 88, 100, 101, 105, 105, 108, 117, 118, 1119, 132, 133, 135, 136, 139. The growth of abduction cases is discussed by J. Bellamy, *Crime and Public Order in England in the Later Middle Ages* (London, 1973) p. 32.

14. I. Bowen (ed) *The Statutes of Wales* (London, 1908) p. 126.

15. R. Flenley (ed) *Calendar*, pp. 64–7, 98, 231.

16. Ifan ab Owen Edwards, *Star Chamber Proceedings*, p. 89.

17. H. Ellis (ed), *Original Letters Illustrative of English History* (London, 1827) vol. iii, pp. 41–48.

18. *State Papers: Domestic Series: Elizabeth*, vol. 107, no. 4: D. Lleufer Thomas, 'Dr. David Lewis's Discourse', *Y Cymmrodor* 1899, vol.

xiii, pp. 128–33; C. A. J. Skeel, *The Council in the Marches of Wales* (London, 1904) pp. 106–8'. Some Elizabethan Documents', *BBCS*, pp. 74–75.

19. *State Papers:Domestic Series: Elizabeth*, vol. 107, no. 4.
20. *Ibid.*
21. P. Williams, *The Council in the Marches of Wales*, p. 260: See also *DNB*, vol. vii, pp. 1104–6.
22. Skeel, *op.cit.*, pp. 108–10.
23. D. Lleufer Thomas, 'Further Notes on the Court of the Marches', *Y Cymmrodor*, 1900, p. 148.
24. D. Lewis, 'The Court of the Council of Wales and the Marches' *Y Cymmrodor*, 1897, pp. 52–3, cites First Discourse, p. 8.
25. J. M. Traherene (ed) *The Stradling Correspondence* (London, 1840) p. 93.
26. P. Williams, *The Council in the Marches of Wales*, pp. 62, 263–4: W. Ll. Williams, 'The King's Court of Great Session in Wales,' *Y Cymmrodor*, XXVI, 1912, pp. 34–35.
27. *Acts of the Privy Council of England*, vol. 9, pp. 94–95.
28. R. Flenley (ed) *A Calendar*, pp. 61–62, 85–92.
29. *Ibid.*, pp. 145, 146, 174, 198.
30. A. Collins (ed) *Letters and Memorials...*, pp. 170–77.
31. *Ibid.*, pp. 135–37.
32. *Ibid.*, p. 143.
33. *Acts of the Privy Council of England*, vol. 10, pp. 116, 158, 161, 189, 209, 226, 101, 229.
34. Ifan ab Owen Edwards (ed), *Star Chamber Proceedings*, pp. 18, 23, 32, 40, 95, 125, 131, 140, 143. R. Flenley (ed) *Calendar*, pp. 98, 178: T. Jones Pierce (ed) *Clennenau Letters and Papers* (Aberystwyth, 1947) p. 31, no. 106.
35. R. Flenley (ed) *A Calendar*, appointment of Whitgift, p. 173.
36. Richard Davies, *A Funeral Sermon* (1577) cited in H. A. Lloyd, *The Gentry of South West Wales 1540–1640*, p. 178.
37. R. Flenley (ed) *A Calendar*, pp. 259–60.
38. *Ibid*, pp. 227–9.
39. *Ibid.*, pp. 227–9.
40. P. Williams, 'The Welsh Borderland under Queen Elizabeth' *WHR* I (1960) p. 27.
41. G. Owen, 'Dialogue', pp. 26–7, 25.
42. Bowen, *Statutes of Wales*, p. lxxviii.
43. T. B. Pugh, 'The Ending of the Middle Ages', p. 579.
44. These figures are calculated on the basis of population estimates for

Wales in 1545/63 in Leonard Owen, 'The Population of Wales in the Sixteenth and Seventeenth Centuries', *THSC*, 1959, pp. 99–113. See also H. A. Lloyd, *The Gentry of South West Wales*, pp. 167–73.

45. *Ibid.*, p. 103.

46. P. Williams, *The Council in the Marches of Wales*, pp. 215–6.

47. Joel Samaha, *Law and Order in Historical Perspective: The Case of Elizabethan Essex* (New York and London, 1974) pp. 168–9.

49. J. S. Cockburn, 'The Nature and Incidence of Crime in England 1550–1800' in J. S. Cockburn (ed) *Crime in England 1550–1800* (London, 1977) p. 53. Figures based on cases indicted before the assizes in the counties of Hertfordshire, Essex and Sussex indicate upsurges in lawlessness in 1572–74, 1585–7, 1596–8 coinciding with periods of economic crisis.

49. G. Williams, *Recovery, Reorientation and Reformation: Wales c 1415–1642* (Cardiff, 1987) pp. 89, 382.

50. T. Herbert & G. E. Jones (eds) *Tudor Wales* (Cardiff, 1988) p. 50.

51. Williams, *Recovery*, p. 422, cites NLW, Penrice and Margam Correspondence, L5.

52. *Stradling Correspondence*, p. 318.

53. P. Williams, *The Council in the Marches of Wales*, pp. 108–9.

54. Williams, *Recovery*, pp. 333, 391, 416.

55. J. J. N. McGurk, 'A Survey of the demands made on the Welsh shires to supply soldiers for the Irish War, 1594–1602', *WHR*, pp. 56–68.

56. On the problem of vagabondage and the Elizabethan criminal world-see A. L. Beier, *Masterless Men* (London, 1985); A. V. Judges (ed) *The Elizabethan Underworld: A Collection of Tudor and Early Stuart Tracts and Ballads* (London, 1965): Gamini Salgado, *The Elizabethan Underworld* (London, 1977): A. L. Beier, 'Vagrants and the Social Order in Elizabethan England', *Past & Present*, 1974, no. 64. F. Aydelotte, *Elizabethan Rogues and Vagabonds* (Oxford, 1913). D. Owen, *Elizabethan Wales: The Social Scene* (London, 1962) pp. 188–189.

57. R. H. Tawney & E. Power (eds) *Tudor Economic Documents* (London, 1924) vol. ii, p. 336.

58. *Ibid.*, vol. iii, p. 412.

59. B. Howells, 'The Lower Orders' in T. Herbert & G. E. Jones, *Tudor Wales*, p. 51.

60. *Ibid.*, p. 50.

61. *Ibid.*, pp. 24–6.

62. Ifan ab Owen Edwards, *Star Chamber Proceedings*, p. 42.

63. W. J. Smith (ed) *Calendar of Salusbury Correspondence 1553–to c*

1700 (Cardiff, 1954) pp. 56–57.

64. H. R. Davies, *The Conway and the Menai Ferries* (Cardiff, 1966) p. 89.

65. P. Williams, 'The Welsh Borderland under Queen Elizabeth', pp. 30–1.

66. Lewis, 'The Court of the Council of Wales and the Marches', pp. 60–1: A. L. Rowse, *The Expansion of Elizabethan England* (London, 1955) pp. 56–7.

67. *Ibid.*

68. P. Williams, *The Council in the Marches of Wales*, pp. 276–77: P. R. Roberts, 'The Act of Union in Welsh History', p. 59.

69. *Ibid.*, p. 347.

70. *Ibid.*, ch. xiii.

71. *Ibid.*, and G. Williams, *Recovery*, p. 347.

72. P. Williams, *The Council in the Marches of Wales*, p. 278.

73. *Ibid.*, p. 304.

74. Ifan ab Owen Edwards, *Star Chamber Proceedings*, pp. 27, 28, 60, 79, 82, 104, 120. Two cases were from Brecon, one from Denbigh, two from Glamorgan, one from Montgomery, and one from Monmouth.

75. W. J. Smith, 'The Salusberies as Maintainers of Murderers', *NLWJ*, vii (1951–1952).

CHAPTER 14: BANDIT TRADITIONS

1. See L. Owen, 'The Population of Wales in the Sixteenth and Seventeenth Centuries', *THSC*, 1958, pp. 99–113. Owen estimates that the population of Merionethshire in 1546/63 was about 10,700 (2,094 households). The population of Mawddwy was 760 (152 households).

2. *Leland's Itinerary in Wales* (ed L. T. Smith) (London, 1906) pp. 76–8.

3. J. Gwynfor Jones, 'Law and Order in Merioneth After the Acts of Union 1536–43', *JMHRS*, 1986, p. 132.

4. R. A. Griffiths, 'Wales and the Marches', in S. B. Chrimes, C. D. Ross and R. A. Griffiths (eds) *Fifteenth Century England 1399–1509* (Manchester, 1972) p. 155.

5. E. Owen (ed) *A Catalogue of the Manuscripts relating to Wales in the British Museum*, vol. iv, p. 820: M. Mahler, *A History of Chirk Castle and Chirkland* (London, 1912) pp. 114–15.

6. *Leland's Itinerary*, pp. 66, 55, 78.

7. *Calendar of the Wynn (of Gwydir) Papers* (ed. J. Ballinger) (Aberystwyth, 1926) p. 1, no. 4. Edward Stanley was MP for Merionethshire in 1542. On the Myttons as lords of Mawddwy see W. R. B. Robinson, 'The Marcher Lords of Wales 1525–1531', *BBCS*, Nov. 1975.

8. I. Bowen (ed) *Statutes of Wales* (London, 1908) pp. 62, 120, 151–152.

9. *Ibid.*, p. 87.

10. *Ibid*, pp. 54–56.

11. Sir John Wynn, *The History of the Gwydir Family* (ed J. Ballinger) (Cardiff, 1927) p. 42.

12. Prys Morris, *Cantref Meirionydd* (Dolgellau, 1900) p. 278.

13. J. Gwynfor Jones, 'Awdurdod Cyfreithiol', *Llên Cymru*, vol. xii, no. 3–4, p. 156.

14. W. Ogwen Williams, *Calendar of the Caernarvonshire Quarter Sessions Records*, vol. 1, pp. liv–lv. J. Gwynfor Jones, *Law and Order in Sixteenth Century Caernarvonshire* (Cardiff, 1994).

15. On Lewis Owen see *DNB*, vol. xiv, pp. 1324–1325: *DWB*, pp. 715: Prys Morris, *op.cit.*, p. 278: *Arch.Camb.*, 1847, p. 129.

16. H. J. Owen, 'Owen Glyn Dŵr's Parliament House at Dolgelley, ' *JMHRS*, 1953/56, vol. 2, pp. 81–88.

17. Prys Morris, *op.cit.*, p. 278.

18. E. A. Lewis & J. C. Davies (eds) *Records of the Court of Augmentation relating to Wales* (Cardiff, 1954) pp. 427, 428, 239, 430, 121: *Arch.Camb.*, 1847, p. 328.

19. J. Gwynfor Jones, 'Lewis Owen, Sheriff of Merioneth and the 'Gwylliad Cochion' of Mawddwy in 1554–55', *JMHRS*, vol. xii, p. 223.

20. E. D. Jones, 'Robert Vaughn of Hengwrt', *JMHRS*, 1949/51, vol. 1, pp. 21–24.

21. L. Dwnn, *Heraldic Visitations of Wales* (Llanddovery, 1845) p. 236: J. Y. W. Lloyd, *The History of Powys Fadog* (London, 1887) vol. 6, pp. 408–12.

22. On John Wynn ap Meredydd see *DWB.*, p. 1097.

23. *Arch.Camb.*, 1847, p. 129.

24. J. Owen, *Marweiddiaid Pechod Mewn Credinwr* (trans H. Jones) (Shrewsbury, 1796) p.1: L. Dwnn, *Heraldic Visitations of Wales* (Llanddovery, 1845) p. 236.

25. E. D. Jones, 'Lewis Owen, Baron of the Exchequer and Vice-Chamberlain of North Wales', *JMHRS*, 1949–51, vol. 1, pp. 110–11.

26. J. Gwynfor Jones, 'Lewis Owen, Sheriff of Merioneth and the

'Gwylliad Cochion' of Mawddwy in 1554–55', pp. 226, 223.

27. J. Gwynfor Jones, 'Law and Order in Merioneth After the Acts of Union 1536–43', p. 128.

28. Prys Morris, *op.cit.*, pp. 84–86: J. C. Morrice (ed) *Barddoniaeth Wiliam Llŷn* (Bangor, 1908) pp. xxviiii, 28, 22.

29. W. Richards, *The Works of Gruffudd Hiraethog* (University of Wales unpublished M.A. dissertation) pp. lxv, lix, 238–40, 327, 218–221.

30. T. Gwynn Jones, *Tudur Aled: Ei Oes A'i Waith* (Cardiff, 1926) vol. i, p. li: T. Parry (ed) *The Oxford Book of Welsh Verse* (Oxford, 1967) pp. 206–8.

31. J. Fisher (ed) *The Cefn Coch MSS* (Liverpool, 1899) p. 223.

32. Prys Morris, *op.cit.*, pp. 104–105, 278: J. Y. W. Lloyd, *History of Powys Fadog* (London, 1887) vol. vi, pp. 409–12.

33. Prys Morris, *op.cit.*, p. 104.

34. *Arch.Camb.*, 1847, p. 129.

35. J. Gwynfor Jones, 'The Merioneth Gentry in the Social Order: Bardic Evidence cc 1540–1640', *JMHRS*, vol. ix, 1983, pp. 278–307, and vol. ix, 1984, pp. 390–419.

36. Prys Morris, *op.cit.*, p. 108.

37. J. C. Morrice (ed) *Barddoniaeth William Llŷn*, pp. 3–6.

38. Dyfrig Davies, *Astudiaeth Destunol o Waith Siôn Mawddwy* (University of Wales unpublished M.A. dissertation, 1944) pp. 173–176.

39. Enid Roberts, *Gwaith Siôn Tudur* (Cardiff, 1978) vol. 1, no. 78.

40. W. Richards, *The Works of Gruffudd Hiraethog* (University of Wales unpublished M.A. dissertation, 1925) pp. ix, 58.

41. Ifan ab Owen Edwards, *Catalogue of Star Chamber Proceedings relating to Wales* (Cardiff, 1929) p. 90: See also H. Gareth Owen, 'Family Politics in Elizabethan Merionethshire', *BBCS*, xviii (1959) pp. 185–191.

42. *Ibid.*, p. 91.

43. *Ibid.*, p. 184.

44. *Ibid.*, p. 186. See also the letter from Griffith Nanney to the Lord President of the Council of Wales and the Marches – *Arch.Camb.*, 1864, pp. 101–5.

45. P. Williams, *The Council in the Marches of Wales* (Cardiff, 1958) pp. 125–6.

46. Prys Morris, *op.cit.*, pp. 279, 376–7, 104, 327.

47. Prys Morris, *op.cit.*, pp. 321.

48. R. Flenley (ed) *Calendar of the Register of the Council of the Marches of Wales 1569–91* (London, 1916) pp. 62, 85–92.

49. *Ibid.*, p. 146.

50. P. Williams, *The Council in the Marches of Wales*, p. 197.

51. E. Lhuyd, *Parochialia, Archeologia Cambrensis*, p. 3.

52. E. Roberts (Elis y Cowper) *Llyfr interlute newydd wedi gosod mewn dull ymddiddanion rhwng gras a natur* (Warrington, 1769).

53. J. Owen, *Marweiddiad Pechod Mewn Credinwyr* (trans. H. Jones 'Maesglasau') (Shrewsbury, 1791, reprinted 1796).

54. T. Pennant, *Tours in Wales* (Caernarfon, 1883) vol. 2, pp. 225–7.

55. *The Cambro-Britain* (1819) vol. 1, pp. 184–5, 266. *Arch.Camb.*, 1852, pp. 308–309; 1854, p. 119. See also the entries in *Arch. Camb.*, 1847, p. 129: *Cymru*, vol. 1, p. 423. The Myvyrian Archeology of Wales (ed Owen Jones – 'Myfyr') (Denbigh, 1870) pp. 703–706. W. Davies, 'Casgliad o Len-Gwerin Meirion', *Eisteddfod Transactions: Eisteddfod Genedlaethol Blaenau Festiniog 1898*, pp. 136, 252–5: G. Ashton, *Guide to Dinas Mawddwy* (Aberystwyth, 1889) pp. 34–5.

56. On Sir Richard Herbert see *DWB*, pp. 347–8: For some of the charges made against him see Peter R. Roberts, 'A Petition Concerning Sir Richard Herbert', *BBCS*, vol. 20, Nov, 1962, pp. 45–9.

57. E. Evans, 'Arwystli and Cyfeiliog in the Sixteenth Century: An Elizabethan Inquisition', *Mont. Coll.*, vol. li, 1949, pp. 23–37.

58. For Edward Herbert see *DNB*, vol. ix, p. 624: *DWB*, p. 348.

59. Ifan ab Owen Edwards, *A Catalogue of Star Chamber Proceedings* (Cardiff, 1929) pp. 120, 122, 125, 127, 128. One incident in this feud, an assault on Richard Herbert at Llanerfyl church, when he was struck by a bill hook 'through to the Pia Mater of the brain', is described in S. L. Lee (ed) *The Autobiography of Edward, Lord Herbert of Cherbury* (London, 1886), p. 4.

60. Ifan ab Owen Edwards, *op.cit.*, pp. 120, 129.

61. S. L. Lee (ed) *The Autobiography of Edward, Lord Herbert of Cherbury* pp. 6–7.

62. H. A. Lloyd, T*he Gentry of South West Wales, 1540–1640* (Cardiff, 1968) p. 208, cites N.L.W. Wales 7/7.

63. Ifan ab Owen Edwards, *op.cit.*, pp. 40–2.

64. George Owen (ed) *The Description of Pembrokeshire* (London, 1906) vol. iii, pp. 92–3.

65. *Ibid.*, p. 93.

66. For the various accounts of Plant Mat see *Arch.Camb.*, 1858, p. 558: Samuel Rush Meyrick, *The History and Antiquities of the County of Cardigan* (Brecon, 1907) p. 240: D. C. Rees, *The History of*

Tregaron (Llandyssul, 1936) pp. 105–7: George Borrow, *Wild Wales* (London, 1955) pp. 401–3.

67. Bowen, *Statutes of Wales*, pp. 128–9.

68. See *DNB*, vol. x, pp. 1052–3: *DWB*, p. 513: Major Francis Jones, 'An Approach to Welsh Genealogy', *THSC*, 1948, pp. 383–5: J. Frederick Jones, 'Thomas Jones of Tregaron, alias Twm Shon Catti', *TCAS*, vol. lxviii, pp. 77–86: R. Isgarn Davies, 'Twm Shon Catti', *CAST*, vol 5, 1926, pp. 100–107: D. C. Rees, *Tregaron, Historical and Antiquarian* (Llandyssul, 1936) pp. 99–105.

69. *The Joker or Merry Companion, to which are added Twmshone Catty's Tricks* (Carmarthen 1763). The Welsh translation is entitled *Casgliad o Gampau a Dichellion Thomas Jones o Dregaron* (1811). Samuel Rush Meyrick collected a number of stories about Twm Siôn Catti for his *History of the County of Cardigan* (1808). These stories were elaborated by William Frederick Deacon, *Twm John Catty, the Welsh Robin Hood* (1822), and *The Welsh Rob Roy* (1823), and by T. J. Llywelyn Pritchard, *The Adventures and Vagaries of Twm Shon Catti* (1828).

70. Meic Stevens (ed) *The Oxford Companion to the Literature of Wales*, pp. 323–324. See also Sam Adams, 'Thomas Jeffrey Llywelyn Pritchard', *Brycheiniog*, vol. xxi, 1984/5, pp. 52–63.

CONCLUSION

1. Rice Merrick, *A Book of Glamorganshire Antiquities (Morganiae Archaiographia)* ed. B. Ll. James (Cardiff, 1984) pp. 67–8.

2. *Ibid.*, pp. 67–8.

3. D. Lleufer Thomas, 'Further Notes on the Court of the Marches', *Y Cymmrodor*, 1900, p. 124.

4. H. Owen (ed) *Description of Pembrokeshire* (1906) vol. iii, p. 24.

5. Glanmor Williams, *Recovery, Reorientation and Reformation: Wales c 1415–1642* (Oxford, 1987) p. 275.

6. A. Collins (ed) *Letters and Memorials of State by Sir Henry Sidney*, vol. 1 (London, 1746) p. 1.

7. *Calendar of State Papers: Ireland 1574–85*, pp. xxxvii–xxxviii.

8. *Ibid*, pp. xxxix. See also Gerard's 'Discourse' in *Y Cymmrodor*, vol xiii (1898) pp. 137–158.

9. 'Early Chronicles of Shrewsbury', ed W. A. Leighton in *Shropshire Archaeological Society Transactions*, vol. iii, p. 276.

10. C. A. J. Skeel, 'The Welsh Woollen Industry in the Sixteenth and Seventeenth Centuries', *Arch.Camb.*, 1922, p. 243, cites Star

Chamber Proceedings, Henry VIII, 25/275. In the Welsh district around Oswestry the prevalence of brigands is alluded to in one place name, recorded in 1602, of Pant y Lladron (Thieves Hollow) in W. J. Slack, *The Lordship of Oswestry 1393–1607* (Shrewsbury, 1951) p. 67.

11. M. Richards, 'The Population of the Welsh Borders', *THSC*, p. 92, cites E. Owen (ed) *Catalogue of Manuscripts relating to Wales in the British Museum* (London, 1903) vol. ii, p. 362.

12. E. J. Miller, 'Wales and the Tudor Drama', *THSC*, 1948, p. 177. In the play 'Sir John Oldcastle' by Munday, Drayton, Wilson and Hathaway, written early in the seventeenth century, one of the antagonists bids his men:

Scour the marches with your Welshman's hooks
That Englishmen may think the devil has come.

13. P. Williams, *The Council in the Marches of Wales under Elizabeth I* (Cardiff, 1958).

14. *Ibid.*, pp. 47, 197–201: F. Bacon, *Works*, vol. ii (London,1870) pp. 567–611, 'The Argument on the Jurisdiction of the Council in the Marches'. See also G. D. Owen, *Wales in the Reign of James I* (Woodbridge, 1988) ch. 1, 'The Council of Wales, its presidents and problems'.

15. P. Roberts, 'Wales and England under the Tudor "union": Crown, principality and parliament 1543–1624' in Claire Cross, et. al (eds) *Law and Government under the Tudors* (Cambridge, 1988) p. 120.

16. See Ciaran Brady, 'Comparable histories? Tudor reform in Wales and Ireland' in Steven G. Ellis and Sarah Barber, *Conquest and Union: Fashioning a British State 1485–1725* (London, 1995). Alexander Grant and Keith J. Stringer, *Uniting the Kingdom* (London, 1995).

17. P. Williams, *The Council of the Marches of Wales under Elizabeth I*, p. 29: *L&P*, vol. xii, no. 177. See also R. Reid, *The King's Council in the North* (London, 1921).

18. M. W. Thompson, *The Decline of the Castle* (Cambridge, 1987) pp. 22–3.

19. *Calendar of State Papers: Ireland 1509–1573*, p. 103.

20. *Calendar of State Papers: Foreign 1560–1561*, p. 336.

21. *Calendar of State Papers: Domestic Addenda 1566–1579*, p. 466.

22. *L&P*, III, i, p. 551.

23. *Calendar of State Papers: Foreign 1564–1565*, p. 388.

24. *State Papers: Ireland*, (S.P. 63), 15, no. 4: instructions to Sidney.

25. See Molyneux's life of Sidney, in R. Holinshed, *Chronicles of England, Scotland and Ireland* (London, 1808) vol. iv, p. 870: Memorandum by Gerard printed in *Analecta Hibernica*, II, 124. See also Perrott's tribute to Marcher government in *State Papers: Ireland*, 36, no. 48, iii.

26. *Calendar of the Carew Manuscripts, 1577*, p. 70: *Calendar of State Papers: Ireland, 1574–1585*, pp. xxxvi–xxxviii.

27. *Calendar of the Carew Manuscripts, 1576*, p. 477.

28. *Calendar of the Carew Manuscripts, 1583*, pp. 369, 395.

29. Ellis and Barber (eds) *Conquest and Union*, pp. 78–9.

30. *Calendar of State Papers: Ireland, 1586–88*, p. 536.

31. *Calendar of State Papers: Ireland, 1599–1600*, p. 363.

32. *Calendar of State Papers: Ireland, 1601–1603*, p. 254; *L&P*, vol. x, no. 31.

33. D. Mathew, *The Celtic People and the Renaissance*, p. 220. On Sir John Perrott see *DWB*, pp. 747–49.

34. D. Lleufer Thomas, 'Further Notes on the Court of the Marches', p. 129. Sir John Davies, *A Discoverie of the True Causes why Ireland was never entirely Subdued* (ed. John Barry) (Irish University Press, 1969) pp. 272, 120.

35. P. Roberts, 'Wales and England under the Tudor "union"', pp. 126–7.

36. Edmund Burke, *Speeches and Letters on American Affairs* (London, 1908).

37. J. A. Froude, *History of England* (London, 1875) vol. iii, pp. 229–30.

38. W. Llywelyn Williams, *The Making of Modern Wales* (London, 1919)

39. T. Gwynn Jones, 'Cultural Bases: A Study of the Tudor period in Wales', *Y Cymmrodor*, xxxi (1921) pp. 161–92.

40. W. Rees, *The Union of England and Wales* THSC, 1937.

41. Peter R. Roberts, 'The "Acts of Union" in Welsh History', pp. 49–73.

42. G. R. Elton, *The Tudor Revolution in Government* (Cambridge, 1953).

43. Ellis and Barber (eds) *Conquest and Union*, ch. 2.

44. Peter Roberts, 'Wales and England under the Tudor "union"', p. 138

45. Norbert Elias, *The Civilizing Process: The History of Manners* (Oxford, 1978) pp. 191–205 'On Changes in Aggressiveness'.

46. P. Corrigan and D. Sayer, *The Great Arch: English State Formation as Cultural Revolution* (Oxford, 1985).

47. H. A. Lloyd, *The Gentry of South West Wales 1540–1640* (Cardiff, 1968) p. 130.
48. A. Fletcher, *Tudor Rebellions* (London, 1968)
49. Alan MacFarlane, *The Culture of Capitalism* (Oxford, 1989) ch. 3.
50. Williams, *Recovery*, pp. 421–2.

Bibliography

ABBREVIATIONS

AAST	*Anglesey Antiquarian Society Transactions*
Arch.Camb.	*Archeologica Cambrensis*
BBCS	*Bulletin of the Board of Celtic Studies*
CAST	*Carmarthenshire Archeological Society Transactions*
CCR	*Calendar of the Close Rolls*
CPR	*Calendar of the Patent Rolls*
DHST	*Denbighshire Historical Society Transactions*
DNB	*Dictionary of National Biography*
DWB	*Dictionary of Welsh Biography*
EHR	*Economic History Review*
FHSP	*Flintshire Historical Society Publications*
JMHRS	*Journal of the Merionethshire Historical and Record Society*
Mon.Coll.	*Montgomeryshire Collection*
NLWJ	*National Library of Wales Journal*
SWMRS	*South Wales & Monmouthshire Record Society*
TCAS	*Transaction of the Cardiganshire Archaeological Society*
TCHS	*Transactions of the Caernarvonshire Historical Society*
TDHS	*Transactions of the Denbighshire Historical Society*
THSC	*Transactions of the Honourable Society of Cymmrodorion*
TRHS	*Transactions of the Royal Historical Society*
WHR	*Welsh History Review*

PRINTED SOURCES

Acts of the Privy Council (London, 1890–)

British Library Harleian Manuscript 433 (ed R. Horrox and P. W. Hammond), (London, 1979, vol. I–IV).

'Biography of Sir Rice ap Thomas', *Cambrian Register*, 1795, pp. 49–144.

Calendar of Ancient Petitions relating to Wales, ed. W. Rees (Cardiff, 1975)

Calendar of Deeds and Documents: Coleman, Crosswood and Hawarden Deeds (Aberystwyth, 1921–31)

Calendar of Letters Relating to North Wales, ed. B. E. Howells (Cardiff, 1967)

Calendar of Papal Letters (London, 1894–)

Calendar of State Papers: Domestic (London, 1856–)
        Foreign (London, 1961–)
        Ireland (London, 1860–)
        Spanish (London, 1862–)
        Venetian (London, 1864–)

Calendar of the Carew Manuscripts (London, 1867–73)

Calendar of the Close Rolls (London, 1892–)

Calendar of the Patent Rolls (London, 1891–)

Calendar of the Wynn (of Gwydir) Papers, ed. J. Ballinger (Aberystwyth, 1926)

Calendar of the Caernarvonshire Quarter Session Records, I, 1541–58, Ed. W. Ogwen Williams (Caernarfon, 1956)

Calendar of the Register of the Queen's Majesty's Council in the Marches of Wales, 1569–91, ed. R. Flenley (London, 1916)

Calendar of the Salusbury Correspondence, 1553 to c 1700, ed. W. J. Smith (Cardiff, 1954)

Catalogue of Manuscripts relating to Wales in the British Museum, ed. E. Owen (1 vol. in 4. London, 1900–22) (except vol.4)

Catalogue of Star Chamber Proceedings relating to Wales, ed. I ab O. Edwards (Cardiff, 1929)

Clenennau Letters and Papers, ed. T. Jones Pierce (Aberystwyth, 1947)

Collins, A., (ed.) *Letters and Memorials ... by Sir Henry Sidney, etc* (London, 1746)

Dictionary of Welsh Biography down to 1940 (London, 1959)

Dodd, A. H., 'A Commendacion of Welshmen', *BBCS*, xix (1960–2), 235–49

Dwnn, Lewys, *Heraldic Visitations of Wales*, ed. S. R. Meyrick (2 vols., Llandovery, 1846)

Ellis, H., (ed.) *Original Letters Illustrative of English History* (II vols., London, 1824–46)

Episcopal Registers of the Diocese of St. David's 1397–1518 (vol I–III) (London, 1917)

Geiriadur Prifysgol Cymru (Cardiff, 1950–)

Herbert, Lord. *An Autobiography*, ed. S. Lee (London, 1886)

Jones, E. G., (ed.) 'History of the Bulkeley Family', *AAST*, 1948

Leland's Itinerary in Wales, ed. L. T. Smith (London, 1906)

Letters and Papers Illustrative of the Reigns of Richard III and Henry VII, ed. J. Gairdner (2 vols., London, 1861–3)

Letters and Papers, Foreign and Domestic, of the Reign of Henry VIII, ed. J. S. Brewer, J. Gairdner, and R. H. Brodie (23 vols., London, 1862–1932)

Mathew, D., 'Some Elizabeth Documents', *BBCS*, VI (1931–3)

Merrick, Rice, *A Booke of Glamorganshire Antiquities*, ed. B. Ll. James (Cardiff, 1984)

Owen, George, *Description of Pembrokeshire* (3 vols., London, 1906)

Paston Letters, ed. J. Gairdner (3 vols., London, 1872)

Pollard, A. F., *The Reign of Henry VII from Contemporary Sources* (3 vols, London, 1913–14)

Powel, D., *The Historie of Cambria* (Shrewsbury, 1774)

Proceedings and Ordinances of the Privy Council of England, ed. H. Nicolas (7 vols., London, 1834–7)

Pryce, A. I., *The Diocese of Bangor in the Sixteenth Century* (Bangor, 1923)

Records of the Court of Augmentation relating to Wales and Monmouthshire, ed. E. A. Lewis and J. C. Davies (Cardiff, 1954)

Rotuli Parliamentorum; ut et Petitiones, et Placita in Parliamento (7 vols., London, 1783–1832)

Royal and Historical Letters during the Reign of Henry IV, ed. F. C. Hingeston (London, 1860)

Salmon, M., *A Source-Book of Welsh History* (Oxford, 1927)

The Statutes of Wales, ed. I. Bowen (London, 1908)

Tudor Economic Documents, ed. R. H. Tawney and E. Power (3 vols., London, 1924

The Stradling Correspondence, ed. J. M. Traherne (London, 1840)

Three Chapters of Letters relating to the Suppression of the English Monasteries, ed. T. Wright (Camden Soc., 1843)

Vergil, Polydore, *The Three Books of Polydore Vergil History* …, ed. H. Ellis (Camden Soc., 1844)

Wynn, Sir John, *The History of the Gwydir Family* (ed J. Ballinger) (Cardiff, 1927).

Wynn, Sir John, *The History of the Gwydir Family and Memoirs* (ed. J. Gwynfor Jones) (Cardiff,1990)

SECONDARY SOURCES

1. Law and Order and Banditry

Aydelotte, F., *Elizabethan Rogues and Vagabonds* (Oxford, 1913)

Baggally, J. W., *The Klephtic Ballads in Relation to Greek History* (Chicago, 1968)

Bellamy, J., *Crime and Public Order in England in the Later Middle Ages* (London, 1973)

Braudel, F., *The Mediterranean*, vol.II (London,1973)

Cockburn, J. S., (ed) *Crime in England 1550–1800* (London, 1977)

Cohn, N., *The Pursuit of the Millennium* (London, 1957)

Corrigan, P. & Sayer, D., *The Great Arch: English State Formation as Cultural Revolution* (Oxford, 1985)

Crosland, J., *Outlaws in Fact and Fiction* (London, 1959)

Dolci, D., *The Outlaws of Partinicio* (London, 1960)

Elias, N., *The Civilising Process* (Oxford, 1982)

Elias, N., *The History of Manners* (Oxford, 1982)

Fletcher, A., *Tudor Rebellions* (London, 1968)

Gaunt, W., *Bandits in a Landscape* (London,1937)

Hale, J., *The Civilization of Europe in the Renaissance* (London, 1993)

Hobsbawm, E. J., *Bandits* (Penguin books, 1969)

Hobsbawm, E. J., *Primitive Rebels* (Manchester, 1963)

Holt, J. C., *Robin Hood* (London, 1982)

Jusserand, J. J., *English Wayfaring Life in the Middle Ages* (London, 1950)

Keen, M., *The Outlaws of Medieval Legend* (London, 1977)

Kiernan, V. G., *State and Society in Europe 1550–1650* (Oxford, 1980)

Lewis, Norman, *The Honoured Society* (London, 1964)

Maffei, Count *Brigand Life in Italy* (London, 1865) 2 vols.

McDonald-Fraser, G., *The Steel Bonnets: The Story of the Anglo-Scottish Border Reivers* (London, 1974)

McIntosh, Marjorie Keniston, *Controlling misbehaviour in England, 1370–1600* (Cambridge, 1998)

Samaha, Joel, *Law and Order in Historical Perspective: The Case of Elizabethan Essex* (New York and London, 1974)

Scott, Sir. W., *Rob Roy* (London, 1893)

Sharpe, J. A., *Crime in Early Modern England 1550–1750* (London and New York, 1984)

Tough, D. L. W., *The Last Years of a Frontier: A History of the Borders during the reign of Elizabeth* (Oxford, 1928)

Weisser, M. R., *Crime and Punishment in Early Modern Europe* (Hassocks, 1979)

William, Glyn, *Y Gwylliaid* (Plas Tan y Bwlch, 1989))

Zagorin, P., *Rebels and Rulers*, vol. I & II (Cambridge, 1982)

2. England and Wales

A Relation of the Island of England … about the year 1500, trans. C. A.

Sneyd (Camden Society, 1847)

Bacon, F., *The History of the Reign of King Henry VII*, ed. F.L.Levy (New York, 1972)

Chrimes, S. B., Ross, C. D., & Griffiths, R. A., (eds) *Fifteenth Century England 1399–1509* (Manchester, 1972)

Chronicon Ade de Usk, ed. E. Maunde Thompson (London, 1904)

Ellis, Steven G. and Barber, Sarah (eds) *Conquest and Union: Fashioning a British State 1485–1725* (London, 1995)

Griffiths, R. A., (ed) Patronage, *The Crown and the Provinces in Later Medieval England* (Gloucester, 1981)

Griffiths, R. A., *The Reign of King Henry VI* (London, 1981)

Griffiths, R. A., *King and Country: England and Wales in the Fifteenth Century* (London, 1991)

Hall, E., *The Union of the Two Noble and Illustre Famelies of York and Lancaster*. ed. H. Ellis (London, 1809)

Harriss, G. L.(ed) *Henry V: The Practice of Kingship* (Oxford, 1991)

Lander, J. R., *Conflict and Stability in Fifteenth Century England* (London, 1969)

Powell, E., *Kingship, Law and Society: Criminal Justice in the Reign of Henry V* (Oxford, 1989).

Ross, C., *Edward IV* (London, 1974)

Somerville, R., *History of the the Duchy of Lancaster, 1265–1603* (London, 1953) vol. 1

Storey, R. L., *The End of the House of Lancaster* (London, 1966).

Warkworth, J., A *Chronicle of the First Thirteen Years of the Reign of Edward the Fourth* (ed. J.O.Halliwell)(London, 1839).

Wolffe, B., *Henry VI* (London, 1981).

Wylie, J. H., *The Reign of Henry V*, vol 1 (Cambridge, 1914).

3. General Studies of Wales

Davies, R.R., *The Age of Conquest: Wales 1063–1415* (Oxford, 1987)

Davies, R. R. et al.(eds.) *Welsh Society and Nationhood* (Cardiff, 1984)

Davies, R. R., *Conquest, Coexistence and Change: Wales 1063–1415* (Oxford, 1987)

Davies, R. R., *Domination and Conquest: The Experience of Ireland, Scotland and Wales 1100–1300* (Cambridge, 1990)

Dictionary of Welsh Biography down to 1940 (London, 1959)

Dodd, A. H., *A Short History of Wales* (1970)

Given, James, *State and Society in Medieval Europe: Gwynedd and Languedoc under Outside Rule* (Ithaca and London, 1990)

Glamorgan County History, vol.III: The Middle Ages, ed T. B. Pugh (Cardiff, 1971)

Glamorgan County History, vol.IV: Early Modern Glamorgan, ed. G. Williams (Cardiff,1974)

Herbert, T., & Jones, G. E., *Tudor Wales* (Cardiff, 1988)

Jones, J. G.(ed) Class, *Community and Culture in Tudor Wales* (Cardiff,1989)

Jones, J. G., *Wales and the Tudor State* (Cardiff,1989)

Jones, J. G., *Concepts of Order and Gentility in Wales 1540–1640* (Cardiff, 1992)

Jones, J. G., *Early Modern Wales c 1525–1640* (Basingstoke, 1994)

Powel, D., *The Historie of Cambria* (Shrewsbury, 1774)

Rees, D., *The Son of Prophecy: Henry Tudor's Road to Bosworth* (London, 1985)

Rees, J. F., *Studies in Welsh History* (Cardiff, 1965)

Rees, W., *An Historical Atlas of Wales* (Cardiff, 1966)

Richards, R., *Cymru'r Oesoedd Canol* (Wrexham, 1933)

Roderick, A. J., *Wales Through the Ages* vol.2 (Llandybie, 1960)

Thomas, W. S. K., *Tudor Wales* (Llandysul, 1983)

Williams, D., *Modern Wales* (London, 1950)

Williams, Glanmor, *Religion, Language and Nationality in Wales* (Cardiff, 1979)

Williams, Glanmor, *Recovery, Reorientation and Reformation: Wales c 1415–1642* (Oxford, 1987)

Williams, Glanmor, *Owain Glyndŵr* (Cardiff, 1993)

Williams, Glanmor, *Henry Tudor and Wales* (Cardiff, 1985)

Williams, Glanmor *Wales and the Acts of Union* (Bangor, 1991)

Williams, G. A., *The Welsh in their History* (London, 1982)

Williams, G. A., *When Was Wales?* (London, 1985)

Williams, P., *The Tudor Regime* (Oxford, 1979)

Williams, W. Ll., *The Making of Modern Wales* (London, 1919)

Williams, W. O., *Tudor Gwynedd* (Caernarfon, 1958)

4. Political History

Adams, S. L., 'The Gentry of North Wales and the earl of Leicester's Expedition to the Netherlands, 1585–1586', *WHR*, vii (no 11) 1974, pp 132–7.

Bradley, A. G., Owen *Glyndŵr and the last struggle for Welsh independence* (London, 1901)

Carr, A. D., *Owen of Wales: The End of the House of Gwynedd* (Cardiff, 1991).

Carr, A. D., 'Welshmen and the Hundred Years War', *WHR*, IV (1968–9)

Chrimes, S. B. et al. (eds.) 'The Reign of Henry VII: Some Recent Contributions', *WHR*, X (1984–5)

Coward, B., *The Stanleys, Lords Stanley and the Earls of Derby, 1385–1672* (Manchester, 1983)

Davies, R. R., *The Revolt of Owain Glyndŵr* (Oxford, 1995)

Davies, R .R., 'Colonial Wales', *Past and Present*, 65 (1974)

Davies, R .R., *Lordship and Society in the March of Wales, 1282–1400* (Oxford, 1978)

Davies, R. R., 'Owain Glyn Dŵr and the Welsh Squirearchy', *THSC*, 1968 (ii)

Davies, R. R., 'Race Relations in Post-Conquest Wales: Confrontation and Compromise', *THSC*, 1974–5

Dodd, A. H., 'Wales's Parliamentary Apprenticeship, 1536–1625', *THSC*, 1942

Edwards, J. G., *The Principality of Wales, 1267–1967* (Denbigh, 1969)

Edwards, P. S., 'The Parliamentary Representation of the Welsh Boroughs in Mid Sixteenth Century', *BBCS*, XXVII (1978)

Edwards, P. S., 'Cynrychiolaeth a Chynnen: Agweddau ar Hanes Seneddol a Chumdeithasol Sir Fôn yn yr 16eg Ganrif', *WHR*, X (1980)

Evans, H. T., *Wales and the Wars of the Roses* (Cambridge, 1915)

Evans, H. T., 'William Herbert, Earl of Pembroke', *THSC*, 1909–1910.

Griffiths, R. A., *Sir Rhys ap Thomas and his Family* (Cardiff, 1993)

Griffiths, R. A., 'Gruffydd ap Nicholas and the Fall of the House of Lancaster', *WHR*, II (1964–5)

Griffiths, R. A., 'Gruffydd ap Nicholas and the Rise of the House of Dinefwr', *NLWJ*, XIII (1964)

Griffiths, R. A., *The Principality of Wales in the Later Middle Ages I. South Wales 1277–1536* (Cardiff, 1972)

Griffiths, R. A., 'The Rise of the Stradlings of St. Donat's', *Morgannwg*, VII (1963)

Heal, F., *The Gentry in England and Wales, 1500–1700* (Basinstoke, 1994).

Jones, G. E., *The Gentry and the Elizabethan State* (Swansea, 1977)

Jones, W. G., 'Welsh Nationalism and Henry Tudor', *THSC*, 1917–18.

Kenyon, J. R., (ed) *Castles in Wales and the Marches* (Cardiff, 1987)

Lewis, E. A., *The Medieval Boroughs of Snowdonia* (London, 1912)

Lloyd, H. A., *The Gentry of South-West Wales, 1540–1640* (Cardiff, 1968)

Lloyd, J. E., *Owen Glendower* (Oxford, 1931)

McGurk, J. J. N., 'A Survey of the Demands made on Welsh Shires … for the Irish War, 1594–1602', *THSC*, 1983

Mitchell, R. J., *John Tiptoft 1427–1470* (London, 1938)

Owen, G. D., *Elizabethan Wales: The Social Scene* (London, 1962)

Owen, G. D., *Wales in the Reign of James I* (Woodbridge, 1988)

Owen, H. G., 'Family Politics in Elizabethan Merionethshire', *BBCS*, XVIII (1959)

Probert, Y., 'Mathew Gough, 1390–1450', *THSC*, 1961

Pugh, T. B., *The Marcher Lordships of South Wales*, 1415–1536 (Cardiff, 1963)

Rawcliffe, C., *The Staffords, Earls of Stafford and Dukes of Buckingham* (Cambridge, 1978)

Rees, D., *Sir Rhys ap Thomas* (Llandysul, 1992)

Rees, D., *The Son of Prophecy: Henry Tudor's Road to Bosworth* (Llandysul, 1985)

Rees, W., *South Wales and the March, 1282–1415* (Oxford, 1924)

Reeves, A. C., *The Lordship of Newport, 1317–1536* (Ann Arbor, Michigan, 1979)

Reeves, A. C., *The Marcher Lords* (Llandybie, 1983)

Roberts, P. R., 'A Breviat of the Effectes devised for Wales', *THSC*, 1974

Roberts, P. R., 'The Union with England and the Identity of 'Anglican' Wales', *TRHS*, XXII (1972)

Robinson, W. R. B., 'The March Lords of Wales, 1525–31', *BBCS*, XXVI

Rowse, A. L., *The Expansion of Elizabethan England* (London, 1955)

Seton-Watson, R. W., (ed) *Tudor Studies* (London, 1924)

Skeel, C. A. J., *The Council in the Marches of Wales* (London, 1904)

Smith, J. B., 'The Last Phase of the Glyn Dŵr Rebellion', *BBCS*, 22, 1966–8.

Smith, J. B., 'The regulation of frontier disputes in fifteenth century Meirionydd', *JMHRS*, vol. 5 (1965–6).

Smith, J. B., 'Cydfodau o'r Bymthegfed Ganrif', *BBCS*, vol. xxi (1966).

Smith, J. B., 'Crown and Community in the Principality of North Wales in the Reign of Henry VII', *WHR*, III (1966–7)

Waters, W. H., *The Edwardian Settlement of North Wales in its Administrative and Legal Aspects* (Cardiff, 1935)

Williams, D., 'The Welsh Tudors', *History Today*, IV (1954)

Williams, P., *The Council of the Marches in Wales under Elizabeth I* (Cardiff, 1958)

Williams, P., 'The Welsh Borderland under Queen Elizabeth', *WHR*, I (1960)

Williams, W. Ll., 'A Welsh Insurrection', *Y Cymmrodor*, XVI (1902)

5. Legal and Constitutional History

Davies, R. R., 'The Survival of the Blood Feud in Medieval Wales', *History*, LIV (1969)

Davies, R. R., 'The Twilight of Welsh Law', *History*, LI (1966)

Davies, R. R., 'The Law of the March', *WHR*, v (1970–1)

Edwards, J. G., *The Principality of Wales 1267–1967: A Study in Constitutional History* (Caernarfon, 1969)

Elton, G. R., *The Tudor Constitution* (Cambridge, 1982)

Elton, G. R., *The Tudor Revolution in Government* (Cambridge, 1953)

Evans, Dafydd, 'Ysgarmes ar Fynydd Llangeinwyr', *NLWJ*, vol.xv, 1987–88, pp 44–52.

Gunn, S. J., 'The Regime of Charles, Duke of Suffolk in North Wales', *WHR*, XII (1984–5)

Hearder, H. and Loyn, H. R., (eds.) *British Government and Administration* (Cardiff, 1974)

Ives, E. W., 'Court and County Palatine in the Reign of Henry VIII: the Career of William Brereton of Malpas', *Transactions of the Historical Society of Lancashire and Cheshire*, 123 (1972)

Ives, E. W., 'Letters and Accounts of William Brereton of Malpas', *The Record Society of Lancashire and Cheshire*, 1976.

Jones, J. G., 'Awdurdod Cyfreithiol a Gweinyddol Lleol yng Ngogledd Cymru yn y Cyfnod 1540–1640 yn ol Tystiolaeth y Beirdd', *Llên Cymru*, XII (1973)

Jones, J. Gwynfor, *Law and Order in Sixteenth Century Caernarvonshire* (Cardiff, 1994)

Lewis, D., 'The Court of the Council of Wales and the Marches', Y *Cymmrodor*, 1897.

Lewis, T. H., 'The Administration of Justice in the Welsh County in its Relations to Other Organs of Justice', *THSC*, 1943–4

Lewis, T. H., 'The Justice of the Peace in Wales', *THSC*, 1943–4

Lowe, D. W., 'The Council of the Prince of Wales … during the Reign of Edward IV', *BBCS*, XXVII (1977–8)

Otway-Ruthven, A. J., 'The Constitutional Position of the Great Lordships of South Wales', *TRHS*, V, VIII (1958)

Owen, H., 'The Administration of English Laws in Wales and the Marches', *Y Cymmrodor*, xiv (1901).

Phillips, J. R. S., *The Justices of the Peace in Wales and Monmouthshire, 1541–1689* (Cardiff, 1975)

Pugh, T. B., 'The Indenture for the Marches between Henry VII and Edward Stafford, Duke of Buckingham', *EHR*, LXXI (1956)

Pugh, T. B. and Robinson, W.R.B., 'Sessions in Eyre in a Marcher Lordship', *SWMRS.*, IV (1957)

Sherrington, E. J., 'The Plea-rolls of the Courts of Great Sessions, 1541–1575', *NLWJ*, XIII (1963–4)

Smith, W. J., 'The Salusburies as Maintainers of Murderers', *NLWJ*, VII (1951–2)

Thomas, D. Lleufer, 'Further Notes on the Court of the Marches', *Y Cymmrodor*, 1900, vol. xiii.

Wade-Evans, A. W., *Welsh Medieval Law* (Oxford, 1909)

Williams, W. R., *The History of the Great Sessions*, 1542–1830 (Brecon, 1890)

Williams, W. R., *The Parliamentary History of Wales, 1541–1895* (Brecon, 1895)

Williams, W. Ll., 'The King's Court of Great Sessions in Wales', *Y Cymmrodor*, XXVI (1912) 1916?

Williams-Jones, K., 'A Mawddwy Court Roll 1415–16', *BBCS*, May 1970.

6. Local histories

Evans, B. M., 'The Commote of Cyfeiliog in the Late-Sixteenth Century', *Mont. Coll.*, IX (1967–8)

Gresham, C., *Eifionydd* (Cardiff, 1973)

Morris, Prys, *Cantref Meirionydd* (Dolgellau, 1890)

Ormerod, G., *The History of the County Palatine and City of Chester* (3 vols., London, 1875–82)

Slack, W. J., *The Lordship of Oswestry, 1393–1607* (Shrewsbury, 1951)

Wright, T., *The History of Ludlow and its Neighbourhood* (London, 1852)

Williams, R., *The History and the Antiquities of the Town of Aberconway* (Denbigh, 1835)

7. Social and Economic History

Anderson, A. H., 'Henry, Lord Stafford (1501–1563) and the Lordship of Caus', *WHR*, 1972–73, vol. 6.

Carr, A. D., 'The Making of the Mostyns', *THSC*,1979

Charles, B. G., *George Owen of Henllys: A Welsh Elizabethan* (Aberystwyth, 1973)

Colyer, R. J., *The Welsh Cattle Drovers* (Cardiff, 1976)

Griffiths, R. A. (ed) *Boroughs of Medieval Wales* (Cardiff, 1978)

Gwyndaf-Jones, R., 'Sir Richard Clough', *TDHS*, XIX, XXII (1970–3)

Jack, R. I., 'The Cloth Industry in Medieval Wales', *WHR*, X (1979–80)

Jones, E. G. (ed.) 'History of the Bulkeley Family', *AAST*, 1948

Jones, J. Gwynfor, 'The Wynn Estate of Gwydir: Aspects of its Growth and Development c.1500–1580', *NLWJ*, vol. xxii, 1981–82.

Jones, R. W., 'England against the Celtic Fringe', *Journal of World*

History, XIII (1971)

Lewis, E. A., 'A Contribution to the Commercial History of Medieval Wales, 1301–1547', *Y Cymmrodor*, XXIV (1913)

Lewis, E. A., 'The Decay of Tribalism in North Wales' *THSC*, 1902–3

Lewis, E. A., 'The Development of Industry and Commerce in Wales during the Middle Ages', *TRHS*, XVII (1903)

Linnard, W., *Welsh Woods and Forests: History and Utilization* (Cardiff, 1982)

Mendenhall, T. C., *The Shrewsbury Drapers and the Welsh Wool Trade in the XVI and XVII Centuries* (Oxford, 1953)

Owen, L., 'The Population of Wales in the Sixteenth and Seventeenth Centuries', *THSC*, 1959

Palmer, A. N. & Owen, E., *A History of Ancient Tenures of Land in Wales and the Marches* (no place of publication given, 1910)

Parry, B. R., 'Huw Nanney Hen (c.1546–1623), Squire of Nannau', *JMHRS*, v (1965–8)

Rees, W., 'The Black Death in Wales', *TRHS*, 1920.

Skeel, C. A. J., 'The Cattle Trade between England and Wales from the Fifteenth Century to the Nineteenth', *TRHS*, iv, IX (1926)

Skeel, C. A. J., 'The Welsh Woollen Industry in the Sixteenth and Seventeenth Centuries', *Arch. Camb.*, 1922

Soulsby, I., *The Towns of Medieval Wales* (Chichester, 1983)

Williams, W. O., 'The Social Order in Tudor Wales', *THSC*,1967 (ii)

8. Religious History

Birch, W. de G., *A History of Margam Abbey* (London, 1897)

Bowen, D. J., 'Englynion o Hiraeth am yr Hen Ffydd', *Efrydiau Catholig*, VI, 1954

Clark, S. and Morgan, P. T. J., 'Religion and Magic in Elizabethen Wales: Robert Holland's Dialogue on Witchcraft', *Journal of Ecclesiastical History*, 27 (1976)

Davies, C. T. B., 'Y Cerddi i'r Tai Crefydd fel Ffynhonnell Hanes', *NLWJ*, XVIII (1974)

Hays, R. W., *The History of the Abbey of Aberconway*, 1186–1537 (Cardiff, 1963)

Hill, C., 'Puritans and the 'Dark Corners of the Land'', *TRHS*, V, XIII (1963)

Jones, G. H., *Celtic Britain and the Pilgrim Movement* (London, 1912)

Lewis, F. R., 'Racial Sympathies of Welsh Cistercians', *THSC*, 1938

Lewis, H. E., 'Welsh Catholic Poetry of the Fifteenth Century', *THSC*, 1911–12

Newell, E. J., *A History of the Welsh Church to the Dissolution of the Monasteries* (London, 1895)

Pryce, A. I., *The Diocese of Bangor in the Sixteenth Century* (Bangor, 1923)

Rees, W., *A History of the Order of St.John of Jerusalem in Wales and on the Welsh Border* (Cardiff, 1947)

Thomas, D. A. (ed) *The Welsh Elizabethan Catholic Martyrs* (Cardiff, 1971)

Williams, D. H., *The Welsh Cistercians* (Tenby, 1984) 2 vols.

Williams, Glanmor, *The Welsh Church from Conquest to Reformation* (Cardiff, 1976)

Williams, Glanmor, 'Bishop William Morgan and the First Welsh Bible', *JMHRS*, VII (1976)

Williams, Glanmor, 'Wales and the Reign of Mary I', *WHR*, X (1980–1)

Williams, Glanmor, *Welsh Reformation Essays* (Cardiff, 1967)

Williams, S. W., *The Cistercian Abbey of Strata Florida* (London, 1889)

Yardley, Edward, *Menevia Sacra* (ed. Francis Green) (London, 1927)

9. Education and Culture

Bartley, J. O., *Teague, Shenkin and Sawney* (Cork, 1954)

Davies, C., *Writers of Wales: Latin Writers of the Renaissance* (Cardiff, 1981)

Davies, W. Ll., 'Phylipiaid Ardudwy', *Y Cymmrodor*, XLII (1932)

Evans, E. V., 'Andrew Boorde and the Welsh People', *Y Cymmrodor*, XXIX (1919)

Harries, F. J., *Shakespeare and the Welsh* (London, 1919)

Harries, F. J., *The Welsh Elizabethans* (Pontypridd, 1924)

Jones, F., 'An Approach to Welsh Genealogy', *TCHS*, 1939

Jones, J. H., 'John Owen: Cambro-Britannus', *THSC*, 1940

Jones, T. G., 'Bardism and Romance', *THSC*, 1913–14

Jones, T. G., 'Cultural Bases: a Study of the Tudor Period in Wales', *Y Cymmrodor*, XXXI (1921)

Williams, W. O., 'The Survival of the Welsh Language after the Union of England and Wales: The First Phase, 1536–1642', *WHR*, II (1964)

10. Poetry and Literature

Ashton, C., *Gweithiau Iolo Goch* (Oswestry, 1896)

Barddoniaeth Wiliam Llŷn, ed. J. C. Morrice (Bangor, 1908)

Cywyddau Iolo Goch ac Eraill, ed. H. Lewis et al. (Cardiff, 1937)

Cywyddau Serch y Tri Bedo, ed. P. J. Donovan (Cardiff, 1982)

Detholiad o Waith Gruffudd ab Ieuan ap Llywelyn Fychan, ed. J. C. Morrice (Bangor, 1910)

Ffwtman Hoff: Cerddi Richard Hughes, Cefnllanfair, ed. Nesta Lloyd (Barddas, 1998)

Fisher, J., *The Cefn Coch Manuscripts* (Liverpool, 1898)

Gwaith Dafydd ap Edmwnd, ed. Thomas Roberts (Bangor, 1914)

Gwaith Dafydd Llwyd o Fathafarn, ed. W. L. Richards (Cardiff, 1964)

Gwaith Guto'r Glyn, ed. I. Williams and J. Ll. Williams (Cardiff, 1939)

Gwaith Huw Cae Llwyd ac Eraill, ed. L. Harris (Cardiff, 1953)

Gwaith Hywel Cilan, ed. I. Jones (Cardiff, 1963)

Gwaith Hywel Swrdwal a'i Fab Ieuan, ed. J. C. Morrice (Bangor, 1908)

Gwaith Ieuan Deulwyn, ed. I. Williams (Bangor, 1909)

Gwaith Iorwerth Fynglwyd, ed. E. I. Rowlands (Cardiff, 1975)

Gwaith Lewys Glyn Cothi, ed. Walter Davies and Ioan Tegid (2 vols. Oxford, 1837)

Gwaith Lewys Glyn Cothi, ed. E. D. Jones (Cardiff and Aber, 1953)

Gwaith Lewys Môn, ed. E.I. Rowlands (Cardiff, 1975)

Gwaith Rhys Brydydd a Rhisiart ap Rhys, ed. J. M. Williams and E. I. Rowlands (Cardiff, 1976)

Gwaith Siôn Tudur, ed. E. P Roberts (2 vols., Bangor, 1978)

Gwaith Tudur Aled, ed. T. Gwynn Jones (2 vols., Cardiff, 1926)

Gwaith Tudur Penllyn ac Ieuan ap Tudur Penllyn, ed. T. Roberts (Cardiff, 1958)

Hen Gwndidau, Carolau a Chywyddau, ed. L. J. Hopkin-James and T. C. Evans (Bangor, 1910)

Henken, Elissa R., *National Redeemer: Owain Glyndŵr in Welsh Tradition* (Cardiff, 1996)

Jackson, K., *Early Welsh Gnomic Poems* (Cardiff, 1961)

Jones, E. D., 'Some Fifteenth-century Poetry relating to Montgomeryshire', *Mont. Coll.*, LIII–LIV (1951–6)

Jones, R. M., 'Y Ddraig Lwyd', in J. E. Caerwyn Williams (ed), *Ysgrifau Beirniadol*, vol. XVIII, (Denbigh, 1992)

Lewis, Saunders, *Meistri a'u Crefft* (Cardiff, 1981)

L'Oeuvre poetique de Gutun Owain, ed. E. Bachellery (2 vols., Paris, 1950–1)

Parry-Williams, T. H. (ed) *Canu Rhydd Cynnar* (Cardiff, 1932)

Rhyddiaith Cymraeg: Detholion o Lawysgrifau a Llyfrau Printiedig, 1547–1618, vol. II, (Cardiff, 1956)

The Poetical Works of Dafydd Nanmor, ed. T. Roberts (Cardiff, 1922)

11. Poetry and Literature (Commentaries)

Bowen, D. J., *Gruffudd Hiraethog a'i Oes* (Cardiff, 1958)
Bowen, D. J., *Barddoniaeth yr Uchelwyr* (Cardiff, 1957)
Bowen, D. J., 'Agweddau ar Ganu'r Unfed Ganrif ar Bymtheg', *THSC*, 1969
Gruffydd, W. J., *Llenyddiaeth Cymru o 1450 i 1600* (Liverpool, 1922)
Gruffydd, W. J., *Llenyddiaeth Cymru: Rhyddiaith o 1546 hyd 1660* (Wrexham, 1926)
Griffiths, M. E., *Early Vaticination in Welsh* (Cardiff, 1937)
Jarman, A. O. H. and Rees, G. (eds) *A Guide to Welsh Literature*, vol. 2 (Swansea, 1979).
Johnston, D., *Medieval Welsh Erotic Poetry* (Cardiff, 1991)
Jones, E. D., *Beirdd y Bymthegfed Ganrif a'u Cefndir* (Aberystwyth, 1984)
Jones, F., 'An Approach to Welsh Genealogy', *THSC*, 1949
Jones, T. Gwynn, *Llenyddiaeth y Cymry* (Denbigh, 1915)
Jones, T. Gwynn, 'Bardism and Romance', *THSC*, 1913–14
Jones, T. Gwynn, 'Cultural Bases: a Study of the Tudor Period in Wales', *Y Cymmrodor*, XXXI (1921)
Jones, W. G., 'Welsh Nationalism and Henry Tudor', *THSC*, 1917–8.
Lewis, T., *Beirdd a Bardd-Rin Cymru Fu* (Aberystwyth, 1929)
Lewis, W. G., 'Herbertiaid Rhaglan Fel Noddwyr Beirdd yn y Bymthegfed Ganrif a Dechrau'r Unfed Ganrif ar Bymtheg', THSC, 1986, pp 33–60.
Morgan, C. Lloyd, 'Prophecy and Welsh Nationhood in the Fifteenth Century', *THSC*, 1985.
Parry, T. (trans. H. I. Bell) *A History of Welsh Literature* (Oxford, 1955)
Prys, R. I., *Hanes Llenyddiaeth Cymreig 1300–1650* (Liverpool, 1883)
Roberts, E., *Dafydd Llwyd o Fathafarn* (Caernarfon, 1981)
Rowlands, E. I., *Poems of the Cywyddwyr: a Selection of Cywyddau, c. 1375–1525* (Dublin, 1976)
Stephens, M. (ed.) *The Oxford Companion to Welsh Literature* (Oxford, 1986)
Williams, D. G., *An Introduction to Welsh Poetry* (London, 1953)
Williams, G. A. 'The bardic road to Bosworth: A Welsh view of Henry Tudor', *THSC*, 1986.